Celebrating the
Midwestern Table

By the Same Author

MORE TASTE THAN TIME
Fast and Flavorful:
New Food Processor Recipes

ABBY MANDEL'S CUISINART
CLASSROOM

CELEBRATING
the Midwestern Table
REAL FOOD FOR REAL TIMES

Abby Mandel

DOUBLEDAY
New York   London   Toronto
Sydney   Auckland

PUBLISHED BY DOUBLEDAY
a division of Bantam Doubleday Dell Publishing Group, Inc.
1540 Broadway, New York, New York 10036

DOUBLEDAY and the portrayal of an anchor with a dolphin are
trademarks of Doubleday, a division of Bantam Doubleday Dell
Publishing Group, Inc.

Book design by Marysarah Quinn
Illustrations by Joanna Roy

Library of Congress Cataloging-in-Publication Data

Mandel, Abby.
Celebrating the midwestern table: real food for real times / Abby
Mandel. — 1st ed.
        p.   cm.
Includes bibliographical references and index.
  1. Cookery, American—Midwestern style.   I. Title.
        TX715.2.M53M36   1996
        641.5977—dc20   95-30377
                CIP

ISBN 0-385-47682-5

This book is dedicated to Holly—my daughter, my critic, and, above all, my friend.
And my deepest gratitude goes to my husband, Bunny Meyer,
who supported me in my efforts to complete this project,
which was so meaningful to me.

CONTENTS

ACKNOWLEDGMENTS

My Great Appreciation to:

The eighty-plus producers and growers from the twelve Midwestern states who, since 1989, have brought their quality specialty items for tasting and sale at The Best of the Midwest Market, a one-day September event in the metropolitan Chicago area. These spirited producers and growers and their diverse foods have inspired this cookbook.

Gordon Sinclair, who, as Chairman of the newly formed Chicago Chapter of the American Institute of Wine and Food in 1987, encouraged me in my desire to showcase the Midwest in terms of its regional food products and persevered with me until the Market became a reality.

Ira Nathanson, who, as senior vice president of Kemper Financial Services, Inc., understood the vision of this regional culinary event and funded the Market with critical seed money for the first three consecutive years.

The entire Board of Directors and the many members of the Chicago Chapter of the American Institute of Wine and Food who have enthusiastically supported and participated in the Market over the years. I am especially grateful to: Marlys Bielunski, Ann Bloomstrand, Jeannette Buerk, Linda Calafiore, Julie Chernoff, Mitch Cobey, Robert Don, Suzanne Florek, Al Harris, Nancy Harris, Mary Hess, Monique Hooker, Meme and Gary Hopmayer, Allen Kelson, Marliss Levin, Larry Levy, Vincent Naccarato, Don Newcomb, Bonnie Rabert, Diane Redding, Colin Reeves, Karen Reidel, Colleen Senn, Elaine Sherman, Jill Van Cleave, Ron and Jeanne Watson, Mara Whitney, and Hans Williman.

Alice Waters, whose leadership, spirit, and special Market efforts helped me to shape the Market.

Janet Connor (formerly in the public relations department of Marshall Field & Company), Susan Lock, and Anne Rashford (both representing the Mayor's Office of Special Events), who helped make the Market a full-scale Chicago event.

The many Chicago-area chefs who have given generously of their time in both resourcing regional products and teaching in the cooking school. I specifically want to thank Mark Baker, Deann and Rick Bayless, Kent Buell, Judy Contino, Toni Cox, David DiGregerio, Joe Doppes, Mark Dorian, Didier Durand, David Foegley, Michael Foley, Scott Foster, Jonathan Fox, David Friedman, Debbie Gold, David Jarvis, Jean Joho, David Koelling, Odessa Piper (Madison, Wisconsin), Yves Roubaud, Peggy Ryan, Michael Smith, Allen Sternweiler, Charlie Trotter, and Charles Weber.

The Women's Board of Ravinia Festival, who

joined forces with the Chicago Chapter of the American Institute of Wine and Food to produce the Market. I want to especially thank Zarin Mehta, executive director of Ravinia Festival, as well as Jean Berghoff, chairman of the Women's Board, Fran Beatty, Joan Freehling, Jean Mc-Clung, and the Women's Board Market Committee for ensuring a successful transition of the Market from Navy Pier to Ravinia Festival.

Susan Lescher, my agent, and Judith Kern, my editor, who recognized my heartfelt mission in publishing this book.

The Best of the Midwest Market

The Best of the Midwest Market was originally organized under the auspices of the Chicago Chapter of the American Institute of Wine and Food, and is now jointly presented by the chapter and the Women's Board of Ravinia Festival. Initially held at Navy Pier in Chicago for three years, the Market now takes place on the grounds of Ravinia Festival in Highland Park, Illinois, and is known as the Best of the Midwest Market at Ravinia.

The Best of the Midwest Market is an extraordinary day-long celebration of the finest, farm fresh produce and local specialty food products from America's heartland. The Market's centerpiece is a bustling market offering participants an opportunity to taste and purchase superior foods directly from nearly 100 of the Midwest's premier producers and growers. The exceptional foodstuffs on display include organic fruits and vegetables, fresh handmade cheeses, specialty meats, farm-raised fish and free-range poultry, traditional breads, local micro-brewed beers, outstanding regional wines, unusual grains and herbs, and other ethnic produced products. The market is a dynamic gathering place for thousands of people; farmers, chefs, food professionals, and consumers, all of whom want to enjoy and learn about quality, locally produced foods.

Education is a key objective of the Best of the Midwest Market. The food festivities include a continuous cooking school featuring eight or more of the Midwest's premier chefs. Another cooking school, just for children, combines fun, hands on learning, and nutritious ingredients. Organized educational forums are held throughout the day on public policy food-related issues such as sustainable agriculture, urban markets, or new food technologies.

Celebrating the
Midwestern Table

INTRODUCTION

Over the years my personal taste—the food I want to cook and the food I want to serve and eat—has evolved more and more in the direction of the earthy, robust flavors of a simpler cuisine. Where in the past, like many a food professional, I looked to Europe and California for culinary inspiration, I have found that there is a wealth of flavor to be mined right here at home in the farmhouse roots of the Midwest where I have lived these past thirty-five years. All it takes to be convinced is a stroll through the special farmers' market events that crop up during the season of growth and harvest. It is here that cooks confront the prime ingredients that lead us right back to the kitchen in a haze of excitement: lamb sausage, farm-raised trout, a plethora of fruits and vegetables, local farmhouse cheeses, specialty lettuces, fresh herbs and edible flowers, homemade flavored vinegars, Midwestern popcorn, smoked pheasant, unusual grains, lake caviar, foraged as well as cultivated exotic mushrooms.

I started down this path by learning to appreciate the terrific flavors of the French and Italian rustic kitchen, flavors based on the vegetable garden, the orchard, the availability of fresh chickens and fish at local open markets. The Midwest offers that same kind of big, broad-shouldered, no-apologies food: long-cooking stews with flavor as deep

as Lake Michigan, steak house brisket you can nudge apart with a fork, homey desserts served in politically incorrect portions, soups that penetrate right to the bone. There's history to it. Consider this midday winter meal of 125 years ago, a time of demanding physical labor: raw oysters, beef soup, broiled fresh cod with egg sauce, roast chicken, mashed potatoes, stewed sweet potatoes, macaroni, turnips, squash or pumpkin pie, eggless plum pudding, plum preserves, assorted fruit, and coffee. This may not sound like sophisticated food, but it isn't stodgy. The end result is a full and satisfying experience because the food tastes just the way you expect it would.

I look around and I see Americans returning to a love of heartland cooking. They might call it "comfort food" because so much of it is attached to happy memories—the berry pies, the buttermilk biscuits, the German potato salad, the corn bread of another time. Even though times change, we needn't leave behind the flavors of our farmhouse roots. No one today is going to sit down to eat a meal fit for 125 years ago. No one has the time to cook that meal, and no one can afford the extra pounds that meal would provide. I have sought out some of those dishes that embody the tastes of the Midwest culinary experience, generated over the years by succeeding waves of European settlers who came here and farmed here and brought their distinct foods to the table. But I have updated the recipes in terms of preparation time as well as fat, salt, and sugar content. The delicious flavors, the ones that taste just the way we expect they should, come right through. The interpretation—and it is certainly fit for the modern kitchen and the modern cook—is my own, but comes from many years of living and studying in the Midwest, of cooking and eating and meeting the people who bring their food products to the farmers' markets.

The food of the Midwest has been well documented across many generations, and I have made use of these resources to establish a solid foundation for my ideas about the Midwestern table. But I haven't approached the writing of this book as an archaeologist committed to excavating the past. I am working more like a painter, my palette loaded with all the glorious foods of this region as well as the long-standing traditions that surround the table. This, then, is my interpretation of the Midwestern table. It is a contemporary table, but one that draws its strength and the depth of its flavors from a past we all share. And like the Midwest, it is a welcoming table that always has room for an extra, unexpected guest.

This book is for the cook who likes to linger in the kitchen, who's there for a special satisfaction, who sees the process of cooking as a personal and creative one, a cook who wants to entertain dinner guests with food that speaks of her own spirit. And that takes time even when the recipes are simple and straightforward. And that should be enjoyable time because the time it takes to prepare a meal for friends and loved ones is the one ingredient in a meal unique to each cook. It flavors the pot. Maybe that should be the subtitle of this cookbook: *The Taste of Time Well Spent.*

Most week nights we might find ourselves relying on the microwave and the freezer, or on take-out taste treats, or on the ease of a restaurant meal. This is the food we need to replenish our batteries. But it isn't necessarily food that brightens our souls. Food that can do that smells like home cooking. It's food with a distinct aroma that fills a house faster than laughter. When you walk into a friend's home for a weekend dinner, it's the smell that greets you at the door, the smell that tells you a soothing, relaxed evening is about to descend upon you. It's the smell of the time a good cook has taken to consider her guests, to plan a meal, to do the shopping, prep the ingredients, then cook and serve the meal. It is what I think of as food from the heart as well as the heartland and I assure you, without fail, everyone lingers long at the table, the conversation unfolds of its own accord, and the evening never seems to end.

I think of these recipes as food fit for family-style dining. I am not necessarily talking about Mom and Dad and the kids gathered around the table. But I am talking about a new, comfortable dining that probably starts with everyone gathering in the kitchen for a glass of chilled wine and the opportunity to offer help, to admire a good cook's labors, and to nibble at a few delectable treats. I'm talking about dining that quickly moves to the table, where big platters of sensual food are passed from hand to hand, about candlelight and fresh flowers to be sure, but about elbows on the table, too. Pretensions won't work here. This food is simply about people as well as for people. And what better way to enjoy it than at a well-appointed table surrounded by friends? That's what these recipes are about.

Because I am, first and foremost, a cooking teacher, I have developed recipes that will deliver their terrific, robust flavors the first time you try them. Time is a precious commodity, and I want you to spend yours wisely and fruitfully when you cook from this book. Look to the sidebars and cooking notes for extra help on achieving the best results and for cutting corners when appropriate. This is familiar, straightforward food, and its appeal is limitless. I think you will discover that the end results are full, satisfying, and great-tasting. It's a little like stepping back to where it all started, the flavor of real food for a real time.

General Guidelines
For Using This Cookbook

My first rule of cooking is to relax and have fun. But trying a new recipe can often seem daunting. So I have put together this list of suggestions to make your use of this book easy and pleasurable. I have specifically created recipes that will yield wonderful, flavorful results the very first time. These general guidelines are sure to help:

❖ Efficiency will make your cooking more enjoyable, so I have included preparation instructions in each recipe's ingredient list. This list tells you whether an onion is minced or sliced or if a tomato is seeded and cut into $1/3$-inch dice. I want you to enjoy the cooking process without stopping to read about these preparatory steps. Your ingredients should be lined up ready to go. Professional chefs call this *mise-en-place*. And what it means are fewer delays . . . and no surprises.

❖ I have stopped using weights to measure the ingredients in this cookbook. Instead you will find cups, teaspoons, or tablespoons. For example, instead of specifying 1 large red onion, about 1 pound, sliced, I have written it as 1 large red onion, sliced, about $2^1/2$ cups. As the seasons change, however, the largest red onion in the produce bin may weigh 12 ounces. Such are the variations in produce. The measured amount is more specific and will hopefully be of practical use to you in these recipes.

❖ You will find the phrase "adjust the seasoning" in every recipe. It may look repetitive but it's key. I want you to taste the recipe at least at that point and make it your own in terms of seasoning.

❖ I have mentioned storage options at the end of each recipe, because do-ahead preparations are enormously practical. For any dish that requires reheating after being refrigerated or frozen, these reheating instructions are included.

❖ When a food processor helps significantly in the preparation of a recipe, this advantage is mentioned in the header of the recipe or is actually spelled out in the body of the recipe instructions. It can be a great time-saver. Knowing about the food processor option in advance will help you make better decisions about how you want to prepare the recipe.

❖ At the back of the book, I have included a list of Midwestern Sources, many from small specialized producers and farmers. These foods have greatly influenced my cooking and my modern sense of the Midwest. I first came to know many of these producers and their foods through my organization of the Best of the Midwest Market, a one-day event that celebrates the best foods in the twelve Midwestern states. Over the past six years this market has expanded its products and grown in stature. Every year I am even more impressed with the excellence as well as the variety of these foods. While the sources list may not be comprehensive, it does represent what I feel to be the best of the Midwest to date.

❖ In those recipes where a particular Midwestern product has inspired me, I specify it. Since many of these products may not be available to you, I have also described the characteristics of that ingredient so you can make an appropriate substitution.

❖ I have also included a Basics chapter that includes key recipes and techniques that are utilized throughout the book but are not specific to any one chapter. These basics are fundamental to my cooking. You can substitute a store-bought food for cooking convenience, but preparing the corresponding basic recipe will make a difference when there is time.

Strawberry Orange Juice

All-Seasons Fresh Fruit Compote

Crunchy Five-Grain Granola

Oatmeal Simmered with Apples

Oat Bran Buttermilk Pancakes with Mixed Berries

Very Wild Rice Waffles with Dried Cranberries

Baked German Pancake with Plums

Amish Scramble with Potatoes and Sausage

The Aunts' Fresh Strawberry Omelet

Spinach Bread Pudding with Capriole Goat Cheese and Bacon

Fried Cornmeal Mush, Thick or Thin

French Toast with Cornflake Crunch

Chunky Apple Muffins

Lemon Cornmeal Blueberry Muffins

Orange Poppy Seed Scones

Onion Breakfast Cake

Baked Apple Dumplings

Keys' Caramel Rolls

Maple-Glazed Canadian Bacon

BUTTERS AND SYRUPS:

Fresh Raspberry Butter

Honey Pecan Butter

Granny Butter

Persimmon Butter

Cranberry Butter

Lemon Maple Butter

Warm Maple Syrup with Fresh Peaches

   Cranberry Variation

Chapter 1
Breakfast Foods

❖

The Midwest way with food comes to us across more than a century, starting in the country, on the farm, and moving into the great Midwestern cities. I get my clearest impression of this heritage when I consider all the possibilities for breakfast. The very soul of this bold-flavored, special food can be found right here at the first meal of the day.

If I close my eyes I can imagine an old farmhouse oak table just off the kitchen in the halcyon days of big breakfasts. The smell of baking muffins eases through the house, beckoning. What would I lay out for a hungry farm crew? In my interpretation, platters of fluffy, steaming pancakes cover the table along with creamy eggs surrounded by rashers of bacon glazed with maple syrup and fresh country sausage; bowls of granola and fruit compote and fried potatoes and savory breakfast cake; piles of Orange Poppy Seed Scones, Lemon Cornmeal Blueberry Muffins, and caramel rolls awaiting Fresh Raspberry Butter, Honey Pecan Butter, or Lemon Maple Butter. Then the pot of coffee is set on the table and its rich, black aroma pulls together all the pieces of the meal.

In this day and age when so much of America has toast and grapefruit and coffee and heads out the door, such a farmhouse breakfast must seem wildly indulgent. But it is from just such Midwest imaginings that I derive my inspiration. The results are breakfast recipes for the contemporary palate and the current attitudes about diet and eating, but recipes that draw directly from that American farmhouse tradition.

Any one dish might do at today's breakfast table. The Amish Scramble with Potatoes and Sausage, say, or the Baked German Pancake with Plums. Dishes such as Onion Breakfast Cake have a curious capacity for fitting into the meal any time of the day. So do Very Wild Rice Waffles with Dried Cranberries, Spinach Bread Pudding with Capriole Goat Cheese and Bacon, and applewood-smoked bacon or Chunky Apple Muffins. And yet, each of these dishes carries with it the special sense of breakfast, a meal with inspired magic.

Strawberry Orange Juice

This juice will bring instant cheer to the most morning-resistant soul. It can be easily doubled or tripled for a crowd. Add yogurt to it, for an entirely different taste.

YIELD: 3 CUPS

*1 pint strawberries, washed, blotted dry with paper
  towels, hulled
1 1/2 cups freshly squeezed orange juice
Honey, maple syrup, or sugar to taste
Orange or strawberry slices, for garnish*

1. Put the strawberries in a blender or a food processor fitted with a metal blade. Puree the strawberries until very smooth. Push the puree through a sieve to remove the seeds.

2. Combine the puree with the orange juice and the sweetener of your choice. The juice mixture can be made several hours ahead and refrigerated.

3. To serve, pour the juice into a chilled glass pitcher; garnish with orange or strawberry slices. Serve chilled.

All-Seasons Fresh Fruit Compote

Fresh fruit on the table in the morning is a welcome sight! The simple syrup in this recipe is an enhancer for most fruit combinations and easy enough to have on hand since it lasts up to 2 weeks in the refrigerator and up to 3 months in the freezer. Double or triple the recipe while you're at it. This specific fruit mix (about 4 cups) spans many months of the year, but don't forget other stalwart fruits in the produce bins—pineapples and bananas. When the fruit selection is very ripe and fragile, it should be mixed with the syrup just before serving. For seasonally perfect fruit, try the more straightforward version in Simply Peaches (page 336).

YIELD: 4 SERVINGS

ORANGE SYRUP:

1 tablespoon orange zest (colored rind), removed with a
    zester or fine grater (see page 14)
1/2 cup fresh orange juice
1/4 cup water
2 tablespoons sugar
1/4 teaspoon pure vanilla extract

FRUIT:

2 very large navel oranges, rind and pith removed,
    orange segments removed from membrane
4 kiwi fruits, peeled, cut into 1/4-inch crosswise slices
1 pint strawberries, washed, blotted dry with paper
    towels, hulled, cut in half vertically
Mint leaves, for garnish (optional)

1. For the orange syrup, put all of the ingredients (except the vanilla) in a small nonaluminum saucepan. Bring to a boil. Simmer, uncovered, for 5 minutes. Let cool. Stir in the vanilla.

2. For the fruit, put the orange segments (and any juice squeezed from the membranes) in a 1 1/2 quart bowl along with the kiwi slices. Pour the syrup over the fruit. Gently toss to coat the fruit. The fruit can be prepared several hours ahead and refrigerated.

3. To serve, add the strawberries to the bowl. Gently toss to mix them. You'll have about 4 cups of fruit total. Chill the mixture 2 hours. Serve chilled, garnished with mint leaves, if you are using them.

Segmenting Citrus Fruit

Cut off the ends of the fruit to make a stable top and bottom. Stand the fruit firmly on a cutting board and trim the peel and white pith away with a sharp flexible knife. You may have to turn the fruit over to get to the peel and pith close to the board. Gently holding the fruit in your hand, cut next to the membranes and remove each segment. Put the segments into a dish, then gather up and squeeze the membranes to release all of the remaining juice over the fruit.

Crunchy Five-Grain Granola

The good taste and great crunch of this addictive granola come from a variety of wholesome grains. This granola also has the added benefit of being fat free—unlike those store-bought mixes that are loaded with oil. Besides making a hearty breakfast when served with milk, this granola is wonderful as a topping for fruit, yogurt, ice cream, and puddings. The recipe recommends specific grain proportions but a total of 4¹/₂ cups in any combination will also work out well. Just remember to choose good-size grains with texture. Also, the dried apples and raisins can be replaced with other dried fruits of your choice.

YIELD: 8 CUPS

¹/₂ cup each: honey, maple syrup, thawed frozen apple juice concentrate

1 tablespoon cinnamon

1 teaspoon each: grated lemon zest, grated orange zest (colored rind), removed with a zester or fine grater (see page 14)

2¹/₂ cups thick-sliced oat flakes (see Note) or regular oat flakes

1 cup each: kamut (see Note), finely snipped dried apples

¹/₂ cup each: flax seeds (see Note), oat bran, raisins

1. Put the racks in the center area of the oven; preheat the oven to 350 degrees. Line 2 jelly roll pans (cookie sheets with sides) with foil. Set aside.

2. Combine the honey, maple syrup, apple juice concentrate, cinnamon, and zests in a 1-quart saucepan. Bring to a boil. Simmer, uncovered, 5 minutes.

3. Put the remaining ingredients in a large mixing bowl. Add the saucepan mixture; toss until well combined. Divide the mixture between the prepared pans, spreading it out evenly.

4. Bake in the oven until well toasted, about 25 minutes, stirring every 10 minutes. (Use a rubber spatula to avoid tearing the foil.) Reverse the pans if the granola is baking unevenly. Cool the granola completely on racks. The granola can be stored in an airtight container in a cool place for up to 3 weeks.

NOTE: These grains are available at health food stores.

Citrus Zest Basics

Lemon and orange zest, sometimes called the rind, is the colorful, thin top layer of the citrus fruit. It's a favorite ingredient of mine. You'll find it in every chapter of this book. Pungent with natural aromatic oils, the zest imparts a fresh flavor to any recipe it's used in.

To get zest from lemons and oranges:

❖ Wash the fruit with soapy water to remove any external chemicals; rinse and dry well.

❖ Remove just the zest with the fine side of a grater or with a zester, a tool available in cookware shops. Zesters are far easier to use than graters. A sharp swivel-bladed vegetable peeler also works well, though a mini food processor or blender is required to mince the rind. This is best done with a small amount of the sugar or flour from the recipe.

❖ Don't expect to get every bit of the zest; there is necessarily some waste.

❖ Avoid removing any of the white rind, or pith, which has a very bitter taste.

❖ Zest removed in advance of its use should be wrapped in plastic to keep it moist. Otherwise it becomes tough as it air-dries.

❖ 1 large lemon yields about 1 tablespoon zest; 1 large orange, about 2 tablespoons zest.

❖ Juice the zested lemon or orange within the next few days since the fruit quickly deteriorates.

Oatmeal Simmered with Apples

This recipe is an adaptation of a simple breakfast dish found in The More-with-Less Cookbook, a collection commissioned by the Mennonite Central Committee. Their cookbook promotes thriftiness and personal health. This delicious version of oatmeal proves that being economical and simple can also be scrumptious.
For a perfect bowl of comfort food, spoon some hot or steamed milk over the oatmeal (using a cappuccino steaming element if you have one) with a sprinkling of brown sugar.

YIELD: 3 1/2 CUPS, ABOUT 4 TO 5 SERVINGS

²/₃ cup old-fashioned oatmeal
2³/₄ cups water
¹/₄ teaspoon salt
1 large tart apple, finely chopped, (unpeeled or peeled, as you wish), about 1¹/₂ cups
¹/₂ teaspoon cinnamon
Freshly grated nutmeg (see page 289)

1. Put the oatmeal, water, and salt in a 1¹/₂-quart saucepan. Bring to a boil. Simmer, uncovered, until thick and creamy, about 10 minutes, stirring occasionally to prevent lumps and sticking.

2. Add the apple, cinnamon, and nutmeg. Simmer until the apple is just tender, about 5 minutes more, stirring often. Serve hot.

3. The oatmeal can be made in advance and refrigerated for up to 3 days. Gently reheat the oatmeal, thinning it with water as necessary for the desired consistency.

Oat Bran Buttermilk Pancakes with Mixed Berries

Berries enhance these light oat bran pancakes. I prefer to sprinkle the berries directly on the pancakes for an even distribution rather than mixing them into the batter. Use 2 cups of berries, no matter whether you use the mix or just one kind. Frozen berries do not need to be thawed before sprinkling them on the pancakes. Serve the pancakes with warm maple syrup passed separately.

YIELD: 3 TO 4 SERVINGS, ABOUT TWENTY 3-INCH PANCAKES

$^1/_2$ cup each: oat bran, cake flour
1 teaspoon baking soda
$^1/_4$ teaspoon salt
2 teaspoons sugar
1 large egg
1 large egg white
$1^1/_4$ cups buttermilk
$1^1/_2$ tablespoons butter, melted
Butter, for cooking pancakes
2 cups mixed berries, washed, blotted dry with paper
    towels: raspberries, strawberries (hulled, quartered),
    blueberries

1. Put the oat bran, flour, baking soda, salt, and sugar in a small bowl. Mix until combined.

2. Put the egg, egg white, buttermilk, and melted butter in a $1^1/_2$-quart mixing bowl. Whisk until well combined. Whisk in the dry ingredients. The batter can be made a day in advance and refrigerated. Stir before using it.

3. Heat a griddle with butter over medium heat. When hot, spoon batter onto the griddle in 3-inch rounds. Sprinkle some of the berries over the batter. Cook until the pancake is bubbly and browned on the edges, about 4 minutes. Use a metal spatula to turn and brown the other side, about 2 to 3 minutes. Keep the cooked pancakes warm in a preheated 200-degree oven while the remaining pancakes are cooked. Serve hot.

Very Wild Rice Waffles with Dried Cranberries

The nuttiness of wild rice highlights this recipe, which is inspired by the delicious waffles served at the Northern Delights Café in the Traverse Bay area of Michigan. I couldn't resist adding dried cranberries to the batter, but the waffles are also good without them. Cooked wild rice freezes very well so it pays to cook more than you need while you're at it. I like serving these waffles with Cranberry Butter (page 39) or Warm Maple Syrup with Cranberries (page 41). Alternately, spreadable fruit, an intensely flavored, not too sweet preserve that is available in supermarkets, works well on them, too.

YIELD: 3 TO 4 SERVINGS, ABOUT 3 3/4 CUPS BATTER, 3 TO 4 WAFFLES

¹/₂ cup each: all-purpose flour, whole-wheat flour
1³/₄ cups well-drained cooked Wild Rice
  (page 360)
¹/₃ cup dried cranberries
2 tablespoons sugar
2 teaspoons baking powder
¹/₂ teaspoon baking soda
¹/₄ teaspoon salt
1¹/₄ cups buttermilk
2 large eggs
4 tablespoons unsalted butter, melted

1. Put the flours, wild rice, cranberries, sugar, baking powder, baking soda, and salt in a large mixing bowl. Mix until combined. In another bowl, put the buttermilk, eggs, and melted butter. Whisk until well combined. Add the buttermilk mixture to the dry ingredients; stir well.

2. Ladle the batter onto a preheated greased waffle iron. Cook the waffles until browned and a little crispy. The waffles can be kept warm in a preheated 200-degree oven while cooking the rest.

Baked German Pancake with Plums

Traditionally, a puffy, oven-baked German pancake is made with apples, but in August I can't resist using prune plums instead because of the tantalizing contrast of tart and sweet tastes. When prune plums are unavailable, any dark plum is fine—but be sure to decrease the sugar if necessary. This recipe makes an ideal breakfast or dessert.

YIELD: 4 BREAKFAST SERVINGS, 6 DESSERT SERVINGS

5 tablespoons unsalted butter

$^1/_3$ cup granulated sugar

$1^1/_2$ teaspoons cinnamon

5 large prune plums, pitted, thinly sliced, about
    $1^3/_4$ cups

$^2/_3$ cup cake flour

$^3/_4$ cup milk

2 tablespoons powdered nonfat dry milk

3 large eggs

1 teaspoon pure vanilla extract

Pinch of salt

1 tablespoon confectioners' sugar, plus additional
    for serving

1. Put a rack in the center of the oven; preheat the oven to 450 degrees.

2. Heat 2 tablespoons of the butter in an 8-inch skillet over medium-high heat. Combine the granulated sugar and cinnamon in a small dish.

3. When the butter is hot, add the plums and half the cinnamon sugar; cook until the plums are still intact but syrupy, about 4 minutes, stirring often. Do not overcook.

4. Put the flour, regular milk, dry milk, eggs, vanilla, salt, and the remaining cinnamon sugar in a bowl, blender, or a food processor fitted with a metal blade. Blend until smooth.

5. Heat the remaining 3 tablespoons of butter in a heavy 12-inch stove-to-oven skillet, preferably cast iron. Brush the butter up the sides of the skillet.

6. When the skillet is very hot, gently pour in half the batter. When the edges bubble, after about 30 seconds, scatter the cooked plums and syrup over the batter. Pour the remaining batter over the plums. Cook 30 seconds more; the pancake should cook for a total of 1 minute on top of the stove. Transfer the skillet to the oven.

7. Bake until puffy and lightly browned, about 15 minutes. Sieve confectioners' sugar over the top. Preheat the broiler.

8. Broil the pancake 8 to 10 inches from the heat until the sugar is caramelized, about 2 minutes. Cut into wedges. Serve the pancake hot with additional confectioners' sugar.

Amish Scramble with Potatoes and Sausage

Mounds of these browned potato slices cooked with onion, sausage, and some wisps of egg come to the table at Das Dutchman Essenhaus restaurant in Middlebury, Indiana. An irresistible sight to behold, they appear to be way more than 1 serving should be but how they disappear! For 50 cents more, the scramble comes with mild Cheddar cheese melted over it. Serve with toast and a side of warm applesauce for morning meals as they do at the restaurant. For lunch or supper, a mixed green salad served with the scramble makes a great meal. The garnish is my addition and is purely optional.

YIELD: 2 TO 3 SERVINGS

1 1/2 medium russet potatoes, peeled, cut into 1/3-inch-
   thick slices, about 3 cups
2 tablespoons peanut oil
1 tablespoon unsalted butter
1/2 teaspoon salt, plus a pinch
Freshly ground pepper to taste
1 small onion, minced, about 1/2 cup
One 4-ounce piece of smoked Thuringer sausage,
   skinned if desired, cut into 1/4-inch slices
1 large egg
2 large egg whites
1 tablespoon water
Minced parsley or snipped fresh chives, for garnish
   (optional)

1. Put the potato slices in a colander. Toss them with your hands under cold running water to wash the surface of the slices. Dry them as thoroughly as possible with paper towels.

2. Heat the oil and butter in a 12-inch nonstick skillet over medium-high heat. When very hot, add the potato slices, 1/2 teaspoon salt, and pepper to taste. Cook, covered, over medium-high heat until the potatoes are almost cooked through and browned, about 9 minutes, turning every 3 minutes to avoid burning. Add the onion and sausage. Gently toss them together. Cook, uncovered, until the potatoes are dark brown on the edges, about 5 to 6 minutes more.

3. Put the egg, egg whites, water, and a pinch of salt in a small dish. Froth with a fork. Add the egg mixture to the skillet. Use a rubber spatula or wooden spoon to move the eggs between the potatoes. Cook until the scramble is well set, about 2 more minutes, stirring it often. Serve hot, garnished with minced parsley or snipped fresh chives, if desired.

The Aunts'
Fresh Strawberry Omelet

When this refreshing omelet first appeared in a volume called The Aunts' Cook Book, *it was considered a dessert, made with heavy cream and 8 whole eggs. I've lightened it by replacing some of the egg yolks with egg whites and eliminating the cream, a good formula to apply to other omelets. The result is a lighter, fluffier breakfast or lunch omelet that makes a perfect foil for the taste of garden fresh strawberries. The aunts who created the original recipe, Emery May Holden and Katherine Davis Holden, wrote their cookbook to ensure that their nieces would marry. It would be hard, indeed, for a suitor to resist this offering.*

YIELD: 2 SERVINGS

1/2 pint fresh strawberries, room temperature, washed, blotted dry with paper towels, hulled

3 tablespoons sugar (use more to taste if the berries are tart)

1 teaspoon finely grated orange zest (colored rind), removed with a zester or fine grater (see page 14)

1 tablespoon fresh orange juice

1 1/2 tablespoons unsalted butter

2 large eggs

6 large egg whites

2 tablespoons water

Strawberries, for garnish

1. Cut half the strawberries into quarters (or into eighths if they are very large). Put the cut strawberries in a small bowl. Toss with 1 tablespoon of the sugar, the grated orange zest, and the orange juice. Set aside.

2. Put the remaining strawberries and 1 tablespoon of the sugar in a food processor fitted with a metal blade or blender. Puree. Set the sauce aside at room temperature.

3. Heat half the butter in a 7-inch nonstick omelet pan over medium high heat.

4. Put the whole eggs, egg whites, water, and the remaining 1 tablespoon of sugar in a mixing bowl. Whisk until smooth.

5. When the butter is sizzling hot but not browned, add half the egg mixture; cook over medium-high heat, shaking the pan back and forth while keeping it flat on the burner.

6. When the bottom is set, in about 3 minutes, stir the remaining uncooked portion rapidly with a fork, holding the tines parallel to the bottom of the pan to avoid disturbing the cooked portion. Continue stirring until almost set, about 1 minute more.

7. With a slotted spoon, arrange half the cut strawberries (reserving the juices) on the half of the

omelet nearest the pan handle. Cook, covered, about 1 minute. Uncover and grasp the handle firmly with your hand turned palm up. Tilt the pan up and insert a spatula under the half of the omelet nearest the handle. Roll onto a heated plate. Keep warm in a preheated 200-degree oven while making the second omelet, using the remaining ingredients.

8. To serve, add the reserved strawberry juices to the room temperature pureed sauce. Spoon the sauce over the omelets, dividing it evenly. Garnish the plate with a few whole strawberries. Serve hot.

Spinach Bread Pudding with Capriole Goat Cheese and Bacon

This savory bread pudding bakes up in the most inviting way—the melted cheese turns bronze on the edges while it stays meltingly soft in the center. Nueske's applewood-smoked bacon makes the difference—this small amount of bacon imparts the perfect smoky taste without being very salty. Nueske's products are processed in Wisconsin and are of excellent quality (see Midwestern Sources, page 371). The mild soft Capriole (see Midwestern Sources, page 374) goat cheese is the perfect choice; if necessary, substitute a similar soft, mild goat cheese. Muenster or any other soft, melting cheese can be substituted for the Monterey Jack. This pudding must be prepared at least 6 hours in advance to allow time for the bread to absorb all the liquid and flavor.

YIELD: 6 SERVINGS

4 lean, thick applewood-smoked bacon slices (see Midwestern Sources, page 376), cut into ¼-inch dice, about ⅔ cup

½ small red onion, chopped, about ¾ cup

5 large eggs

6 large egg whites

¾ cup milk (regular or 2 percent)

¾ teaspoon salt

Freshly ground pepper to taste

Two 10-ounce packages frozen chopped spinach, thawed completely, drained, and squeezed dry

2 cups firm-textured white bread cubes (about ½-inch cubes)

2¼ ounces soft, mild goat cheese, crumbled (or if it's very soft, pinch off small bits)

1 cup shredded Monterey Jack cheese

1. Grease a 4½-cup-capacity shallow baking dish. Set aside along with a baking sheet.

2. Put the bacon and onion in a 10-inch nonstick skillet. Cook over medium-high heat until the bacon is crisp, about 8 minutes, stirring often. Use a slotted spoon to transfer the contents of the skillet to a triple thickness of paper towels. Blot with paper towels. Set aside.

3. Meanwhile, put the eggs, egg whites, milk, salt, and pepper in a mixing bowl. Whisk until frothy. Use a wooden spoon to stir in the spinach. Stir in the bread cubes and bacon mixture.

4. Transfer the mixture to the prepared dish. Dot the surface evenly with the crumbled goat cheese. Evenly sprinkle Monterey Jack cheese over the surface. Cover and refrigerate for at least 6 hours or overnight.

5. Put a rack in the center of the oven; preheat the oven to 350 degrees. When ready to bake, place the refrigerated dish on the baking sheet. Bake, uncovered, until the edges are brown and puffy, about 1 hour. To serve, cut the pudding into serving portions. Serve hot.

Fried Cornmeal Mush, Thick or Thin

Fried mush is a kissing cousin to polenta. Like its Italian counterpart, it should be crisp on the outside while remaining soft within. Das Dutchman Essenhaus in Middlebury, Indiana, serves its fried mush with maple syrup or with tomato gravy made from tomato juice and flour—accompanied by a side order of regular or Canadian bacon. Before frying, you can cut the mush as thick or thin as you like.

YIELD: ONE 7 1/2-INCH LOAF

4 cups water
1¼ teaspoons salt
1 tablespoon vegetable oil
1¼ cups yellow cornmeal
3 tablespoons flour
Peanut oil, for frying
Warm maple syrup, for serving

1. Grease a 4-cup-capacity (7½ × 3½-inch) bread pan. Set aside.

2. Put the water, salt, and oil in a small saucepan. Bring to a boil. Meanwhile, combine the cornmeal and flour in a small dish. Reduce the water mixture to a simmer and slowly add the cornmeal mixture in a thin, steady stream, whisking constantly. Cook gently, stirring often, until it is very thick, about 3 minutes.

3. Transfer the hot mixture to the prepared loaf pan; smooth the surface with a spatula. Cool it completely, then refrigerate until it is chilled. The loaf can be kept refrigerated up to 3 days.

4. To cook, cut the chilled mush into slices of the desired thickness. Heat a ⅛-inch depth of peanut oil in a skillet over medium-high heat. When it is hot, without crowding, add the chilled slices and brown both sides, about 4 minutes per side. Use tongs to transfer the slices to a double thickness of paper towels. The slices can be kept warm in a preheated 200-degree oven while any remaining slices are being cooked. Sprinkle the slices lightly with salt. Serve hot with warm maple syrup.

French Toast with Cornflake Crunch

Several years ago, when the new, stylish Hyatt Regency Suites Hotel opened in Chicago, Steve Peterson was the chef with a back-to-basics cooking style. He introduced this delicious version of French toast, which has an appealing crunch of cornflakes on one side and a garnish of sliced strawberries and orange segments. Serve it with Maple-Glazed Canadian Bacon (page 34), sausage, or bacon and pass warm maple syrup separately.

YIELD: 4 SERVINGS

3 large eggs
2 large egg whites
$^1/_2$ cup fresh orange juice
$^1/_2$ cup confectioners' sugar, plus additional for garnish
1 tablespoon cinnamon
2 teaspoons pure vanilla extract
Pinch of salt
$2^2/_3$ cups cornflakes
8 thick (about $^3/_4$-inch) slices day-old egg bread, brioche, or challah
3 tablespoons unsalted butter
Sliced strawberries, orange segments (see page 12), for garnish

1. Put the eggs, egg whites, orange juice, confectioners' sugar, cinnamon, vanilla, and salt in a mixing bowl. Whisk until well mixed. Spread $^1/_3$ cup of the cornflakes on the center of a piece of plastic wrap.

2. Dip a slice of bread quickly into the egg mixture, coating both sides. Place the bread onto the cornflakes. Use a fork to press the top of the bread lightly to embed the cornflakes into the underside. It should be solidly coated. Set the bread slice aside, cornflake side down. Working quickly, repeat the dipping process with the remaining slices of bread, using about $^1/_3$ cup of cornflakes per slice.

3. Divide the butter between 2 large nonstick griddles or skillets. Melt over medium heat until it is hot. Transfer the slices, cornflake side down, to the griddles. Cook until both sides are browned, about 4 minutes each side. (Lacking sufficient cooking surface, you can dip the slices and coat them with cornflakes as batches are cooked, keeping the cooked slices warm in a preheated 200-degree oven.) Serve hot, cornflake side up. Lightly sieve confectioners' sugar over the toast. Garnish the plate with strawberries and orange segments.

Chunky Apple Muffins

These muffins are moist with an abundance of diced apples. The batter is light-textured—almost like a cake—making them a good option for tea or dessert, sprinkled with confectioner's sugar. Any extra muffins can be successfully frozen.

YIELD: 15 MEDIUM MUFFINS

³/₄ cup sugar

¹/₄ cup vegetable oil

¹/₂ cup buttermilk

1 large egg

2 large egg whites

1 teaspoon pure vanilla extract

2 medium Granny Smith apples, cut in ¹/₃-inch dice,
    about 2 cups

1¹/₂ cups flour

2 teaspoons baking powder

¹/₂ teaspoon each: baking soda, cinnamon

¹/₄ teaspoon salt

1. Put a rack in the center of the oven; preheat the oven to 375 degrees. Place paper liners into 15 standard muffin cups or grease the muffin cups. Set aside.

2. Put the sugar and oil in an electric mixer. Mix until it is smooth. Add the buttermilk, egg, egg whites, and vanilla to the sugar mixture. Mix until it is smooth.

3. Put the apples in a small mixing bowl. Toss them with ¹/₂ cup of flour. Add the remaining flour, baking powder, baking soda, cinnamon and salt to the electric mixer bowl. Combine well. Stir the apples into the batter with a wooden spoon.

4. Spoon the batter into the prepared muffin cups, filling about two-thirds full.

5. Bake until the muffins are golden brown and a toothpick inserted in the center comes out clean, about 28 minutes. Transfer them in the pan to a wire rack. Let muffins rest 10 minutes before removing them from the cups. Serve warm.

6. The muffins can also be frozen for as long as 3 months. After they have cooled, put them in a single layer on a cookie sheet and place in the freezer. Once frozen solid, pile them into a plastic bag, securely tied. Then pop this bag inside another (also securely tied) to keep that fresh taste and to eliminate any freezer odors. It is not necessary to thaw the muffins before reheating them. The muffins can be reheated in a preheated 300-degree oven for about 10 to 14 minutes or gently in a microwave oven for 20-second increments on medium power (50 percent) until warm. The microwave timing will depend on how many muffins are reheated at the same time. Serve warm.

Lemon Cornmeal Blueberry Muffins

Even with the addition of cornmeal, these muffins are extremely light-textured. The glaze makes the muffins very lemony, also pleasantly moist. Let the batter stand about 15 minutes before baking the muffins; this waiting period produces puffier muffins.

YIELD: 12 MUFFINS

MUFFINS:
Grated zest (colored rind) of 2 large lemons, removed
    with a zester or fine grater (see page 14), about 2
    tablespoons
1 cup sugar
$1/2$ cup vegetable oil
1 large egg
1 cup buttermilk
$1^1/2$ cups flour
$1/3$ cup cornmeal
1 teaspoon baking soda
Scant $1/4$ teaspoon salt
1 cup blueberries

GLAZE:
3 tablespoons fresh lemon juice
$1^1/2$ tablespoons sugar

1. Put a rack in the center of the oven; preheat the oven to 375 degrees. Line 12 standard-size muffin cups with paper liners or grease them. Set aside.

2. Put the zest, sugar, oil, and egg in a mixing bowl. Use a wooden spoon to mix well. Stir in the buttermilk, then the flour, cornmeal, baking soda, and salt. Fold in the blueberries. Let the batter rest for 15 minutes before baking the muffins. Ladle the batter into the muffin cups, filling them seven-eighths full.

3. Bake until the muffins are lightly browned and a toothpick inserted into the center comes out clean, about 22 minutes. Let them cool in the pan for 5 minutes before dipping them in the glaze.

4. Meanwhile, make the glaze. Stir the lemon juice and sugar together in a small bowl. Be sure the sugar dissolves. Quickly dip the tops of the warm muffins into the glaze. Let the muffins rest 15 minutes before removing them from the cups and serving them. The muffins can be frozen for up to 3 months. After they have cooled, put them in a single layer on a cookie sheet and place in the freezer. Once frozen solid, pile them into a plastic bag, securely tied. Then pop this bag inside another (also securely tied) to keep that fresh taste and to eliminate any freezer odors. It is not necessary to thaw the muffins before reheating them. To reheat, place the muffins in a preheated 300-degree oven for 10 minutes or in a microwave oven for increments of 20 seconds on medium power (50 percent) until warm.

Orange Poppy Seed Scones

Scones are a close relative to biscuits but slightly sweeter. Here, the citrus zest and juices flavor the scones while the poppy seeds provide a nice bite. Serve them with flavored butters (pages 35–40) and/or preserves for breakfast, tea, or with a late morning cappuccino. The recipe can be easily doubled or tripled.

YIELD: 8 SCONES

SCONES:
1 1/2 cups cake flour
3 tablespoons sugar
3/4 teaspoon baking powder
1/4 teaspoon baking soda
1/8 teaspoon salt
1 tablespoon poppy seeds
1/2 tablespoon each: grated lemon and orange zest
   (colored rinds), removed with a zester or fine grater
   (see page 14)
4 tablespoons unsalted butter, at room temperature
1/3 cup buttermilk
1 tablespoon each: fresh lemon juice,
   fresh orange juice

GLAZE:
1 large egg
1 tablespoon sugar
1/4 teaspoon salt

1. Put a rack in the center of the oven; preheat the oven to 425 degrees. Grease a baking sheet; sprinkle it lightly with water (the moisture keeps the scones from sticking). Set aside.

2. For the scones, put the flour, sugar, baking powder, baking soda, salt, poppy seeds, and zests in a mixing bowl. Use a fork to mix the ingredients. Cut the butter into 4 pieces. Scatter on flour mixture. Use a pastry blender or 2 knives to cut the butter into the flour until the mixture is crumbly.

3. Combine the buttermilk and juices in a cup. Add them to the mixing bowl. Use a fork to mix just until all the flour mixture is moistened; the dough will be a mass of lumps. Do not overmix. Gather the lumps into a ball, compacting it to hold it together. The dough will be moist.

4. Turn the dough onto a floured board. Knead the dough, folding and pressing it back on itself, until it holds together and is smooth, about 30 seconds. Pat the dough into a 7 1/4-inch-diameter circle, about 1/2 inch thick.

5. For the glaze, put the egg, sugar, and salt into a small dish. Use a fork to mix well until frothy.

6. Brush the surface of the dough with the glaze. Cut the dough into 8 equal-size pie-shaped wedges. Place the scones 1 inch apart on the prepared baking sheet.

7. Bake until the tops are just lightly browned, about 10 minutes. Do not overbake. Serve warm or at room temperature.

Onion Breakfast Cake

This intriguing recipe was originally a dessert called Zweibelkuchen, *appearing in the sweets section of* The United States Regional Cook Book, *edited by Ruth Berolzheimer (Culinary Arts Institute, Chicago, 1947). However, when I made it, I found that it was perfectly suited to any time of the day, from morning to late night, although it's more of a savory than a dessert. It has a sweet balance that works well with the onion and bacon topping. The yeast base, quickly mixed ahead and refrigerated overnight, has a tender, spongy texture with the addition of the whipped egg white. For a gracious late breakfast, serve it with sliced ham or smoked turkey and a fresh fruit salad. Later in the day, it's intriguing on a buffet table or served as a side dish with roasted chicken and warm applesauce for a simple homespun meal.*

YIELD: ONE 9 1/2-INCH ROUND, 6–8 SERVINGS

DOUGH:

1 package dry yeast
3 tablespoons sugar
1/2 cup warm milk (about 105 to 115 degrees)
1 1/4 cups flour
2 tablespoons unsalted butter, softened
1/4 teaspoon salt
1 large egg, separated

TOPPING:

2 tablespoons unsalted butter
2 medium Spanish onions, thinly sliced,
  about 4 cups
1 tablespoon flour
2 large eggs
1/2 teaspoon salt
1/4 teaspoon freshly grated nutmeg (see page 289)
3 thin slices cooked applewood-smoked bacon (see
  Midwestern Sources, page 376), crumbled, about
  1 1/2 tablespoons

1. For the dough, stir the yeast and 1/2 tablespoon of the sugar into the milk; let it stand until foamy, about 5 minutes.

2. Put the flour, remaining sugar, butter, salt, and egg yolk in a 2-quart mixing bowl. Use a wooden spoon to combine it well. Add the yeast mixture; mix until combined. Use the mixer to whip the egg white until it holds its shape but is still moist. Fold the egg white into the batter. Cover the bowl with plastic wrap and refrigerate overnight.

3. Generously grease the bottom and sides of a 9 1/2-inch springform pan.

4. On a well-floured board, roll the dough out to fit the prepared pan and place the dough in the pan. Let it rest 30 minutes at room temperature. The dough will not rise.

5. Meanwhile, make the topping. Heat the butter in a large skillet over medium-high heat. When it is hot, add the onions and cook until softened, about 5 minutes, stirring often. Stir in flour.

6. Transfer the onions to a mixing bowl. Put the eggs, salt, and nutmeg in a small bowl. Use a fork to froth the mixture. Add to the onions. Mix until combined.

7. Put a rack in the center of the oven; preheat the oven to 375 degrees.

8. When ready to bake, spread the onion mixture (it's okay if it's still warm) over the dough. Sprinkle with the bacon.

9. Bake until the cake is lightly browned on the edges, about 50 minutes. Let it rest 10 minutes on a wire rack. Serve warm, cut into wedges.

10. The cake can be made a day ahead, cooled completely, and refrigerated, covered airtight. To reheat, bake, covered, in a preheated 375-degree oven until it is warmed through, about 15 minutes. Or, alternately, remove the cake from the pan, place it on a microwavable platter, and gently reheat in a microwave oven on medium power (50 percent) until just warm but not hot and steamy, about 2 to 3 minutes.

Baked Apple Dumplings

From Joan Bilderback of Woodstock, Illinois, comes a real old-fashioned, down-home recipe. She writes, "When I was growing up there was an apple tree in our backyard. This was before the days of home freezers so apple season was eagerly anticipated. My mother and grandmother, both wonderful cooks, prepared apples in many delicious ways. I think this had to be my favorite of all those apple dishes." Here is their recipe for apple dumplings. What makes this delicious apple recipe so appealing to me is its versatility; consider it a brunch side dish with ham, Canadian bacon, and eggs or a supper accompaniment to fried chicken. With a scoop of ice cream, it's definitely in the dessert category. Whatever role it has in your meal, just be sure to serve it warm.

YIELD: 6–8 SERVINGS

SUGAR SYRUP:
$1^1/_2$ cups water
1 cup sugar
1 teaspoon fresh lemon juice

DUMPLINGS:
4 tablespoons unsalted butter
$1^3/_4$ cups flour
1 teaspoon baking powder
$^3/_4$ teaspoon salt
2 tablespoons sugar
$^1/_2$ cup water
$1^1/_4$ teaspoons cinnamon
4 small tart apples, peeled, halved, cored (if the apples are large, use only 2, cutting them into quarters)
2 small tart apples, peeled, cored, coarsely chopped, about 1 cup
1 tablespoon melted unsalted butter, for brushing
Heavy cream, for serving (optional)

1. Put a rack in the center of the oven; preheat the oven to 350 degrees. Set aside a shallow $7^1/_2$-cup-capacity round or shallow square ovenproof baking dish and a cookie sheet.

2. For the syrup, put all the ingredients in a small saucepan. Bring to a boil. Simmer, uncovered, for 5 minutes. Set aside.

3. Meanwhile, for the dumplings, cut $2^1/_2$ tablespoons of the butter into the flour, baking powder, salt, and sugar in a food processor fitted with the metal blade or with a pastry blender. Add the water. Mix until the dough just begins to clump together. Transfer the dough to a floured board. Compact the dough with your hands. Knead the dough, folding and pressing it back on itself, until it holds together and is smooth. Cut the dough in half; then each half into quarters. (You should have 8 equal size pieces.) Take a piece of dough into your hand and gently pat it into a 3-inch round. (Flour your hands for easier handling if the dough is sticky.) Lightly sprinkle the dough with cinnamon. Place an apple half (or quarter), rounded side down, on the center of the dough. Wrap the dough around the apple, gently easing the dough so it covers the apple completely. Repeat the process with the remaining dough, cinnamon, and apples.

4. Arrange the covered apples in a single layer, cut side down, in the baking dish, spacing them evenly. Spoon the chopped apples into the spaces. Pour the syrup over the dumplings. Sprinkle with the remaining cinnamon; dot with the remaining 1½ tablespoons of butter. Place the dish on the cookie sheet (to catch any juices).

5. Bake until the dumplings are lightly browned, about 1 hour, 10 minutes. Brush them with melted butter. Set them on a rack to cool at least 30 minutes before serving. Serve warm, with cream if desired.

6. The dumplings can be made several hours ahead and kept at room temperature. To serve, reheat in a preheated 350-degree oven until they are warmed through, about 15 minutes.

Spice Up Your Morning Coffee:

- ❖ Shake a generous dash of cinnamon onto ground coffee before brewing.
- ❖ Make hot chocolate with strong hot coffee instead of water.
- ❖ Serve it *mit Schlag*—with a froth of real whipped cream spooned on top— or steamed 1 percent milk.

Keys' Caramel Rolls

For those of you who are reluctant to make your own bread dough, here's a recipe using ready-made frozen white bread dough, available in most supermarkets. Interestingly enough, the popular original Keys Restaurant in St. Paul, Minnesota, (at last count there were six others in the Minneapolis–St. Paul area) uses frozen dough for their irresistible caramel rolls. Soft and squishy, this dough is just the right texture for the huge (big enough to cut into slices) mouthwatering, caramelized mounds that they serve to a constantly clamoring crowd. A waiting line is commonplace for Keys' hearty, Midwestern specialties, these rolls included. The official recipe includes pecans and raisins, but the rolls I tasted did not have them—and I personally didn't miss them!

YIELD: 4 VERY LARGE CARAMEL ROLLS

6 tablespoons milk
1 stick unsalted butter
1 cup packed light brown sugar
$^1/_3$ cup small pecan halves (optional)
1 pound frozen white bread dough, thawed according to package instructions
$^1/_4$ cup sugar
2 teaspoons cinnamon
$^1/_3$ cup raisins (optional)

1. Grease a 9-inch square pan. Set aside.

2. Put the milk, 6 tablespoons of the butter, and the brown sugar in a small saucepan. Bring to a simmer. Cook over medium-high heat, stirring often, until the butter is melted and the mixture is smooth, about 4 minutes. Transfer the mixture to the prepared pan, spreading it evenly over the bottom. If using pecans, scatter them, rounded side down, within 1 inch of the outer edge of the pan. Set aside.

3. On a lightly floured board, roll the dough into a rectangle, about 14 inches by 6 inches. Melt the remaining 2 tablespoons of butter. Brush the butter over the surface of the dough. Combine the sugar and cinnamon in a small dish. Sprinkle it evenly over the surface (it seems as if it is too much but it's okay). If using raisins, scatter them evenly over the surface. Gently press them into the dough with a rolling pin. Cut the dough in half lengthwise. Starting with the short end, carefully roll up each half compactly. Pinch the dough together to secure the end. Cut it in half crosswise. Place the cut side down in the pan, spacing the rolls evenly. Brush the remaining melted butter over the top of the rolls. Cover the pan loosely with plastic wrap. Let the rolls rise in a warm place until they are doubled, 40 to 60 minutes. (Or alternately, the rolls can be prepared to this point and refrigerated overnight. Remove them from the refrigerator in the morning and let them rise as described above, taking somewhat longer, until they are doubled, about 2 hours total. Remove the plastic.

4. Put a rack in the center of the oven; preheat the oven to 350 degrees.

5. Bake the rolls until they are well browned, about 30 minutes. Set the pan on a wire rack for 15 minutes, then invert the rolls onto foil, reapplying any caramel sauce and pecans that stick to the baking pan. Let them cool at least 20 more minutes before serving.

6. The rolls can be made a day ahead and kept at room temperature in a cake tender, or wrapped airtight and frozen for up to 3 months. It is not necessary to thaw the rolls before reheating them. To serve, reheat, uncovered, in a preheated 350-degree oven until the rolls are warmed through, about 12 minutes (about 16 minutes, if frozen).

Maple-Glazed Canadian Bacon

A lightly sweetened syrup gives a bronze patina to slices of Canadian bacon.

YIELD: 6 SERVINGS

3 tablespoons pure maple syrup
1 tablespoon light brown sugar
2¹/₂ teaspoons Dijon mustard
1 teaspoon fresh lemon juice
Pinch of salt
One 8-ounce piece of applewood-smoked Canadian
*   bacon (see Midwestern Sources, page 376), cut into*
*   six ³/₈-inch-thick slices*

1. Put the syrup, sugar, mustard, lemon juice, and salt in a small bowl. Mix until smooth.

2. Brush one side of each slice of bacon with the glaze. Place the bacon, glazed side down, on a large nonstick griddle. Cook over medium-high heat until the bottom is browned and syrupy, 3 to 4 minutes. Brush the top of the bacon and turn the slices over. Cook until the other side is browned, about 3 minutes longer. Transfer the bacon to a platter and brush with any remaining glaze. Serve hot.

Nueske's Meats

When it comes to applewood-smoked bacon, Canadian bacon, slab ham, and other smoked meats, Nueske's Hillcrest Farm Meats, located in Wittenberg, Wisconsin, does it best. The quality is so good that the simplest pan-frying is all that's required to bring out subtle and very appealing flavors. Use for breakfast and other meals during the day. See Midwestern Sources, page 376.

Fresh Raspberry Butter

Fruit butters add a welcome brightness to the morning meal . . . and other informal meals as well. They are easy to make and freeze well; they're a quick idea for capturing the flavors of seasonal fruit. Spread these butters on toast, muffins, rolls, pancakes, or waffles. In early summer and fall, when raspberries are at their peak, this brightly colored butter should be a regular on your breakfast table. The microwave variation yields a more intense flavor and color because it isn't necessary to use any water in the cooking.

YIELD: 1/2 CUP

1 cup raspberries
2 tablespoons each: water, confectioners' sugar
1 tablespoon sugar
1 stick unsalted butter, softened
A few drops of fresh lemon juice
1 teaspoon raspberry or blackberry liqueur (optional)

1. Put the raspberries, water, and confectioners' sugar in a small pot. Bring to a boil. Simmer, uncovered, over medium heat until syrupy, about 5 minutes. Watch carefully to avoid burning. (Alternately, cook in a microwave and omit the water. Put the raspberries and confectioners' sugar in a 1-quart microwave dish. Cook on high, uncovered, until syrupy, about 4 minutes.) Press the raspberries through a fine sieve to remove any seeds.

2. Put the raspberry syrup in a small food processor fitted with a metal blade, a blender, or a 1-quart mixing bowl. Add the remaining ingredients and mix until smooth. Transfer the butter to a ramekin for serving. Chill. To serve, let the butter soften slightly at room temperature until it is spreadable.

3. Covered airtight, the butter can be refrigerated for up to 3 days or frozen for up to 3 months.

Honey Pecan Butter

Toasting pecans greatly enhances their flavor. Toast more than you need while you're at it as you can keep them frozen, ready to use whenever you need them. To give this butter an extra dimension, try using an exotic fruit honey like raspberry or cranberry honey. It's especially good spread on cornmeal mush as pecans and cornmeal have a special affinity for one another.

YIELD: 1 1/3 CUPS

1 cup pecans, toasted (page 358)
1 stick unsalted butter, softened
1/3 cup honey

1. Put the pecans and the remaining ingredients in a small food processor fitted with a metal blade or in a blender. Blend until smooth. Transfer the butter to a ramekin. Chill. To serve, let the butter soften slightly at room temperature until it is spreadable.

2. Covered airtight, the butter can be refrigerated for up to 3 days or frozen for up to 3 months.

Granny Butter

*The tartness of Granny Smith apples makes a nicely flavored butter
for biscuits, muffins, and toast.*

YIELD: ABOUT 1/2 CUP

Granny Smith apple, peeled, cored, chopped ($^1/_2$ cup)
3 tablespoons water (optional)
6 tablespoons unsalted butter, softened
$^1/_4$ teaspoon allspice
2 tablespoons sugar
Pinch of salt

1. Soften the apple in the microwave oven on high power (100 percent) in a microwavable dish for about 2 minutes or, uncovered, in a small saucepan with 3 tablespoons of water over medium heat, about 6 minutes.

2. Put the apple, along with the butter, allspice, sugar, and salt, in a small food processor fitted with a metal blade or in a blender. Mix until smooth. Transfer the butter to a ramekin. Chill. To serve, let the butter soften slightly at room temperature until it is spreadable.

3. Covered airtight, the butter can be refrigerated for up to 3 days or frozen for up to 3 months.

Persimmon Butter

Persimmons are a huge crop in the Midwest with the harvest occurring in late fall; when ripe, they have a mild but intriguing flavor that is different from that of any other fruit. Quite unlike Japanese persimmons, they are small, with a large pit. These persimmons are time-consuming to pit and puree so it's fortunate that frozen persimmon pulp is available by mail. (see Midwestern Sources, page 378). The flour in this recipe makes the butter smoother without adding any taste of its own.

YIELD: 1 SCANT CUP

³/₄ cup pureed fresh (or thawed frozen) persimmon pulp
¹/₂ stick unsalted butter, softened
2 tablespoons sugar
2 teaspoons flour
Pinch of salt

1. Put all the ingredients in a food processor fitted with a metal blade or in a blender. Process until smooth, about 3 minutes. The texture will be slightly rough. Transfer the butter to a ramekin. Chill. To serve, let the butter soften slightly at room temperature until it is spreadable.

2. Covered airtight, the butter can be refrigerated for up to 3 days or frozen for up to 3 months.

Cranberry Butter

*This makes a truly festive holiday spread for biscuits and quick breads. The same quantity
of cooked cranberries can also be used, but the sugar should be adjusted according to taste.*

YIELD: 1/2 CUP

6 tablespoons unsalted butter, softened
$^1/_3$ cup raw cranberries
3 tablespoons confectioners' sugar

1. Put all the ingredients in a small food processor
fitted with a metal blade or in a blender. Process
until smooth, about 2 minutes, stopping as
necessary to scrape down the sides of the container.
Transfer the butter to a ramekin. Chill. To serve, let
the butter soften slightly at room temperature until
it is spreadable.

2. Covered airtight, the butter can be refrigerated
for up to 3 days or frozen for up to 3 months.

Lemon Maple Butter

*This butter is especially good on Lemon Cornmeal Blueberry Muffins (page 26)
and Lemon Popovers (page 272).*

YIELD: ABOUT 2/3 CUP

4 tablespoons unsalted butter, softened
1 tablespoon fresh lemon juice
3 tablespoons maple syrup
1 tablespoon grated lemon zest (colored rind), removed
    with a zester or fine grater (see page 14)
1 tablespoon confectioners' sugar

1. Put all the ingredients in a small food processor
fitted with a metal blade or in a blender. Process
until smooth. Transfer the butter to a ramekin.

Chill. To serve, let the butter soften slightly at
room temperature until it is spreadable.

2. Covered airtight, the butter can be refrigerated
for up to 3 days or frozen for up to 3 months.

Warm Maple Syrup with Fresh Peaches

Adding fresh fruit to maple syrup makes an especially delicious pancake or waffle topping. If you like, you can substitute an equal amount of bananas, blueberries, raspberries, or strawberries for the peaches. Always serve the fruit syrup slightly warm.

YIELD: 2 CUPS

2 ripe but firm small peaches, peeled and thinly sliced, about 1²/3 cups
2 teaspoons fresh lemon juice
²/3 cup pure maple syrup

Toss the peaches with the lemon juice in a saucepan. Just before serving, add the maple syrup and heat over medium-low heat. Adding the syrup just before serving keeps the peaches from wilting too much.

Cranberry variation: Simmer 1¹/3 cups raw cranberries in the maple syrup just until they pop, about 5 minutes (slightly longer if frozen). Omit the lemon juice, and add brown sugar to taste.

Herbed Spiced Pecans

Pepper Cheese Pastry "Puffs"

Crispy Garlic Red Potato Skins

Smoked Salmon Spread with Horseradish and Capers

Eggplant Basil Sandwiches

Cornmeal Chive Pancakes with Great Lakes Golden Caviar

Sauerkraut Balls with Mustard Mayonnaise

Spinach and Feta Cheese Strudel

Wild Rice Pancakes with Chutney and Sour Cream

Warm Cranberry-Glazed Brie Cheese

Basket of Crudités with Anchovy and Mustard Vinaigrettes

Warm Fantome Farm Goat Cheese in Herbed Garlic Oil
   with Crusty Bread Slices

Chapter 2
Appetizers

❖

One of the things I love most about entertaining is that no matter what, just about everybody ends up in the kitchen. And little wonder. It's where so many delicious things happen, a center of friendly, creative energy. While I put the finishing touches on a meal, I like to serve small taste treats that go well with a glass of wine.

My idea of an appetizer is something that is easy to prepare and delivers big flavor in a small package. The idea here isn't to fill but to entice. This calls for simple, practical dishes while eschewing the precious and complicated.

Warm Cranberry-Glazed Brie Cheese can hardly be called an inspiration of the Midwest tradition, but it does rely on major products of the Midwest, cranberries as well as the Wisconsin Brie. So too do Wild Rice Pancakes with Chutney and Sour Cream and Crispy Garlic Red Potato Skins. Lots of vegetables here, a Basket of Crudités enlivened with Anchovy and Mustard Vinaigrettes. And that means crunch, snap, flavor explosion, and color. Great Lakes Golden Caviar begs your attention on top of cornmeal pancakes. The horseradish for which Illinois is so famous finds a delightful partnership with smoked salmon and capers. The flavors and textures of simple appetizers intermingle and entangle, and the dinner guests, enchanted by now, are pulled that much closer to the table.

Herbed Spiced Pecans

These pecans are great to have on hand in the freezer for nibbles with drinks. The key to their success is the quality of the pecans; sample one before you start the recipe to make sure that they are not rancid or stale. You can substitute walnut halves (equal quantity) for the pecans, if you wish.

YIELD: 4 CUPS

2 large egg whites
2 tablespoons olive oil
1/4 cup light corn syrup
2 teaspoons each: dried rosemary, chili powder, dried
    thyme leaves, ground cumin
1 teaspoon salt
Pinch of cayenne pepper
1 pound large pecan halves

1. Put a rack in the center of the oven; preheat the oven to 325 degrees. Line a jelly roll pan (a cookie sheet with sides) with foil. Set aside.

2. Put the egg whites and oil together in 1¹/₂-quart bowl. Whisk until frothy. Add the remaining ingredients except the pecans; mix well. Add the pecans. Toss until they are evenly coated with the egg-white mixture.

3. Spread the pecans in a single layer on the prepared pan.

4. Bake until the pecans are deeply browned, about 25 to 27 minutes, stirring them twice during baking to allow the nuts to brown evenly. Watch them carefully to prevent burning.

5. Transfer the hot nuts to a clean piece of aluminum foil, separating any that stick together. Allow them to cool completely.

6. The nuts can be kept in an airtight container at room temperature up to a week, or frozen for as long as 2 months. If the nuts lose their crispness, refresh them in the oven. Spread them in a single layer on a jelly roll pan; bake in a preheated 300 degree oven until they are heated through, about 8 to 10 minutes. Let them cool completely before serving.

Easy Finger Foods . . .

❖ Bowls of fresh, high-quality lightly salted nuts.

❖ Interesting olives, such as Niçoise, Picholine, Calamata, served in separate bowls, marinated in olive oil with orange or lemon zest, garlic, and mixed herbs.

❖ Smoked salmon (insist on tasting a sample before buying it; make sure it's well flavored and not salty) served on thin-sliced lightly toasted pumpernickel or rye bread, or in Belgian endive leaves. A lemon wedge and coarsely cracked pepper are all that are needed to complement the finest salmon. A small bowl of crème fraîche to dollop on the top wouldn't detract.

❖ Paper-thin sliced smoked ham or prosciutto (Lupi is the best-tasting Parma ham), trimmed of visible fat, wrapped around wedges of cantaloupe or pear (dipped in lemon juice to prevent discoloring, patted dry), fresh fig halves, cheese sticks, blanched asparagus, or marinated artichoke hearts.

❖ Cooked shrimp served with a Mustard Mayonnaise (page 54).

❖ Fresh oysters on the half-shell served on ice with lemon wedges and spicy cocktail sauce.

❖ A cheese tray of assorted, ripe, room-temperature cheeses with thin-sliced French bread. Garnish with Gaelax leaves (available at the florist), clusters of grapes, and shiny apples and pears that can be cut into wedges by your guests.

❖ Herbed soft cheese piped into Belgian endive leaves, garnished with a snip of pimiento or a basil leaf.

❖ Crudités are always appealing to the health-minded; they have so much potential for colorful presentation, arranged in a lettuce-lined basket with the simplest curry mayonnaise (add a dash of lemon) served in a hollowed-out red pepper.

Pepper Cheese Pastry "Puffs"

Easy enough, these tasty freezer-ready pastries puff up like little pillows, filling the bill for cocktail nibbles without interfering with the dinner to follow. Don't skimp on the cheese; buy Parmigiano-Reggiano, available in Italian food stores and many specialty food markets. The quality of cheese makes all the difference.

YIELD: 36 PUFFS

1 sheet frozen puff pastry, thawed according to package directions
¹/₂ cup finely grated imported Parmesan cheese
1 teaspoon coarsely cracked black pepper
Pinch of cayenne pepper
¹/₂ teaspoon ground cumin

1. Put a rack in the center of the oven; preheat the oven to 400 degrees. Set aside a large cookie sheet.

2. On a lightly floured board, roll the pastry sheet into a 12-inch square.

3. Put the cheese, peppers, and cumin in a small bowl; mix well. Spread the mixture evenly over the pastry. Use your fingers to gently press it into the pastry.

4. Use a pizza cutter or a sharp knife to cut the dough into 2-inch squares. The puffs can be baked immediately or frozen, wrapped airtight, for as long as 3 months. It is not necessary to thaw them before baking.

5. Place the puffs, in a single layer, on the cookie sheet. Bake until they are puffed and well browned, about 12 minutes. Transfer them to a cooling rack. The puffs can be served after 5 minutes or cooled completely and stored in an airtight container for as long as 2 days.

Crispy Garlic Red Potato Skins

These potato skins lack the fat that is typical of their preparation but not any of the anticipated satisfaction. Delicious as they are plain, they are even better sprinkled with grated imported Parmesan cheese. These potatoes can also be filled with many flavorful mixtures. I tested this recipe with baking potatoes (russets) as well as small red potatoes; the red potatoes were more attractive, with a more appealing, tender texture for appetizers. Small new brown potatoes can be substituted for the red potatoes. Double or triple this recipe for a crowd.

YIELD: 12 POTATO SKIN HALVES

6 small red potatoes, scrubbed
1 large egg white
1 tablespoon olive oil
3 large cloves garlic, minced, about 1¹/₂ tablespoons
¹/₄ teaspoon salt
Freshly ground pepper to taste
2 tablespoons shredded imported Parmesan cheese
    (Parmigiano-Reggiano), for sprinkling

1. Put a rack in the center of the oven; preheat the oven to 450 degrees.

2. Bake the potatoes on a baking sheet until tender, about 40 minutes. Allow them to cool until they are easy to handle. The potatoes can be baked a day ahead and refrigerated after they are completely cool.

3. Cut the potatoes in half lengthwise and scoop out the center with a small melon baller, leaving a ¹/₈-inch-thick shell. (Use the scooped potato in soups or fried potatoes.)

4. Put the egg white, olive oil, garlic, salt, and pepper in a small bowl. Whisk until very frothy. Brush the inside of the skins with the mixture. Set aside remaining mixture. Place the potatoes in a single layer on a baking sheet.

5. Bake in the 450-degree oven until they are crisp and only lightly browned, about 20 to 25 minutes.

6. Lightly brush the skins with the egg-white mixture again. Evenly sprinkle them with Parmesan cheese, pressing it lightly into place with the back of a spoon.

7. Return the skins to the 450-degree oven and bake until the cheese is melted and the skins are deeply browned on the edges, about 6 minutes. Serve hot.

Smoked Salmon Spread with Horseradish and Capers

Smoked salmon varies greatly in quality and taste. I prefer a lightly smoked salmon that is nationally distributed by Duck Trap River Fish Farm in Maine (800-828-3825). When you buy smoked salmon, ask to taste a small sample first so that you know it has a good flavor and is not overly salty. This spread is piquant without being too sharp; serve it spread on pickling or English cucumber slices, toasted thin-sliced white bread or pumpernickel, or crackers.

YIELD: 1 1/2 CUPS

¹/₂ pound smoked salmon
1 cup light sour cream
2 teaspoons drained horseradish
¹/₂ teaspoon fresh lemon juice
3 tablespoons minced red onion
2 tablespoons snipped chives, *plus additional for garnish*
1 tablespoon drained capers

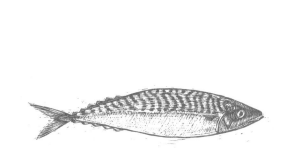

Put the salmon, sour cream, horseradish, lemon juice, and red onion in a blender or in a food processor fitted with the metal blade. Mix until smooth. Stir in the 2 tablespoons of chives and the capers. Refrigerate until well chilled, at least 4 hours. The spread can also be made a day ahead and refrigerated. Mound the salmon mixture in a shallow serving bowl. Smooth the surface with a knife. Garnish with additional snipped chives. Place the bowl on a large plate surrounded by cucumber slices, toast, or crackers.

Eggplant Issues

To some, the purple skin of eggplant is one of its most prized assets. Others disagree. So the question of whether eggplant should be peeled or not is more a matter of choice than of necessity. However, if the skin is thick and heavy, it is always a good idea to peel it. If you leave the peel on, make sure to cook the eggplant long enough to soften the skin.

Another eggplant issue that isn't etched in stone is whether or not to salt it before using. Eggplant very often—especially if it is quite mature—holds a lot of bitter-tasting liquid. Salting the cubed or sliced eggplant and letting it drain for at least 30 minutes will remove the liquid and hence the unpleasant taste. Another benefit to salting is that it allows you to cook the eggplant with far less fat. Unsalted eggplant soaks up cooking oil like a sponge. Salted, it will soak up much less oil in the cooking. I try to be pragmatic. Although it does add another step to the preparation, salting eggplant generally guarantees that the dish will not taste bitter and can be cooked with less fat.

Eggplant Basil Sandwiches

These sandwiches are scrumptious; crisply fried eggplant slices enclose a creamy cheese filling flecked with fresh basil. They are best served slightly warm, not hot, with or without a dab of Sweet Tomato Marmalade (page 125) or a very thick tomato sauce. Serve them as little nibbles with drinks or as a first course at the table. To make them bite-size and easy to handle with drinks, select long, slender Japanese eggplants or quarter large sandwiches after cooking them.

YIELD: 10 TO 12 SANDWICHES

Salt for eggplant, plus ³/₄ teaspoon
1 slim medium eggplant, peeled, cut crosswise into
   ¹/₄-inch-thick slices, about 4 cups (20 to 24 slices)
8 ounces light cream cheese, softened
¹/₂ cup minced fresh basil leaves
³/₄ cup soft bread crumbs
¹/₄ teaspoon cayenne pepper
2 large eggs
Vegetable oil, for cooking

1. Lightly salt the eggplant slices. Put them in a colander. Weight them with a heavy object. Leave them in the sink for at least 30 minutes. Pat them dry just before using.

2. Put the cream cheese and basil in a small bowl. Mix until smooth.

3. Combine the bread crumbs, ³/₄ teaspoon salt, and the cayenne pepper on a sheet of waxed paper. Put the eggs in a pie plate or shallow dish; froth them with a fork.

4. Spread a slice of eggplant with the herbed cheese, using about 2 teaspoons on the smaller slices and up to a tablespoon or more on the larger ones. Sandwich with another slice of eggplant. Dip the sandwiches first in the beaten eggs, then in the crumbs so they are well coated. Repeat with all the eggplant.

5. Heat a ¹/₈-inch depth of oil in a large nonstick skillet over medium heat. When very hot, fry the sandwiches, in batches so they aren't crowded, until crisp and golden on both sides, about 3 minutes per side. The sandwiches can be kept warm in a preheated 225-degree oven while the rest are being cooked. Serve warm (not hot).

Cornmeal Chive Pancakes with Great Lakes Golden Caviar

Tender little chive-flecked cornmeal pancakes lay the foundation for a layer of crème fraîche or sour cream and a small dollop of golden caviar, a great Midwestern product from the Carolyn Collins Caviar Company (see Midwestern Sources, page 375). The contrast of the slightly sweet pancakes with the delicious not-too-salty golden caviar is a great combination. The pancakes can be served at room temperature. If they are made in advance and refrigerated or frozen, they should be reheated to restore their original texture.

YIELD: TWENTY-FOUR 2 1/2-INCH PANCAKES

2 large eggs
3 tablespoons yellow cornmeal
2¹/₂ teaspoons sugar
2 teaspoons snipped chives
¹/₂ teaspoon baking soda
¹/₄ teaspoon salt
1 cup sour cream (light or regular)
Unsalted butter, for cooking
¹/₃ cup crème fraîche or sour cream, for serving
3 to 4 teaspoons golden caviar, for serving

1. Put the eggs, cornmeal, sugar, chives, baking soda, and salt in a small mixing bowl. Stir until smooth. Gently fold in the sour cream. The batter can be used right away or refrigerated overnight.

2. Melt enough butter to coat the bottom of a nonstick griddle. When the butter is hot, add a scant tablespoon of batter for each pancake, spreading it in neat 2¹/₂-inch circles with the back of a spoon. Cook over medium heat until the top is covered with air bubbles, about 3 minutes. Turn and brown the other side, about 3 minutes.

3. To serve, the pancakes should be at room temperature. Spread each pancake with crème fraîche or sour cream, leaving a small border of the pancake exposed. Top with a small dollop of caviar.

4. Pancakes can also be made a few hours in advance and kept at room temperature, or refrigerated overnight, or frozen. To refrigerate or freeze, stack the pancakes between squares of waxed paper and wrap the stack airtight in a plastic bag. Thaw in the plastic bag before reheating. Arrange refrigerated or thawed pancakes in a single layer on a cookie sheet. Bake in a preheated 200-degree oven until they are heated through, about 8 minutes. This reheating restores the pancakes' texture, although they are served at room temperature.

Caviar

The Caspian Sea and the Great Lakes have one wonderful thing in common—sturgeon, the enormous ancient fish that provides both veal-like fillets and the world's finest caviar.

A hundred years ago the American caviar industry was booming. At the end of the nineteenth century, 25 million pounds of sturgeon was being harvested per year, according to historian and writer Wesley Marx. Then, overfishing and a sharp increase in water pollution brought the sturgeon to near extinction. By 1920 the industry was all but dead.

In the last decade, this sad state of affairs has turned around, thanks to stricter fishing and pollution regulations and the advent of aquatic farms. The Carolyn Collins Caviar Company (see Midwestern Sources, page 375) in Chicago, Illinois, has been at the forefront of the American freshwater-caviar movement. Carolyn Collins produces caviar from Canadian lake sturgeon and hackleback sturgeon as well as from such lake fish as trout, whitefish, chinook and coho salmon, bowfin, and paddlefish.

Collins offers her caviar in a variety of forms: smoked, infused with liqueur, and as caviar butter. Her products turn up in some of Chicago's finest restaurants and have been praised for their smooth, fresh taste and low salt content.

Sauerkraut Balls with Mustard Mayonnaise

These appetizers are a specialty in many parts of the Midwest, especially in the State of Ohio. Paired with beer, they are delicious informal fare along with a selection of sausages and cheeses. They can be made early in the day and reheated in the oven. The food processor does a fast job of this preparation by mincing the parsley, bread for crumbs, garlic, and onion, as well as coarsely chopping the ham and sauerkraut, in that sequence, without your ever having to wash the work bowl.

YIELD: 2 DOZEN 1 1/2-INCH BALLS

SAUERKRAUT BALLS:

1 tablespoon vegetable oil

1 medium clove garlic, minced, about $^3/_4$ teaspoon

1 small onion, minced, about $^2/_3$ cup

6 ounces ham, preferably honey-baked, trimmed, coarsely chopped, about $1^1/_2$ cups

1 pound sauerkraut, rinsed, patted dry, coarsely chopped, about 2 cups

1 teaspoon dry mustard

$^1/_2$ to $^2/_3$ cup finely textured fresh bread crumbs

Freshly ground pepper to taste

2 tablespoons minced parsley

1 large egg white, frothed with a fork

FOR FRYING:

$^1/_2$ cup flour

1 large egg, frothed with a fork

1 cup finely textured fresh bread crumbs

Peanut oil, for frying

MUSTARD MAYONNAISE:

$^2/_3$ cup light mayonnaise

1 tablespoon plus 1 teaspoon Dijon mustard

1. For the sauerkraut balls, heat the oil in a small nonstick skillet over medium-high heat. When it is hot, add the garlic and onion. Cook until the onion is softened, about 3 minutes, stirring it often. Transfer the mixture to a 1-quart mixing bowl along with the remaining ingredients (start with only $^1/_2$ cup crumbs). Mix well. Add the remaining crumbs if the mixture is too wet to hold together. Use your hands to shape the mixture into $1^1/_2$-inch balls.

2. For frying, put the flour, egg, and bread crumbs in separate shallow dishes. Dip each ball first in the flour, then the beaten egg, and finally in the bread crumbs.

3. Heat a 2-inch depth of oil to 375 degrees (or, to test the temperature, be sure a bread crumb sizzles in the oil before frying the balls). Fry the balls, in batches, until they are brown and crisp, about 3 minutes, turning them as necessary to brown evenly. Place the balls on a double thickness of paper towels. They can be kept warm in a preheated 200-degree oven while you are frying the remaining balls.

4. For the mustard mayonnaise, put the ingredients in a small dish. Mix until combined. The mustard mayonnaise can be made 2 days ahead, covered airtight, and refrigerated. Let come to room temperature before using. Serve with the hot sauerkraut balls, passing the mustard mayonnaise separately.

5. The balls can be fried in advance, cooled, and refrigerated for several hours. To reheat, place them in a single layer on a cookie sheet. Bake in a preheated 350-degree oven until they are sizzling and crisp, about 20 to 25 minutes.

Sauerkraut

A Midwestern cook without a sauerkraut recipe was an anomaly in the nineteenth century. Historically, sauerkraut holds a significant place in the Midwest, especially on German and Amish tables. One third of the cabbage grown for sauerkraut in this country comes from Wisconsin.

When making your own sauerkraut, equipment is key. You need a cabbage shredder, a wooden mallet, an oversize oak barrel or crock, and a proper cellar for storing the finished product. Also, lots of time.

Making sauerkraut is so involved, I recommend using the bottled or bagged product, located in the refrigerator sections of supermarkets; it's far superior to canned sauerkraut.

A century ago homemade sauerkraut would be served as a side dish, boiled with spareribs, or combined with bacon and onions to make a complete meal. These are still good ideas.

Spinach and Feta Cheese Strudel

This flavorful spinach combination is an hors d'oeuvre favorite. Usually folded into time-consuming individual packets, this mixture is rolled up in phyllo leaves. The egg white mixed with oil and garlic replaces the melted butter that is typically brushed between phyllo layers and over the shaped roll. This mixture not only reduces the fat but, more importantly, makes the strudel very crisp and more flavorful.

YIELD: ABOUT SIXTEEN 1-INCH APPETIZERS

1½ tablespoons olive oil

¼ cup minced red onion

One 10-ounce package frozen chopped spinach, thawed
    but not squeezed dry

¾ teaspoon minced garlic

¼ teaspoon finely chopped orange zest (colored rind),
    removed with a zester or fine grater (see page 14)

⅛ teaspoon finely chopped fresh rosemary

3 ounces feta cheese, crumbled, about ¾ cup

¼ teaspoon salt

Freshly ground pepper to taste

1 large egg white

4 sheets phyllo, thawed

1. Put a rack in the center of the oven; preheat the oven to 375 degrees. Lightly grease a baking sheet. Set aside.

2. Heat ½ tablespoon of the olive oil in a large skillet over medium heat. When hot, add the onion. Cook until it is softened, about 2 minutes. Add the spinach and half of the garlic. Cook until the spinach is almost but not quite dry, about 2 to 4 minutes, stirring it often. Remove it from the heat. Transfer the mixture to a large bowl to cool. When it is cool, mix in the orange zest, rosemary, feta, salt, and pepper. The filling can be made several hours in advance and refrigerated.

3. Put the egg white, the remaining olive oil, and the remaining garlic in a small bowl. Whisk it until frothy.

4. To assemble, lay a piece of plastic wrap that is 4 inches longer than the phyllo on a work surface. Lay 1 sheet of phyllo on the plastic; cover the remaining sheets with a damp towel so they don't dry out. Brush the phyllo with the egg-white mixture. Cover it with another phyllo sheet, brush it with the egg mixture and continue layering in this manner until all 4 sheets (the top sheet should also be brushed) are used. Set aside unused egg mixture.

5. Arrange the filling in a 2-inch-wide row down the long side of the phyllo. Using the plastic wrap to help you, make one turn of the phyllo. Tuck under the ends, neaten the roll, and finish rolling it up into a compact cylinder. Cut the roll in half. Brush the surface of both halves with the remaining egg-white mixture. The strudel can be baked immediately or wrapped airtight and frozen for up to 2 months. Do not thaw it before baking.

6. Place the strudel on the prepared baking sheet. Bake it uncovered, until golden, about 18 to 20 minutes, or slightly longer if it is frozen. Use a serrated knife to cut the hot strudel at an angle into 1-inch-wide slices. Serve hot, warm, or at room temperature.

Wild Rice Pancakes with Chutney and Sour Cream

These crispy wild rice pancakes are very lightly bound with egg and the smallest amount of flour so they are almost lacy, with an earthy flavor and rough texture. Served with sour cream and chutney, they are delicious nibbles, easy to handle as finger food at a cocktail party. Served plain, they make an interesting side dish with meat, game, or poultry.

YIELD: TWENTY-FOUR 2-INCH PANCAKES

2¹/₂ cups cooked Wild Rice (page 360)
1 medium shallot, minced, about 2 tablespoons
2 large eggs
1¹/₂ tablespoons flour
¹/₂ teaspoon dried dill
¹/₂ teaspoon salt
Freshly grated nutmeg to taste (see page 289)
Unsalted butter, for frying
¹/₂ cup light sour cream
¹/₄ cup mango chutney

1. Put the cooked rice, shallot, eggs, dill, salt, and nutmeg in a small bowl. Stir until combined.

2. Heat 1 tablespoon of butter on a nonstick griddle or large nonstick skillet over medium heat. When it is hot, use 1 scant tablespoon of the rice mixture to form the pancakes. With the back of a spoon, spread the mixture into neat, flat rounds. Cook, turning once, until they are set, about 3 minutes per side. Repeat with the remaining rice mixture, adding more butter as necessary.

3. To serve, top each pancake (more textured side up) with 1 teaspoon sour cream and ¹/₂ teaspoon chutney. Serve warm or at room temperature.

4. The pancakes can be made 2 days in advance and refrigerated, or wrapped airtight and frozen for as long as 2 months. To reheat the pancakes, bring them to room temperature, still wrapped. When ready to reheat them, unwrap and place them in a single layer on a baking sheet. Bake in a preheated 325-degree oven until they are warm, about 10 minutes.

Brie

Besnier America (see Midwestern Sources, page 374), a French cheese company, has built a production facility in Belmont, Wisconsin; they make a great plain Brie as well as other varieties, including herbed and cracked-pepper Brie. A perfectly ripened Brie should be soft inside but not too runny. If you find that your Brie is not quite soft enough, you can soften it slightly in the microwave oven. Though this won't modify the taste, the texture will be more like that of a ripened Brie. Place the cheese on a microwave-safe plate; cook in the microwave oven on medium (50 percent power) just until it is softened, in 30-second increments, watching carefully to avoid melting it. And by the way, the white rind of Brie cheese is edible.

Warm Cranberry-Glazed Brie Cheese

No matter the year's trend in food and eating, I always make this Brie for holiday get-togethers, much to everyone's delight. Fortunately, the preparation can all be done ahead. The cranberry mixture is actually a mild chutney. It's a sensational coupling of flavors, colors, and textures that has wide appeal. For a festive holiday presentation, surround the Brie with a circle of holly leaves.

YIELD: 16 TO 20 SERVINGS

3 cups raw cranberries
$1/3$ cup dried currants
$3/4$ cup packed light brown sugar
$1/3$ cup water
$1/8$ teaspoon each: dry mustard, ground allspice, ground cloves, ground ginger, crushed red pepper flakes
One 2.2-pound Brie cheese (8 inches in diameter)
Plain crackers and/or toasted thin baguette slices, for serving

1. Line a baking sheet with heavy-duty foil. Set aside.

2. Put the cranberries, currants, brown sugar, water, and spices in a nonaluminum pan. Cook over medium-high heat, uncovered, until most of the berries have popped, about 8 minutes. Cool the mixture to room temperature. The glaze can be made up to a week ahead and refrigerated, or it can be frozen for up to 3 months.

3. Use a sharp, flexible paring knife to remove the top rind from the cheese, but try not to cut through the rind on the side or the cheese will ooze out of the cracks as it bakes. The cheese can be prepared 3 days ahead to this point, wrapped airtight, and refrigerated.

4. To assemble, place the cheese on the prepared baking sheet. Spread a thick layer of cranberry glaze over the top. The cheese can be assembled up to several hours in advance and kept at room temperature.

5. Put a rack in the center of the oven; preheat the oven to 300 degrees. Bake just until the cheese is soft, not oozing, about 12 minutes. The cheese is best served warm, but it is also good served at room temperature. Use the foil to transfer the cheese to a large platter, then gently tear the foil to remove it. Circle the cheese with plain crackers and/or toasted thin baguette slices.

Basket of Crudités

This presentation of crudités celebrates vegetables. Inspired by the tall wicker baskets brimming with whole vegetables at Le Maschou, a simple, rustic, wood-grill restaurant in Old Cannes, France, that could easily fit into the Midwestern countryside, these crudités are not set up for cocktail parties but as a dazzling first course. Since the vegetables are presented whole, it's necessary that each guest be seated at the table with a plate and a sharp knife to cut off a portion of each vegetable and pass it on. The two vinaigrettes are thick, tangy sauces. The experience makes for a wonderful, prolonged, shared first course—perfect for the participation of up to 8 people—and a great show-stopper. This is an easy and creative artistic endeavor.

YIELD: DEPENDS ON VEGETABLE SELECTION

SELECT VEGETABLES
FROM THE FOLLOWING:
Whole red, green, and yellow peppers; tomatoes; slender seedless cucumbers; bunches of young carrots with greens; celery hearts with greens; kohlrabi; small fennel bulbs with tops; heads of Belgian endive; small zucchini and summer squash; scored large mushrooms; bunches of spring or green onions; small cooked beets; small heads of red leaf lettuce and curly endive; bunches of radishes with their leaves; wedges of red cabbage (all vegetables should be washed and blotted dry with paper towels)
Hard-cooked brown eggs in the shell
Parsley clumps, for garnish
Anchovy Vinaigrette and Mustard Vinaigrette (recipes follow), for serving

1. Arrange a selection of colorful, contrasting vegetables in a tall basket lined with a linen towel, stuffed at the bottom with florists' oasis (blocks of porous material) so the vegetables end up at the top of the basket, fully exposed. Cover the oasis with cabbage or lettuce leaves.

2. Fill in any openings around the edge of the basket with clumps of curly parsley.

3. Pass the vinaigrettes—thick and delicious—in separate pitchers or bowls with small ladles. (And forget a salad. It's redundant when the meal starts with these crudités.)

Anchovy Vinaigrette

YIELD: 1/2 CUP

1 medium shallot, minced, about 1 tablespoon
One 1.75-ounce tin flat anchovies, well rinsed,
   patted dry
1 tablespoon red wine vinegar
$^1/_2$ tablespoon fresh lemon juice
$^1/_2$ cup olive oil
Salt and freshly ground pepper to taste

Put all the ingredients in a blender. Combine
until smooth. The vinaigrette can be made
only a day ahead (the anchovy taste becomes
too dominant) and refrigerated, covered
airtight.

Mustard Vinaigrette

YIELD: 2/3 CUP

1 medium shallot, minced, about 1 tablespoon
1 tablespoon red wine vinegar
$^1/_2$ cup olive oil
1$^1/_2$ tablespoons Dijon mustard
Salt and freshly ground pepper to taste

Put all the ingredients in a blender. Combine
until smooth. The vinaigrette can be made
several days ahead and refrigerated, covered
airtight.

Warm Fantome Farm Goat Cheese in Herbed Garlic Oil with Crusty Bread Slices

It's easy to understand why this starter is a signature dish at Odessa Piper's L'Étoile restaurant in Madison, Wisconsin. Here, it's set up as an appetizer for guests to help themselves. Appealingly simple and great tasting, this goat cheese from Ann Topham's and Judy Borre's small Wisconsin goat cheese production at Fantome Farm (see Midwestern Sources, page 374) is marinated, warmed through, spread on croutons, and garnished with chopped brine-cured black olives. The cheese needs to be prepared at least 24 hours (or even 36) before rest of recipe can be completed. If you don't have access to fresh goat cheese, just shape a firmer goat cheese into 4-ounce rounds and marinate them the same way. The infused garlic and herb oil is a great base for salad dressings and other marinades long after the cheese has been served. Just be sure to keep the oil refrigerated.

YIELD: 4 TO 6 SERVINGS

GOAT CHEESE:
16 ounces fresh goat cheese
1 tablespoon kosher salt
2 cups extra-virgin olive oil
8 medium cloves garlic, minced, about 2¹/₂ tablespoons
8 bay leaves
4 teaspoons each: dried rosemary, basil, and oregano leaves

ACCOMPANIMENTS:
12 baguette slices, ¹/₃ inch thick
Infused oil from above
Salt
24 brine-cured black olives, pitted, finely chopped, (L'Étoile uses an olive mix of Moroccan, Calamata, and black Greek)

1. For the cheese, divide it into 4 equal (4-ounce) portions or 6 equal (2²/₃-ounce) portions.

Gently form each portion into a ball. Roll the balls in kosher salt. Wrap each one in cheesecloth and secure it with string. Suspend them by the string from a knife set across a bowl. It's not necessary to cover the bowl. Let the whey drip from the cheese for 12 hours at room temperature. To have firmer cheese, keep them suspended for another 24 hours under refrigeration.

2. Combine the oil, garlic, bay leaves, rosemary, basil, and oregano in a jar large enough to hold the cheese balls. Unwrap the balls. Add them to the oil mixture and marinate overnight or up to 1 month, refrigerated.

3. For the accompaniments, preheat the oven to 300 degrees. Arrange the bread slices in a single layer on a cookie sheet. Brush them lightly with the infused oil. Sprinkle them with salt. Bake until they are crisp and golden, about 20 minutes. Let them

cool completely. The bread can be made a day ahead and stored in an airtight container at room temperature.

4. Preheat the oven to 425 degrees. Remove the cheese from the oil. Put each ball in an individual baking or soufflé dish. Drizzle $\frac{1}{2}$ teaspoon infused oil over each. Bake until the oil just bubbles, about 8 minutes. Center the dishes on a large serving platter. Garnish the cheese with olives. Arrange the croutons attractively on the platter. Serve hot or warm.

Smile and Say Cheese . . .

Although due praise of its foods and cooking has been much slower coming to the Midwest than to either coast, there has never been any doubt about the preeminence of its cheese production. In fact, the Midwest makes more cheese than any other region of the country. And these cheeses are good! Wisconsin tops the nation's cheese-producing states, but Iowa, Minnesota, Missouri, Ohio, and South Dakota all fall within the top ten of volume producers. Brick, Colby, Baby Swiss, and blue have become Midwest signature cheeses.

Many of the Midwest's cheese producers are small and specialized and work in a painstaking manner to produce unique farmhouse cheeses (see Midwestern Sources, page 374).

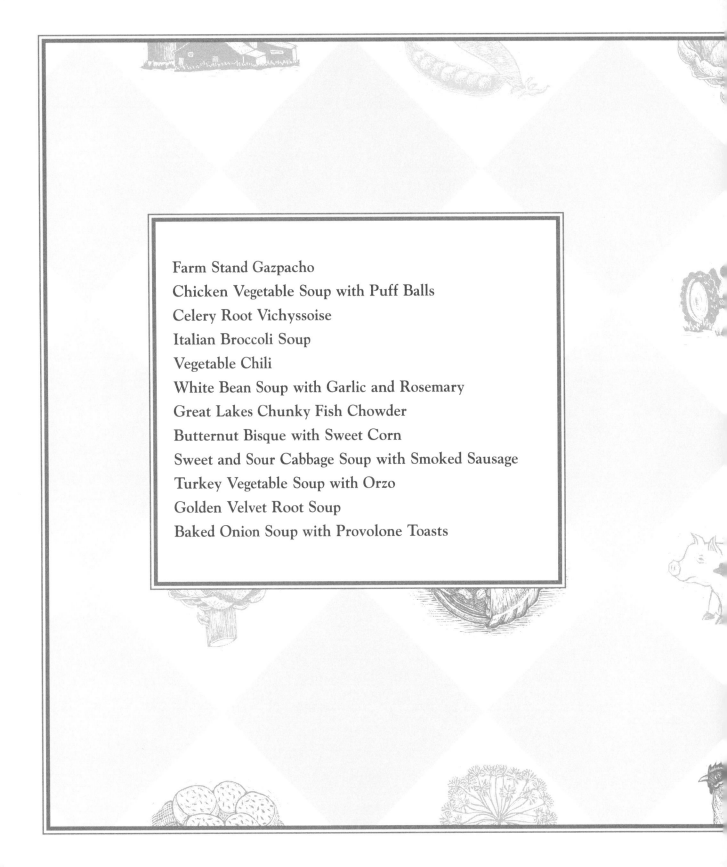

Farm Stand Gazpacho

Chicken Vegetable Soup with Puff Balls

Celery Root Vichyssoise

Italian Broccoli Soup

Vegetable Chili

White Bean Soup with Garlic and Rosemary

Great Lakes Chunky Fish Chowder

Butternut Bisque with Sweet Corn

Sweet and Sour Cabbage Soup with Smoked Sausage

Turkey Vegetable Soup with Orzo

Golden Velvet Root Soup

Baked Onion Soup with Provolone Toasts

Chapter 3
Soups

❖

Midwest winters can last half the year and burrow right down to your bones. So it is no small wonder that this is the land of hearty soups, one of the ultimate comfort foods. A great soup penetrates right to the heart.

But there's more to soups than their sensual impact. They are individual celebrations as well, steaming exaltations of the bounty of backyard gardens, of favorite foraging spots and farmers' markets, of roadside stands. To sit down on a cold winter evening to a meal built around a thick soup is to be reminded that there is more to the year than wind and snow, that there is a time when the earth is alive and the sun beats down and the crops simply grow and grow.

The Chicken Vegetable Soup with Puff Balls is both fabulous and fun. The Vegetable Chili has been fortified with bulgur wheat instead of meat. The Sweet and Sour Cabbage Soup with Smoked Sausage draws from the deep well of regional ethnic tradition. Add a terrific bread, a salad, maybe some cheese: you not only have the makings of a wonderful meal, you have something to soothe a long winter's soul.

Gazpacho

If you are long on gazpacho, you can strain the soup gently (just before using it) without pressing on the vegetables. And you can use the gazpacho vegetables as a salsa garnish on more than a tortilla. Here are some ideas:

❖ As a topping on baked potatoes.

❖ As the tomato base of a pizza.

❖ As a cold or hot sauce (it's unexpectedly good warmed through) on seafood, omelets, grilled chicken breasts, and many grilled vegetables, such as onions, mushrooms, zucchini, and eggplant.

❖ Tossed with fresh herbs into cooked rice or pasta.

❖ As the tomato component in a quick ratatouille.

❖ Mixed into a vinaigrette or mayonnaise.

❖ Combined with corn or black beans, diced peppers, sliced green onions, and minced herbs for a corn relish or bean salad.

Farm Stand Gazpacho

The fresh vegetables in this gazpacho can be gathered up at any farmers' market or stand. Freshness is key to the success of this soup. Sun-ripened sweet tomatoes form the base; if they lack flavor, add 1 to 2 tablespoons of tomato paste or ketchup until the tomato liquid is full-flavored. Once you've unloaded the vegetables on the counter, the soup can be ready in a flash since there's no cooking and the food processor does the work most efficiently. (Cut vegetables into 1-inch pieces before chopping them in the food processor.) Gazpacho is not a candidate for freezing but it will keep several days in the refrigerator. Just adjust the seasoning before serving. Surprisingly, it's delicious served chilled or hot. Since this soup is basically a vegetable salad, it's best served with sandwiches and cold meats or as the opener to a simple grilled dinner.

YIELD: ABOUT 5 1/2 CUPS, 8 TO 11 SERVINGS

$1/2$ small red onion, halved

1 medium carrot, scrubbed

$1/2$ large red pepper, seeded

2 small pickling cucumbers, scrubbed, unpeeled

3 large ripe tomatoes, halved, seeded

$1/2$ cup fresh basil leaves, plus additional for garnish

1 large ear of corn, kernels cut from the cob, about 1 cup

2 cups seasoned tomato juice (Clamato works well)

$1/2$ teaspoon sugar

Salt, freshly ground pepper, and hot pepper sauce to taste

1 to 2 tablespoons ketchup or tomato paste (optional)

1. Cut the onion, carrot, red pepper, and cucumbers into 1-inch chunks. Put 1 cup of chunks into the food processor work bowl fitted with the metal blade. Pulse off/on until the vegetables are finely chopped. Transfer them to a 2-quart mixing bowl. Repeat the process with the remaining vegetables.

2. In the same work bowl (without washing it), puree the tomatoes with $1/2$ cup of the basil until the mixture is smooth. Add it to the vegetables along with the corn, tomato juice, sugar, and seasonings. Stir until well combined. Taste for a full-bodied tomato flavor. Add the ketchup or tomato paste if needed to improve the flavor. The gazpacho can be made 3 days ahead, covered airtight, and refrigerated.

3. To serve, stir well. Adjust the seasoning. Serve chilled or hot, garnished with fresh basil leaves. To serve hot, heat gently to retain the crunchy texture of the vegetables.

Chicken Vegetable Soup with Puff Balls

Chicken soup has popular appeal. This particular version starts with a stock made with a roasting chicken, a few simple vegetables, and a 2-to-1 ratio of water to lower-salt chicken broth to achieve a deep chicken flavor. Be sure to make the stock base long enough in advance so that, after it's refrigerated, the congealed fat can be easily removed. Alternately, as a shortcut, you can make a stock with the vegetables and 6 cups lower-salt chicken broth, cooking them together until the vegetables are tender. In either case, puree these softened vegetables into the soup base. The meat from the roasting chicken measures about 6 cups; use 2 cups in the soup and reserve the rest for a salad. For the soup itself, the vegetables are quickly shredded in a food processor and cooked in under 10 minutes. The soup can be made in advance and quickly reheated. Don't forget the puff balls; they really make the difference.

YIELD: ABOUT 3 1/2 QUARTS SOUP, ABOUT 10 SERVINGS

CHICKEN STOCK BASE:

One 6-pound roasting chicken, cut into 8 pieces,
   rinsed, patted dry
1 medium Spanish onion, peeled, quartered
2 each: medium carrots, celery ribs, scrubbed, cut into
   2-inch chunks
1 bay leaf
$2^3/4$ cups lower-salt chicken broth
$5^1/2$ cups water

CHICKEN SOUP:

1 large rutabaga, peeled, split, shredded, about 6 cups
2 each: medium carrots and parsnips, peeled, shredded,
   about $1^1/2$ cups each
$1/2$ teaspoon each: ground cumin, salt
2 cups diced cooked chicken (from above,
   cut into $3/4$-inch dice)
Pinch of cayenne pepper
5 large green onions, thinly sliced, about $1^1/4$ cups
4 large romaine lettuce or spinach leaves, julienned,
   about 2 cups

Freshly ground pepper to taste
Puff Balls (recipe follows)

1. For the stock base, combine all the ingredients in a large stockpot. Bring it to a boil. Simmer, covered, for $1^1/2$ hours. Use tongs to transfer the chicken pieces to a large bowl. Cover the chicken with foil until it is cool enough to handle, or refrigerate until you are ready to use it. Remove the meat from the bones in chunks, discarding the skin, fat, and gristle. Refrigerate the cooled stock until the fat solidifies; remove and discard the fat. Discard the bay leaf. Use a slotted spoon to transfer the vegetables to a food processor fitted with the metal blade or to a blender. Puree the vegetables until smooth. Stir the pureed vegetables back into the stock. The stock can be refrigerated for up to 2 days or frozen for as long as 3 months.

2. For the soup, put the shredded vegetables, the cumin, and the salt in a large pot along with the stock. Bring to a boil. Simmer, covered, until the vegetables are tender, about 8 minutes. Add the chicken meat. Heat through. Add the cayenne.

3. Stir in the green onions and julienned lettuce or spinach leaves. Adjust the seasoning. Ladle over a warm puff ball centered in each heated shallow soup dish. Serve hot.

4. The soup can be made ahead and refrigerated overnight, covered airtight or frozen for up to 3 months. To serve, gently heat until hot.

Soup Stock or Not?

The best thing you can do for a pot of homemade soup is to make it with rich, salt-free stock. Making stock is not at all complicated (see Basics, page 357). Once it's on the stove, it takes very little attention. And since your butcher may give you beef, veal, and chicken bones just for the asking, making stock is a matter of good economy. Stocks freeze very well so you'll have repeated dividends for your investment of time. Store them in convenient 1- or 2-cup-capacity containers.

But it's likely that you'll use canned broth some of the time. Lower-salt or salt-free broth is the best choice. Even when using lower-salt broth, I rarely find that additional salt is needed in the finished soup. Always taste the soup at the end of cooking, then add a bit of salt as needed. Another hint—refrigerate the broth before you open the can. The fat will solidify on top so it can be easily removed before pouring the broth into the soup pot.

Puff Balls

These are the puffiest cloudlike dumplings. They are easy to make and transform any simple broth-based soup into a heartier meal. This recipe was a true find in a cookbook entitled Cooking for the Joyful Eater, *published in about 1919 by the First Presbyterian Church of Mankato, Minnesota. This is Mrs. Gus Kleinschmidt's puff ball recipe, virtually unchanged except for the subtle addition of curry, which helps marry the puff balls with the medley of vegetables in the soup. They can be made a day ahead and held in the refrigerator without becoming heavy, although they are sublime when freshly made. Be sure to mix the batter just until it comes together; do not overmix it. If you want to make fewer than 10 balls, the recipe is easily divided in half.*

YIELD: TEN 3-INCH BALLS OR 10 SERVINGS

1 cup flour
1½ teaspoons baking powder
1 teaspoon sugar
1 teaspoon curry powder
¼ teaspoon salt
Freshly ground pepper to taste
2 tablespoons milk
2 large eggs
3 tablespoons unsalted butter, melted

1. Bring a large quantity of salted water to a boil in a 5-quart pot. Keep the water at a simmer.

2. Put the flour, baking powder, sugar, curry powder, salt, and pepper in a 2-quart bowl. Mix well. Put the milk, eggs, and melted butter in a small bowl. Use a whisk to mix well. Slowly pour the milk mixture into the dry ingredients, stirring with a wooden spoon until just smooth. Do not overmix. This is a stiff batter.

3. To form the puff balls, dip a tablespoon into a glass of cold water, then into the batter for a level measure. Gently roll the batter with your fingertips into a rough, not super-smooth, ball. Place it on a plate. Repeat with the remaining batter.

4. Gently drop the balls into the simmering salted water. Simmer, covered, 3 minutes. Use a slotted spoon to gently turn the balls over in the water to be sure they cook completely. Simmer until they are puffy and tender, about 3 to 5 minutes more.

5. The balls can be served immediately or made a day ahead and refrigerated. Use a slotted spoon to gently transfer the balls from the water to heated soup dishes if serving immediately.

6. If making ahead, arrange them in a single layer in a large shallow baking dish with a 1-inch depth of the cooking water. Cover loosely with foil. Let them cool. Refrigerate overnight. Let them come to room temperature before using. Gently reheat the puff balls in the soup. Use a slotted spoon to transfer the puff balls to the soup bowls. Handle carefully or they will break into pieces.

Soup Substance

As I slice and chop vegetables during the week, the little leftover bits and pieces—at least those that I don't nibble on—go into a bag in the produce drawer, destined at some time to become a pot of soup. Often, the contents turn into a treasure. Who ever expected leftover celery root to end up in one of my favorite pureed soups, Celery Root Vichyssoise? The Butternut Bisque with Sweet Corn had a similar genesis. Those vegetables just happened to be collecting in the soup bag. What happened to them is serendipity at its best. Here's a helpful formula for soups based on pureed vegetables, aiming for a medium consistency: use 2½ cups of vegetable puree to about 5 to 6 cups stock or lower-salt broth.

Celery Root Vichyssoise

Celery root provides a welcome dimension in this soothing mix of ingredients. Celery root is a natural partner with potatoes (mashed potatoes and celery root are a simple and delicious preparation). The density of the celery root puree and the nonfat dry milk makes it possible to use the least amount of cream for that essential creaminess characteristic of vichyssoise. The food processor is invaluable in preparing this soup; it slices the vegetables and then purees them after they are cooked. Although vichyssoise is typically served chilled, I also like this version served hot.

**YIELD: ABOUT 8 CUPS,
10 TO 16 SERVINGS**

1 tablespoon vegetable oil
1 medium Spanish onion, sliced, about 2 cups
1 medium leek, white part only (use trimmed green
    ends for other soups), split, washed, sliced, about
    2 cups
2 large red potatoes, peeled, sliced, about 4 cups
1 medium celery root, peeled, sliced, about 1 1/2 cups
6 cups Chicken Stock (page 364) or lower-salt broth
1/3 cup nonfat dry milk
2 to 4 tablespoons heavy cream
1/4 teaspoon freshly grated nutmeg (see page 289)
Salt and freshly ground white pepper, to taste
2 tablespoons snipped fresh chives, for garnish

1. Heat the oil in a 3-quart pot over medium-high heat. When it is hot, add the onion and leek. Cook until softened, about 5 minutes, stirring often.

2. Add the potatoes, celery root, and stock or broth. Bring to a boil. Simmer, covered, until the vegetables are very soft, about 30 to 40 minutes.

3. Strain the vegetables from the liquid, reserving both. Put the vegetables with the nonfat dry milk in the food processor fitted with a metal blade or in a blender. Mix until pureed. Add a little reserved cooking liquid to smooth out the puree even more.

4. Stir this pureed mixture into the remaining liquid. (The soup can be strained at this point, if desired.) Add 2 to 4 tablespoons cream, for desired creaminess. Add the nutmeg, and salt and pepper to taste. Adjust the seasoning. The soup can be refrigerated up to 3 days, or frozen for as long as 3 months, covered airtight.

5. To serve, this soup is good chilled or hot. Stir well; adjust the seasoning. Gently reheat, if serving hot. Garnish with the chives.

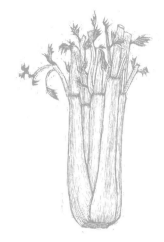

Italian Broccoli Soup

This soup is loaded with broccoli; it makes a great Sunday night supper with a crusty loaf of bread, Italian sausages, and an array of mustards. The food processor is the best bet for getting through these vegetables quickly; chop them in batches without washing the bowl of the processor in between. After the vegetables are chopped, the cooking takes a mere 20 minutes. This soup is best served the day that it's made . . . or the following day . . . because the broccoli flavor becomes strong and dominant as it stands.

YIELD: ABOUT 9 CUPS, 8 TO 10 SERVINGS

1 tablespoon olive oil

2 large cloves garlic, minced, about 1 tablespoon

1 medium red onion, finely chopped, about 1¹/₂ cups

1 medium rib celery, finely chopped, about ¹/₂ cup

2 medium carrots, scrubbed, coarsely chopped, about ²/₃ cup

1 bunch broccoli, stems peeled, stems and florets coarsely chopped, about 6 cups

6 to 8 cups Chicken Stock (page 364) or lower-salt chicken broth

1 teaspoon each: dried thyme, dried tarragon

Pinch of red pepper flakes

¹/₂ cup orzo or other small pasta such as tripolini

3 cups julienned fresh young spinach leaves

Finely shredded imported Parmesan (Parmigiano-Reggiano) cheese, for serving

1. Heat the oil in a 3-quart pot over medium-high heat. When hot, add the garlic, onion, celery, and carrots. Cook, uncovered, until heated through and fragrant, about 5 minutes, stirring often to avoid scorching.

2. Add the broccoli, 6 cups of the stock or broth, the thyme, tarragon, red pepper flakes, and the orzo. Bring to a boil. Simmer, uncovered, until the pasta is al dente, about 10 minutes. Add the

spinach. Stir well until combined. Add the remaining stock or broth as needed for consistency. The soup should be thick. Adjust the seasoning. The soup can be served immediately. Serve hot. Pass the cheese separately.

3. The soup can also be made a day ahead and refrigerated. To serve, gently reheat. Add water as needed for consistency. Adjust the seasoning.

Vegetable Chili

This is a highly flavorful, crunchy, and substantial chili. As with most chilis, it's best made at least a day ahead so the flavors have a chance to develop fully. The food processor fitted with the metal blade chops all these vegetables in rapid succession. Small items, such as garlic, should be dropped first through the feed tube into a dry work bowl with the machine running and processed until finely minced. The other vegetables should be chopped using the pulse on/off motion so their texture is controlled. Cut large vegetables into 1-inch chunks and chop them in 1 cup batches. The drained, canned tomatoes should be pureed last since their liquid will moisten the work bowl and blade, interfering with the chopping of the fresh vegetables.

YIELD: 9 1/2 CUPS, 6 TO 8 MAIN-COURSE SERVINGS

1 tablespoon oil
4 large cloves garlic, minced, about 2 tablespoons
1 large Spanish onion, minced, about 3 cups
2 medium carrots, chopped, about $^2/_3$ cup
1 large zucchini, chopped, about 2 cups
One 15$^1/_4$-ounce can red kidney beans, drained, washed, coarsely chopped
One 14$^1/_2$ ounce can whole tomatoes, drained, liquid reserved, tomatoes coarsely chopped
One 6-ounce can tomato paste
4$^1/_2$ to 5$^1/_2$ cups Vegetable Stock (page 367) or broth
1$^1/_2$ tablespoons light brown sugar
2 teaspoons ground cumin
2 tablespoons chili powder
1 teaspoon each: dried oregano, salt
$^1/_2$ cup each: bulgur wheat, corn kernels (fresh, frozen, or canned)
Light sour cream or lowfat yogurt, thinly sliced green onions, and cilantro leaves, for serving

1. Heat the oil in a 3-quart nonaluminum pot over medium-high heat. When hot, add the garlic, onion, carrots, and $^1/_2$ cup of the zucchini. Cook until the onion is softened, about 4 minutes, stirring often.

2. Add the kidney beans, tomatoes, tomato liquid, tomato paste, 4 cups of the vegetable broth, the brown sugar, cumin, chili powder, oregano, and salt. Stir until combined. Simmer 40 minutes, covered, stirring often.

3. Add the remaining zucchini, the bulgur wheat, and the corn kernels. Simmer 15 minutes more. Add the remaining vegetable stock as necessary for medium thick consistency. Adjust the seasoning. Serve hot. Pass light sour cream or lowfat yogurt, sliced green onions, and cilantro leaves in separate bowls.

4. The chili can be made up to 4 days ahead and refrigerated, or frozen for as long as 3 months, covered airtight. To serve, gently reheat, adding more broth or water for the desired consistency. Adjust the seasoning.

White Bean Soup with Garlic and Rosemary

Canned beans work well in this soup, making this recipe a quick and easy preparation. The soup makes a great winter meal when accompanied by a mixed green salad with cherry tomatoes and a loaf of warm crusty bread. One suggestion: leftover lamb is delicious in the soup if you happen to have it.

YIELD: 6 CUPS, 4 TO 6 MAIN-COURSE SERVINGS

1 tablespoon olive oil, plus 1 tablespoon warm olive oil, for drizzling over the soup
3 large cloves garlic, minced, about 1^1/$_2$ tablespoons
1 medium onion, minced, about 1^1/$_4$ cups
Three 15^1/$_2$-ounce cans Great Northern beans (about 4^1/$_2$ cups cooked beans), rinsed with cold water, drained well
2 to 3 teaspoons dried rosemary
2 to 3 cups Vegetable Stock (page 367) or broth
1^1/$_2$ teaspoons balsamic vinegar
Salt and red pepper flakes to taste
1^1/$_2$ tablespoons snipped chives, for garnish

1. Heat 1 tablespoon of oil in a 3-quart pot over medium-high heat. Add the garlic and onion. Cook until the onion is softened, about 4 minutes, stirring often.

2. Put the beans (reserve ^{1}/$_2$ cup whole beans) with the rosemary in a blender or food processor fitted with a metal blade. Puree until smooth.

3. Transfer the pureed mixture along with the whole beans to the pot. Add 2 cups of the vegetable stock or broth, the vinegar, salt, and red pepper flakes. Simmer, covered, for 20 minutes. Add more stock or broth as needed for the desired medium thick consistency. Adjust the seasoning. Serve hot, each serving drizzled with oil and garnished with snipped chives.

4. The soup can be made 2 days ahead and refrigerated, or frozen for as long as 3 months, covered airtight. To serve, gently reheat, adding broth or water as needed for the desired consistency. Adjust the seasoning.

Freezing Soup

Most soups freeze well. If you're freezing a large quantity, divide it into several smaller containers. If you're short on plastic freezer containers, freeze the soup until it is solid, then remove it from the container in one solid block. Double wrap it in plastic bags, label, and quickly put it back into the freezer.

❖

Reheating Soup

The microwave oven is ideal for reheating 2 servings of soup. Put the soup right into microwavable serving bowls; cook on high power (100 percent) until hot, about 3 to 4 minutes. If the soup is frozen, put it into a microwavable dish. Cook it on high power (100 percent) until it has thawed. The length of time will depend on the quantity of frozen soup, but it should take less than 10 minutes. Once liquid, ladle the soup into individual serving bowls and finish on high (100 percent) power.

For reheating and serving large quantities of frozen soup, put the frozen chunk of soup into a pot. Cook, covered, over medium heat until thawed, stirring occasionally to prevent sticking or burning. Adjust the consistency and seasoning before serving.

Great Lakes Chunky Fish Chowder

This simple, comforting chowder captures the flavor of Great Lakes fish and is a most delicious focus for an informal summer meal. Serve it with Lemon Cornmeal Blueberry Muffins (page 26) and a condiment salad of Pickling Cucumbers, Tomatoes, and Basil (page 99). Any mild skinless fillets will work well in this recipe.

YIELD: ABOUT 5 3/4 CUPS, 5 TO 6 MAIN-COURSE SERVINGS

2 thick slices lean applewood-smoked bacon
   (see Midwestern Sources, page 376),
   cut into ¼-inch dice, about ⅓ cup
1 tablespoon unsalted butter
1 large onion, chopped, about 2 cups
2 medium ribs celery, diced, about 1 cup
5 small red potatoes, unpeeled, cut into ¼-inch dice,
   about 2½ cups
One 8-ounce bottle clam juice
1 cup water
½ teaspoon salt
Freshly grated nutmeg (see page 289)
   and pepper to taste
2 cups milk (2 percent or regular)
2 tablespoons cornstarch mixed with 2 tablespoons milk
1 cup well-drained corn kernels (cut off the cob,
   frozen, or canned)
1 pound skinless walleye, bass, or northern pike fillets,
   cut into ½-inch chunks

1. Cook the bacon in a 2-quart pot over medium-high heat until crisp, about 2 minutes, stirring often.

2. Add the butter to the pot. When it is hot, add the onion and celery. Cook until the onion is softened, about 4 minutes, stirring often.

3. Add the potatoes, clam juice, water, salt, nutmeg, and pepper to the pot. Bring to a boil.

Simmer, covered, until the potatoes are tender, about 20 minutes.

4. Add the milk and cornstarch mixture and the corn. Gently cook until the soup is hot and slightly thickened, about 6 minutes, stirring often. Do not let the chowder boil.

5. The chowder can be made 2 days ahead to this point and refrigerated. It does not freeze successfully. Gently reheat the chowder until it is hot, but not boiling.

6. Add the fish. Cook until the fish is opaque, about 1 to 2 minutes. Adjust the seasoning. Serve hot.

Butternut Bisque with Sweet Corn

Here, pureed butternut squash makes a smooth, thick bisque. A very small amount of cream—3 tablespoons in 9¹/₂ cups of soup—rounds out the flavors and gives the soup a perfect balance.

YIELD: 9 1/2 CUPS, 10 TO 16 SERVINGS

1 tablespoon oil
3 medium leeks, white part only, thinly sliced (reserve
   green parts for another soup), about 3 cups
2 large cloves garlic, split
1 large butternut squash, peeled, seeded, cut into
   2-inch chunks, about 7 cups
4 to 4¹/₂ cups Chicken Stock (page 364)
   or lower-salt broth
¹/₂ teaspoon each: freshly grated nutmeg (see page 289),
   ground cumin, salt
Freshly ground pepper to taste
1¹/₄ cups corn kernels (fresh, frozen, or canned)
3 tablespoons heavy cream
Snipped fresh chives, for garnish

1. Heat the oil in a 3-quart pot over medium-high heat. When hot, add the leeks and garlic. Cook until they are softened, about 3 minutes, stirring often.

2. Add the squash, 4 cups of the broth, the nutmeg, cumin, salt, and pepper. Simmer, covered, until the squash is very soft, about 25 minutes.

3. Strain the vegetables from the liquid, reserving both. Put the vegetables in a blender or in a food processor fitted with a metal blade. Puree until very smooth. Add a little cooking liquid to make the mixture even smoother.

4. Return this mixture and all of the reserved liquid to the pot. Add the corn and cream. Stir until combined. Add the remaining broth as needed for desired medium thick consistency. Adjust the seasoning. Serve hot, garnished with snipped chives.

5. The soup can be made a few days ahead and refrigerated, or frozen for as long as 3 months, covered airtight. If made ahead, add garnish just before serving. To serve, gently reheat. Adjust the seasoning.

Sweet and Sour Cabbage Soup
with Smoked Sausage

There are so many robust flavors in this soup that the ingredients can be quickly combined and simmered together; no preliminary sautéing is necessary. The recipe can be easily doubled or tripled to serve a crowd.

YIELD: 9 TO 10 CUPS, 8 MAIN-COURSE SERVINGS

1 large onion, chopped, about 2 cups
$^1/_2$ medium cabbage, cored, sliced, about 5 cups
2 medium carrots, cut into $^1/_2$-inch slices, about $^3/_4$ cup
10 ounces smoked Polish sausage, cut into $^1/_2$-inch slices
One 28-ounce can stewed tomatoes, pureed with their
    liquid
$^1/_3$ cup packed light brown sugar
4 cups Chicken Stock (page 364) or lower-salt broth
$^1/_2$ teaspoon each: allspice, paprika
Salt and freshly ground pepper to taste

1. Put all the ingredients in a 3-quart nonaluminum pot. Bring to a boil. Simmer, covered, until the carrots and cabbage are tender, about 20 minutes. Adjust the seasoning. Serve hot.

2. The soup can be made 2 days ahead and refrigerated, or frozen for up to 3 months, covered airtight. To serve, gently reheat. Adjust the seasoning.

Turkey Vegetable Soup with Orzo

This is a thick and sustaining rich soup that makes a great supper. It's no different from any other broth-based soup; the depth of flavor in the broth makes the soup. The turkey stock is a separate step, which helps to develop this essential characteristic. Serve the soup with Peppered Buttermilk Biscuits (page 267) or Pizza Batter Bread (page 264).

YIELD: ABOUT 8 CUPS, 6 TO 8 SERVINGS

4 cups Turkey Stock (page 365)
2 cups lower-salt chicken broth, plus additional broth or
  water as needed for consistency
2 medium ribs celery, diced, about 1 cup
2 medium carrots, peeled, diced, about ³/₄ cup
2 medium parsnips, peeled, diced, about ³/₄ cup
2 small onions, diced, about 1¹/₃ cups
¹/₄ teaspoon dried thyme leaves
1¹/₂ cups diced cooked turkey
¹/₂ cup orzo
Salt and freshly ground pepper to taste
2 tablespoons minced fresh parsley

1. Put the turkey stock, chicken broth, vegetables, and thyme leaves in a 3-quart pot. Bring the liquid to a boil. Simmer, covered, for 20 minutes. Add the turkey and orzo. Mix well. Simmer, covered, until the orzo is tender, about 12 more minutes. Add more broth or water as needed for the desired medium thick consistency. Adjust the consistency and seasoning. Stir in the parsley. Serve hot.

2. The soup can be made 2 days ahead and refrigerated, or frozen for up to 2 months, covered airtight. If soup is made ahead, add parsley just before serving. To serve, heat through. Adjust the consistency and seasoning.

Golden Velvet Root Soup

Smooth as velvet, this soup has a creamy finish without any cream; the roots do it with the help of a little nonfat dry milk! The nutmeg lifts and rounds out the flavors. The thinner the vegetable slices (use the thin processor slicing disc), the more quickly they cook.

YIELD: ABOUT 4 1/4 CUPS, 6 TO 8 SERVINGS

1 tablespoon safflower oil
1 large onion, sliced, about 2 1/2 cups
2 large parsnips, peeled, sliced, about 1 2/3 cups
1 large rutabaga, peeled, sliced, about 2 cups
4 medium carrots, peeled, sliced, about 2 cups
4 to 4 1/2 cups Chicken Stock (page 364)
    or lower-salt broth
2 tablespoons nonfat dry milk
1/2 teaspoon freshly grated nutmeg (see page 289),
    plus additional, for garnish
Salt and freshly ground pepper to taste

1. Heat the oil in a 2-quart pot over medium-high heat. When hot, add the vegetables. Cook, uncovered, until they are hot and fragrant, about 5 minutes, stirring occasionally.

2. Add 3 1/2 cups of the stock or broth. Bring to a boil. Simmer, covered, until the vegetables are very soft, about 25 to 28 minutes.

3. Strain the solids from the liquid, reserving both. Put the solids with the nonfat dry milk in a food processor fitted with a metal blade or in a blender. Puree until very smooth. Return the mixture and reserved liquid to the pot. Stir well. Add more broth as needed for the desired consistency; the soup should be thick. Add 1/2 teaspoon of the nutmeg. Adjust the seasoning. Serve garnished with a light sprinkling of nutmeg. The soup is good chilled or hot.

4. The soup can be made 2 days ahead and refrigerated, or frozen for up to 3 months, covered airtight. If soup is made ahead, add garnish just before serving. Stir well. Adjust the seasoning. Gently reheat, if serving hot.

Baked Onion Soup with Provolone Toasts

Onion soup can run the gamut from mostly broth to totally laden with onions. Here, it's about halfway—loads of onions but enough broth to sustain them. Slowly sweating and then caramelizing the onions are essential steps for a sweet, rich-tasting onion soup. There's time involved but it's well worth it. The classic Gruyère cheese can be substituted for the provolone in this recipe.

YIELD: ABOUT 6 CUPS, 4 MAIN-COURSE SERVINGS

SOUP:
1 tablespoon each: butter, vegetable oil
3 large Spanish onions, thinly sliced, about 9 cups
1/4 teaspoon salt
Freshly ground pepper to taste
2 teaspoons sugar
1³/4 cups Chicken Stock (page 364) or lower-salt chicken broth
3¹/2 cups Beef Stock (page 366) or beef broth

CROUTONS:
Four ¹/2-inch-thick baguette slices
1 clove garlic, split
1 cup grated provolone cheese

1. Set aside 4 individual, deep, ovenproof soup bowls or *marmites* on a baking pan.

2. For the soup, heat the butter and oil in a 3-quart pot over medium-high heat. When hot, add the onions, salt, and pepper. Toss until mixed well. Press a piece of waxed paper over the onions to cover them completely. Gently cook, covered, until the onions are very soft, about 30 minutes, stirring occasionally. Remove the paper. Stir in the sugar. Cook over medium-high heat until the onions take on a light brown color and are caramelized. This will take about 20 minutes, watching carefully and stirring as the edges caramelize. Often, you may want to remove the pot from the heat for better control as you stir the edges into the onion mixture.

3. Add chicken and beef stocks or broths. Simmer, covered, for 40 minutes. Adjust the seasoning. The soup can be made a few days ahead and refrigerated.

4. For the croutons, preheat the oven to 250 degrees. Arrange the bread in a single layer on a baking sheet. Bake until lightly toasted, about 15 minutes a side. Remove from the oven and rub with the cut edges of the garlic. The croutons can be toasted several hours ahead and kept at room temperature.

5. Put the oven rack 6 inches from the broiler; preheat the oven to broil. Heat the soup on top of the stove until very hot. Place a crouton in each bowl. Ladle boiling soup over the bread. Sprinkle each serving with cheese, dividing it evenly.

6. Broil until the cheese is browned and sizzling, about 2 minutes. Serve hot.

DINNER SALADS:
Herb Garden Salad with Tomato and Olive Vinaigrette
Wilted Spinach Salad Tossed with Capriole Goat Cheese
   and Spiced Walnuts
Simple Lettuce Salad with Fresh Ginger Vinaigrette
Tart Apple Salad with Belgian Endive and Watercress
Mixed Greens with Pears, Crumbled Tolibia Blue Cheese, and Pine Nuts
Watercress Salad with Ripe Melon and Nueske Applewood-Smoked Ham

SUBSTANTIAL SALADS:
Summer Macaroni Salad with Crisp Garlic Bread Crumbs
Greek Orzo Salad with Shrimp
Warm Sweet and Sour Chicken and Wild Rice Salad
Couscous Vegetable Salad
Chef's Slaw
Barley Salad with Spicy Sausage, Peas, Celery, and Carrots
Turkey and Rice Salad with Dried Tart Cherry Vinaigrette

CONDIMENT SIDE DISH SALADS:
Pickling Cucumbers, Tomatoes, and Basil
Sweet Corn Confetti Salad
Speck's "Best Ever" German Potato Salad
Oil Lamp Cucumber Salad
Curried Celery Root and Apple Salad
Sweet and Sour Red Cabbage Slaw with Cracked Pepper
Farmhouse Coleslaw with Buttermilk-Dill Dressing
Red Cabbage Slaw with Broccoli and Red Pepper
Cranberry Relish Mold with Pineapple Dressing

VINAIGRETTES:
Basic Vinaigrette
   Cracked Pepper Variation
Lemon Thyme Vinaigrette
Zinfandel's Strawberry Vinaigrette

Chapter 4
Salads

❖

In the old Midwest cookbooks, compilations of the recipes of church basement potlucks, salads tend to show up as combinations of condiments: pickled cucumbers, preserved corn, slaw, potato salad. Nowhere will you find the likes of a Turkey and Rice Salad with Dried Tart Cherry Vinaigrette. And yet I think a modern salad such as this rises out of that same church-basement spirit. What has changed are the ingredients we have at hand.

Bitter greens, for instance. Watercress and arugula lend balance to a salad and work well with fruits, cheeses, and tangy vinaigrettes. And then there are salads that rely on macaroni, on orzo, on couscous. These are substantial salads that sit at the center of a meal, not at one end or the other.

Yet it is just this versatility that I find so intriguing. At the beginning of a meal a good salad stimulates the appetite. At the end of a meal it tends to settle and define all that has come before. At the center of the meal, salad has a friendly, casual nature unlike any other food on the table. There's a soothing quality to salad whether it is a small-sized dinner salad, a substantial main course, or a condiment side dish.

Such a broad and creative palate has plenty of room for Curried Celery Root and Apple Salad or Wilted Spinach Salad Tossed with Capriole Goat Cheese and Spiced Walnuts, Greek Orzo Salad with Shrimp, or Farmhouse Coleslaw with Buttermilk-Dill Dressing, Warm Sweet and Sour Chicken and Wild Rice Salad, or Herb Garden Salad with Tomato and Olive Vinaigrette. Unlike any other part of the meal, salad reflects the inspiration of the cook.

Greens Are Not Last Minute . . .

Many cooks think that preparing greens is a last-minute effort. Not so. Fresh greens without any dark brown or faded yellow spots can be washed, refrigerated, and crisped 2 to 3 days before serving. A lettuce spinner is a great asset, spinning most of the water from washed greens without bruising them in the process.

Here's how to wash and crisp greens in advance:

❖ Wash the greens, and gently spin dry or gently blot with paper towels to remove the excess moisture.

❖ Wrap drained greens in dry paper towels.

❖ Enclose towel-wrapped greens in plastic bags, seal airtight, and refrigerate.

❖ If the towels become too wet, replace them with dry ones. Very wet towels accelerate spoilage of the greens while damp towels keep greens crisp up to 3 days.

Herb Garden Salad with Tomato and Olive Vinaigrette

This salad is intended to take advantage of summer herb gardens. Wonderfully robust, it works well as a starter with grilled meals and is a most satisfying main-dish salad (for 2 to 3) on a hot summer day.

YIELD: 6 FIRST-COURSE SERVINGS

SALAD:
3 cups mixed herb leaves (basil, thyme, mint)
7 cups torn romaine leaves (torn into small pieces)
2 cups stemmed arugula leaves

VINAIGRETTE:
2 medium cloves garlic, minced, about 1 1/2 teaspoons
2 tablespoons fresh lemon juice
3 teaspoons balsamic vinegar
1/2 cup extra-virgin olive oil
1/2 teaspoon each: Dijon mustard, sugar
1 tablespoon water
1/4 teaspoon each: salt and freshly ground pepper
2 firm, ripe, medium tomatoes, seeded, cut into 1/2-inch dice, about 1 1/2 cups
1/2 medium red onion, cut into 1/2-inch dice, about 1 cup
8 Calamata olives, pitted, flesh cut into small pieces
2 teaspoons capers
Freshly grated imported Parmesan (Parmigiano-Reggiano) cheese, for serving

1. For the salad, wash the herbs and lettuces. Gently spin off the water. Put in a large bowl, wrap in paper towels. Chill several hours.

2. For the vinaigrette, put the garlic, lemon juice, balsamic vinegar, oil, mustard, sugar, water, salt, and pepper into a 1-quart bowl. Whisk together. Add the tomatoes, onion, olives, and capers. Toss together. Let the dressing stand at room temperature for 2 to 3 hours before using. The vinaigrette can be made a day ahead and refrigerated. Let it come to room temperature before using.

3. To serve, pour the room-temperature vinaigrette over the chilled greens; toss. Adjust the seasoning. Serve the salad in a large bowl or divide it among 6 chilled salad plates. Serve immediately. Pass the cheese separately.

Wilted Spinach Salad Tossed with Capriole Goat Cheese and Spiced Walnuts

Here, the wilted spinach salad is worked into a more sophisticated, tasty mix. Serve this salad as a first course or following the main course; it has too much flavor to be served with the meal. It will also make a great main course for lunch or supper. Most (not all) of the bacon fat is replaced with olive oil, giving it a more subtle bacon flavor. The Capriole goat cheese (Midwestern Sources, page 374) is soft, mild, and sweet, a perfect complement to the other ingredients in the salad. Find a similar type of goat cheese in your market.

YIELD: 4 FIRST-COURSE SERVINGS

SALAD:
1 large red bell pepper, roasted (page 359), cut into
   julienne strips
1/2 pound stemmed young spinach leaves, washed and
   gently spun dry, about 6 to 7 cups
3 ounces soft goat cheese, crumbled
1/2 cup Spiced Walnuts (recipe follows)

VINAIGRETTE:
2 thick slices bacon, preferably applewood-smoked (see
   Midwestern Sources, page 376) cut in 1/4-inch dice,
   about 1/3 cup
1/4 cup each: balsamic vinegar, water
2 tablespoons extra-virgin olive oil
1/4 teaspoon salt
Freshly ground pepper to taste

1. For the salad, put all the ingredients (except the walnuts) in a large bowl. Tear spinach leaves, if large. Chill until ready to use. Set the walnuts aside at room temperature.

2. For the vinaigrette, sauté the bacon in a nonstick skillet until crisp. Use a slotted spoon to transfer the bacon to a paper towel. Pour off the fat but do not wipe the pan.

3. Add the vinegar, water, olive oil, salt, and pepper to the same skillet. Bring to a boil. Remove from the heat. Set aside. The vinaigrette can be used immediately or made several hours ahead and kept at room temperature. Gently reheat before using.

4. To serve, pour the hot vinaigrette over the salad. Toss well to coat the salad with the vinaigrette. Toss in half of the walnuts. Adjust the seasoning. Serve the salad in a bowl or divide it among 4 salad plates, arranging each attractively. Garnish with the reserved bacon and remaining walnuts. Serve warm.

Spiced Walnuts

These walnuts freeze well, so it's a good idea to make more than you need. They are a flavorful garnish on simple green salads.

YIELD: 1/2 CUP

¹/₂ cup walnut halves
¹/₂ teaspoon olive oil
¹/₈ teaspoon salt
¹/₄ teaspoon each: dried rosemary, chili powder

1. Put a rack in the center of the oven; preheat the oven to 350 degrees. Set aside a cookie sheet.

2. Put the walnuts in a small bowl. Toss with the olive oil until they are well coated. Combine the remaining ingredients in a small dish. Add to the walnuts. Mix well. Spread the walnuts in a single layer on the cookie sheet.

3. Bake until lightly browned, about 12 minutes, watching carefully to avoid burning. Cool on a wire rack.

Finishing Touches to Salads . . .

Once a salad is tossed, these final details make a difference:

- ❖ Arrange the salad on chilled plates. When a salad is large, serve it on a dinner plate; it looks better and is much easier to eat.
- ❖ Garnish salads with minced parsley. Parsley is a hardy, versatile, and fragrant herb, a good value compared to other herbs. To mince it, take a bunch of parsley, twist off the leafy tops, wash them (discard stems or save for stocks or soups), and air-dry, spread out on a paper towel. Once completely dry, put the tops in a food processor fitted with a metal blade. Pulse on/off in short spurts until the parsley is minced, just a matter of seconds. Store the minced parsley in an airtight plastic bag and refrigerate up to 5 days.
- ❖ Other fresh herbs are also a great enhancement on salads, but they are more perishable than parsley. Buy them shortly before using them. Options include mint, tarragon, oregano, chives, basil, cilantro, and dill.
- ❖ Garnish simple green salads with Parmesan cheese. Buy the best (Parmigiano-Reggiano) in a store with a high turnover of cheeses so that you know the cheese is fresh. Leave the cheese whole if you have a small grater that can be easily handled at the table, but try to use all the cheese before it gets rock-hard. Otherwise, Parmesan cheese freezes well. Grate the cheese when you purchase it. Portion the grated cheese in small plastic bags, seal airtight, and freeze. Parmesan cheese should be at room temperature when used as a garnish on a salad.
- ❖ At the table, pass a pepper grinder that grinds medium coarse: not too fine and not too coarse. That's the final touch of all!

Simple Lettuce Salad with Fresh Ginger Vinaigrette

This is a bold-flavored salad; its refreshing flavor and crunch are especially welcome on hot summer nights. Serve it as a starter to simple grilled main courses or Asian-inspired meals.

YIELD: 6 FIRST-COURSE SERVINGS

SALAD:

6 cups cut-up iceberg lettuce (cut into 1½-inch squares)
3 cups watercress leaves
1½ cups radish sprouts,* top 1 inch only

VINAIGRETTE:

3 tablespoons minced peeled fresh ginger
1 tablespoon each: oriental sesame oil, paprika
   (preferably Hungarian), sugar
¾ cup rice vinegar
⅓ cup peanut oil
¾ teaspoon salt
Freshly ground pepper to taste

Radish sprouts resemble red alfalfa sprouts, although their stems are a little thicker. They have green leaves, a red stem at base, and a distinct radish flavor. They are available at greengrocers and in the produce section of specialty supermarkets.

1. For the salad, wash the lettuce, watercress, and sprouts. Gently spin off the water. Combine all the ingredients in a large bowl and cover with paper towels. Refrigerate until well chilled and crisp.

2. For the vinaigrette, put all the ingredients in a blender or a food processor fitted with the metal blade. Blend until combined. The vinaigrette can be made a day ahead and refrigerated. Let it come to room temperature before using.

3. To serve, toss the chilled salad with the vinaigrette to coat evenly. Adjust the seasoning. Serve in the large bowl or divide among 6 chilled salad plates. Serve immediately.

Tart Apple Salad with
Belgian Endive and Watercress

This salad has come a long way from the Waldorf salad that inspired it. It's light and refreshing, a lift to almost any meal, especially when it's the first course. I like the straightforward flavors of this salad, but toasted walnuts, crumbled blue or Roquefort cheeses, typical garnishes on winter apple salads, can be sprinkled on top. To get a head start on the salad, toss the apple slices in a little vinaigrette to keep them from turning brown; they will keep for about 1 hour in the refrigerator.

YIELD: 4 FIRST-COURSE SERVINGS

VINAIGRETTE:

1 small shallot, minced, about 1 tablespoon
3 tablespoons apple cider
2 tablespoons red wine vinegar
1/4 cup vegetable oil
1 teaspoon each: Dijon mustard, grated orange zest
    (colored rind), removed with a zester or fine grater
    (see page 14)
1 tablespoon honey
1/4 teaspoon salt
Freshly ground pepper to taste

SALAD:

4 medium heads Belgian endive, cut into 1/3-inch
    crosswise slices, washed, gently spun dry, chilled,
    about 6 cups
2 1/2 cups watercress leaves
2 large Granny Smith apples, unpeeled, cored,
    thinly sliced, about 3 1/2 cups
Salt and freshly ground pepper to taste

1. For the vinaigrette, combine the ingredients in a blender or a food processor fitted with the metal blade. The vinaigrette can be made a day ahead and refrigerated. Let it come to room temperature before using.

2. For the salad, wash the endive and watercress. Gently spin off the water. Put them in a large bowl, and cover with paper towels. Keep chilled until serving time.

3. To serve, add the apples to the greens. Toss the salad with the vinaigrette. Adjust the seasoning. Serve immediately, on a large chilled platter or on 6 chilled dinner plates, arranging it attractively.

Mixed Greens with Pears, Crumbled Tolibia Blue Cheese, and Pine Nuts

Here, pears are peeled, diced, and tossed in a little of the honey mustard vinaigrette, which enhances their flavor and keeps them white. The mixed greens are best tender and young; they should include some bitter leaves such as curly endive or arugula, which balance the flavors of the sweet pears and pungent cheese. Tolibia blue cheese (see Midwestern Sources, page 375) has a nice deep flavor without being harsh; it crumbles into small particles which distribute the flavor evenly.

YIELD: 6 FIRST-COURSE SERVINGS

VINAIGRETTE:

1 large shallot, minced, about 2$\frac{1}{2}$ tablespoons

1 tablespoon Dijon mustard

2 tablespoons each: red wine vinegar, honey

$\frac{1}{2}$ cup safflower oil

1 tablespoon water

$\frac{1}{8}$ teaspoon salt

$\frac{3}{4}$ teaspoon coarsely cracked pepper

SALAD:

12 cups torn mixed greens, including red leaf, Boston, curly endive, and arugula, washed, gently spun dry or blotted

2 large ripe firm pears, unpeeled, cored, and cut into $\frac{1}{2}$-inch dice, about 4 cups

Salt and freshly ground pepper to taste

$\frac{1}{3}$ cup crumbled Tolibia blue cheese

$\frac{1}{4}$ cup pine nuts, toasted (page 358)

1. For the vinaigrette, put all the ingredients in a small jar. Close it securely and shake vigorously to mix. The vinaigrette can be made a day ahead and refrigerated. Use it chilled. Shake it well before using.

2. For the salad, put the greens into a large shallow bowl. Cover with paper towels. Keep them chilled until you are ready to use them. The diced pears can be tossed with a scant $\frac{1}{4}$ cup of vinaigrette 2 hours before using and refrigerated.

3. To serve, toss the greens with the remaining vinaigrette. Serve the salad on a large chilled platter or divide it among 6 chilled serving plates. Season the greens lightly with salt and pepper. Scatter the pears over the greens; garnish with the crumbled blue cheese, then the pine nuts. Serve immediately, chilled.

Watercress Salad with Ripe Melon and Nueske Applewood-Smoked Ham

This combination—melon and applewood-smoked ham—is inspired by the Italian classic, melon and prosciutto. Here, the melon and ham are julienned and tossed into contrasting, slightly bitter watercress leaves for a most refreshing first-course salad. It's a satisfying cool supper in the hot summer months, serving only two as a main course. Nueske's ham is nicely smoked and less salty than most.

YIELD: 4 FIRST-COURSE SERVINGS

SALAD:

6 cups stemmed watercress leaves, washed, gently spun dry or blotted

2 medium Belgian endives, cut into 1/2-inch crosswise slices, about 3 cups

1 cup each: julienned ripe cantaloupe, julienned applewood-smoked ham (see Midwestern Sources, page 376)

1/4 cup diced red onion

VINAIGRETTE:

2 tablespoons each: balsamic vinegar, extra-virgin olive oil

1/2 teaspoon honey

1/4 teaspoon salt

Freshly ground pepper to taste

1. For the salad, put all the ingredients in a large bowl. Toss until combined. Chill. The salad can be refrigerated for up to 3 hours. Cover with plastic wrap.

2. For the vinaigrette, put all the ingredients into a small bowl. Whisk until they are combined. The vinaigrette can be mixed a day ahead and refrigerated. Let it come to room temperature before using.

3. To serve, pour the vinaigrette over the chilled salad. Gently toss to coat the salad with the vinaigrette. Adjust the seasoning. Serve the salad on a small platter or divide it among 4 chilled salad plates, arranging it attractively. Serve immediately, chilled.

Salad-Styling Tips

There's more to putting a salad together than mixing a perfect vinaigrette. Select crisp greens, colorful garnishes, and fresh herbs to create an eye-catching and delicious presentation.

Use a mixture of different lettuces or a chiffonade of shredded romaine and leaf lettuce. For color contrast, add thinly sliced red cabbage. Bitter greens such as frisee, arugula, and watercress enhance both taste and texture.

Fresh garnishes such as red or yellow cherry tomatoes and bell peppers in any shade are always appealing. Herb blossoms, such as chives, basil, and thyme, as well as nasturtium blossoms, lend a wonderful touch.

Summer Macaroni Salad with Crisp Garlic Bread Crumbs

Garlic bread crumbs add an inviting crunch to this summer macaroni salad that highlights the best seasonal tastes—sun-ripened tomatoes, red peppers, and basil. The small amount of sugar brings out the natural sweetness of the tomatoes and red pepper. Contrary to most pasta salads, this one does not require much reviving before serving because chilled pasta absorbs much less of the flavors in the salad than hot pasta.

YIELD: 4 MAIN-COURSE SERVINGS

VINAIGRETTE:
10 large basil leaves, minced, about 1 tablespoon
2 large cloves garlic, minced, about 1 tablespoon
6 tablespoons olive oil
$1/4$ cup balsamic vinegar
1 teaspoon salt
$1/2$ teaspoon sugar
$1/4$ teaspoon red pepper flakes

SALAD:
6 ripe medium tomatoes, outer shells only,
    cut into $1/2$-inch dice, about 4 cups
1 large red bell pepper, seeded, roasted (page 359),
    cut into $1/2$-inch dice, about $3/4$ cup
8 ounces macaroni, cooked, rinsed with cold water,
    tossed with $1/2$ teaspoon oil, chilled

BREAD CRUMBS:
1 tablespoon olive oil
1 small clove garlic, minced, about $1/2$ teaspoon
$1/2$ cup fresh white or whole-wheat bread crumbs
Pinch of salt

$1 1/2$ tablespoons julienned basil leaves, for garnish

1. For the vinaigrette, put all the ingredients in a 2-quart mixing bowl. Whisk until combined.

2. For the salad, put the tomatoes, pepper, and macaroni in the bowl with the vinaigrette. Gently toss until combined.

3. For the bread crumbs, heat the oil in a small nonstick skillet over medium-high heat until hot. Add the garlic and crumbs. Cook until the bread is browned and crispy, about 4 minutes, stirring often to prevent burning. Add the salt. Stir well. Let cool.

4. The salad can be made in advance to this point. Refrigerate the macaroni salad, covered airtight. Store the cooled crumbs at room temperature, wrapped airtight. If chilled, let the salad come to room temperature before serving.

5. To serve, mix salad well; adjust the seasoning. Serve the salad in a shallow bowl or divide it among 4 serving plates. Garnish with the julienned basil. Sprinkle 2 tablespoons of bread crumbs on each serving.

Greek Orzo Salad with Shrimp

All the traditional components of a Greek salad combine with shrimp and orzo, a rice-shaped pasta, to make a most delicious summer pasta salad. Using chilled pasta ensures that the salad will taste as good as when it was mixed—even 24 hours later.

YIELD: 4 MAIN-COURSE SERVINGS

VINAIGRETTE:

3 tablespoons minced fresh dill
1 medium clove garlic, minced, about ³/4 teaspoon
2 tablespoons each: fresh lemon juice, olive oil
1 tablespoon red wine vinegar
¹/4 teaspoon each: salt, coarsely cracked pepper

SALAD:

1 ripe large tomato, outer shell only, cut into ¹/3-inch
   dice, about ²/3 cup
3 large green onions, thinly sliced, about ³/4 cup
3¹/2 ounces feta cheese, preferably a less salty variety,
   cut into ¹/3-inch dice
20 cooked shelled jumbo shrimp, about 1 pound total,
   each cut into 4 pieces
12 Calamata olives, pitted, flesh cut into thirds
2 cups cooked orzo, rinsed in cold water, tossed with ¹/2
   teaspoon oil, chilled
Red leaf lettuce for serving
Dill sprigs and Calamata olives, for garnish

1. For the vinaigrette, put all the ingredients in a 2-quart mixing bowl. Whisk until combined.

2. For the salad, add the tomato, green onions, cheese, shrimp, olives, and orzo to the vinaigrette. Gently toss until combined. The salad can be made a day in advance to this point and refrigerated, covered airtight. If chilled, let the salad come to room temperature before serving.

3. To serve, toss gently; adjust the seasoning and lemon balance as needed. Arrange the lettuce leaves on a platter or on 4 individual serving plates. Mound the salad on the lettuce leaves or divide evenly on the individual serving plates. Garnish with dill sprigs and olives.

Warm Sweet and Sour Chicken and Wild Rice Salad

This warm chicken and wild rice salad makes a wonderful winter lunch or Sunday night supper. The microwave oven warms it up as if just freshly cooked. The salad can also be served at room temperature or chilled. Wild rice freezes beautifully, so it makes good sense to cook more than you need; it's great to have on hand for an array of salads, side dishes, soups, and casseroles. Turkey can be substituted for the chicken, if you wish.

YIELD: 4 MAIN-COURSE SERVINGS

CHICKEN:
3 large chicken breast halves, skinned, boned, trimmed, about 5 to 6 ounces each
1/2 cup lower-salt chicken broth
Salt and freshly ground pepper to taste

SALAD:
2 cups cooked Wild Rice (page 360)
1/2 red medium onion, minced, about 3/4 cup
1 large tart apple, cored, unpeeled, cut into 1/4-inch dice, about 2 1/3 cups
1/2 large red bell pepper, seeded, cut into 1/4-inch dice, about 3/4 cup
1/2 cup each: currants, toasted pecan pieces (page 358)
2 tablespoons each: balsamic vinegar, olive oil
Scant 1/2 teaspoon salt
Freshly ground pepper to taste
Red leaf lettuce leaves, for serving

1. For the chicken, place the breasts, one at a time, between 2 sheets of plastic wrap. Use a meat pounder or heavy pot to make them uniform in thickness. Place them in a single layer in a 9-inch skillet. Add the chicken broth. Lightly season top side of each breast. Cook, covered, over medium-high heat for 3 minutes. Turn them once. Lightly season top side of each breast. Simmer the chicken until just cooked through; the juices should run clear when the breasts are pierced with the tip of a knife, about 7 minutes total. Do not overcook the chicken.

2. Let the chicken cool in the broth. When the chicken is cool enough to handle, cut it into 1-inch chunks. Transfer the chunks to a bowl. Reserve the broth for another use; it can be frozen.

3. For the salad, add the rice, onion, apple, red pepper, currants, pecans, vinegar, oil, salt, and pepper to the bowl with the chicken. Toss together. Adjust the seasoning and vinegar balance. The salad can be served immediately or covered airtight and refrigerated overnight.

4. To serve, the salad can be warm, room temperature, or chilled. To serve warm, gently reheat in a nonstick skillet, stirring often. (Alternately, reheat in a microwave oven, covered, in a microwave dish on medium power [50 percent] until just warm, about 3 to 5 minutes, stirring once halfway through.) Adjust the seasoning.

5. Arrange the lettuce leaves on a serving platter or on 4 dinner plates. Mound the salad on the lettuce leaves or divide it evenly on individual serving plates. Serve immediately, if warm.

Couscous Vegetable Salad

This is a flavorful vegetable couscous salad. It's versatile, too, filling the vegetable-grain slot from picnics to buffets. Paired with simply grilled fish, lamb, beef, or poultry, the meal is complete. Couscous is a granular semolina, which, when precooked, is quickly prepared.

YIELD: 4 TO 5 SIDE-DISH SERVINGS

1 cup quick-cooking couscous
1/4 cup dried currants
2/3 cup boiling Vegetable Stock (page 367)
   or vegetable broth
3/4 tablespoon olive oil
3 tablespoons pine nuts
2 medium zucchini, shell only, finely diced,
   about 2 cups
1 large shallot, peeled, coarsely chopped, about
   2 1/2 tablespoons
1 large green onion, including green tops, trimmed,
   thinly sliced, about 1/4 cup
Scant 1/2 teaspoon salt
1/2 large red bell pepper, seeded, finely diced,
   about 2/3 cup
2 to 3 tablespoons fresh lemon juice
1/2 teaspoon ground cumin

1. Place the couscous and currants in a 1-quart mixing bowl; pour the boiling stock or broth over them. Stir with a fork; let the mixture rest for 5 minutes.

2. Heat the oil in a 10-inch nonstick skillet over medium heat. When hot, add the pine nuts; lightly brown, about 5 minutes, stirring often. Use a slotted spoon to transfer the browned nuts to paper towels. Set aside.

3. Add the zucchini, shallot, green onion, and salt to the same skillet; cook over high heat, stirring often, just until the vegetables begin to soften, about 2 minutes. Add the red pepper; cook 1 more minute.

4. Stir the couscous mixture, 2 tablespoons of the lemon juice, and the cumin into the vegetables. Cook until just heated through, about 1 minute. Remove from the heat. Add the reserved pine nuts, stir well, and adjust the seasoning. Add the remaining lemon juice as needed. The salad can be refrigerated up to 2 days.

5. The couscous can be served warm, at room temperature, or chilled. Stir well. Adjust the seasoning. To serve warm, gently reheat in a 12-inch nonstick skillet over medium heat for 3 minutes or in a microwave oven on medium power (50 percent) until warm, about 2 to 3 minutes. Adjust the seasoning. Mound on a serving platter. Serve immediately.

Chef's Slaw

Here, many of the typical components of a chef's salad are mixed with thin cabbage slices that becomes a chef's slaw. As chef's salads go, this one is unusual because it can be prepared a day in advance of serving. Double or triple the recipe as needed.

YIELD: 4 MAIN-COURSE SERVINGS

SALAD:

8 cups packed thinly sliced green cabbage
1 medium red onion, cut into $^1/_4$-inch dice, about 1 cup
20 large firm cherry tomatoes, quartered
4 ounces each: sliced Swiss cheese, sliced ham or
    salami, cut into julienne strips
$^1/_4$ cup crumbled blue cheese
2 cups diced or julienned cooked chicken or turkey

VINAIGRETTE:

3 tablespoons each: red wine vinegar, fresh lemon juice
$^1/_3$ cup safflower oil
1 tablespoon water
1 tablespoon plus 1 teaspoon Dijon mustard
$^1/_8$ teaspoon salt
Freshly ground pepper to taste

1. For the salad, toss all the ingredients in a large mixing bowl until combined.

2. For the vinaigrette, combine all the ingredients in a small dish.

3. Toss the salad and vinaigrette together. The slaw can be made a day ahead and refrigerated, covered airtight.

4. To serve, toss well to mix; adjust the seasoning. Serve chilled in a bowl.

Charting Cabbage . . .

Cabbage, along with broccoli, brussels sprouts, and cauliflower, belongs to a class of vegetables known as crucifers. Evidence suggests that crucifers may help reduce the risk of developing certain types of cancer. In addition, cabbage is a good source of vitamins, especially C and A. Red cabbage has more vitamin C than green, but less of A. Both add a great deal of fiber to the diet and crunch to a salad. And finally, cabbage is low in calories, so low that you could eat an entire pound of cabbage for about 110 calories.

Barley Salad with Spicy Sausage, Peas, Celery, and Carrots

Barley, like many grains, takes a long time to cook (although quick-cooking barley, which has an appealing texture, takes only 10 minutes) and freezes well. Keep cooked barley on hand in the freezer to add to salads, soups, casseroles, and side dishes.

**YIELD: ABOUT 4 1/2 CUPS,
4 MAIN-COURSE SERVINGS**

SALAD:
2 cups water
1/2 cup barley, regular or quick-cooking
8 ounces smoked sausage, cut into 1/2-inch pieces
8 ounces mushrooms, quartered, about 2 cups
1 large rib celery, diced, about 1 cup
1/4 cup diced red onion
1 cup each: frozen thawed tiny peas, diced carrots

VINAIGRETTE:
1 1/2 tablespoons red wine vinegar
3 tablespoons olive oil
2 tablespoons water
1 tablespoon Dijon mustard
1/4 teaspoon salt
1/2 teaspoons dried tarragon
Freshly ground pepper to taste

1. For the salad, bring the water to a boil in a medium pot. Stir in the barley and bring to a boil again. Cover, then simmer barley until tender, about 45 to 50 minutes for regular barley, about 10 minutes for quick-cooking barley. Drain off any excess liquid.

2. Cook the sausage in an 8-inch nonstick skillet over medium-high heat about 6 minutes, until browned. Use a slotted spoon to transfer the sausage to paper towels. Blot any excess fat. Place in a large bowl along with the remaining salad ingredients.

3. For the vinaigrette, mix all the ingredients in a small bowl. Add the vinaigrette to the salad and toss well. The salad can be served immediately or covered airtight and refrigerated overnight.

4. The salad can be served warm, at room temperature, or chilled in a serving bowl. To serve chilled, toss well; adjust the seasoning, mustard, and vinegar. To serve warm, gently reheat in a nonstick skillet over medium heat for about 3 minutes or in the microwave oven on medium power (50 percent) until just warm, not hot, about 2 to 3 minutes. Serve immediately.

Turkey and Rice Salad with Dried Tart Cherry Vinaigrette

Rice is the basis of this salad, so the more interesting the rice, the better the salad. Basmati, brown, and wild rice are all earthy-tasting, offering an interesting flavor and texture. They can be mixed with white rice, if you choose. This is a great leftover dish—just as good with cooked chicken, lamb, and beef. The salad is also delicious without any meat at all, served as a partner to cold meats. Plumping dried tart cherries (dried cranberries can be substituted) in the mixture of balsamic vinegar and water imparts great flavor to the vinaigrette, making it unnecessary to use very much oil. Olive oil can be substituted for the walnut oil; the taste will be different but still very good.

YIELD: 6 MAIN-COURSE SERVINGS

SALAD:

4 cups cooked and chilled rice—Basmati, brown, or
 Wild Rice (page 360) (or a mixture of these)
1 medium Granny Smith apple, unpeeled, cored,
 cut into 1/2-inch dice, about 2 cups
1 1/2 cups diced cooked turkey or chicken, beef, or lamb
2 medium ribs celery, cut into 1/2-inch dice, about 1 cup
6 small green onions, thinly sliced, about 3/4 cup
1/2 cup coarsely chopped walnuts, toasted (page 358)

VINAIGRETTE:

1 cup dried tart cherries (or dried cranberries)
6 to 8 tablespoons balsamic vinegar
2/3 cup water
Scant 1/2 teaspoon each: cinnamon, salt
1/4 teaspoon cayenne pepper
2 tablespoons walnut oil

Red leaf lettuce leaves, for serving

1. For the salad, put all the ingredients in a 3-quart bowl. Toss until combined. Set aside.

2. For the vinaigrette, heat the dried tart cherries, 6 tablespoons of the vinegar, the water, cinnamon, salt, and cayenne in a small nonaluminum saucepan just to the boil. Pour the vinaigrette over the salad. Gently toss. Stir in the walnut oil. Adjust the vinegar balance and the seasoning. The salad can be served immediately or covered airtight and refrigerated overnight. Before using, stir it well; adjust the seasoning.

3. To serve, arrange the lettuce on a serving platter. Mound the salad attractively on the lettuce. Serve cold or at room temperature.

Pickling Cucumbers, Tomatoes, and Basil

Pickling cucumbers, loaded up in fall produce bins, have a sweet taste and firm texture without an abundance of seeds. An English cucumber, peeled, quartered lengthwise and thinly sliced, can be substituted for the pickling cucumbers. This condiment salad brings into play other seasonal ingredients—sun-ripened tomatoes and fresh basil. A flavorful salad that is easy to make, it can be doubled or tripled to serve a crowd. And it tastes better the day after it's made.

YIELD: 4 SIDE-DISH SERVINGS

SALAD:

4 medium pickling cucumbers, peeled and thinly sliced
    into rounds, about 2 cups
1 large ripe but firm tomato, outer shell only, cut into
    $^1/_3$-inch dice, about $^3/_4$ cup
3 tablespoons minced red onion

VINAIGRETTE:

3 tablespoons finely julienned basil leaves
1 tablespoon olive oil
2 tablespoons apple cider vinegar
1 teaspoon sugar
$^1/_2$ teaspoon salt
Freshly ground pepper to taste

1. For the salad, combine all the ingredients in a
1$^1/_2$-quart bowl. Set it aside.

2. For the vinaigrette, combine all the ingredients
in a small dish. Stir until combined. Add to the
salad. Toss well to coat the salad ingredients.
Refrigerate the salad covered airtight for at least 6
hours, preferably overnight.

3. To serve, toss the salad well. Drain off any excess
liquid. Adjust the seasoning. Mound in a bowl or
divide evenly among 4 chilled salad plates. Serve
chilled.

Sweet Corn Confetti Salad

Here, seasonal young sweet corn is put to the test. The corn is cut off the husk and, without cooking it, mixed with zucchini, red pepper, green onions, and jicama for a colorful salad. If this is your first taste of raw corn, it's surprisingly luscious—sweet and a little al dente. Leftover cooked corn can be substituted, as well as frozen or canned corn; the salad just won't have the same crunch. This salad can be served right after it's mixed or held a day in the refrigerator. To serve, spoon the salad into small Romaine lettuce leaves or Belgian endive leaves. This is a great salad for a barbecue; arrange the lettuce leaves on a large serving platter as they are easy to pick up in the hand. side dish

YIELD: 4 SIDE-DISH SERVINGS

SALAD:

2 large ears young corn, kernels cut off the cob,
   about 2 cups
1/2 cup each: diced zucchini, diced seeded red bell pepper
3 large green onions, thinly sliced, about 3/4 cup
1 cup diced peeled jicama

VINAIGRETTE:

2 tablespoons vegetable oil
1/4 cup white vinegar
1 jalapeño pepper, seeded (wear gloves), minced, about
   1 tablespoon
1 teaspoon ground cumin
1 1/2 teaspoons sugar
1/2 teaspoon salt

Small romaine lettuce leaves from the heart or Belgian
   endive leaves, for serving

1. For the salad, put all the ingredients in a 2-quart bowl. Mix until combined.

2. For the vinaigrette, put all the ingredients in a small bowl. Whisk until combined. Add the vinaigrette to the salad. Toss it well. Adjust the seasoning. The salad can be made a day ahead and refrigerated, covered airtight.

3. To serve, toss the salad well and adjust the seasoning. Spoon into the lettuce leaves. Arrange on a platter. Serve chilled.

Speck's "Best Ever" German Potato Salad

Hot German-style potato salad is the perfect foil for a gutsy winter meal of pan fried smoked sausage and Baked Sweet and Sour Red Cabbage (page 204), all accompanied by a glass of chilled beer! The following potato salad recipe is adapted from How America Eats *by Clementine Paddleford (Charles Scribner's, 1960); it was deemed "the best ever" when served to many St. Louis generations at Speck's, a century-old coffeehouse on Market Street, now extinct. The egg whites add that "special something that no other potato salad ever had."*

YIELD: 4 TO 5 SIDE-DISH SERVINGS

16 small red potatoes, about 2 pounds total, scrubbed
4 thick slices applewood-smoked bacon (see Midwestern Sources, page 376), cut into $1/4$-inch dice, about $2/3$ cup
2 small onions, minced, about 1 cup
2 tablespoons flour
$1/2$ cup each: cider vinegar, water
2 teaspoons sugar
$1/2$ teaspoon celery seed
1 teaspoon salt
Freshly ground pepper to taste
2 large egg whites
$1/3$ cup minced fresh parsley

1. Boil the potatoes in salted water to cover until barely tender (not mushy), about 20 to 22 minutes. Drain. Set the potatoes aside until they are just cool enough to handle.

2. Meanwhile, brown the bacon in an 8-inch nonstick skillet, about 3 minutes. Drain all but 1 tablespoon of the fat from the skillet.

3. Add the onions to the skillet. Cook over medium heat until hot, about 2 minutes. Stir in the flour. Add the vinegar, water, sugar, celery seed, salt, and pepper. Gently cook until the mixture is thickened, about 4 minutes. Keep it hot.

4. Put the egg whites in a small bowl. Froth them with a fork. Set aside.

5. To assemble, peel the warm potatoes. Cut the potatoes into $1/3$-inch-thick slices. Put them in a large bowl. Pour the hot dressing over them. Gently toss them until mixed. Add the egg whites. Toss gently. Adjust the seasoning. Add the parsley. Serve the salad warm. It's best eaten when freshly mixed; however, it can be made up to 3 hours ahead and refrigerated.

6. To serve salad that has been chilled, gently reheat, covered, in a 10-inch nonstick skillet over medium heat until warm, about 2 to 3 minutes, or, alternately, in a microwave oven on medium power (50 percent) until the potatoes are just warmed through, about 2 minutes. Serve immediately, mounded in a bowl.

Oil Lamp Cucumber Salad

This is an old-fashioned cucumber salad inspired by the condiment salad offerings at the roadside Oil Lamp restaurant in New Paris, Indiana. The cucumbers have a great piquant flavor and end up being only slightly creamy as the collected juices and cream are drained off before serving. However, the sour cream isn't wasted; the remaining cream gives just the right finish to the salad. Double or triple this recipe for a crowd.

YIELD: 3 TO 4 SIDE-DISH SERVINGS

1 large English cucumber, peeled, thinly sliced,
   about 2 cups
1 small onion, minced, about $1/2$ cup
$1/3$ cup light sour cream
2 tablespoons plus 1 teaspoon cider vinegar
2 teaspoons sugar
Scant $1/4$ teaspoon salt
Freshly ground pepper to taste
2 teaspoons snipped fresh chives

1. Put the cucumbers in a 2-quart bowl. Set aside.

2. Put the remaining ingredients (except the chives) in a small bowl. Combine until well blended. Add to the cucumbers and toss until well combined. Refrigerate for at least 4 hours until the salad is well chilled, or for up to 2 days, covered airtight.

3. To serve, toss the salad until it is well mixed. Drain all liquid (if you have leftover salad, you'll find more collected juices each time you want to serve it—always drain before serving). Toss the cucumbers with the chives. Adjust the seasoning. Serve chilled.

Curried Celery Root and Apple Salad

This salad has a slightly sweet edge derived from the apple and currants. It goes well with cold grilled chicken, leftover turkey (great on a turkey sandwich with Cranberry Mustard, page 349), roast leg of lamb, and baked ham. Celery root is a very firm vegetable; the shredding disk of the food processor does the best job of shredding it.

YIELD: 4 TO 6 SIDE-DISH SERVINGS

DRESSING:
1/2 cup light mayonnaise
2 tablespoons each: water, fresh lemon juice
1 tablespoon plus 1 teaspoon curry powder (preferably Madras)

SALAD:
1 large celery root, peeled, shredded, about 2 cups
2 medium Granny Smith apples, unpeeled, cored, shredded, about 2 cups
1/2 cup dried currants

1. For the dressing, put all the ingredients in a large mixing bowl. Whisk until combined.

2. For the salad, put the ingredients into the bowl with the dressing. Toss well to coat the salad with the dressing. The salad can be made 2 days ahead and refrigerated, covered airtight.

3. To serve, toss well; adjust the seasoning. Serve chilled, in a bowl.

Sweet and Sour Red Cabbage Slaw with Cracked Pepper

Red cabbage slaw has a hidden asset; it improves as it stands. Here, it's combined in a sweet and sour dressing that's low in fat, a perfect accompaniment to a wide array of sandwiches. The ultra-thin slicing disc of the processor does a quick professional job with the cabbage and onion.

YIELD: 6 SIDE-DISH SERVINGS

1 medium red cabbage, quartered, cored, thinly sliced,
  about 10 cups
1 small red onion, halved, thinly sliced, about 1 cup
$^1/_4$ cup each: honey, water
5 tablespoons red wine vinegar
2 tablespoons safflower oil
$^3/_4$ teaspoon dried thyme
1 teaspoon salt
$2^1/_2$ teaspoons coarsely cracked pepper

1. Combine all the ingredients in a large bowl. Toss until combined. Adjust the seasoning and vinegar. The slaw can be made a day in advance and refrigerated, covered airtight.

2. To serve, toss well. Adjust the seasoning. Serve chilled, in a large bowl.

Farmhouse Coleslaw with Buttermilk-Dill Dressing

This coleslaw is intended for hamburgers, hot dogs, bratwursts, barbecued chicken, and ribs although it's not heavy with dressing as it's typically made. If you prefer a thicker dressing, you can increase the amount of mayonnaise to your taste. The food processor is the best equipment for coleslaw; it mixes the dressing, then slices the cabbage and celery, and shreds the carrots and radishes, all without washing the work bowl.

YIELD: 8 SIDE-DISH SERVINGS

DRESSING:

2 large cloves garlic, minced, about 1 tablespoon

$^1/_2$ cup fresh dill leaves

1 cup buttermilk

$^2/_3$ cup light mayonnaise

2 tablespoons cider vinegar

1 tablespoon plus 1 teaspoon sugar

$^3/_4$ teaspoon salt

Freshly ground pepper

COLESLAW:

1 medium cabbage, cored, very thinly sliced, about 10 cups

3 medium ribs celery, thinly sliced, about 1 $^1/_2$ cups

2 large carrots, shredded, about 2 $^1/_2$ cups

8 large radishes, shredded, about 1 $^1/_3$ cups

1 medium red onion, cut into small dice, about 2 cups

1. For the dressing, put all the ingredients in a food processor fitted with the metal blade or in a blender. Process until combined. Transfer to a 3-quart mixing bowl.

2. For the cole slaw, put all the ingredients in the mixing bowl with the dressing. Toss until the slaw is coated with the dressing. Chill. The slaw can be refrigerated up to 6 hours, covered airtight.

3. To serve, toss well, drain off any excess liquid, and adjust the seasoning. Mound in a bowl or divide evenly between 8 chilled salad plates. Serve chilled.

Red Cabbage Slaw with Broccoli and Red Pepper

This slaw is robustly flavored yet somewhat refined at the same time; it's the fresh basil that does it. The broccoli stems are peeled, shredded (use the shredding disk of the food processor), and included in the slaw mix. Chill the slaw for several hours before serving it; the broccoli florets need some time to absorb the dressing.

YIELD: 8 TO 10 SIDE-DISH SERVINGS

VINAIGRETTE:

1/2 cup fresh basil leaves

1/3 cup light-tasting olive oil

3 tablespoons each: honey, balsamic vinegar

1/4 cup each: red wine vinegar, water

1 teaspoon each: salt, coarsely ground pepper

COLESLAW:

1 medium red cabbage, cored, very thinly sliced, about
   10 cups

1 medium bunch broccoli, florets trimmed and
   separated into tiny pieces, stems peeled and shredded,
   about 6 cups total

1 large red bell pepper, cut into 2-inch-long fine
   julienne, about 1 1/2 cups

6 large green onions, thinly sliced, about 1 1/2 cups

1. For the vinaigrette, put the basil leaves, olive oil, honey, vinegars, water, salt, and pepper in a food processor fitted with the metal blade or in a blender. Mix until the basil is minced. Transfer to a 4-quart bowl.

2. For the coleslaw, put all the ingredients into the bowl with the dressing. Toss until well mixed. Chill at least 4 hours or up to 8 hours before serving.

3. To serve, toss well, drain off any excess liquid, and adjust the seasoning. Serve chilled in a large bowl.

Cranberry Relish Mold with Pineapple Dressing

Back in the fifties, a co-worker was proud of this recipe and the whole office made it for their Thanksgiving dinner. It was a great success! Subsequently, gelatin salads fell out of favor, but I have continued to serve it, much to my family's delight. This cranberry relish mold is especially crunchy, refreshing, and not too sweet. It's also quick and easy to make in a food processor. I've opted to leave out the marshmallows that were in the original recipe. If you omit the nuts, it's definitely lowfat. This recipe must be made at least a day ahead, allowing time for the fresh cranberry flavor to round out and deepen.

YIELD: 12 SERVINGS

One 12-ounce bag of fresh cranberries, about 4 cups
   (if frozen, it is not necessary to thaw them),
   coarsely chopped in a food processor
1/3 cup sugar
One 6-ounce package raspberry Jell-O
1 cup each: hot water, cold water
1 cup each: finely chopped celery and walnuts
3 tart medium apples, unpeeled, cored, finely chopped,
   about 6 cups
2 teaspoons fresh lemon juice
Decorative leaves (such as galax or lemon), for garnish
Pineapple Dressing (recipe follows)

1. Lightly oil a 7 to 8-cup-capacity ring mold. Set aside.

2. Combine the chopped cranberries and sugar in a 2-quart mixing bowl; set aside for at least 10 minutes to draw out the juices.

3. Meanwhile, put the gelatin and 1 cup hot water in a 1-quart bowl. Stir until the gelatin is dissolved. Add the remaining cold water. Add the cranberries and juices, celery, walnuts, apples, and lemon juice.

Mix well. Transfer the mixture to the prepared mold. Cover the mold and refrigerate overnight. The salad can be made up to 3 days ahead, covered airtight, and refrigerated.

4. To serve, invert the ring mold on a serving platter. Loosen the contents by placing a hot, wet towel on top of the mold. If the mold is not easily released, keep reapplying hot, wet towels on the inverted mold. Once it is unmolded, the cranberry relish can be held in the refrigerator for several hours. Decorate the platter with the leaves. Serve the pineapple dressing in a separate dish with a small ladle; top each serving with a small dollop.

Pineapple Dressing

This creamy pineapple sauce is a lower fat version of the cooked fruit dressings typically served with gelatin molds.

YIELD: 12 SERVINGS

1 tablespoon each: unsalted butter, flour
3/4 cup unsweetened pineapple juice (one 6-ounce can)
1 large egg, separated
1 large egg white
Pinch of salt
1/3 cup sugar
2 tablespoons plain nonfat yogurt
1 to 3 tablespoons fresh lemon juice

1. Melt the butter in a 1-quart nonaluminum saucepan over medium-high heat. When it is hot, whisk in the flour and cook for 2 minutes. Slowly whisk in the pineapple juice. Cook until thickened, about 3 minutes, stirring constantly.

2. Put the egg yolk into a small dish. Froth the yolk with a fork. Stir in a little of the hot juice mixture. Whisk the egg mixture slowly into the juice mixture in the saucepan. Simmer, about 2 minutes, until thickened, stirring constantly. Remove from the heat.

3. Use a mixer to beat the 2 egg whites with the salt until frothy. With the mixer running, add the sugar by the tablespoon, letting each tablespoon incorporate before adding the next. Continue to beat until the whites are shiny, smooth, and just hold their shape. Whisk a little whipped egg white into the mixture in the saucepan, then whisk in the remaining whites.

4. Return the saucepan to the stove and cook, whisking slowly and constantly for about 2 minutes, until the mixture comes to a boil (it will puff more than boil). Remove from the heat. Use a spatula to immediately transfer the sauce to a 2-cup bowl. Refrigerate the sauce until it is chilled. Stir in the yogurt and 1 tablespoon of the lemon juice until it is smooth. Adjust the lemon juice to taste. The sauce can be made a day ahead and refrigerated, covered airtight.

5. To serve, stir well. Serve chilled in a small bowl with a ladle.

Basic Vinaigrette

This basic vinaigrette has a wide range of uses and can be the base of many variations. The oil and vinegar you select will change its character to suit any salad. Safflower oil is tasteless but very light, so it's a good oil to mix with other more flavorful oils such as walnut or hazelnut. Sometimes using all olive oil will seem too heavy, so again, you might mix it with some safflower oil. The water helps to make the vinaigrette less harsh tasting.

For the vinegar, use red wine, sherry, white wine, or cider vinegar, or lemon juice. The dressing can be used plain or flavored with a variety of herbs and/or a range of savory condiments.

YIELD: 1 GENEROUS CUP DRESSING

³/₄ cup oil of your choice, or a combination as suggested above
¹/₄ cup vinegar
2 tablespoons cold water
1 teaspoon each: Dijon mustard, salt
Freshly ground pepper to taste

Use a whisk to mix the oil, vinegar, water, mustard, salt, and pepper. Or put the ingredients in a jar. Tightly close it. Shake until well mixed. For a thicker consistency (which I prefer), mix the vinaigrette in the processor or blender. The dressing can be covered airtight and refrigerated for up to 2 weeks.

Cracked Pepper Variation: Replace the freshly ground pepper with 1 tablespoon coarsely cracked black pepper.

Lemon Thyme Vinaigrette

This is a tangy vinaigrette for summer green salads. Mix the vinaigrette in the processor or blender for a thick consistency.

YIELD: 1 1/4 CUPS DRESSING

1 small clove garlic, minced, about ¹/₂ teaspoon

1 small shallot, minced, about 1 tablespoon

1 teaspoon grated lemon zest (colored rind), removed
   with a zester or fine grater (see page 14)

2 tablespoons fresh lemon juice

1 tablespoon each: red wine vinegar, Dijon mustard

¹/₂ cup canola or safflower oil

2 teaspoons fresh thyme leaves

1 teaspoon sugar

¹/₂ teaspoon each: salt, freshly ground pepper

¹/₃ cup cold water

Put all the ingredients except the water in a food processor fitted with the metal blade or in a blender. Process, adding the water slowly, until combined and smooth. The dressing can be made 5 days ahead and refrigerated, covered airtight. Let it come to room temperature before using.

Zinfandel's Strawberry Vinaigrette

Strawberry vinegar is commercially available, but I urge you to make your own (see Note); it will be a boon to your summer salads. Easy to make, it's full of bright, deep flavor without being harsh, one of those vinegars you could successfully use on salads with only a touch of oil. Thanks to Susan Goss and Rick Bayless, co-owners and chefs of Zinfandel, in Chicago, for this delicious twist on vinegar.

YIELD: 1 1/2 CUPS DRESSING

1/2 cup strawberry vinegar (see Note)
1 cup vegetable oil such as corn, canola, or safflower
   (I used safflower)
1/3 cup halved ripe strawberries
1 tablespoon plus 1 teaspoon clover honey
1 scant teaspoon salt
1/4 teaspoon freshly ground pepper

Put all the ingredients in a blender and puree until smooth. The dressing should have the consistency of a loose mayonnaise. Adjust the seasoning if necessary; the dressing should be tangy. It can be made ahead and stored in a covered, nonreactive container in the refrigerator. Let it come to room temperature before using.

NOTE: If strawberry vinegar is unavailable, substitute a mild white wine vinegar and increase the strawberries to 1/2 cup when you make the dressing. Or, better yet, make your own strawberry vinegar by putting a quart of very ripe (even blemished) strawberries in a nonreactive container and covering them with a mild white wine vinegar. After a week or so, strain, bottle, and store in a dark, cool place.

Salad Oils . . .

A very important and expensive component of salads is oil. Extra-virgin olive oil and walnut oil can cost as much as a bottle of fine wine. You'll want to handle these oils properly so they don't become rancid.

❖ First, buy oil where there is likely to be a fast turnover. Oil can easily turn rancid as it sits on the shelf. Make sure that what you've bought is fresh. Even if you've never tasted the specific oil before, you'll immediately recognize an off-flavor.

❖ Store it in a cool place, away from the light. For large quantities or infrequent use, the refrigerator is ideal, except that many oils will become solid at such a low temperature. If you keep oil in the refrigerator, remember to take it out about 30 minutes before you're ready to use it.

❖ The freezer is the best place to store oils you don't use very often. I pour walnut oil into small glass jars, label, and freeze them.

Family Baked Steak

Grilled Horseradish Hamburgers

Grilled Tenderloin on a Bed of Herbed Sweet and Sour Onions
  with Red Peppers

Rib Roast with Fresh Garlic Seasoning Salt

Brisket of Beef with Caramelized Onion Sauce

Meat Loaf with Greens

Cabbage Layer Cake Casserole with Sweet Tomato Marmalade

Lazy Man's Beef Stew

Lee's Lamburgers

Barbecued Herbed Leg of Lamb

Grilled Herb-Rubbed Lamb Chops on Greens

Spring Lamb Stew with Leeks and Root Vegetables

Braised Veal Shanks with Vegetables

Grilled Veal Chops with Lemon, Capers, and Sage Onions

Swedish Roast Pork Stuffed with Prunes, Apples, and Lingonberries,
  with Lingonberry Fruit Sauce

Carolyn's Sweet and Spicy Ribs

Venison Stew with Red Onions, Dried Cranberries, and Wild Mushrooms

Myrna's Scandinavian Venison Meatballs

SAUCES TO ACCOMPANY MEATS:
Woodland Port Wine Sauce

Horseradish Sauce

Chapter 5

Meat and Game Meats

❖

You would hardly recognize the beef that once made the Chicago stockyards famous if you compared it to its modern cousins. Long gone are the deep veins of fat marbled in the meat. They say that today's pork more closely resembles that brought to the first colonies in America—long and lean—than the pork of a hundred years ago. And it has taken a modern look at diet to see in venison a meat so devoid of fat that it may well be considered spa food. What remains unchanged is the central role the Midwest has always played in providing the nation with high-quality meat products.

The meat that once claimed the spotlight in any meal now takes a backseat. And that makes it special. Something of a treat, an occasional indulgence. So I find that what I look for in meat recipes are those flavors that take me right back to the comfort zone. I'm not looking for a lot of meat on my plate, but the essence of meat in a moderate portion.

A Grilled Tenderloin on a bed of Herbed Sweet and Sour Onions with Red Peppers, a Barbecued Herbed Leg of Lamb, a Rib Roast with Fresh Garlic Seasoning Salt, or simply hamburgers resplendent with horseradish . . . with dishes such as these I feel I am making the absolute most of the occasional meat dish I put on the table. Those times I cook meat, for myself or for my guests, I want the effort and the indulgence to really count.

So you will find Meat Loaf with Greens in this chapter, and Spring Lamb Stew with Leeks and Root Vegetables, and Myrna's Scandinavian Venison Meatballs, and Brisket of Beef with Caramelized Onion Sauce. You can taste the big flavors in the titles.

Family Baked Steak

This is the perfect dish for a family Sunday night supper! The success of this recipe depends on a top-quality well-trimmed 1½-inch-thick sirloin or T-bone steak. Season the steak and prepare the sauce, refrigerating both until it's time to cook the steak. Alternately, the steak can be seared and refrigerated overnight with the sauce spread over it. Either way, it's a great do-ahead.

YIELD: 6 SERVINGS

STEAK:

One 1½-inch-thick sirloin steak, about 2¾ pounds, well trimmed of all visible fat
¾ teaspoon each: minced garlic, freshly ground pepper
½ teaspoon salt

SAUCE:

1 large onion, quartered, thinly sliced, about 2½ cups
1 large green bell pepper, cored, seeded, quartered, thinly sliced, about 1¼ cups
1 cup ketchup
1 tablespoon Worcestershire sauce
¾ teaspoon ground cumin
Dash of Tabasco sauce
Freshly ground pepper to taste

1. For steak, combine the garlic, pepper, and salt. Rub this mixture over the entire surface of the steak. Put the steak in a plastic bag, seal it tightly, and refrigerate for at least 2 hours or as long as overnight.

2. Put a rack 4 inches from the broiler; turn on the broiler. Set aside a shallow broiling pan and an 8-cup-capacity shallow baking dish.

3. Remove the steak from the plastic bag; put it on the broiling pan.

4. Sear the steak under the hot broiler on both sides, about 2 to 3 minutes per side. Transfer to the reserved baking dish.

5. For the sauce, combine all the ingredients in a 1-quart saucepan. Gently simmer until the onion and pepper are just beginning to soften, about 7 minutes. Pour the sauce over the steak. The steak can now be baked immediately or refrigerated overnight. If you refrigerate it, bring it to room temperature before baking.

6. Move the rack to the center of the oven; preheat the oven to 375 degrees.

7. Bake the steak for 30 minutes, basting midway with the juices that collect in the bottom of the dish. Use a sharp knife to cut through the steak and check for medium rare. If the steak requires more cooking for your taste, lower the temperature to 325 degrees and continue baking, basting once more, until the meat is cooked as desired. Remove from the oven. Allow the steak to rest for 10 minutes before slicing.

8. To serve, cut across the grain into ¼-inch slices. Arrange on a warm platter; spoon the sauce over the meat. Serve hot.

Burger Basics

All hamburgers are not created equal. The most memorable ones are those cooked with the same care and attention that goes into more elaborate preparations.

- ❖ Start with a good cut of beef. Round or shoulder is the best, but lean chuck is also acceptable. Some fat is essential in hamburgers for both the flavor and the juiciness it adds. For juicy burgers 20 percent fat is about right.

- ❖ How to season a hamburger can be a volatile issue. Some feel that little bits of onion and green pepper should dot the meat; others think anything more than salt and pepper is heresy. I use a little seasoned salt and some freshly ground pepper mixed into the meat, and let the burger speak for itself.

- ❖ The very best burgers have been grilled over a charcoal flame, with just the smallest amount of presoaked mesquite or hickory chips thrown in to add their smoke. The fire should not be so hot that it flares up and chars the burgers.

- ❖ Pan sautéing is quite good. Use a heavy pan and a moderately high heat. Be sure to deglaze the pan to make a simple sauce. Set the cooked burgers aside and pour a small amount of red wine or beef stock in the pan. Boil over high heat until all the browned bits of meat dissolve into the sauce, stir in a little butter and pour these juices over the burgers.

- ❖ Don't skimp on the buns. Buy good-quality rolls that are soft inside and have a nice crust. Butter and grill or broil them until they are crisp and golden.

- ❖ Make sure whatever condiments you like, from ketchup to chopped onion and sweet pickle relish, are set on the table.

Grilled Horseradish Hamburgers

Horseradish and beef are longtime partners although they are rarely combined in a burger. If you have fresh horseradish, grind it fine and add it to taste. Serve with Chili Bean Bake (page 238) and Sweet and Sour Red Cabbage Slaw with Cracked Pepper (page 104).

YIELD: 4 BURGERS

1 pound lean ground beef
1 large egg white
2 tablespoons ketchup
1 tablespoon plus 1 teaspoon drained prepared white
 horseradish
2 teaspoons Dijon mustard
Scant $1/2$ teaspoon salt
Freshly ground pepper to taste
Barbecue sauce (store-bought), for serving

1. Use a fork to combine all of the ingredients except the barbecue sauce in a mixing bowl. Gently shape the mixture into 4 equal burgers. Cover with plastic wrap and refrigerate for at least 2 hours or up to 6 hours to allow the burgers to firm up.

2. Prepare a medium-hot barbecue fire with a few chunks of water-soaked mesquite wood. Or, alternately, put the broiler rack 6 inches from heat source and preheat the broiler.

3. Grill the burgers over a medium-hot fire (or broil them) until they are very browned on one side. Use a spatula to carefully turn them. Grill (or broil) to the desired doneness. Serve hot, with barbecue sauce on the side.

Grilled Tenderloin on a Bed of Herbed Sweet and Sour Onions with Red Peppers

Because tenderloin is a bland cut of beef, it should be marinated overnight to give it flavor. The best quality meat will also make a difference. For enhanced smokiness, add a few pieces of water-soaked applewood, hickory, or mesquite to the barbecue, whether it's fueled by charcoal or gas.

YIELD: 6 TO 8 SERVINGS

One 3-pound piece of tenderloin, trimmed of visible fat
2 large cloves garlic, minced, about 1 tablespoon
1 large shallot, minced, about 2¹/₂ tablespoons
¹/₂ tablespoon each: Dijon mustard, balsamic vinegar
¹/₄ cup each: olive oil, minced mixed fresh herbs
    (basil, thyme, and rosemary)
¹/₂ teaspoon salt
1 teaspoon coarsely cracked pepper
Herbed Sweet and Sour Onions and Red Peppers
    (recipe follows)
Fresh herb sprigs, for garnish

1. Put the meat in a large plastic food bag. Combine the garlic, shallots, mustard, vinegar, oil, herbs, salt, and pepper in a small dish. Add them to the meat. Secure the bag close to the meat so the marinade coats the surface of the meat. Place the bag in a dish. Refrigerate overnight, turning the bag occasionally.

2. When ready to cook, let the meat rest at room temperature for 1 hour. Prepare a medium-hot barbecue fire with a few chunks of water-soaked mesquite wood. Or alternately, put the broiler rack 8 inches from the heat source and preheat the broiler to medium-high heat. Drain the meat, reserving the marinade. Sprinkle the meat lightly with additional salt.

3. Grill over a medium-hot fire or broil until cooked as desired, brushing with the reserved marinade and turning as necessary. It may take as long as 15 to 20 minutes to cook the meat; an instant-reading thermometer should register 125 degrees for medium rare, 130 degrees for medium. Serve the steak hot or at room temperature.

4. To serve, let the meat rest for at least 10 minutes, loosely covered with foil, before cutting it into thin slices. If serving it at room temperature, slice the meat as close to serving time as possible. Overlap the slices attractively on the herbed sweet and sour onions and red peppers. Spoon the pan juices that have accumulated after cooking over the meat. Garnish the platter with fresh herb sprigs.

Herbed Sweet and Sour Onions with Red Peppers

This is a convenient do-ahead preparation. Be sure to add the fresh herbs after the final reheating. This mixture is also a great garnish for lamb, pork, and baked fish.

YIELD: 6 SERVINGS

1 tablespoon olive oil
1 medium Spanish onion, thinly sliced,
    about 2 cups
1 tablespoon sugar
2 tablespoons balsamic vinegar
$^{1}/_{2}$ teaspoon each: Dijon mustard, salt
1 large red bell pepper, roasted (page 359), seeded,
    cut into julienne strips, about $^{3}/_{4}$ cup
3 tablespoons minced mixed fresh herbs
    (basil, thyme, and rosemary)
1 tablespoon unsalted butter

1. Heat the oil in a 10-inch nonstick skillet over medium-high heat. When it is hot, add the onion and sugar. Cook until the onion is lightly colored but not dark brown, about 10 minutes, stirring often. Add the vinegar, mustard, and salt. Cook until the onion is very soft, about 7 minutes more, stirring often. Add the red pepper and heat through. Adjust the seasoning. The recipe can be made a day ahead to this point and refrigerated.

2. To serve, gently reheat the onion mixture and toss in the herbs. When it is hot, stir in the butter. Adjust the seasoning. The mixture can be served hot or at room temperature.

Best Bets for Beef

Beef is back in a big way! People have come to realize that it is possible to eat beef and still maintain a healthy diet. Here are some healthy meat-eating tips:

❖ Trim all visible fat from the meat.
❖ Select the lowfat cuts such as the round, sirloin tip, and flank steaks.
❖ Down-size the portions. Where 12-ounce steaks were once the norm, nutritionists now recommend 3-ounce portions. If this seems too skimpy, pair the meat with pasta or rice.
❖ Consider buying the new, lean-bred beef. It has a fraction of the fat found in traditional cuts of beef while maintaining all the flavor. It cooks differently, so be sure to read the instructions on the package.

Rib Roast with Fresh Garlic Seasoning Salt

There are many commercial seasoning blends available on the supermarket shelves, but this fresh garlic mix has much more flavor. For the best flavor, rub the seasoning salt on the surface of the meat the night before . . . or at least 4 hours before roasting it. Serve with pan juices, Horseradish Sauce (page 145), or Double-Baked Potatoes with Horseradish (page 212). The Woodland Port Wine Sauce (page 144) would complement the meat nicely. One of the easiest ways to finely mince fresh garlic is to use the food processor fitted with a metal blade; be sure the blade and work bowl are dry. Turn the processor on, drop the garlic cloves through the feed tube; process until all the garlic is minced as fine as possible.

YIELD: 6 TO 8 SERVINGS

GARLIC SEASONING MIX:
3 large cloves garlic, minced very fine,
    about 1¹/₂ tablespoons
1¹/₂ tablespoons salt
¹/₂ teaspoon each: paprika, turmeric, cumin,
    ground thyme, freshly ground pepper
One 3-rib roast, trimmed, about 6 to 7 pounds
2 tablespoons safflower oil
Salt and freshly ground pepper to taste

1. Set aside a shallow roasting pan.

2. For the garlic seasoning mix, put all the ingredients in a small dish and combine well.

3. Wipe the roast dry with paper towels. Rub the surface with the oil. Rub the garlic mixture over the entire roast. Place the roast in the reserved pan. Refrigerate 3 hours. The roast can also be prepared to this point a day ahead and refrigerated. Let it come to room temperature before roasting.

4. Put a rack in the lower third of the oven; preheat the oven to 450 degrees.

5. Roast the beef until it is seared, about 30 minutes. Decrease the oven temperature to 325 degrees. Continue to roast about 1¹/₄ hours more for medium rare (an instant-reading thermometer should read 125 degrees; the temperature will increase at least 10 degrees on standing). Tent the meat with foil after removing it from the oven. Let the roast rest at least 15 minutes before carving.

6. To serve, use a sharp carving knife or electric knife to cut off the ribs and slice the meat. Arrange on a warm serving platter. Spoon the skimmed pan juices over the meat. Lightly sprinkle with salt and pepper. Pass the Horseradish Sauce separately, if using it; or spoon some of the Woodland Port Wine Sauce over the meat, with the rest passed in a sauceboat.

Brisket of Beef with Caramelized Onion Sauce

Slow cooking results in a well-flavored, fork-tender brisket and the garlic and onions sweeten as they cook. It's best to make the brisket ahead so it can be refrigerated; the flavors improve and the solidified fat can be removed easily. The caramelized onions and onion sauce can also be made in advance and refrigerated. Once sliced and sauced, the brisket can also be frozen. When you have house guests, this is a great recipe for your entertaining needs; it reheats to perfection, works well on the buffet table, and makes irresistible sandwiches. Serve the brisket with Warm Russet Potato Pancakes (page 214), Mashed Potatoes with Celery Root and Parsnip (page 210), or Toasted Barley and Mushroom Risotto (page 231).

YIELD: 10 TO 12 SERVINGS

2 large cloves garlic, minced, about 1 tablespoon,
  plus 12 large cloves garlic, peeled
1 tablespoon each: salt, sweet paprika
2 teaspoons dry mustard
1 teaspoon freshly ground pepper
1 beef brisket, well trimmed, 6 to 7 pounds;
  or 2 first-cut briskets, about 3^1/$_2$ pounds each
2 medium Spanish onions, halved, thinly sliced,
  about 4 cups
1 cup water
Caramelized Onion Sauce (recipe follows)

1. Put a rack in the center of the oven; preheat the oven to 350 degrees. Line a large shallow roasting pan with heavy-duty aluminum foil, extending the foil flaps beyond the sides of the pan so the meat can be completely enclosed during baking. Set aside.

2. Put the minced garlic in a small dish with the salt, paprika, mustard, and pepper. Combine well. Rub this mixture over both sides of the meat.

Spread half the onion slices and half the whole garlic cloves on the center area of the foil. Place the meat over them. Top the meat with the remaining onions and whole garlic cloves. Carefully pour the water around the meat (do not pour it over the meat). Bring up the foil flaps and crimp the edges together to seal tightly.

3. Bake until the meat is tender, 4 to 5 hours. Test for tenderness with a fork or a sharp paring knife. Once cooled, the brisket should be refrigerated overnight or as long as 3 days. Discard the fat. Reserve the onions, garlic, and pan juices for the caramelized onion sauce.

4. Use an electric knife (or a sharp carving knife) to cut the meat across the grain into thin slices.

Arrange the sliced meat in a large, shallow, ovenproof dish just large enough to hold it. Spoon the caramelized onion sauce over the meat.

5. The brisket can be prepared in advance to this point, refrigerated overnight, or frozen for 3 months, covered airtight. Bring it to room temperature before reheating. To reheat, cover the dish loosely with aluminum foil. Bake in a preheated 350-degree oven until it is hot, about 40 minutes. Serve hot.

Kansas City–Style Beef Brisket . . .

For beef brisket in the Kansas City–style, rub the meat with dry seasonings, then slow-cook it over a pan of hot water in a smoker or pit barbecue. Depending on the weight of the brisket, the cooking may take 4 to 6 hours. An instant-reading thermometer should register 160 degrees and the meat should be fork-tender. If the brisket is trimmed of almost all its fat, be sure to lay some thin slices of beef fat on top while it cooks so it doesn't dry out. A good barbecue sauce is key for enjoying the brisket; tune up a commercial variety with cumin, garlic, sautéed onion, brown sugar or honey and cayenne pepper until you have developed the best flavor.

Caramelized Onion Sauce

YIELD: 10 SERVINGS

2 tablespoons vegetable oil
4 medium Spanish onions, halved, thinly sliced, about 8 cups
¼ teaspoon salt
Cooked onions and garlic from the brisket
1½ tablespoons flour
1 cup skimmed brisket pan juices
¼ cup tomato paste
2 tablespoons each: dry vermouth, light brown sugar
1 cup water
2 tablespoons unsalted butter
Freshly ground pepper to taste

1. Heat the oil in a 12-inch nonstick skillet over medium heat. When it is hot, add the sliced onions. Cook, stirring occasionally, until the onions are tan and lightly caramelized but not browned, about 20 to 25 minutes. Stir in the salt. Set aside. The onions can be cooked 2 days ahead and refrigerated, covered airtight.

2. Use a slotted spoon to transfer the onions and garlic that cooked with the brisket (not the caramelized onions) to a blender or a food processor fitted with a metal blade. Add the flour. Puree the mixture until it is smooth. Add the skimmed brisket pan juices, tomato paste, vermouth, and sugar. Mix well.

3. Transfer to a 1-quart saucepan. Stir in the water. Stir over medium-high heat until the sauce is thickened, about 4 minutes. Cut the butter into 3 pieces. Add 1 piece at a time, stirring until each is melted. Add the reserved caramelized onions and heat through. Adjust the seasoning with salt and pepper.

Meat Loaf with Greens

Here, mustard greens and spinach leaves lighten up the classic meat loaf. It's a tasty main course for an informal supper and it's a great option for picnics. Leftovers make the best sandwiches. The food processor shortcuts the preparation; use it if you have one. Ground lean lamb can be substituted for the beef, if you prefer it.

YIELD: 6 TO 8 SERVINGS

1½ tablespoons vegetable oil
3 large garlic cloves, minced, about 1½ tablespoons
4 large green onions, thinly sliced, about 1 cup
2 medium ribs celery, chopped, about 1 cup
1 packed cup each: spinach leaves, mustard greens,
    stems trimmed on both, leaves roughly cut
¾ teaspoon salt
1½ pounds lean ground beef
12 ounces breakfast sausage
¾ cup soft bread crumbs
2 large eggs
¾ cup ketchup
2 tablespoons milk
1½ teaspoons Worcestershire sauce
1 teaspoon ground cumin
¼ teaspoon red pepper flakes
Freshly ground pepper to taste

1. Put a rack in the center of the oven; preheat the oven to 375 degrees. Set aside a 9 × 13-inch baking pan.

2. Heat the oil in a 12-inch nonstick skillet over medium-high heat. When hot, add the garlic, green onions, celery, spinach leaves, mustard greens, and ¼ teaspoon of the salt. Cook until the celery is softened, about 6 minutes, stirring often. Transfer the mixture to a large mixing bowl. Let it cool slightly.

3. Add the ground beef, sausage, bread crumbs, eggs, ¼ cup of the ketchup, the milk, Worcestershire sauce, cumin, red pepper flakes, the remaining ½ teaspoon salt, and the pepper to the bowl. Mix all ingredients thoroughly with a fork. To test the seasoning, fry a small amount of the mixture or, alternately, cook a small amount in the microwave oven. Adjust the seasoning.

4. Mound the mixture in the reserved pan. Use your hands to shape it into an 8 × 6-inch oval. Gently press to compact the loaf as much as possible. The recipe can be prepared a day ahead to this point. Cover the loaf and refrigerate. When you are ready to bake, spread the loaf with the remaining ½ cup ketchup.

5. Bake until the loaf is well browned and sizzling, about 1 hour, 10 minutes. Remove from the oven and use a flexible spreader to smooth the ketchup coating.

6. To serve, the meat loaf can be hot, at room temperature, or chilled. Use a sharp knife or an electric knife to cut it into ¾-inch-wide slices.

Cabbage Layer Cake Casserole with Sweet Tomato Marmalade

Inspired by stuffed cabbage, this sweet and sour cabbage recipe is much easier to assemble since forming individual packets is not involved. Instead, the cabbage head is boiled until the outer leaves are soft enough to remove and use as layers between the meat filling. The cabbage heart remains firm; some of it is chopped and mixed in with the meat. The finely minced prunes add the perfect sweetness to the meat; people who shy away from prunes will not detect them. This is one of those dishes that benefits from being refrigerated for up to 3 days in the refrigerator before serving; this gives the flavors a chance to meld. It's best to serve this cake right from the casserole. As with most cakes, the first slice is not always perfect.

YIELD: 6 TO 8 SERVINGS

CABBAGE CAKE:
1 large head green cabbage, about $2^{1}/_{2}$ pounds
4 quarts boiling salted water
1 tablespoon vegetable oil
3 large garlic cloves, minced, about $1^{1}/_{2}$ tablespoons
1 medium Spanish onion, minced, about 2 cups
1 cup soft bread crumbs
12 pitted large prunes, minced
$1^{1}/_{2}$ pounds ground lean pork, beef, or veal
1 large egg
2 large egg whites
1 teaspoon allspice
2 teaspoons Dijon mustard
$1^{3}/_{4}$ teaspoons salt
Freshly ground pepper to taste

SWEET AND SOUR SAUCE:
One $14^{1}/_{2}$-ounce can stewed tomatoes
  (with no salt added)
2 tablespoons each: dark brown sugar, cider vinegar

$^{1}/_{2}$ teaspoon each: Worcestershire sauce, salt
Sweet Tomato Marmalade (recipe follows), for garnish

1. Put a rack in the center of the oven; preheat the oven to 350 degrees. Set aside a 3 to 4-quart heavy casserole with a lid.

2. For the cake, cut an X about $^{1}/_{2}$-inch deep into the cabbage core. Cook in boiling water until cabbage leaves are pliable, about 10 minutes, and drain. When the cabbage is cool enough to handle, remove the large outer leaves, which will have softened; you will have about 12. Cut out the thick, hard veins from these leaves. Chop part of the remaining cabbage, enough to measure $1^{3}/_{4}$ cups. Reserve the rest for another use.

3. Heat the oil in a 10-inch nonstick skillet over medium-high heat. When it is hot, add the garlic and onion. Cook until they are very soft, about 6 minutes, stirring often.

4. Transfer the cooked garlic and onion to a large mixing bowl. Add the remaining cake ingredients, including the chopped cabbage but not the whole leaves. Use a fork to mix well. To test the seasoning, cook a small amount of the mixture in a skillet or in a microwave oven. Adjust the seasoning.

5. To assemble, arrange 3 cabbage leaves to cover the bottom of the casserole. Add a third of the meat mixture, spreading it evenly. Layer 3 more leaves, covering the meat. Repeat layering, ending with cabbage. Lightly compress the mixture with your hands.

6. For the sweet and sour sauce, mix all the ingredients in a food processor fitted with the metal blade or in a blender. Pour the mixture over the cabbage cake.

7. Bake, covered, for 2 hours. Let the cabbage cake cool 2 hours with the cover askew. Then refrigerate.

8. The cake can be made 3 days ahead and refrigerated. To reheat, bake, covered, in a preheated 350-degree oven until hot, about 45 minutes. Cut into wedges, spoon some of the casserole juices over the top, and garnish with a dollop of sweet tomato marmalade. Pass the remaining marmalade.

Sweet Tomato Marmalade

YIELD: ABOUT 1 3/4 CUPS

2 tablespoons safflower oil
1 large clove garlic, minced, about ¹/₂ tablespoon
1 small onion, minced, about ¹/₂ cup
4 medium tomatoes, cored, seeded, coarsely chopped, about 3 cups
2 tablespoons tomato paste
2 teaspoons brown sugar
¹/₄ teaspoon ground cumin
³/₄ teaspoon salt
Freshly ground pepper to taste

1. Heat 1 tablespoon of the oil in a medium-size nonaluminum pot over medium heat. When hot, add the garlic and onion. Cook gently until softened but not browned, about 10 minutes.

2. Add the tomatoes, tomato paste, sugar, cumin, salt, and pepper. Cook, uncovered, over very low heat until thick, about 30 to 50 minutes. Stir often, especially toward the end of cooking to avoid burning. If any liquid remains at the end of the cooking time, increase the heat to high and quickly boil it off. Stir in the remaining oil. Adjust the seasoning. Serve hot.

3. This marmalade can be refrigerated for up to 4 days, or frozen for up to 3 months, covered airtight. Before using, gently reheat in a saucepan or in a microwave oven on high power (100 percent) for 1 minute.

Lazy Man's Beef Stew

Usually stews are prepared in a specific sequence—the meat is browned, set aside in the casserole; the vegetables are sautéed in the same pan, then set aside with the meat. The pan is deglazed with the liquids used in the stew so that all the flavorful bits adhering to the pan are incorporated. Here, all the ingredients cook together in the casserole from beginning to end (save for the potatoes, which are added during the last hour or so of cooking so they don't fall apart). The result? Flavorful and easy! Serve with Curried Celery Root and Apple Salad (page 103) or Farmhouse Coleslaw with Buttermilk-Dill Dressing (page 105).

YIELD: 6 TO 7 SERVINGS

2 pounds stewing beef, cut into 1¼-inch cubes,
    trimmed of visible fat
3 tablespoons flour
¾ teaspoon salt
¼ teaspoon freshly ground pepper
3 medium onions, diced, about 4½ cups
3 large carrots, peeled, cut into 1¼-inch chunks,
    about 3 cups
2 large parsnips, peeled, cut into 1¼-inch chunks,
    about 2 cups
2 medium turnips, peeled, cut into 1¼-inch chunks,
    about 2 cups
¾ cup tomato sauce
¾ cup spicy barbecue sauce
⅔ to 1 cup Beef Stock (page 366) or broth
¼ cup dry red wine
6 small red potatoes, scrubbed, halved

1. Put a rack in the center of the oven; preheat the oven to 350 degrees. Set aside a 4-quart casserole with a lid.

2. Put the beef, flour, salt, and pepper in a plastic food bag. Shake to mix the ingredients and coat the meat. Empty the contents of the bag into the casserole.

3. Add the onions, carrots, parsnips, and turnips to the casserole. Toss together until mixed. Combine the tomato sauce, barbecue sauce, ⅔ cup of the beef broth, and the red wine in a bowl. Add to the casserole. Mix well.

4. Bake, covered, for 1½ hours. Add the potatoes. Use 2 large spoons to mix the stew. Bake, covered, until the meat is tender, about 1 hour longer. Gently mix the stew. Adjust the beef broth and seasoning as needed. Serve hot.

5. The stew can be made 2 days ahead and refrigerated, or it can be frozen, covered airtight, for as long as 2 months. Let it come to room temperature before reheating, covered, in a preheated 350-degree oven, until bubbling, about 45 minutes. Adjust the seasoning.

Lee's Lamburgers

Some great recipes come from friends' spur-of-the-moment improvisations. One summer night, a friend grabbed a large handful of mint leaves and chopped them into ground lean lamb with sweet onion and seasonings. It's a great burger. If you're using a food processor to mix the ingredients, the mint and onion will be chopped to the right consistency along with the meat. Be sure to use the pulse on/off motion to control the texture. Serve these burgers with sautéed (or grilled) new potatoes sprinkled with fresh dill, warm pita bread, and a Herb Garden Salad with Tomato and Olive Vinaigrette (page 85) garnished with diced feta cheese.

YIELD: 4 BURGERS

1 pound ground lean lamb
¹/₂ medium sweet onion, coarsely minced, about 1 cup
¹/₃ cup minced fresh mint leaves
Generous ¹/₄ teaspoon salt
Freshly ground pepper to taste

1. Use a fork to combine all the ingredients in a mixing bowl. Alternately, use a food processor fitted with the metal blade and pulse on and off just a few times until mixed together. Gently shape the mixture into 4 equal burgers. They can be made several hours ahead and refrigerated, covered with plastic wrap.

2. Prepare a medium-hot barbecue fire with a few chunks of water-soaked mesquite wood. Or, alternatively, put the broiler rack 7 inches from the heat source and preheat the broiler. Grill or broil the burgers until cooked on one side. Use a spatula to turn them and cook to the desired doneness, about 6 to 8 minutes altogether for medium rare. Insert a sharp paring knife into the center to check for doneness. Serve hot.

Barbecued Herbed Leg of Lamb

This recipe takes some thinking ahead so the meat can marinate long enough to absorb the flavors of the marinade. Otherwise, it's a quick preparation. Because the lamb is butterflied, it grills easily and slices attractively. Any leftovers are great in a salad or sandwich.

YIELD: 4 TO 6 SERVINGS

1 large clove garlic, minced, about ¹/₂ tablespoon
Zest (colored rind) of 1 large lemon, removed with a
    zester or fine grater (see page 14),
    about 1 tablespoon
¹/₃ cup each: fresh lemon juice, olive oil
2 teaspoons each: Dijon mustard, dried rosemary
³/₄ teaspoon salt
Freshly ground pepper to taste
Butterflied half leg of lamb, boned, about 4 pounds,
    trimmed of fat
Lemon slices, for garnish

1. Combine the garlic, lemon zest, lemon juice, oil, mustard, rosemary, ³/₄ teaspoon salt, and pepper in a large plastic food bag. Add the lamb and seal the bag tightly against the meat. Refrigerate for at least 12 hours or up to 2 days, turning the bag occasionally to make sure the marinade seeps into the folds of the meat.

2. Prepare a medium-hot barbecue fire with a few chunks of water-soaked mesquite wood. Or, alternately, put the broiler rack 7 inches from the heat source and preheat the broiler.

3. Remove the lamb from the marinade. Let the excess drip off. Discard the marinade. Lightly season the lamb with additional salt and pepper.

4. Grill or broil the meat until it is cooked as desired, turning at least once. To test it, insert an instant-reading thermometer halfway through the thickest part of the meat. The reading for medium rare is 125 degrees (the temperature will increase at least 10 degrees while the meat is resting). Do not overcook. Let the meat rest on a warm platter, covered with foil, for 20 minutes before slicing it.

5. To serve, use a sharp carving knife or an electric knife to cut the lamb across the grain on the diagonal into thin slices. Arrange the slices on a warm platter, spoon on the juices, and garnish with lemon slices.

Grilled Herb-Rubbed Lamb Chops on Greens

Hot herbed lamb chops served on a chilled salad of mixed arugula, Bibb lettuce, and fresh basil leaves make an elegant presentation that is full of flavor and interesting contrasts. Pair it with White Beans with Two Tomatoes (page 236) for a great meal. This recipe is easily doubled or tripled.

YIELD: 4 SERVINGS

SALAD:

6 cups loosely packed greens, a mix of trimmed arugula
   leaves, Bibb lettuce, and fresh basil, washed,
   gently spun dry
12 Calamata olives, pitted, flesh cut in fine julienne
1/4 cup light-tasting olive oil
2 tablespoons each: balsamic vinegar, water
1 1/2 teaspoons each: Dijon mustard, honey
1/8 teaspoon salt
Freshly ground pepper to taste

LAMB CHOPS:

2 large cloves garlic, minced, about 1 tablespoon
2 teaspoons each: crushed dried rosemary, ground
   thyme, sugar
Scant 1 teaspoon salt
Freshly ground pepper to taste
1 1/2 tablespoons olive oil
Eight 1 1/2-inch-thick loin lamb chops, about 6 to 8
   ounces each, well trimmed
White Beans with Two Tomatoes (page 236)

1. For the salad, put the greens and olives in a mixing bowl and refrigerate. Keep chilled until ready to use. Mix the remaining salad ingredients in a small dish and set aside. The dressing can be made a day ahead and refrigerated; bring it to room temperature before using.

2. For the lamb chops, put the garlic, rosemary, thyme, sugar, salt, pepper, and oil into a small dish. Mix into a paste. Rub the paste over both sides of the chops. Set them aside at room temperature for 30 minutes.

3. To serve, prepare a hot barbecue fire with a few chunks of water-soaked mesquite wood. Or, alternately, put the broiler rack 6 inches from the heat source and preheat the broiler. Grill or broil the chops to the desired doneness. Toss the greens and olives with the dressing. Adjust the seasoning. Divide the salad between 4 dinner plates, arranging it attractively on one side. Arrange 2 lamb chops on each salad. Spoon the simmered White Beans with Two Tomatoes on the other side of the plate. Serve hot.

Spring Lamb Stew with Leeks and Root Vegetables

*Don't be put off by the long ingredient list; this is a one-pot meal with great flavors.
It's a lamb stew with a light flavor that results from the port wine, carrots, and parsnips,
all sweet and mild ingredients. The cumin adds an interesting tang and the cilantro
a fresh finish. Serve a mixed green salad with a Cracked Pepper Vinaigrette (page 109)
and a warm crusty loaf of French or Italian bread. Lemon Angel Cake with Lemon Yogurt
Glaze (page 282) is the perfect finish.*

YIELD: 6 SERVINGS

LAMB:

2 tablespoons olive oil

2 pounds lamb from the leg, cut into 1-inch cubes,
    trimmed of all visible fat

1 teaspoon salt

Freshly ground pepper to taste

VEGETABLES:

1 tablespoon olive oil

3 large cloves garlic, minced, about 1 1/2 tablespoons

2 medium leeks, trimmed of tough green parts, split,
    washed, thinly sliced, about 4 cups

8 ounces mushrooms, trimmed, cut into 1/2-inch-thick
    slices, about 3 cups

7 slender carrots, peeled, cut into 1/2-inch-thick diagonal
    slices, about 3 cups

6 medium parsnips, peeled, cut into 1/2-inch-thick
    diagonal slices, about 2 1/4 cups

3 large russet potatoes, scrubbed, split lengthwise,
    cut into 3/4-inch-thick slices, about 6 cups

1 1/3 cups Beef Stock (page 366) or broth

1 cup ruby red port wine

1/4 cup water

1 teaspoon ground cumin

1/8 to 1/4 teaspoon cayenne pepper

Salt to taste

1/3 cup minced fresh cilantro, for garnish

1. Put a rack in the center of the oven and preheat
the oven to 350 degrees. Set aside a heavy 5-quart
casserole with a lid.

2. For the lamb, heat 1 tablespoon of the oil in the
casserole over a medium-high heat until it is hot.
Pat the meat dry with paper towels; season the
meat with the salt and pepper. In 2 batches, brown
the meat in a single layer without crowding the
pan, about 3 minutes per batch, stirring often. Heat
the remaining oil before browning the second
batch. Set both batches aside.

3. For the vegetables, heat the oil in the same
casserole. Add the garlic, leeks, and mushrooms.
Cook until they are softened, about 5 minutes,
stirring often. Add the reserved lamb with its
juices, along with the carrots, parsnips, potatoes,
beef stock, port wine, water, cumin, and cayenne
pepper. Mix well until combined; bring to a boil.

4. Once the stew is boiling, use the back of a wooden spoon to push the vegetables and the meat into the liquid (it's okay if the liquid does not completely cover the ingredients).

5. Bake, covered, for 30 minutes. Uncover, gently stir, and press the vegetables and meat back into the liquid. Bake the stew, uncovered, until the meat is tender, about 45 minutes more. Salt to taste. Garnish with cilantro. Serve hot.

6. This stew can be made ahead and refrigerated for up to 3 days, or frozen for up to 3 months, covered airtight. Thaw before cooking. To serve, gently reheat the stew, covered, in a preheated 350-degree oven, until hot, about 40 minutes, adding water as needed for desired consistency of sauce. Adjust the seasoning.

Braised Veal Shanks with Vegetables

This makes a most satisfying meal, full-flavored and soothing at the same time. Try to make this recipe at least a day ahead so the flavors have a chance to develop. This dish makes a great homespun presentation; the shanks are served on a big platter with Gremolata Fettuccine nestled underneath with the vegetables and braising juices spooned over the top.

YIELD: 6 SERVINGS

VEAL SHANKS:

3 tablespoons flour

3/4 teaspoon each: dried thyme, dried marjoram, salt

Freshly ground pepper to taste

6 veal shanks with bone-in, about 9 ounces each, about 1 1/2-inches thick and 3 inches across, rinsed, patted dry

1 1/2 tablespoons olive oil

VEGETABLES:

1 1/2 tablespoons olive oil

3 large cloves garlic, minced, about 1 1/2 tablespoons

1 medium leek, trimmed of dark green leaves (save for making a soup), split lengthwise, washed, cut into thin slices, about 2 cups

6 small carrots, peeled, cut into 1-inch-thick diagonal slices, about 2 1/3 cups

1 large fennel bulb, cut into 1/3-inch dice, about 4 cups

8 medium mushrooms, trimmed, quartered, about 2 cups

1 to 1 3/4 cups Chicken Stock (page 364) or lower-salt broth

3/4 cup dry white wine

2 1/2 tablespoons tomato paste

Gremolata Fettuccine (page 247), for serving

1 tablespoon minced parsley, for garnish

1. Put a rack in the center of the oven; preheat the oven to 375 degrees. Set aside a shallow baking dish or pan just large enough to hold the veal shanks in a single layer.

2. For the veal shanks, combine the flour, herbs, salt, and pepper in a large plastic food bag. Shake to combine. Add the shanks in batches; shake to coat the shanks lightly but evenly, then set aside. Add the leftover seasoned flour in the plastic bag to the baking dish.

3. Heat the oil in a 12-inch nonstick skillet over medium-high heat. When hot, swirl the oil over the bottom of the pan. Add the veal shanks; brown them on both sides, about 6 minutes total. Transfer the shanks to the reserved baking dish, arranging them in a single layer.

4. For the vegetables, add the oil to the same skillet. When hot, add the garlic, leek, carrots, fennel, and mushrooms. Cook, uncovered, until the leek is limp, about 4 minutes, stirring often. Transfer the vegetables to the baking dish, arranging them over and around the shanks.

5. Add 1 cup of the chicken stock or broth, the dry white wine, and the tomato paste to the skillet. Bring the liquid to a boil. Stir until combined. Pour the liquid over the vegetables and meat. Cover the baking dish with foil.

6. Bake until the meat is fork tender, almost falling off the bones, about 1½ to 2 hours, turning the meat midway during cooking. If the pan becomes too dry, add the remaining broth as needed.

7. The recipe can be made 2 days ahead to this point and refrigerated, or frozen for as long as 3 months, covered airtight. Bring to room temperature before reheating. Bake, covered, in a preheated 300-degree oven until hot, about 40 minutes, adding the remaining stock or broth as needed. Adjust the seasoning.

8. Mound the Gremolata Fettuccine on a large warm platter, top with the shanks, arranging the vegetables attractively over the meat. Sprinkle with parsley. Serve hot.

Grilled Veal Chops
with Lemon, Capers,
and Sage Onions

Here, veal chops are grilled and topped with a marmaladelike onion mixture, flavored to complement the veal. The topping would also work on chicken breasts or fish fillets. Serve the veal chops with Green Beans and Shallots (page 191) and Mashed Potatoes with Celery Root and Parsnip (page 210). A salad of Mixed Greens with Pears, Crumbled Tolibia Blue Cheese, and Pine Nuts (page 90) would be perfect served following this main course.

YIELD: 4 SERVINGS

ONIONS:
2 teaspoons olive oil
2 large onions, julienned, about 4 cups
1 1/2 teaspoons sugar
1/2 teaspoon salt
Freshly ground pepper to taste
1 cup Chicken Stock (page 364)
  or lower-salt broth
Grated zest (colored rind) of 1 large lemon, removed
  with a zester or fine grater (see page 14),
  about 1 tablespoon
2 teaspoons snipped fresh sage
2 tablespoons fresh lemon juice
1 1/2 teaspoons capers
2 teaspoons butter

VEAL CHOPS:
Four 1-inch-thick veal chops, trimmed
2 teaspoons olive oil
Salt and freshly ground pepper to taste

Sage sprigs, for garnish

1. For the onions, heat the oil in a 12-inch nonstick skillet over medium-high heat. When hot, add the onions, sugar, salt, and pepper. Cook, uncovered, until the edges are seared, about 8 minutes, stirring occasionally to prevent burning.

2. Add the stock or broth, zest, and snipped sage. Simmer, uncovered, until the onions are softened and the liquid is almost evaporated, about 12 minutes. Add the lemon juice and capers. Stir in the butter until melted. Adjust the seasoning. The onions can be used immediately or refrigerated overnight. Gently reheat and adjust the seasoning before using.

3. For the veal chops, prepare a hot barbecue fire with a few chunks of presoaked mesquite wood. Or, alternatively, put the broiler rack 6 inches from the heat source and preheat the broiler.

4. Rub the veal chops with the oil; season both sides with salt and pepper. Grill over the hot barbecue or broil, turning once, to the desired doneness (about 4 to 6 minutes on each side for medium rare).

5. To serve, place the veal chops on a warm platter; top with the warm onions, divided evenly. Garnish the platter with sage sprigs. Serve hot.

Swedish Roast Pork Stuffed with Prunes, Apples, and Lingonberries, with Lingonberry Fruit Sauce

Once trimmed of most of its surface fat, the center-cut pork roast is lean and luscious, especially when it's stuffed with this medley of fruit. It's a festive (and practical) cut of meat that's easy to set up ahead of time and pop into the oven just before your guests arrive. The sauce itself can be prepared in advance; before serving, just reheat it and add the skimmed pan juices and the final swirl of butter. The pork roast is easier to handle in 2 pieces rather than 1 long roast. Serve with Wild Rice (page 360) and Green Beans and Shallots with Dill (see variation, page 191).

YIELD: 8 SERVINGS

PORK ROAST:
1 large Granny Smith apple, peeled, cored, thinly sliced, about 1$\frac{1}{2}$ cups
16 pitted large prunes
2 tablespoons lingonberry preserves
1 cup plus 2 tablespoons dry sherry
Two 2-pound center-cut pork roasts with pockets, trimmed of all but a very thin layer of surface fat
$\frac{3}{4}$ teaspoon salt
Freshly ground pepper to taste

LINGONBERRY FRUIT SAUCE:
3 large Granny Smith apples, peeled, thinly sliced, about 4$\frac{1}{2}$ cups
1 cup each: beef broth, lingonberry preserves
2 tablespoons dry sherry
Skimmed pan drippings from the pork
2 tablespoons unsalted butter

1. For the pork roast, put a rack in the lower third of the oven; preheat the oven to 375 degrees. Line a shallow roasting pan with foil. Set aside.

2. Put the apple, prunes, lingonberry preserves, and 2 tablespoons of the sherry in a bowl; mix until combined. Divide the fruit among the pockets in the pork roasts, placing 8 prunes in a line down the center of each. Close the pockets and secure roasts with string. Season the roasts with salt and pepper and place them in the prepared pan. The recipe can be prepared a day ahead to this point and refrigerated, covered airtight. Let the roast come to room temperature before cooking.

3. Roast, uncovered, for 30 minutes. Baste the meat as it cooks with the dry sherry. Roast until an instant-reading thermometer registers 170 degrees, about 45 minutes more. Pour off the drippings and skim the fat from the pan juices. Tent the meat with foil until the sauce is finished.

4. Meanwhile, for the lingonberry fruit sauce, put the apple slices in a large skillet along with the beef broth, lingonberry preserves, and 2 tablespoons dry sherry. Simmer, uncovered, until the apples are just tender, about 10 minutes. This can be made several hours ahead and the apples kept at room temperature.

5. To finish the sauce, add the skimmed pan drippings and heat well. Stir in the butter until it is melted. Adjust the seasoning.

6. To serve, use a sharp carving knife or an electric knife to cut the meat into $1/3$-inch-thick slices. Arrange the slices, overlapping, on a warm serving platter. Spoon the hot fruit sauce over the meat. Serve hot.

Carolyn's Sweet and Spicy Ribs

Carolyn Buster, a great Midwest chef, fine-tunes every recipe she turns out; this one is no exception. These ribs are simmered in an herbed beer mixture, which flavors them and removes most of their fat. Luckily, this step can be done a day ahead so the final grilling is a quick 10-minute procedure. Serve with Oven Country "Fries" (page 213) or baked potatoes with Chive Cream (page 215).

YIELD: 6 SERVINGS

BARBECUE SAUCE:

1 cup store-bought barbecue sauce
¹/₃ cup Dijon mustard
¹/₄ cup packed dark brown sugar
2 teaspoons each: soy sauce, Thai fish sauce
    (nuoc nam)
1 teaspoon chili paste
    (or hot sauce according to taste)

RIBS:

6 racks baby back ribs, well trimmed,
    about 1¹/₄ pounds each
Four 12-ounce cans light beer
2 large onions, sliced, about 5 cups
8 large cloves garlic, peeled and split
1 teaspoon each: dried thyme, rosemary, basil, salt,
    freshly ground pepper
2 bay leaves
3 whole cloves
1 cup honey, for brushing

1. For the barbecue sauce, combine all the ingredients in a 1-quart bowl. Refrigerate at least overnight or for up to 3 days. Before using, stir well. Adjust the seasoning; the sauce should be spicy.

2. Place the ribs, meaty side down, in a roasting pan (cut them in half as necessary to fit them in).

Add the beer and enough water to just cover the ribs. Add the onions, garlic cloves, herbs, salt, pepper, bay leaves, and cloves, and distributing them evenly. Shake the pan to combine. Bring the liquid to a boil on top of the stove, cover with foil, and simmer gently until the ribs are very tender, about 1 hour.

3. Use tongs to transfer the hot ribs to heavy-duty foil. Blot them with paper towels. Immediately brush both sides with honey. Reapply any honey that drips onto the foil. The ribs can be prepared a day ahead to this point and refrigerated, covered.

4. To finish, let the ribs and barbecue sauce come to room temperature. Prepare a medium-hot barbecue fire with a few chunks of water-soaked mesquite wood, or alternately, put the broiler rack 8 inches from the heat source and preheat the broiler. Brush both sides of the ribs generously with the barbecue sauce.

5. Place the ribs meaty side down on the hot grill or meaty side up in the broiler. Grill or broil until they are heated through and bronzed (not burned), about 5 to 10 minutes, depending on the heat. Use tongs to turn them. Brush sauce on the browned side and grill or broil until the underside is

browned, about 5 minutes more. Brush more sauce on both sides.

6. To serve, transfer the ribs to a warm serving platter. Serve hot. Pass the remaining barbecue sauce separately.

Basic Barbecue . . .

❖ Grill on a clean, oiled rack.

❖ It's best to clean the rack right after grilling when the rack is still hot. Wear long oven mitts and use a wire bristle brush to scrape the rack clean, dipping the brush in water if the food persists in sticking to the rack (be careful of the steam).

❖ Oil the rack before heating the barbecue. Be sure that the rack is well cleaned. The easiest way to oil a rack is to use vegetable cooking oil spray; alternately, dip an old towel in vegetable oil and grease the rack.

❖ Always place food to be grilled on a hot rack.

❖ Prior to grilling, drain marinated foods to avoid excessive flare-ups.

❖ Score thick center portions of fish fillets so they cook uniformly; this also decreases cooking time.

❖ Various hardwoods enhance the flavor of barbecued foods. Hickory, oak, and mesquite woods are especially good with beef, lamb, and pork. For chicken and seafood, choose apple, maple, cherry, and alder.

Venison Stew with Red Onions, Dried Cranberries, and Wild Mushrooms

This venison stew is a richly seasoned tart-sweet mix of dried cranberries, wild mushrooms, and ruby red port wine. Served over Mashed Potatoes with Celery Root and Parsnip (page 210) or buttered Wild Rice (page 360), it's a great main course for a winter dinner party. Stewing beef can be substituted for the venison, if you prefer. Whichever your choice, be sure to make the stew at least a day ahead so the flavors have a chance to develop.

YIELD: 6 SERVINGS

VENISON:
1/4 cup flour
1 1/4 teaspoons salt
Freshly ground pepper to taste
2 pounds venison stew meat, trimmed,
    cut into 3/4-inch cubes
1 1/2 tablespoons each: unsalted butter,
    vegetable oil

VEGETABLES:
1 teaspoon each: unsalted butter, vegetable oil
1 large red onion, thinly sliced, about 2 1/2 cups
2 large cloves garlic, minced,
    about 1 tablespoon
1 1/4 cups each: ruby red port wine, Beef Stock
    (page 366) or broth
1 cup dried cranberries
1 1/2 teaspoons sugar
Pinch of allspice
8 ounces shiitake mushrooms, stems trimmed,
    caps quartered (white cultivated mushrooms
    can be substituted for the wild mushrooms),
    about 3 cups

1. Put a rack in the center of the oven; preheat the oven to 350 degrees. Set aside a 1 1/2-quart-capacity casserole with a lid.

2. For the venison, combine the flour, salt, and pepper in a plastic food bag. Pat the meat dry with paper towels. Toss the meat with the seasoned flour until it is evenly coated, shaking off any excess flour. Set the meat on a work surface. Put any remaining seasoned flour into the casserole.

3. Heat 3/4 tablespoon each of the butter and oil in a 12-inch nonstick skillet. When it is very hot, sear half the meat on all sides, about 1 1/2 minutes total. Transfer the meat to the casserole. Add the remaining butter and oil and brown the remaining meat. Toss the browned meat with any flour in the casserole.

4. For the vegetables, heat the butter and oil in the same skillet over medium-high heat. When it is hot, add the onion and garlic. Cook until the onion is softened, about 4 minutes. Add the port, beef stock or broth, dried cranberries, sugar, and allspice. Bring the liquid to a boil. Pour the mixture over the venison. Toss until mixed well.

5. Bake, covered, for 1¹/₂ hours. Add the mushrooms, mix well, and continue to bake, covered, until the meat is tender, about 30 to 60 minutes longer. Adjust the seasoning. Serve hot.

6. The stew can be made a day ahead and refrigerated, or frozen for up to 3 months, covered airtight. Thaw if frozen. Gently reheat, covered, in a preheated 350-degree oven until hot, about 30 minutes, adding a little water as needed. Adjust the seasoning.

Myrna's Scandinavian Venison Meatballs

Wild venison gives these meatballs a deep, rich flavor. You can substitute 1 pound each of ground beef and veal for the venison (and omit the sugar) for a milder flavor that is also delicious. These are most quickly prepared in the food processor; the recipe must be divided into 2 batches for a standard-size processor.

YIELD: 6 TO 8 SERVINGS

MEATBALLS:

1 1/2 cups fresh bread crumbs

3/4 cup milk

1/2 medium Spanish onion, minced, about 1 cup

2 large eggs, frothed with a fork

1 3/4 teaspoons salt

1/4 teaspoon each: sugar, ground allspice, freshly grated
    nutmeg (see page 289)

1/2 teaspoon freshly ground pepper

2 pounds ground venison

1/2 pound ground lean pork

4 tablespoons unsalted butter

GRAVY:

Unsalted butter, if needed

1 medium Spanish onion, chopped, about 1 3/4 cups

2 1/2 tablespoons flour

2 cups Beef Stock (page 366) or broth

1/2 cup heavy cream

Salt and freshly ground pepper to taste

1. For the meatballs, put the bread crumbs in a 2-quart bowl. Add the milk. Soak the bread crumbs 10 minutes. Add the onion, eggs, seasonings, venison, and pork. Use a large fork to combine the ingredients. The consistency should be light and fluffy.

2. Moisten your hands with water and gently shape the mixture into 2-inch-diameter meatballs, then smooth them out by lightly rolling them between your moistened palms. Place them in a single layer on a cookie sheet; refrigerate until firm, at least 3 hours.

3. Heat 2 tablespoons of the butter in a 12-inch nonstick skillet over medium-high heat. When very hot, add the meatballs, in batches, without crowding them. Brown them on all sides, about 5 minutes, shaking the pan to avoid sticking. Use a slotted spoon to transfer them to paper towels. Repeat with the remaining meatballs, adding more butter as needed. Reserve the drippings in the skillet. Transfer the meatballs to a 4-quart ovenproof dish.

4. For the gravy, you will need 3 tablespoons drippings (spill off any excess or add butter to make 3 tablespoons). Heat the drippings and, when hot, add the onion. Cook over medium heat until soft, about 6 minutes, stirring often. Add the flour and cook 2 minutes, stirring constantly. Gradually mix in the stock or broth and the cream. Simmer, uncovered, until thickened, about 10 minutes, stirring often. Adjust the seasoning.

5. To assemble, pour the gravy through a strainer onto the meatballs, pressing firmly on the onions to release all the flavor. Serve hot.

6. The meatballs can be prepared up to 2 days ahead and refrigerated, or frozen for as long as 3 months, covered airtight. Let them come to room temperature before reheating. Bake, covered, in a preheated 275-degree oven until hot, about 45 minutes. Adjust the seasoning.

Woodland Port Wine Sauce

This sauce adds flavor and a festive touch to simply-roasted or grilled meats—
beef, pork, lamb, or veal.

YIELD: 1 1/2 CUPS, ABOUT 6 SERVINGS

1 tablespoon olive oil
3 tablespoons unsalted butter
1 large clove garlic, thinly sliced, about 1/2 tablespoon
3 large shallots, thinly sliced, about 1/2 cup
8 ounces thinly sliced trimmed wild mushrooms (I used
*   mixed cremini and shiitake), about 3 cups*
3/4 cup Beef Stock (page 366) or broth
1 1/4 cups ruby red port wine
1 teaspoon cornstarch mixed with 1 tablespoon water
Salt and freshly ground pepper to taste

1. Heat the oil and 1 tablespoon of the butter in a 10-inch nonstick skillet over medium-high heat. When hot, add the garlic and shallots. Cook until the shallots are softened, about 2 minutes, stirring often. Add the mushrooms. Cook until they are limp, about 2 minutes, continuing to stir often.

2. Add the beef stock or broth and the port wine. Bring to a boil. Simmer, uncovered, until the mixture is reduced to 1 3/4 cups, about 5 minutes.

3. Stir in the cornstarch mixture. Cook until the sauce thickens slightly, about 3 minutes. Stir in 1/2 tablespoon of the remaining butter until it is melted, repeating this by the 1/2-tablespoon until all of the remaining butter has been stirred and melted into the sauce. Season with salt and pepper to taste. The sauce can be made several hours ahead and kept at room temperature.

4. To serve, gently reheat until hot. Adjust the seasoning. Serve hot, spooned over sliced meat or passed in a gravy boat.

Horseradish Sauce

*Sharp and bright-tasting, this sauce is the perfect complement for roast beef as well as
Boiled Chicken and Sausage in the Pot (page 157).*

YIELD: 1 CUP

³/₄ *cup heavy cream, chilled*
3 to 4 tablespoons each: Dijon mustard,
  white horseradish
2 teaspoons minced parsley, for garnish

Use a mixer to whip the cream until it is thick.
Add 3 tablespoons each of the mustard and
horseradish. Mix well. Add the remaining mustard
and horseradish as needed to your taste. Chill well.
Serve chilled, garnished with minced parsley.

Roast Capon with Garlic and Tarragon

Flattened Chicken Breasts with Piquant Basil Sauce

Orange-Roasted Chicken on Tossed Greens

Oven "Fried" Chicken

Sherry Chicken Casserole

Chicken Vesuvio

Boiled Chicken and Sausage in the Pot

Glazed Cornish Hens with Wild Rice, Pecan,
  and Dried Cranberry Stuffing

Terri's Thanksgiving Turkey with Giblet Gravy

Poached Turkey Breast

Sweet-Spiced Turkey Breast, Roasted on Onions and Raisins

Skewered Turkey, Red Peppers, and Onions

Duck Breasts with Red Onion Cranberry Relish

Chapter 6
Poultry

❖

Good chicken today is so plentiful and readily available at reasonable cost that it is hard to imagine it as ever being special. And yet, in the 1928 national election the pledge of the Republican party was "once in every week, a chicken in every pot." Those days may be behind us, but the days of homespun, full-flavored, hearty ways of cooking chicken are not. They are as relevant now as ever before. The Midwest has always had a tasty way with poultry, and I have let my inspiration be my guide.

Consider a sumptuous update such as Orange-Roasted Chicken on Tossed Greens, or Chicago's own Chicken Vesuvio. Here you have chicken and potatoes roasting together until both become crisp, then the addition of a last-minute garnish of garlic, oregano, parsley, and dry white wine. When you sit down at the table you can't help wondering how so few ingredients could deliver so much flavor. But that's what is so wonderful about looking back at our homespun hearty past. Those simple pleasures are there to be rejuvenated.

With Oven "Fried" Chicken you capture the unique pleasure of fried chicken, but you lose the fat. Glazed Cornish Hens with Wild Rice, Pecan, and Dried Cranberry Stuffing all but define those bold flavors I think of as Midwestern. Terri's Thanksgiving Turkey with Giblet Gravy addresses the issue of modern tastes and time constraints while still lingering over a Thanksgiving of a hundred years back.

Roast Capon with Garlic and Tarragon

Robust seasoning brings out the best in this capon; set it up the night before if you can. Compared to a fryer, a capon boasts much richer flavor, provides 6 generous portions, and roasts only a little longer in the oven. Roast 2 capons simultaneously if you like to have great leftover chicken on hand. Serve the capon with Goose Island Honey-Roasted Root Vegetables (page 198), Roasted Acorn Squash with Garlic, Honey, and Thyme (page 194), or Maple Carrots and Leeks (page 195).

YIELD: 6 SERVINGS

GARLIC MIXTURE:

3 large cloves garlic, minced, about 1¹/₂ tablespoons

3 tablespoons chopped fresh tarragon leaves

1 tablespoon salt

¹/₂ teaspoon each: paprika, ground thyme, freshly ground pepper

CAPON:

1 large capon, about 6¹/₂ pounds, washed, blotted dry

1 tablespoon olive oil

3 large cloves garlic, peeled, split lengthwise

1 medium onion, peeled, quartered

2 fresh tarragon sprigs

Snipped fresh tarragon and tarragon sprigs, for garnish

1. Line a shallow roasting pan with foil. Set it aside.

2. For the garlic mixture, mix all the ingredients in a small dish. Set aside.

3. For the capon, rub the surface with the oil. Place the capon on its back. With your fingers, separate the skin from the flesh around the breast area, starting at the cavity. Be careful not to tear the skin. Push 3 split garlic cloves under the skin, cut side down, over each breast. Spread the garlic mixture on the surface and in the cavity. Place the onion and 2 tarragon sprigs in the cavity. Place the capon in the prepared pan, tent it with foil, and refrigerate overnight.

4. Put a rack in the lower third of the oven; preheat the oven to 450 degrees.

5. Remove the foil from the capon and roast for 30 minutes. Reduce the oven temperature to 400 degrees. Roast the capon until the juices run clear rather than pink when the meat between the thigh and breast is pierced with a knife, about 30 to 40 minutes longer. Let the capon rest 10 minutes before serving. Remove any seared garlic particles with a paper towel. Garnish the top of the capon with snipped fresh tarragon and tarragon sprigs.

Serving Whole Chicken . . .

Carving a whole chicken is as straightforward a task as roasting it. I highly recommend cutting a chicken into parts with poultry or kitchen shears (the latter are more practical since they can be used for many other preparations).

To carve a whole chicken:

❖ Let the chicken rest breast side up, tented with foil, on a warm platter for 10 minutes before carving.

❖ Use poultry or kitchen shears to cut through the ball joints of the thighs. Remove the leg and thigh in 1 piece. Then cut through the joint to separate the leg from the thigh.

❖ Use a sharp knife to remove the wings along with the lower third of the breast. This makes the wing portion a useful serving.

❖ For ease in slicing the breast meat, remove the wishbone from inside the neck cavity. Thinly slice the meat, starting at an angle.

❖ Arrange the chicken pieces and slices attractively on a warm serving platter. Serve immediately.

❖ When the chicken is a small fryer, cut it into serving halves or quarters: use shears to remove the strip of backbone; then cut up the chicken as desired.

How to Get More From Less . . .

Pounding half a skinned and boned chicken breast into a uniformly thin, flat portion—technically called a *paillard*—makes this small quantity of chicken seem like it's much more than it is. And it's easy to do:

❖ Before pounding, chill the chicken breast (it's easier to handle), trim all visible fat, and remove any gristle or tendons. Place the chilled chicken breast between 2 sheets of plastic wrap (waxed paper is not practical because there is less control and the paper tears easily). Flatten gently with a meat pounder, a heavy pot, or any other heavy object with a smooth 4-inch-diameter base, until breast is a uniform 1/8 inch thick. Start in the center and work outward, pounding the meat firmly but gently without tearing it. These *paillards* can be refrigerated up to 2 days, or frozen for up to 2 months, separated by plastic wrap and wrapped airtight. Because they are so thin, they thaw quickly.

Flattened Chicken Breasts with Piquant Basil Sauce

Flattened (skinned and boned) chicken breasts—paillards—make a great quick meal. In the interest of using very little oil, the breasts themselves are oiled instead of the skillet, assuring that they will not stick. The key to their success is seasoning them well before sautéing them, then saucing them with an intensely flavored mixture, such as this piquant basil sauce, to perk up the bland white meat. Once the breasts are pounded, they can be kept frozen for about a month, ready for a spur-of-the-moment meal.

YIELD: 4 SERVINGS

4 large skinned, boned chicken breast halves, about
   4 ounces each, trimmed, chilled
2 teaspoons honey
2 tablespoons Dijon mustard
¹/₄ cup balsamic vinegar
6 tablespoons lower-salt chicken broth
2 teaspoons olive oil
¹/₄ teaspoon salt
Freshly ground pepper to taste
2 tablespoons julienned basil leaves

1. To flatten the chicken breasts, place a breast between 2 pieces of plastic wrap. Use a meat pounder, a heavy pot, or any heavy object with a smooth, 4-inch-diameter base, to flatten it to about ¹/₈-inch uniform thickness. Repeat with the remaining breasts. The breasts can be flattened a day in advance and refrigerated or frozen for up to 1 month; stack one on top of the other, wrapped in plastic, to keep them from sticking together. Enclose the stack in a large plastic bag. If frozen, the breasts do not need to be thawed before cooking; they will just take 30 seconds longer to cook.

2. Combine the honey, mustard, vinegar, and chicken broth in a small dish and set aside.

3. Brush or rub ¹/₄ teaspoon of the oil on the top side of each breast; season with salt and pepper. Heat a 12-inch skillet over medium-high heat. When hot, cook 2 breasts at a time, oiled side down, until lightly browned, for about 2¹/₂ minutes. Then, carefully brush or rub ¹/₄ teaspoon oil on the top (uncooked) side, sprinkle lightly with salt and pepper; turn, and brown the second side for another 2¹/₂ minutes. Cover the skillet for the last 30 seconds to be sure the chicken is cooked through. Do not overcook. (Test for doneness by inserting the point of a sharp paring knife into the center of the meat; it should be moist but not pink.) Transfer the breasts to a warm platter, tent with foil, and repeat with the remaining breasts.

4. To serve, add the honey mixture to the hot skillet. Cook to thicken, about 5 seconds. Add the warm breasts, spooning the sauce over them. As soon as they are warmed through, transfer them to a warm serving platter and garnish with the julienned basil. Serve hot.

Orange-Roasted Chicken on Tossed Greens

Here, broiler halves are glazed with orange juice concentrate sauce and roasted until deeply browned. The garlic becomes mild and sweet in the roasting pan, giving only a subtle flavoring to the final sauce. The pan juices, removed of their fat, are used as a dressing for the greens as well as a sauce for the chicken.

YIELD: 4 SERVINGS

2 broilers, about 2³/4 pounds each, split, backbone
  removed, washed, patted dry
Salt and freshly ground pepper to taste
12 large cloves garlic, split
One 6-ounce can frozen orange juice concentrate,
  thawed
1¹/2 cups Chicken Stock (page 364) or lower-salt broth
2 teaspoons balsamic vinegar
¹/4 teaspoon cayenne pepper
1 small fennel bulb, trimmed, cut into small dice,
  about 1³/4 cups
5 cups torn-up mixed greens, including some bitter
  greens such as arugula, frisée, or watercress,
  washed, blotted dry with paper towels, crisped

1. Put a rack in the center of the oven; preheat the oven to 450 degrees. Line a large shallow roasting pan with heavy-duty foil. Set aside.

2. Sprinkle the entire surface of the chicken with salt and pepper. Place the chicken, skin side up, in a single layer in the prepared pan. Scatter the garlic in the pan.

3. Roast the chicken for 30 minutes. Meanwhile, combine the orange juice concentrate, chicken stock or broth, balsamic vinegar, and cayenne pepper in a small mixing bowl. After 30 minutes, remove the chicken from the oven and pour this mixture into the pan. Continue to roast, basting

the chicken often with these pan juices as they cook and thicken, until the chicken is well browned and cooked through, about 20 to 30 minutes longer.

4. Use a spatula to release the chicken from the pan, transfer it to a heated platter and tent with foil. Put the pan juices and garlic in a fat-skimming cup or in a small dish. Remove all of the fat. Mix the garlic and skimmed juices in a blender or food processor fitted with a metal blade until the garlic is pureed.

5. Transfer the garlic mixture to a small pan, adding a little water as needed to make it the consistency of heavy cream. Add the fennel to the pan and bring to a boil. Remove from the heat and adjust the seasoning.

6. To serve, cut the chicken into serving portions. Place the chilled greens in a large bowl. Toss the greens with the hot sauce and fennel, reserving a few tablespoons of sauce (not fennel) to spoon over the chicken. Arrange the tossed greens on a large serving platter. Season the greens lightly with salt and pepper. Place the chicken over the greens. Spoon the reserved sauce over the chicken. Serve hot.

Fowl Tips

Here are some key tips on the care and cooking of chicken:

- ❖ Keep chicken refrigerated until ready to cook.

- ❖ Wash chicken with cold water, patting it dry with paper towels. Discard the towels.

- ❖ Use hot, soapy water to wash off work surfaces and knives after preparing chicken to prevent any bacteria from the raw chicken from coming in contact with other foods.

- ❖ To remove skin from cut-up chicken, carefully dry each piece so it doesn't slip out of your grasp. It's not necessary to use a knife. Just pull the skin off with your hands (or use paper towels for a firmer grasp), trimming any remaining fat with a knife.

- ❖ To brown chicken, it must be moisture-free so blot it dry. Use a nonstick skillet and heat the oil (or oil and butter) over medium-high heat. When it's very hot, add the chicken pieces, rounded side down, in a single layer, without crowding. When well browned on the underside, turn with a spatula or tongs. Turn only once. To avoid overcrowding, brown chicken in batches.

- ❖ To make sure chicken is fully cooked but still moist, pierce the thigh meat (which takes longer to cook than the white meat) with a knife. The juices should run clear rather than pink.

Oven "Fried" Chicken

This "fried" chicken has everything going for it: great garlic flavor, a lowfat oven-baked crispy crust without skin, and serving ease—it's great hot or cold. Cooking the garlic before adding it to the rest of the coating ingredients makes it less sharp. A food processor or blender makes fast work of this preparation. If you're not a garlic fan, it can be omitted entirely.

YIELD: 4 SERVINGS

BREAD CRUMB COATING:
5 large garlic cloves, minced, about 2$\frac{1}{2}$ tablespoons
1 tablespoon olive oil
1$\frac{1}{3}$ cups fresh fine-textured bread crumbs
2 tablespoons yellow cornmeal
Grated zest of 1 large lemon (colored rind), removed
    with a zester or fine grater (see page 14), about
    1 tablespoon
$\frac{1}{2}$ teaspoon salt
$\frac{1}{4}$ teaspoon freshly ground pepper

CHICKEN:
2 tablespoons Dijon mustard
1 tablespoon water
2 teaspoons honey
4 each: chicken thighs, drumsticks
                or
2 each: chicken thighs, drumsticks, breasts
Salt and freshly ground pepper to taste

1. Put a rack in the center of the oven; preheat the oven to 400 degrees. Lightly grease a jelly roll pan (cookie sheet with sides). Set aside.

2. For the bread crumb coating, combine the minced garlic and oil in a small skillet. Heat the oil until the garlic is fragrant but not browned, watching closely to make sure it doesn't burn.

Combine the garlic and oil with the remaining coating ingredients. The crumb mixture should be a fine and uniform texture. Transfer the crumbs to a pie plate or a shallow soup dish.

3. For the chicken, combine the mustard, water, and honey in a pie plate or a shallow soup dish. Set aside. Remove the skin from the chicken pieces by pulling it off with your hands; use paper towels for a firm grasp on the skin. Trim away any visible fat.

4. Piece by piece, coat the chicken with the mustard mixture. Season it lightly with salt and pepper, then dip the pieces in the crumb mixture to coat them evenly. The coating should not be too thick. If it is, gently brush away the excess. Gently pat the crumbs in place. Arrange the chicken in the prepared pan, meatier side up.

5. Bake until crisp and browned, about 30 minutes for breasts, 45 minutes for thighs and drumsticks.

6. To serve, the chicken can be hot, at room temperature, or chilled.

Sherry Chicken Casserole

This is the ubiquitous chicken casserole from the fifties in lower-calorie form. Light and appealing, it's perfect served with Apple Chutney with Dried Cranberries (page 352) and a refreshing condiment salad such as those on pages 99–108. If you're cooking the chicken specifically for the casserole, a 3½-pound chicken will yield the right amount. Cooked turkey is easily substituted for the chicken.

YIELD: 6 TO 8 SERVINGS

SAUCE:

3 tablespoons unsalted butter
1 large stalk celery, thinly sliced, about ½ cup
1 small onion, chopped, about ¾ cup
8 medium mushrooms, quartered, about 2 cups
3 tablespoons flour
¼ cup dry sherry
3 cups Chicken Stock (page 364) or lower-salt broth
Generous pinch of freshly grated nutmeg (see page 289)
Few drops of hot pepper sauce
Salt and freshly ground pepper to taste

CASSEROLE:

2 cups corn kernels, fresh, frozen (thawed), or canned
   (well drained)
1 cup frozen tiny peas, thawed
3 ounces egg noodles, cooked according to package
   directions, drained
3 cups cubed cooked chicken (cut into 1½-inch cubes)
Salt to taste

TOPPING:

1 cup fresh bread crumbs
½ cup grated imported Parmesan cheese
1 tablespoon butter, melted

1. Put a rack in the center of the oven; preheat the oven to 350 degrees. Grease a 10-quart casserole or soufflé dish. Set aside.

2. For the sauce, heat the butter in a 2-quart saucepan over medium-high heat. When it is hot, add the celery, onion, and mushrooms. Cook until the vegetables are softened, about 5 minutes, stirring often. Sprinkle the flour over the vegetables and stir until combined. Slowly add the sherry and stock or broth to the pan. Use a wooden spoon to stir the mixture constantly until it is thick and smooth, about 3 minutes. Add the nutmeg, hot pepper sauce, and salt and pepper to taste. Transfer the mixture to a large mixing bowl.

3. For the casserole, combine all the ingredients with the sauce in the bowl and mix well. Adjust the seasoning. Transfer the mixture to the prepared casserole; use a spatula to spread it out evenly.

4. For the topping, toss the bread crumbs, cheese, and butter together in a small dish. Sprinkle the topping evenly over the surface of the casserole. The recipe can be made a day ahead to this point, covered airtight, and refrigerated, or frozen up to 3 months, and thawed in the refrigerator.

5. Bake, uncovered, until the casserole is hot and the top is golden brown, about 40 to 50 minutes (slightly longer if chilled). Let it rest 10 minutes before serving. Serve hot.

Chicken Vesuvio

A Chicago invention and a favorite, chicken Vesuvio appears on the menus of most family-style Italian restaurants in Chicago. Always robust and laden with garlic, this version is also crispy (including the potatoes)! It's adapted from the Chicago landmark restaurant Gene & Georgetti's, where chicken Vesuvio has been served for more than 55 years at the same 500 North Franklin Street location.

YIELD: 4 SERVINGS

1 large fryer, 3½ to 4 pounds, cut into 8 pieces, washed, blotted dry with paper towels, trimmed of all visible fat
4 medium Idaho potatoes, peeled, quartered lengthwise
¼ cup olive oil
1 teaspoon salt
Freshly ground pepper to taste
1 large clove garlic, minced, about ½ tablespoon
2 teaspoons dried oregano leaves
3 tablespoons minced fresh parsley
2 tablespoons dry vermouth (or any dry white wine)

1. Put a rack in the center of the oven; preheat the oven to 425 degrees. Grease a large (12 × 18-inch), heavy, shallow roasting or baking pan to hold the chicken and potatoes in a single layer. Set aside.

2. Blot the potatoes dry with paper towels. Transfer them to the prepared roasting pan.

3. Add the chicken to the potatoes. Drizzle the oil over the top and toss the chicken and potatoes until they are well coated with oil. Sprinkle with salt and pepper. Toss again to be sure the seasonings are well distributed. Arrange the chicken, meatier side down, and the potatoes in a single layer.

4. Bake 30 minutes, then use a spatula to gently release the chicken and potatoes from the pan and turn them. Continue baking until both are lightly browned, about 25 minutes more. Increase the oven temperature to 475 degrees. Bake until the chicken and potatoes are well browned and crisp, about 10 minutes longer, watching carefully to prevent burning. Meanwhile, combine the garlic, oregano, and parsley in a small dish. Measure out the dry vermouth.

5. Working quickly, use tongs to transfer the chicken and potatoes to a large heated serving platter. Immediately sprinkle the chicken and potatoes with the garlic, oregano, parsley, and wine; gently toss until well mixed. Lightly sprinkle with salt and freshly ground pepper, and serve hot.

Boiled Chicken and Sausage in the Pot

This is one of my favorite one-pot meals, totally homespun and flavorful. It's actually a soup with chicken, sausage, and a wonderful variety of vegetables, all cooked simultaneously in the same pot. Whether you serve it from the pot it is cooked in (I use a large copper casserole for cooking and serving), an elegant tureen, or a platter with the broth passed separately, you will find this meal warm and welcoming on the table. It is best cooked just before serving; luckily, it requires no attention as it simmers. The vegetables can be prepared in advance, only to be dropped into the pot at cooking time. Be sure to serve it with Horseradish Sauce.

YIELD: 4 SERVINGS

1 tablespoon olive oil
4 chicken legs with thighs, separated at the joint
4 smoked sausages, about 12 ounces total
1 large clove garlic, minced, about 1/2 tablespoon
1 large Spanish onion, minced, about 3 cups
6 cups Chicken Stock (page 364) or lower-salt broth
4 small turnips, peeled, each stuck with a clove
6 small zucchini, cut into 1-inch chunks, about 8 cups
8 small new red potatoes
1/2 small head of cabbage, cored, cut into 4 wedges
4 medium carrots, peeled, cut into thirds
1 bay leaf
Salt and freshly ground pepper to taste
Horseradish Sauce (page 145), for serving

1. Heat the oil in a 6-quart pot over medium-high heat. When hot, add the chicken and brown on all sides. When browned, push it to the edge of the pan. Add the sausage and cook until browned. Remove the sausage and set it aside. Leave the chicken in the pan, pushed to the side.

2. Stir the garlic and onion into the pan. Cook over high heat until they are softened, about 2 minutes. Add the stock or broth, the vegetables and the bay leaf to the pan. Gently stir together all the ingredients in the pan, including the chicken. Bring the liquid to a boil over high heat and simmer, covered, until the vegetables are tender, about 25 minutes. Return the sausage during the last 10 minutes of cooking. Taste the liquid and adjust the seasoning.

3. To serve, use tongs and a slotted spoon to transfer the chicken, sausage, and vegetables to a large tureen or a warm serving platter, grouping each kind of vegetable separately on the platter. Discard the bay leaf. Skim the fat from the broth—a gravy strainer works very well. If serving from a tureen, ladle all the skimmed broth over the mixture; for the platter, moisten the meat and vegetables with some of the broth and pass the remaining broth separately. Serve hot. Pass the horseradish sauce separately.

Glazed Cornish Hens with Wild Rice, Pecan, and Dried Cranberry Stuffing

Cornish hens still deliver great value for the relatively little money and effort spent on them. They're impressive served whole when they're not too large—no more than 22 ounces each. Here, they are stuffed with a nicely balanced wild rice mixture that is both crunchy and flavorful. The glaze burns easily and is best brushed on during the last 10 minutes of roasting. These hens make a great focus for a fall dinner party when served with Roasted Acorn Squash with Garlic, Honey, and Thyme (page 194) and Green Beans and Shallots (page 191).

YIELD: 6 SERVINGS

6 Cornish hens, about 22 ounces each, thawed if frozen
Salt and freshly ground pepper to taste
Wild Rice, Pecan, and Dried Cranberry Stuffing
    (recipe follows)
³/4 cup orange marmalade
¹/4 cup soy sauce
1 tablespoon finely minced fresh ginger
Pinch of cayenne pepper
Clusters of watercress, for garnish

1. Put a rack in the lower third of the oven; preheat the oven to 450 degrees. Line a large shallow roasting pan with foil. Set aside.

2. Wash the hens well and blot them dry with paper towels. Season the cavities lightly with salt and pepper. Stuff the hens, overlapping the skin to close the opening and tying the legs together with a string. Place the hens in the prepared pan, breast side up. Season the skin lightly with additional salt and pepper.

3. Roast the hens until they are lightly browned, about 30 minutes; slightly longer if they were chilled. Don't worry if they appear dry as they roast; the glaze will moisten them.

4. While the hens are roasting, put the marmalade, soy sauce, ginger, and cayenne pepper in a mini food processor fitted with a metal blade or in a blender. Mix until the glaze is as smooth as possible.

5. When the hens are lightly browned, lightly brush the glaze over them, reserving any remaining glaze for a final brushing. Roast until the skin is well browned, about 8 to 10 minutes more, watching closely to avoid burning. Remove the hens from the oven. Generously brush the remaining glaze over the hens. Use a sharp paring knife to neatly slit the skin and meat between the breast and thigh area to let the glaze permeate the meat. Cover the hens loosely with foil and let them rest 10 minutes before serving.

6. To serve, arrange the hens on a heated serving platter, garnish with clumps of watercress leaves, and serve hot.

Wild Rice, Pecan, and Dried Cranberry Stuffing

This stuffing also makes a great rice casserole, baked, covered, in a 350-degree oven for 40 minutes. Serve it with meat, game, and poultry.

YIELD: ENOUGH FOR 6 CORNISH HENS

2 teaspoons vegetable oil

3 small ribs celery, cut into $^1/_4$-inch dice, about 1 cup

2 medium onions, finely minced, about 2$^1/_2$ cups

Grated zest (colored rind) of 2 large oranges, removed with a zester or fine grater (see page 14), about 2 tablespoons

$^3/_4$ cup dried cranberries

$^3/_4$ teaspoon salt

Freshly ground pepper to taste

3 cups cooked Wild Rice (page 360)

Heat the oil in a 12-inch nonstick skillet over medium-high heat. When hot, add the celery, onions, orange zest, cranberries, salt, and pepper. Stir-fry until all the ingredients are heated through and fragrant, about 3 minutes. Add the rice and stir until combined. Adjust the seasoning. The stuffing can be made up to 2 days ahead, covered airtight, and refrigerated.

Terri's Thanksgiving Turkey with Giblet Gravy

This method of roasting a turkey came about by necessity one Thanksgiving Day when a dear friend, Terri D'Ancona, called frantically to say that all was in readiness for her 25 dinner guests save the turkey, which she had forgotten to put in the oven. Knowing that many of the French chefs with whom I had worked used very high oven temperatures for roasting poultry, I devised the following method. Not only did it put a large, stuffed turkey on the table in a grace-saving 3¹/₂ hours but it produced a turkey of amazing moistness . . . without any basting. Since then, I roast turkey only this way! To get set to roast the turkey, make the stock and stuffing and piece together the heavy-duty foil sheets that encase the bird during roasting—and actually steam it. The turkey should be stuffed just before roasting. Try to buy a fresh, high-quality turkey—it makes all the difference. Be sure to remove all the stuffing from the cavities before refrigerating the leftover turkey carcass.

YIELD: 12 TO 14 SERVINGS

TURKEY:
One 16- to 18-pound turkey
³/₄ teaspoon each: paprika (preferably Hungarian), salt,
    freshly ground pepper
Old-Fashioned Sausage, Wild Rice,
    and Mushroom Stuffing (recipe follows)
2 tablespoons vegetable oil
2 tablespoons melted unsalted butter, for final brushing
Giblet Gravy (page 162)
Sliced oranges and watercress, for garnish

1. Put a rack in the lowest level in the oven; preheat the oven to 475 degrees. You will need a large roasting pan. Cut three 3-foot lengths of heavy-duty foil. Working on a large, flat surface, place the foil lengths side by side to make a wide sheet that will be pieced together, about 36 × 36 inches square. Form this continuous sheet by double folding the long edges together. Make sure the seams are securely sealed; the foil must be airtight. To shape the foil to the pan without tearing it, invert the roasting pan; center the foil over the pan and gently press the foil around it. Remove the foil. Turn the pan over and carefully fit the foil in the pan without tearing it. Set it aside.

2. Rinse the body and neck cavities of the turkey (be sure to save the giblets for the gravy); drain and pat dry with paper towels. Combine the seasonings in a small dish. Sprinkle the seasoning into both cavities, reserving a little for the surface. Loosely spoon the stuffing into the cavities. Do not pack the stuffing or it will become too compact during roasting. Put any extra stuffing in a 2-quart casserole (bake, covered, in 350-degree oven for 40 minutes). Tie the turkey legs together, skewer both cavities to close them, and tuck in the wings. Blunt the points of the skewers with a small clump of foil to prevent tearing the foil around the turkey.

3. Place the turkey, breast side up, in the pan. Rub

the turkey with the oil and sprinkle with the remaining seasoning. Bring the foil up over the sides of the turkey, leaving airspace on the sides and top so the skin won't tear during roasting. Double fold the foil edges to form an airtight package.

4. Roast 2½ hours. Carefully open the foil; beware of hot steam escaping. Brush the breast and legs with the melted butter. Tent the foil loosely over the legs and thighs (to prevent them from drying out) but leave the breast exposed. Continue to cook until the breast is deeply browned and an instant-reading thermometer registers 170 degrees (insert the thermometer into the thigh meat right next to the breast). Remove the turkey from the oven. Use a bulb baster to transfer the drippings and pan juices to a 2-cup measure. Bring the foil sides up to cover the turkey and let it stand 30 minutes before carving. Meanwhile, make the giblet gravy.

5. To serve, use a sharp carving knife or an electric knife to cut off the legs, thighs, and wings and to slice the turkey. Arrange the turkey on a large heated serving platter, leaving a space in the center. Spoon the stuffing from the cavities and casserole into the center. Garnish the platter with orange slices and clumps of watercress. Serve hot. Pass the giblet gravy separately in a gravy boat.

Old-Fashioned Sausage, Wild Rice, and Mushroom Stuffing

I prefer a well-seasoned stuffing, one that stands on its own in a casserole, with leftovers and on sandwiches. Thus, the "hot" sausage and packaged herb-seasoned stuffing mix. Cultivated mushrooms can be substituted for the wild mushrooms. Wild rice, cooked al dente, provides the perfect texture for this stuffing.

YIELD: ABOUT 12 CUPS, ENOUGH FOR AN 18-POUND TURKEY PLUS A 2-QUART CASSEROLE

2 tablespoons unsalted butter
One 12-ounce package breakfast sausage, preferably "hot," crumbled
Turkey liver, diced (optional)
Diced cooked meat from Turkey Gravy Stock (page 162)
2 medium Spanish onions, minced, about 4 cups
2 large ribs celery, diced, about 1½ cups
3½ cups sliced, trimmed wild mushrooms (3½ ounces shiitake mushrooms, 6 ounces cremini mushrooms)
3 cups cooked Wild Rice (page 360)
One 8-ounce package herb-seasoned stuffing mix
1 cup small cubes day-old white bread
3 to 6 tablespoons Turkey Gravy Stock (page 162) or lower-salt chicken broth
Red pepper flakes, salt, and freshly ground pepper to taste

1. Heat the butter in a large 4-quart sauté pan (a skillet with high sides) or in a wide pot over medium-high heat. When hot, add the sausage, liver, if using, onion, and celery. Cook until the sausage is cooked through, about 8

minutes, stirring often. Add the mushrooms and cook until they are just beginning to become limp, about 4 minutes. Remove from the heat.

2. Add the rice, seasoned stuffing mix, and bread cubes. Use 2 large wooden spoons to mix all the ingredients together. Add 3 to 6 tablespoons stock, just enough to moisten the stuffing; do not make it wet. Season with the red pepper flakes, salt, and pepper. The stuffing can be made a few hours in advance and kept at room temperature.

Giblet Gravy

The secret to a good gravy is a flavorful stock. Since the turkey gravy stock is made with chicken broth (instead of water), it has a great depth of flavor.

YIELD: 2 CUPS

3 tablespoons turkey fat drippings
1/4 cup plus 2 tablespoons flour
Enough skimmed pan juices and Turkey Gravy
  Stock (recipe follows) to make 2 cups, heated
  and kept warm
Diced turkey giblets, reserved from the
  Turkey Gravy Stock
A few drops Kitchen Bouquet, if needed for color
Salt and freshly ground pepper to taste

Heat the drippings in a 1-quart saucepan over medium heat. When hot, stir in the flour. Cook until lightly colored, about 4 minutes, stirring constantly. Slowly add the warm juices and stock, stirring constantly. If there are stubborn lumps, mix the gravy in the blender or in a food processor fitted with a metal blade until smooth. Stir in the giblets. Adjust the color with Kitchen Bouquet and season to taste. Keep the gravy warm until serving time. Pass in a gravy boat.

Turkey Gravy Stock

YIELD: ABOUT 2–2 1/2 CUPS

Turkey heart, gizzard, and neck
1 small onion, split
2 each: medium carrots and celery ribs,
  cut into 1-inch chunks
3²/₃ cups lower-salt chicken broth
  (two 14¹/₂-ounce cans)
1 bay leaf
4 peppercorns

Put all the ingredients in a 3-quart pot and bring to a boil. Simmer, covered, until the gizzard is tender, about 1¹/₂ hours. Strain, reserving the turkey parts. Trim the giblets; cut them and the neck meat into small dice. The stock can be made up to 2 days ahead; combine the stock and diced giblets and refrigerate. Wrap neck meat separately, refrigerate and add to stuffing. When ready to use for gravy, strain out and reserve the giblets. Save any leftover stock for the Turkey Vegetable Soup with Orzo (page 79); it can be kept a few days refrigerated or frozen for up to 3 months, covered airtight.

Poached Turkey Breast

This easy preparation ensures having turkey breast meat on hand for sandwiches, salads, and casseroles. Serve it with Cranberry Mustard (page 349) or Fresh Cranberry Relish (page 355). This is Jimmy Adkins's recipe and it's a breeze to make. It only takes an hour to cook a 6-pound turkey breast on the bone, with no attention from the cook. If the turkey breast is smaller, it takes less time. An instant-reading thermometer is useful for determining when the turkey breast is fully cooked. Lacking a thermometer, use a knife to penetrate the thickest part of the meat to be sure the juices run clear rather than pink. (It will be necessary to remove the turkey breast from the liquid in order to see the juices; afterward, replace the meat in the liquid for 20 minutes' standing time.) The poaching liquid can be boiled down and used as a stock in soups and sauces.

YIELD: 1 WHOLE TURKEY BREAST

1 whole turkey breast on the bone, about 6 pounds
2 each: large onions, carrots, celery ribs,
    all cut into chunks
2 bay leaves
Several parsley sprigs
1 teaspoon salt

1. Put the turkey breast in a large stockpot. Cover it with water and add the remaining ingredients. Bring the water to a boil. Gently simmer, covered, for 1 hour or until an instant-reading thermometer registers 155 degrees when inserted into thickest part of the meat; the temperature will increase at least 20 degrees on standing. Remove from the heat and let the turkey stand 20 minutes in its liquid. Skim the foam and small particles off the surface of the liquid. Remove the meat and reserve the liquid. The meat can be sliced immediately for serving or wrapped airtight and refrigerated for as long as 2 days. Once the meat is removed from the bone, it can also be frozen, wrapped airtight.

2. Boil the liquid vigorously, uncovered, until it is reduced to about 8 cups of mildly flavored stock. Strain and reserve the stock for soup-making or sauces. The stock can be refrigerated for up to 3 days, or frozen for as long as 3 months, either in ice cube trays for individual portions (once frozen, pop the cubes out and wrap them airtight in plastic bags) or in larger airtight containers.

Sweet-Spiced Turkey Breast,
Roasted on Onions and Raisins

The inspiration for the delicious range of flavors in this recipe comes from Rick and Deann Bayless's wonderful cookbook Authentic Mexican (Morrow, 1987). Here, a sweet spice paste is rubbed into the turkey breast to give the normally bland meat a mild but delicious zest. A great way to eat this is to wrap a soft corn tortilla around the thin turkey slices, onions, raisins, and rice cooked with cumin. Or you can skip the tortillas and serve it with Toasted Barley and Mushroom Risotto (page 231). This recipe makes great leftovers. While you're at it, double the recipe; just be sure each turkey breast is separately wrapped in foil. Roasting the turkey in a foil-pack at a very high temperature ensures remarkably moist meat. An instant-reading thermometer is infallible for determining when the meat is cooked but still juicy.

YIELD: 6 TO 8 SERVINGS

SPICE PASTE AND TURKEY:
3 large cloves garlic, minced, about 1¹/₂ tablespoons
2 large green onions, minced, about ¹/₂ cup
*1 teaspoon each: cinnamon, allspice, coarsely cracked
    pepper*
1¹/₄ teaspoons salt
1 tablespoon safflower oil
*1 large, boned, skinned turkey breast, about 2¹/₄
    pounds, flattened slightly between sheets of plastic
    wrap with a meat pounder or heavy pot*

ONIONS AND RAISINS:
1 large Spanish onion, thinly sliced, about 3 cups
¹/₂ cup golden raisins
2 tablespoons cider vinegar

Salt to taste
1 tablespoon minced fresh parsley

1. Put a rack in the center of the oven; preheat the oven to 500 degrees. Set aside a sheet of heavy-duty foil, large enough to enclose the turkey breast, and a shallow roasting pan.

2. For the spice paste and turkey, combine the garlic, green onions, spices, and oil in a small dish. Wash the turkey breast and dry it with paper towels. Rub the paste evenly into the entire surface of the turkey. The turkey can be roasted immediately or refrigerated overnight, covered airtight.

3. For the onions and raisins, place them (onion slices separated into rings) in the center of the foil. Sprinkle the vinegar over them. Place the turkey breast on top of the onions and raisins. Tent the turkey in an airtight foil package, leaving a small amount of space between the foil and the breast. Place the turkey foil-pack in the reserved pan.

4. Roast until an instant-reading thermometer inserted halfway through the thickest portion of the turkey registers 160 degrees, about 30 to 35 minutes. Don't open the foil to test the temperature; just insert the thermometer right through the foil.

5. Carefully open the foil to release the steam. Let the turkey rest 10 to 20 minutes, loosely covered, before cutting it into thin diagonal slices. Arrange the slices on a warm platter. Spoon the juices, onions, and raisins over the top. Sprinkle lightly with salt and minced parsley. Serve it hot, at room temperature, or chilled.

Skewered Turkey, Red Peppers, and Onions

The turkey breast meat becomes so tender as it marinates that it's hard to believe it's not expensive veal. The meat, onions, and red peppers are slightly caramelized on the surface during the broiling or grilling. Serve this on a bed of Lightly Spiced Pilaf (page 225) with Cranberry Mustard (page 349) on the side.

YIELD: 6 SERVINGS

^{1}/$_2$ cup balsamic vinegar

2 tablespoons olive oil

^{1}/$_3$ cup honey

1^1/$_4$ teaspoons dried thyme

^{1}/$_2$ teaspoon each: crushed dried rosemary, salt

Freshly ground pepper to taste

^{1}/$_2$ large, skinned, boned turkey breast, about 1^3/$_4$ pounds, trimmed of all visible fat and gristle, cut into 1^3/$_4$-inch cubes (you should have about 24 cubes)

2 large Spanish onions, peeled, split, each half cut into 6 equal-size chunks

2 large red bell peppers, cut into 24 1^1/$_2$-inch squares

1. To marinate the skewered ingredients, put the vinegar, olive oil, honey, thyme, rosemary, salt, and pepper in a large plastic food bag. Shake the bag to mix the ingredients. Add the turkey cubes, onion chunks, and red pepper squares to the bag. Secure the bag tightly around the ingredients. Turn the bag to coat all the ingredients with the marinade. Refrigerate overnight, turning the bag occasionally.

2. Put the broiler rack 7 inches from the heat source and preheat the broiler. Line a shallow roasting pan with foil. Set it aside. Set aside 6 long skewers. Alternately, the brochettes can be grilled. Prepare a hot barbecue fire with a few chunks of water-soaked mesquite wood.

3. To assemble, drain and reserve the marinade. Divide the turkey, onion chunks, and red pepper squares among the skewers, alternating turkey, onion, and red pepper squares and leaving a slight space around the turkey to let it cook through.

4. For the broiler, place the skewers on the prepared broiler pan. Broil until the turkey meat is seared and just cooked through, about 10 minutes total, turning once midway through broiling. Baste often with the reserved marinade. Alternately, for the barbecue, grill the brochettes over a hot fire, turning and basting them with the reserved marinade until cooked through, about 10 to 12 minutes.

5. To serve, sprinkle the brochettes lightly with additional salt and pepper. Serve them hot, arranged on large warm serving platter. Drizzle with any pan juices (discard the uncooked marinade).

Talking Turkey

Turkey is an excellent source of high-quality protein as well as iron, B vitamins, and niacin. Both calorie and cholesterol counts are appealingly low. A 3½-ounce serving of skinless turkey breast has a mere 115 calories, 23 grams of protein—more than a third of the recommended daily requirement—and under 2 grams of fat.

Turkey is now readily available in convenient parts. Look for:
- Turkey breast, either whole with the bone in or as boneless breast halves.
- Breast tenderloins, fillets of white breast meat.
- Drumsticks, thighs, and drumstick steaks for those who prefer dark meat.
- Ground turkey, usually a mix of light and dark meat that is much lower in fat and calories than beef. And it can be used the same way—as burgers, in meat loaf, meat sauces, chili, casseroles, tacos, and pizza.
- Turkey sausage, spiced for the breakfast table, also works in stuffings and casseroles.

Leftover Turkey

Leftover turkey meat will taste better if it's left on the bone until you use it. Once it has been cut, it quickly dries out. Wrapped tightly, either in a jumbo food bag or aluminum foil, leftovers will keep in the refrigerator for up to 3 days. To freeze turkey meat, remove the meat from the bone, wrap it in convenient-size foil packets, put the packets in a plastic bag, seal airtight, and freeze for up to 2 months. Thaw, still wrapped, in the refrigerator.

Duck Breasts with
Red Onion Cranberry Relish

*These duck breasts are topped with a deep-red, sweet-tart tangle of red onion and
cranberry relish. I especially like serving them with the Sautéed Wild Rice with Fennel,
Currants, and Orange (page 226) for a festive meal. Luckily, packaged duck breasts are
easy to find in the market; they are practical and extremely quick to prepare. Here, the
breasts are cooked without the skin so that they're far less fat-laden than a whole roasted
duck. Each half breast typically weighs about 4 ounces, an adequate serving once it is sliced
and arranged on the plate. Although the last-minute cooking is short, this recipe can also be
prepared completely in advance and reheated at serving time. Chicken breasts would work,
too, cooked in the same manner as the duck, but a few minutes longer until cooked
through. Or, if you prefer a game meat, serve the relish with broiled venison chops.*

YIELD: 6 SERVINGS

RED ONION CRANBERRY RELISH:
1 tablespoon safflower oil
1 medium red onion, thinly sliced, about 2 cups
1/2 cup each: fresh cranberries, dried cranberries
6 tablespoons water
1 1/2 tablespoons sugar
1/2 cup dry red wine
1/4 teaspoon salt
Freshly ground pepper to taste
2 teaspoons unsalted butter

DUCK:
2 teaspoons each: safflower oil, unsalted butter
3/4 teaspoon cinnamon
1/4 teaspoon allspice
1/2 teaspoon salt
Freshly ground pepper to taste
3 boneless duck breasts, about 10 ounces each, split,
    skinned, trimmed of all visible fat

12 orange slices, each centered with a clove, for garnish

1. For the relish, heat the oil in an 8-inch nonstick
skillet over medium-high heat. When hot, add the
onion and both cranberries. Cook, covered, until
the onion softens, about 7 minutes, stirring often to
avoid burning. Add the water and sugar and mix
well. Cook, uncovered, until the mixture is thick
and syrupy, about 7 minutes more, stirring often.

2. Add the wine, salt, and pepper. Bring to a boil.
Lower the heat to a simmer and stir in the butter
until melted. Adjust the seasoning and sugar
(adding a pinch more sugar if the wine tastes highly
acidic), and remove from the heat. The relish can
be made up to 3 days ahead and refrigerated.
Gently reheat in a saucepan or in the microwave
oven.

3. For the duck, heat the oil and butter in a 12-inch nonstick skillet over medium-high heat. Combine the cinnamon, allspice, salt, and pepper in a small dish. Sprinkle half the mixture over the top of the duck breasts, dividing it evenly. When the oil and butter are hot, place the breasts seasoned side down in the skillet. Sprinkle the remaining seasoning over the unseasoned side of the breasts. Cook, uncovered, turning only once when the underside is browned, until rare (about 3 minutes altogether) or medium (about 5 minutes altogether). The meat tends to be tough when cooked well done.

4. To serve, cut each breast on a slight angle, into thin slices. Arrange on a warm serving platter, reassembling the breast in its original shape but fanning out the slices. Top the breasts with the hot relish, dividing it evenly. Garnish the platter with orange slices. Serve hot.

5. Alternately, to cook the duck ahead and reheat it at serving time, brown both sides quickly for 1½ minutes altogether. Slice for serving and use a metal spatula to transfer the sliced breasts to a shallow baking dish. Garnish with the relish, cover, and refrigerate for as long as overnight. Before proceeding, spill off the accumulated liquid in the pan. Then reheat, covered, in a preheated 350-degree oven for 20 to 25 minutes, until the duck is hot and cooked to the desired doneness. Serve hot.

Chapter 7

Fish and Shellfish

❖

Even a casual reading of the old cookbooks demonstrates a long tradition in the Midwest of the special pleasures that can be found in fish and shellfish, be that fried smelts or shucked oysters. As they did with so many other foods, our forebears in this region were inclined to take simple flavors and make them stand up on the plate. There is magic in the traditional fish boil, after all—how can so few ingredients cooked in such an alarming way yield such delicious results? Such is the wellspring of my inspiration for this chapter.

Traditionally in the Midwest a fish or shellfish dish would have been part of a much larger meal, a single course where many more were likely to follow. The way we eat today, a single entree and a salad often make up the meal. Fish and shellfish fit so well with this change in diet. You end up eating a meal that is lighter, packed with nutrition, and explosive with flavor. The other benefit, and one not to be overlooked in this day and age, is the short time it takes to prepare truly exciting fish and shellfish dishes. Simplicity is the key in these recipes, and I think you will find that it unlocks a world of dining pleasure.

First, you start with the highest possible quality fresh fish or shellfish, ample reason in and of itself to get to know your fishmonger. Then you do to it as little as possible as quickly as possible. I cook fish at high temperature because this seals in the natural moistness. But there is a trick. Don't let the fish cook too long, just to the point of being done. And that's *before* you can flake it with the tines of a fork. These are the fundamentals of how I cook fish and shellfish, and probably why I think it works so well for entertaining. No muss, no fuss.

What could be better than a lovely fillet of broiled fish splashed with freshly squeezed lemon juice and a dusting of seasoning? What could be simpler to prepare yet speak to the senses with such bold authority? I'm thinking here of seared and broiled whitefish, one of the prized catches from Lake Superior.

But while considering the likes of Mackerel Fillets with Vegetables, or Baked Salmon with Fresh Tomatoes and Capers, or Grouper with Sweet and Sour Onions, don't overlook the shellfish options. In its prime, shellfish has an incomparable sweetness. Spiced Shrimp in Beer is a snap to prepare but delivers a flavor that suggests otherwise. The same is true of Pan-fried Scallops with Sweet and Sour Mustard Glaze.

Oysters Midas in-the-Shell

Oyster lovers will find this preparation mouthwatering. Served sizzling hot (which is easy to do), these oysters have great flavor. Their presentation is especially appealing with bright watercress leaves peeking out from under and a deep bronze Parmesan with crumbled bacon on top. Serve with Double-Baked Potatoes with Horseradish (page 212) and The Blackhawk's Creamed Spinach (page 209). These make a great first course as well, serving 8.

YIELD: 4 SERVINGS

24 each: oyster shells, medium oysters
1 cup oyster liquor or clam broth
¹/₂ cup light mayonnaise
¹/₄ cup grated imported Parmesan cheese (Parmigiano-Reggiano)
¹/₂ teaspoon each: Dijon mustard, fresh lemon juice
Scant ¹/₈ teaspoon cayenne pepper
2 teaspoons each: minced fresh parsley, snipped fresh chives
2 cups watercress leaves
2 thick slices applewood-smoked bacon (see Midwestern Sources, page 376), diced very small, browned, about 2 tablespoons cooked, for garnish
Watercress sprigs, for garnish

1. Arrange the oyster shells on a baking sheet. Set aside.

2. Put the oysters in a small saucepan with the oyster liquor or clam broth. Cook, uncovered, over medium-high heat until they are just plumped, about 3 minutes. Do not overcook. Set the oysters aside in the liquid.

3. Combine the mayonnaise, cheese, mustard, lemon juice, pepper, parsley, and chives in a small dish. Set aside.

4. To assemble, divide the watercress leaves among the shells. Drain the oysters and blot them dry with paper towels. Put ¹/₂ teaspoon of the mayonnaise mixture in the center of each shell. Place an oyster in the shell. Use a generous teaspoon of the mayonnaise mixture to coat each oyster. Sprinkle each with bacon. The oysters can be prepared several hours ahead to this point and refrigerated.

5. Put the broiler rack 6 inches from the heat source and preheat the broiler. Broil the oysters until well browned, about 1 to 2 minutes.

6. To serve, use tongs to arrange the oysters on a large warm platter. Garnish with watercress. Serve sizzling hot.

Oysters

Oysters have been a prominent factor in Midwestern dining since the mid-nineteenth century. Some nineteenth-century cookbooks actually devoted entire chapters to oysters. And these mollusks weren't just for the wealthy. Everyone loved them. Englishman Charles Mackey wrote in 1859 that the rich were those who "consume oysters and Champagne" while the poor "consume oysters and lager bier." Abraham Lincoln was a great oyster fan and often threw oyster parties in Springfield, Illinois.

For shipping across country, live oysters were packed in watered-down straw inside huge barrels, then repeatedly soaked and drained. This fooled the oysters into thinking they were in low tide.

Shrimp de Jonghe

A highly seasoned garlicky shrimp dish, shrimp de Jonghe has been a Chicago specialty since the turn of the century, when it was invented by two Belgians named De Jonghe. It makes a great meal served with steamed rice. Served in smaller portions (3 to 4 shrimp per serving) it can also be an enticing first course.

YIELD: 6 SERVINGS

SAVORY GARLIC CRUMB TOPPING:
5 tablespoons unsalted butter
4 large cloves garlic, minced, about 2 tablespoons
4 medium shallots, minced, about ¹/₄ cup
¹/₃ cup dry vermouth (or dry white wine)
3 cups fresh bread crumbs
²/₃ cup minced parsley leaves
1 teaspoon paprika (preferably, Hungarian)
¹/₄ teaspoon salt
Pinch of cayenne pepper

SHRIMP:
36 uncooked shelled jumbo shrimp, back vein removed, washed
³/₄ cup each: lower-salt chicken broth, dry vermouth (or dry white wine)
1 tablespoon olive oil

Lemon wedges, for serving (optional)

1. Generously butter 6 individual shallow baking dishes just large enough to hold 6 shrimp in a single layer, slightly overlapping. Set aside along with a baking sheet.

2. For the crumb topping, heat the butter in an 8-inch nonstick skillet over medium-high heat.

When hot, add the garlic and shallots. Cook until hot and fragrant but not browned, about 1 minute. Add the dry vermouth and simmer until the mixture is thick, about 1 minute. Transfer to a food processor fitted with a metal blade.

3. Add the remaining topping ingredients to the processor. Pulse on/off until mixed. Taste the crumbs. They should be very spicy; adjust the seasoning as necessary.

4. For the shrimp, arrange 6 shrimp, overlapping, in each prepared baking dish. Combine the broth and vermouth. Spoon 4 teaspoons of liquid into each dish. Tuck 2 tablespoons of crumbs around the shrimp in each dish. Sprinkle ¹/₄ cup crumbs over each dish. Drizzle each with ¹/₂ teaspoon of oil. Place the dishes on the reserved baking sheet. The shrimp can be prepared to this point several hours ahead and refrigerated.

5. Put the rack in the lower third of the oven; preheat the oven to 450 degrees. Bake the shrimp until browned and sizzling, about 12 to 14 minutes. Serve hot, with lemon wedges if desired.

Spiced Shrimp in Beer

Beer makes shrimp both piquant and sweet, enhancing them so much that it's surprising shrimp are not cooked in beer more often. Serve these over buttered rice or noodles, using every drop of the delicious sauce. It's more fun to leave the shells on the shrimp, although I do recommend splitting them down the back, which lets you remove the vein, allows the shrimp to absorb more flavor, and makes them much easier to eat. So roll up your sleeves and use your fingers. Green Beans and Shallots with Dill (see variation, page 191) and Red Cabbage Slaw with Broccoli and Red Pepper (page 106) are ideal accompaniments.

YIELD: 4 SERVINGS

20 large shrimp, shells on, about 1 pound
1 1/2 tablespoons safflower oil
2 large cloves garlic, minced, about 1 tablespoon
1 medium red onion, cut into 1/2-inch dice,
     about 2 cups
1 1/2 cups beer
1/2 teaspoon each: cumin seed, mustard seed, salt
1/2 tablespoon light brown sugar
Freshly ground pepper to taste
Hot buttered rice or pasta, for serving

1. Use kitchen shears to split the shrimp shells along the back, leaving the shell in place and the tail intact. Remove the veins and wash the shrimp well. Set aside.

2. Heat the oil in a 9-inch nonstick skillet over medium heat. When hot, add the garlic and onions. Cook until the onions are very soft and fragrant, about 5 minutes. Stir often.

3. Add the beer, cumin and mustard seeds, salt, sugar, and pepper. Bring the liquid to a boil. Simmer, covered, for 5 minutes. This liquid can be made a day ahead and refrigerated. Reheat before cooking the shrimp.

4. Add the shrimp, in a single layer, to the hot liquid. Simmer, uncovered, until the shrimp are opaque, about 1 minute, turning them once. Do not overcook. Serve hot over rice or noodles, dividing the shrimp and sauce evenly.

Pan-Fried Scallops with Sweet and Sour Mustard Glaze

Lemon slices and delicate threadlike tangles of lemon zest garnish this piquant scallop preparation. The cooking is best done at the last minute, taking well under 10 minutes. Serve the scallops with Lemon Noodles with Poppy Seeds (page 248), plain buttered noodles, or steamed rice.

YIELD: 6 SERVINGS

1 tablespoon each: unsalted butter, safflower oil

1³/₄ pounds sea scallops, rinsed, blotted dry with
   paper towels

¹/₃ cup seasoned rice vinegar

1 tablespoon Dijon mustard

4 teaspoons honey

3 tablespoons fresh lemon juice

Pinch of cayenne pepper

Salt to taste

Grated zest of 2 large lemons (colored rind), removed
   with a zester, about 2 tablespoons, for garnish
   (see page 14)

2 lemons, scored, thinly sliced, for garnish

1. Heat the butter and oil in a 12-inch nonstick skillet over medium-high heat. When it is hot, brown the scallops on one side, cooking until they are just opaque (do not overcook), about 3 minutes, depending on their size. Use a slotted spoon to remove the scallops as they are cooked; set them aside on a warm platter.

2. Add the vinegar to the hot skillet (watch out for splatter). Boil over high heat until the liquid is reduced to 3 tablespoons, about 2 minutes. Add any scallop juices that may have accumulated on the plate along with the mustard, honey, lemon juice, and cayenne. Stir well until combined.

3. Simmer until the glaze is very thick and coats the spoon, about 2 minutes. Return the scallops to the pan and stir to coat them with the glaze. Cook only to heat them through, about 20 seconds. Do not overcook. Adjust the salt.

4. To serve, arrange the hot scallops, browned side up, on a large warm platter. Lightly drizzle the scallops with the glaze; top them with the lemon rind threads, garnish with the lemon slices, and serve hot.

Fried Lemon-Battered Fish Fillets

Crisp and light-tasting, these fillets are easy to prepare, even though they require last-minute cooking. The club soda (or sparkling mineral water) gives this thin batter a delicate crust. Serve these fillets with Oven Country "Fries" (page 213) or baked potatoes with Chive Cream (page 215) and Asparagus with Balsamic Vinegar (page 193). Another choice would be the Curried Garden Rice Casserole (page 228).

YIELD: 4 SERVINGS

6 tablespoons club soda
1 tablespoon plus 1 teaspoon fresh lemon juice
1 teaspoon Worcestershire sauce
$^1/_2$ cup flour
$^3/_4$ teaspoon salt
Freshly ground pepper to taste
Four 4-ounce mild fish fillets, such as striped bass,
    walleye pike, red snapper, or tilapia
1 tablespoon each: unsalted butter, olive oil, for frying
Lemon wedges and Tartar Sauce (page 361), for serving

1. Put the club soda, lemon juice, Worcestershire sauce, flour, salt, and pepper in a Pyrex pie plate or a shallow soup dish. Mix until combined.

2. Rinse the fillets in cold water and pat them dry with paper towels. Set aside on paper towels.

3. Heat $^1/_2$ tablespoon each of the butter and oil in a 10-inch nonstick skillet over medium-high heat. When it is hot, dip 2 fillets in the batter to coat them. Put them in the skillet and fry until they are lightly brown and crisp on both sides, about 3 minutes per side. Transfer the fillets to a warm plate and keep them warm in a preheated 200-degree oven. Heat the remaining butter and oil until hot; coat and fry the remaining fillets.

4. To serve, arrange the fillets on a warm serving platter. Garnish with lemon wedges. Serve hot. Pass the tartar sauce separately.

Seafood Smarts

❖ **How to tell if fish really is fresh? Fresh fish will smell sweet, with a faint, pleasant suggestion of the water. If it has a strong, fishy smell, reject it. It's too old. The flesh should feel firm and somewhat elastic and should be moist and translucent. If you're buying whole fish, the eyes should be clear and protruding, and the scales tight.**

❖ **Once home, try to use fish as soon as possible. For short-term storage in the refrigerator, remove it from its original wrapping. Rewrap it in plastic, and store it in the coldest part of the refrigerator.**

❖ **If you don't know a lot about fish and seafood, ask questions. Your fishmonger can describe the various characteristics of his fish—taste, texture, fat content, and suitable cooking methods—and also direct you to appropriate recipe substitutions.**

Balsamic-Glazed Salmon Fillets

Balsamic vinegar adds a delicious tartness to this glaze, perfect for a mild fish. Don't worry about the amount of garlic, it sweetens as it cooks, leaving only a trace of garlic but a nice depth of flavor. This recipe can be easily doubled for a large party; just be sure all the fillets are roughly the same thickness so that they cook evenly. Serve with Stuffed Onions with Garlicky Spinach (page 208) and buttered orzo.

YIELD: 6 SERVINGS

2 large garlic cloves, sliced paper-thin, about 1 tablespoon
1 tablespoon each: olive oil, honey
1 tablespoon plus 1 teaspoon Dijon mustard
$^1/_3$ cup balsamic vinegar
$^1/_4$ teaspoon salt
Freshly ground pepper to taste
Six 5-ounce salmon fillets, washed, patted dry with paper towels
2 tablespoons julienned fresh basil, for garnish

1. Put a rack in the lower third of the oven; preheat the oven to 475 degrees. Line a jelly roll pan (cookie sheet with sides) with foil. Set aside.

2. In a small saucepan, cook the sliced garlic in the oil over medium heat until it is soft, about 3 minutes, stirring often. Do not brown. Add the honey, mustard, vinegar, salt, and pepper. Stir until well combined. Simmer, uncovered, until slightly thickened, about 3 minutes. This glaze can be made 2 days ahead and refrigerated. Gently reheat before using.

3. Arrange the salmon fillets, skin side down, in a single layer on the prepared pan. Brush with the warm glaze.

4. Bake until the fillets are sizzling and browned, about 10 to 14 minutes, depending on their thickness. To be sure that they're cooked, use a small paring knife to cut through the thickest part. Do not overcook. When done, brush the fillets with the remaining glaze and sprinkle them very lightly with additional salt and pepper.

5. To serve, use a spatula to transfer the fish to a warm serving platter, garnish them with julienned basil, and serve hot.

Baked Whitefish Fillets with Tarragon Mustard, Tarragon-Tomato Relish

Lake Superior whitefish is sweet and mild. Here, a tarragon mustard is brushed over the fillets, which are baked at a high temperature, then topped with a tarragon-tomato relish. Serve these with Corn Flan with Onions and Bacon (page 197).

YIELD: 4 SERVINGS

TARRAGON-TOMATO RELISH:
2 large plum tomatoes, seeded and diced, about ²/₃ cup
2 small green onions, sliced, about ¹/₄ cup
1¹/₄ teaspoons seasoned rice vinegar
1 teaspoon snipped fresh tarragon

TARRAGON MUSTARD:
2 tablespoons olive oil
2 teaspoons snipped fresh tarragon
1 tablespoon Dijon mustard
1 teaspoon fresh lemon juice
Pinch of salt
Freshly ground pepper to taste

WHITEFISH:
Four 6-ounce whitefish fillets, washed, patted dry with paper towels
Salt and freshly ground pepper to taste

1. Put the rack in the center of the oven; preheat the oven to 450 degrees. Set aside a shallow baking pan large enough to hold the fillets in a single layer.

2. For the relish, put all the ingredients in a small dish and mix well. The relish can be used immediately or it can rest for up to 2 hours at room temperature.

3. For the mustard, put all the ingredients in a small dish and mix well. This mixture can also be used immediately or it can be refrigerated overnight.

4. Arrange the whitefish fillets, skin side down, in the pan. Coat the surface of each with a thin layer of the tarragon mustard. Lightly sprinkle with salt and pepper.

5. Bake until sizzling and lightly browned around the edges, about 12 to 14 minutes, depending on the thickness of the fillets.

6. To serve, use a metal spatula to transfer the fillets to a warm serving platter. Top each fillet with the relish, dividing it evenly. Serve hot or warm.

Sizzling Fillets, Simple Mustard Mayonnaise

Fresh is key in this simple preparation. Fresh fish fillets are dipped in a light coating of seasoned flour, seared on the stove, then finished off in a 500-degree oven until cooked through and sizzling. Served with lemon wedges and a mustard mayonnaise typically used for stone crab claws, the fish is light and appealing.

YIELD: 6 SERVINGS

$1/4$ cup flour
$3/4$ teaspoon each: salt, freshly ground pepper
12 fresh fish fillets, about $2^1/2$ ounces each, such as
    striped bass, sole, tilapia, flounder, washed, patted
    dry with paper towels
$1^1/2$ tablespoons each: unsalted butter, vegetable oil,
    for cooking
Simple Mustard Mayonnaise (recipe follows) and
    lemon wedges, for serving

1. Put a rack in the center of the oven; preheat the oven to 500 degrees. Line a jelly roll pan (cookie sheet with sides) with foil or lightly grease it. Set aside.

2. Sift the flour, salt, and pepper into a shallow dish or pie plate. Coat the fish fillets with the flour mixture, shaking off any excess.

3. Heat 1 tablespoon each of the butter and oil in a 12-inch nonstick skillet over medium-high heat. When it is very hot, add the fillets in batches, rounded side down. Cook them until they are well browned on one side, about 2 minutes. Turn and brown the other side, about 1 minute more. Use a metal spatula to transfer them, rounded side up, to the prepared baking sheet. Add more butter and oil, if needed, and continue to cook the remaining fillets.

4. When the fillets are all cooked, place the baking sheet in the oven. Bake until the fillets are sizzling, about 3 minutes for thin fillets, longer if they are thick. Be careful not to overcook the fish. Serve them hot, with lemon wedges and a dollop of Simple Mustard Mayonnaise on the side.

Simple Mustard Mayonnaise

YIELD: 6 SERVINGS, ABOUT 1/2 CUP

$1/2$ cup light mayonnaise
1 tablespoon Dijon mustard
$1/2$ teaspoon sugar

1. Combine all the ingredients. Chill. The mayonnaise can be made up to 2 days ahead and refrigerated. Serve chilled.

Baked Salmon with Fresh Tomato and Capers

Mild-flavored salmon is garnished with a perfectly balanced fresh tomato and caper sauce. The fresh basil is a great flavor accent and also brightens the presentation. This salmon dish can be served hot, at room temperature, or chilled. Served hot, try it with The Blackhawk's Creamed Spinach (page 209) and Warm Russet Potato Pancakes (page 214) as side dishes.

YIELD: 6 SERVINGS

TOMATO AND CAPER SAUCE:

2 tablespoons light olive oil

1 large clove garlic, minced, about ¹/₂ tablespoon

3 large shallots, minced, about ¹/₂ cup

2 tablespoons dry white wine or dry vermouth

6 large plum tomatoes, outer shells only, cut into ¹/₃-inch dice, about 2 cups

1 tablespoon capers, drained

Pinch of sugar

¹/₂ teaspoon salt

Freshly ground pepper to taste

2 tablespoons unsalted butter

SALMON:

Six 5- to 6-ounce uniformly thick fresh salmon fillets

1 tablespoon olive oil

Salt and freshly ground pepper to taste

4 large basil leaves, cut into fine julienne, for garnish

1. Put a rack in the lower third of the oven; preheat the oven to 450 degrees. Line a jelly roll pan (cookie sheet with sides) with foil. Set aside.

2. For the sauce, heat the oil in a 10-inch nonstick skillet over medium heat. When it is hot, add the garlic and shallots. Cook until they are softened, about 4 minutes. Add the wine or vermouth and simmer 1 minute. Add the tomatoes, capers, sugar,

salt, and pepper. Heat just until warmed through. Stir in the butter until it is melted. Remove from the heat. Adjust the seasoning. This sauce can be made several hours ahead and kept at room temperature. Gently reheat before using it.

3. For the salmon, wash the fillets and dry them with paper towels. Place the fillets, skin side down, in a single layer on the prepared jelly roll pan. Rub the surface of the fillets with oil. Season generously with salt and pepper.

4. Bake until the fish is sizzling and lightly browned around the edges, about 8 to 10 minutes. To be sure that they are cooked, use a small paring knife to cut through the thickest part. Do not overcook.

5. To serve, use a metal spatula to transfer the fillets to a large, warm serving platter. Spoon the warm sauce over them and garnish with the julienned basil. Serve hot, at room temperature, or chilled. If serving chilled, refrigerate the fillets up to 3 hours with the sauce on them.

Grouper with Sweet and Sour Onions

Fish dishes rarely come better than this rendition of grouper, perfectly enhanced by a seductive mix of sweet and sour onions and a garnish of toasted pine nuts. Chef Paul Lo Duca, the chef and co-owner of Mare and Vinci, two excellent Italian restaurants in Chicago, fine-tuned this recipe when he was the chef at Carlucci's. The grouper can be grilled or broiled.

YIELD: 4 SERVINGS

ONIONS:

3 tablespoons olive oil

4 large onions, cut into julienne strips, about 5 1/2 cups

1/2 teaspoon salt

Freshly ground pepper to taste

1/2 cup golden raisins

1/4 cup sugar

1/2 cup balsamic vinegar

1 1/2 cups red wine vinegar

FISH:

Four 5-ounce grouper fillets

2 tablespoons extra-virgin olive oil

Salt and freshly ground pepper to taste

1/4 cup pine nuts, toasted (page 358), for garnish

1 tablespoon snipped fresh chives, for garnish

1. For the onions, heat the olive oil in a 12-inch skillet over high heat. When it is hot, add the onions, salt, and pepper. Cook over high heat until the onions are a light brown and lightly caramelized, about 7 minutes, stirring as needed to prevent sticking or burning.

2. Add the raisins, sugar, and vinegars to the onions. Gently simmer, uncovered, over low heat until the mixture is thick and the liquid evaporated, about 25 to 30 minutes. The onions can be cooked several hours ahead and kept at room temperature. Gently reheat and adjust the seasoning before using.

3. For the fish, prepare a hot barbecue fire with a few chunks of presoaked mesquite wood. Alternatively, put the broiler rack 8 inches from heat source and preheat the broiler. Rub the surface of the fillets with 1 tablespoon of the oil. Season with salt and pepper. Grill over hot coals (skin side up) or broil (skin side down). If grilling, use a spatula to carefully turn the fish once. If broiling, do not turn them. Grill or broil until they are cooked through and browned, about 7 to 10 minutes. Do not overcook.

4. To serve, spoon the hot onion mixture onto a large warm platter. Arrange the fish over the onions. Drizzle the remaining tablespoon of oil over the fillets. Garnish with pine nuts and chives. Serve hot.

Glazed Stuffed Fish with Shrimp and Bread Crumb Stuffing

The high oven temperature keeps this fish deliciously moist, but be sure not to overbake it. The flesh should be firm to the touch but it should not be so well cooked that it flakes with a fork. This recipe can be completely assembled a few hours before serving and refrigerated until time to cook it. For fearless fish cooks, the head also keeps the fish flesh moist, but its appearance doesn't appeal to everyone. The fish can be cooked without the head; just tuck the stuffing neatly into the cavity. Red snapper can be substituted for the sea bass. Serve the fish with steamed rice mixed with green onions and steamed carrots.

YIELD: 3 SERVINGS

SHRIMP AND BREAD CRUMB STUFFING:

1 tablespoon plus 2 teaspoons olive oil
1 cup loosely packed fresh bread crumbs
1 small clove garlic, minced, about $^1/_2$ teaspoon
1 medium rib celery, cut into small dice, about $^1/_2$ cup
1 small onion, cut into small dice, about $^1/_2$ cup
$^1/_4$ pound peeled, deveined shrimp, cut into a small dice, about $^2/_3$ cup
$^1/_8$ teaspoon each: dried thyme, grated orange zest (colored rind), removed with a zester or fine grater (see page 14), salt
Freshly ground pepper to taste

GLAZE:

2 teaspoons each: olive oil, Worcestershire sauce
$2^1/_2$ tablespoons orange juice
1 teaspoon Dijon mustard
$^1/_8$ teaspoon dried thyme
Freshly ground pepper to taste

One $2^1/_4$ pound whole sea bass, gutted, scaled, butterflied, washed, patted dry with paper towels
Orange slices and parsley sprigs, for garnish

1. Put a rack in the center of the oven; preheat the oven to 450 degrees. Set aside a 9 × 13-inch shallow baking pan.

2. For the stuffing, heat 2 teaspoons of the oil in an 8-inch nonstick skillet over medium-high heat until hot. Tip the pan to spread the oil. Add the bread crumbs and garlic. Cook until the crumbs are browned, not burned, about 1 to 2 minutes, stirring constantly. Remove from the pan and set aside.

3. Add the remaining oil to the same skillet. When hot, add the celery and onion. Cook until the onion is fragrant, about 3 minutes. Add the shrimp, thyme, orange zest, salt, and pepper. Mix well. Cook just until the shrimp is opaque, about 2 minutes, stirring constantly. Remove from the heat. Stir in the reserved garlic crumbs. Set aside.

4. For the glaze, combine all the ingredients in a small dish.

5. Fill the cavity of the fish with the stuffing. Place the fish in the reserved baking pan. The fish can be prepared to this point and refrigerated for up to

4 hours. When ready to bake, brush the fish with the glaze.

6. Bake until the fish is cooked through and the flesh is firm but not flaking (test by inserting a sharp paring knife into the thickest part of the fish), about 30 minutes. Brush with any remaining glaze.

7. To serve, place the fish on a heated platter. Garnish the platter and head (if using it) with orange slices and parsley. Serve hot.

Mackerel Fillets with Vegetables

Oceanique, a restaurant in Evanston, Illinois, that specializes in fish, serves these fillets cooked in a vegetable-and-herb-laden stock, which not only makes for great flavor but also for a vibrant presentation. Ono or kingfish can be substituted for the Spanish mackerel, which is somewhat lighter and sweeter than American mackerel. The white pearl onions are labor-intensive to peel but they are worth it. The fillets are served at room temperature, making this recipe an excellent choice for buffets and summer entertaining.

YIELD: 6 SERVINGS

VEGETABLES AND STOCK:
2 large tomatoes, skinned, shells only cut into $1/3$-inch
 dice, about $1^1/2$ cups
$1/2$ cup each: thinly sliced white pearl onions, celery,
 and slender carrots
5 cups well-seasoned Quick Fish Stock (page 368)
$3^1/2$ tablespoons sherry wine vinegar
$1/4$ cup minced fresh parsley
2 tablespoons minced fresh tarragon

FISH:
Six 5-ounce Spanish mackerel fillets, skin intact
Salt and freshly ground pepper to taste
3 tablespoons olive oil
Lemon wedges, for garnish

1. Set aside a shallow nonaluminum baking pan just large enough to hold the fish in a single layer.

2. For the vegetables and stock, put the diced tomatoes, sliced onions, celery, carrots, and fish stock in a large nonaluminum skillet. Simmer, uncovered until carrots are just tender, about 10 minutes. Cool the mixture quickly. Either set it over ice or pour it into a shallow stainless-steel pan and refrigerate it until chilled. This stock can be made a day ahead and refrigerated. Just before

using, add the vinegar, parsley, and tarragon to the chilled stock. Mix well.

3. Put a rack in the center of the oven; preheat the oven to 400 degrees.

4. For the fish, rub the surface of the fillets with salt and pepper. Rub the oil over the filleted surface of the fish and on the bottom of the baking pan. Place the fish, skin-side-up, in the prepared pan. Ladle the stock around the fish. Place a piece of parchment paper or waxed paper over the fish.

5. Bake until the fish is just cooked, about 15 to 20 minutes, depending on the thickness of the fillets. To be sure that they are cooked, use a small paring knife to cut through the thickest part. Do not overcook. Remove the fish from the oven and leave in the pan with the stock to cool to room temperature. This will take about 20 minutes, and the fish will cook somewhat more. Strain the vegetables from the stock (save the stock for soups and cooking fish).

6. To serve, place the room-temperature fillets on a platter with the vegetables arranged attractively over them. Garnish the platter with lemon wedges.

Door County's Fish Boil

Door County's most famous culinary spectacle is the fish boil, a beloved Wisconsin tradition akin to the New England clambake that draws hungry crowds to a bubbling cast-iron cauldron full of fish, potatoes, and onions. Though a tourist attraction today, fish boils were started over 100 years ago in Wisconsin by practical-minded Scandinavian settlers as an efficient way of feeding a hot outdoor meal to logging crews while taking advantage of Door County's three most abundant resources: potatoes, onions, and fish.

In the last 25 years, the fish boil has become a symbol of the county. Practically every visitor to the peninsula partakes. A typical fish boil recipe calls for 100 pounds each of fish and potatoes, a good amount of onions, and 40 pounds of salt. Surprisingly, the fish tastes neither salty, oily, nor mushy, in thanks, they say, to the dramatic boil-over that leaves the fish perfectly cooked, fresh, and sweet.

SIDE DISHES:
Green Beans and Shallots
    Dill Variation
    Basil Variation
Stir-Fried Broccoli and Carrots
Asparagus with Balsamic Vinegar
Roasted Acorn Squash with Garlic, Honey, and Thyme
Maple Carrots and Leeks
Corn Flan with Onions and Bacon
Goose Island Honey-Roasted Root Vegetables
Sautéed Woodland Mushrooms with Sliced Green Onions
Spiced Squash Pancakes
Harvest Ratatouille
Baked Sweet and Sour Red Cabbage
Corn Fritters
Grilled Portobellos with Garlic Oil
Stuffed Onions with Garlicky Spinach
The Blackhawk's Creamed Spinach
Mashed Potatoes with Celery Root and Parsnip
Double-Baked Potatoes with Horseradish
Oven Country "Fries"
Warm Russet Potato Pancakes
Chive Cream

MAIN DISHES:
Aunt Mary's Stuffed Artichokes
Eggplant Rolatini
Spaghetti Squash Lasagna
Pizza Bread Pudding

Chapter 8
Vegetables

❖

What better representation of abundance can there be than a cornucopia overflowing with vegetables? And yet, in turning the pages of historic Midwest cookbooks, I find scant mention of vegetables. And when I do, they are generally cooked to mush and buried under a white sauce.

I love vegetables. I love their variations of color, texture, and flavor; the way fresh peas in spring bring a tired winter palate back to life; the way bean soups in winter soothe their way deep into the soul. When the farmers' markets are burgeoning during the growing season, you will find me at the vegetable stands.

I use Midwest staples in this chapter—corn, potatoes, carrots, cabbage, squash—then let my enthusiasm lead the way. Corn Flan with Onions and Bacon, for example. There will be no leftovers. Or Maple Carrots and Leeks. Or Roasted Acorn Squash with Garlic, Honey, and Thyme.

But there are other treats here as well, all of them simple to prepare. I'm thinking of the Asparagus with Balsamic Vinegar, of Sauteed Woodland Mushrooms with Sliced Green Onions, of Aunt Mary's Stuffed Artichokes, of Spiced Squash Pancakes.

Some of these dishes take center stage on the dining table, others are meant to complement. All of them, however, stand right out with lively flavors and make any meal exciting.

Green Beans and Shallots

Try to buy fresh young beans (not haricots verts) that are not old or overgrown. As straightforward as this vegetable combination is, it's especially delicious with young tender beans. The thinly sliced shallots are added to the boiling water just when the beans are cooked. Use the ultra-thin slicing disc of the food processor to cut the shallots into paper-thin slices. During the Thanksgiving and Christmas holiday season, add ¼ cup pomegranate seeds to the skillet just before serving.

YIELD: 4 SERVINGS

1¹/₂ quarts salted water
1¹/₂ pounds young green beans, stem ends trimmed, washed
3 large shallots, sliced paper-thin, about ¹/₂ cup
1 tablespoon unsalted butter
Scant ¹/₄ teaspoon salt
Freshly ground pepper to taste

1. Bring 1¹/₂ quarts of salted water to a boil. Add the beans slowly to keep the water at a boil. Cook, uncovered, until the beans are just tender (do not overcook—test by tasting a bean), about 6 to 7 minutes. Add the sliced shallots. Drain immediately into a colander. To preserve the green color and to keep the texture of the beans, put the colander under cold running water until the vegetables feel cold to the touch. They can be cooked several hours ahead and kept at room temperature.

2. To serve, heat the butter in a 12-inch nonstick skillet over medium-high heat. When very hot, add the vegetables, salt, and pepper. Heat through, shaking the pan to mix the vegetables, about 2 minutes. Adjust the seasoning. Serve hot.

Dill Variation: Just before serving, gently toss 1 tablespoon snipped fresh dill into green beans.

Basil Variation: Just before serving, gently toss 1 tablespoon julienned fresh basil leaves into green beans.

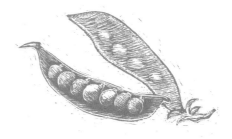

Stir-Fried Broccoli and Carrots

This is a flavorful vegetable mix . . . colorful, too.

YIELD: 3 TO 4 SERVINGS

1 cup packaged "shortcut" carrots, split horizontally
   (or 1 cup sliced carrots)
4 cups broccoli florets
1¹/₂ teaspoons oriental sesame oil
1 large clove garlic, minced, ¹/₂ tablespoon
1 tablespoon grated orange zest (colored rind), removed
   with a zester or fine grater (see page 14)
¹/₄ cup orange juice
A pinch of red pepper flakes
Salt to taste

1. Bring a large pot of salted water to a boil over high heat. Add the carrots and cook 1 minute. Add the broccoli florets. Cook, uncovered, until both are just barely tender, about 2 to 3 minutes. Drain immediately into a colander. To preserve the color and keep the texture, put the colander under cold running water until the vegetables feel cold to the touch. They can be cooked several hours ahead and kept at room temperature.

2. To serve, heat the oil in a nonstick wok or a 10-inch nonstick skillet over medium-high heat. When hot, add the garlic, orange zest, carrots, and broccoli. Stir-fry the vegetables until they are heated through, about 3 minutes. Add the orange juice and red pepper flakes. Cook until the vegetable mixture is hot, about 2 minutes. Adjust the salt. Serve hot.

Asparagus with Balsamic Vinegar

This simple preparation flatters asparagus without overpowering its delicate taste.

YIELD: 6 SERVINGS

2¹/₂ pounds asparagus
2¹/₂ tablespoons unsalted butter
2¹/₂ teaspoons balsamic vinegar
¹/₂ teaspoon salt
Freshly ground pepper to taste

1. Trim the white woody ends from the asparagus; peel the stems with a vegetable peeler.

2. Bring 12 cups salted water to a boil in a 10¹/₂-inch sauté pan (a skillet with straight sides) or a pot wide enough to hold the asparagus lying down. When the water boils, add the asparagus. Simmer, uncovered, just until tender, from 3 to 8 minutes depending on their thickness. Watch carefully—do not overcook. Use tongs to transfer the asparagus to a colander. To preserve the green color and keep the texture, put the colander under cold running water until the asparagus feel cold to the touch. Drain and pat dry. The asparagus can be cooked several hours ahead and kept at room temperature.

3. To serve, heat the butter in the same pan over medium-high heat. When hot, stir in the vinegar. Add the asparagus and cook until hot, 2 to 3 minutes, shaking the pan occasionally so that the asparagus heat evenly. Add the salt and pepper and shake pan gently until mixed. Adjust the seasoning. Serve hot.

Roasted Acorn Squash with Garlic, Honey, and Thyme

These wedges are good enough to eat plain as finger-food snacks; the skin becomes so soft that it's edible. They also make great plate garnishes. Very large garlic cloves are necessary, as smaller ones dry up and become hard. The garlic cloves flavor the squash and make a nice presentation. Use these wedges to garnish platters of Grilled Veal Chops with Lemon, Capers, and Sage Onions (page 134), Orange-Roasted Chicken on Tossed Greens (page 152), or Toasted Barley and Mushroom Risotto (page 231).

YIELD: 3 TO 4 SERVINGS

2 large acorn squashes, split, seeds and membrane
  removed, each half cut lengthwise into quarters,
  patted dry with paper towels
3 tablespoons olive oil
8 very large cloves garlic, unpeeled
2 tablespoons honey
Salt and freshly ground pepper to taste
1/2 teaspoon dried thyme leaves

1. Put the rack in the lower third of the oven; preheat the oven to 400 degrees. Set aside a large baking pan just large enough to hold the squash wedges in a single layer.

2. Put the oil in the baking pan. Place the pan in the oven until the oil is hot, about 10 minutes. Tip the pan to coat the bottom with oil. Place the squash and garlic in a single layer in the pan.

3. Roast for 30 minutes. Then drizzle the honey over the squash. Use a spatula to release and turn the squash. Shake the pan to distribute the honey. Bake until the squash is just tender but not mushy, about 20 to 30 minutes more, depending on the size of the squash wedges.

4. To serve, put the wedges in a bowl. Toss with salt, pepper, and thyme. Serve hot.

Maple Carrots and Leeks

These carrots are simple . . . and simply delicious.

2 tablespoons unsalted butter

2 small leeks, dark green leaves trimmed (save for
   soup), split lengthwise, washed, blotted dry,
   thinly sliced, about 1 1/2 cups

16 medium carrots, thinly sliced, about 8 cups

1/2 to 2/3 cup water

3 tablespoons pure maple syrup

1/4 teaspoon salt

1. Heat the butter in a 12-inch nonstick skillet over medium-high heat. When it is hot, add the leeks. Cook, stirring often, until they are softened, about 4 minutes. Remove and set aside half of the leeks.

2. Add the carrots, 1/2 cup water, the maple syrup, and salt to the leeks remaining in the skillet. Simmer, covered, until the carrots are tender, about 17 minutes. Add the remaining water as necessary if the mixture becomes too dry. The vegetables can be cooked up to 2 days ahead, refrigerating the carrots and reserved leeks separately.

3. To serve, gently reheat the carrots in the same skillet. When they are hot, stir in the reserved leeks. Heat through and adjust the seasoning. Serve hot.

Grilling Corn

Grilling freshly picked corn is one of summer's best pleasures. It's a terrific way to enjoy it with a taste of the fire, and nothing could be more simple. Soak the corn in its husks in cold water for about 30 minutes. Leave the silk on. It gets singed in the process of grilling and gives the corn a nice smoky taste. Place the corn on the grill over a low-to-medium fire; the corn actually steams. Turn it every 5 minutes for a total of about 20 minutes. To serve, carefully remove the husks and silk (I use paper towels as a pot holder to help handle the heat). You can place the corn right on a warm platter and take it to the table, or put it back on the grill for 5 minutes, brushed with a little butter and sprinkled with salt.

Corn Flan with Onions and Bacon

This corn dish is perfect to serve when whole ears may be too awkward to handle. The flan has very little custard, just enough to hold the corn and onions together. Nueske's applewood-smoked bacon makes the difference in taste; alternately, use bacon that is mildly smoked and not overly salted. This is a do-ahead recipe with two options; the flan can be mixed a day ahead, refrigerated overnight, and baked the next day, or it can be fully baked a day ahead and reheated at serving time, depending on your schedule.

YIELD: 6 SERVINGS

1 tablespoon unsalted butter
1 large sweet onion, minced, about 2 cups
1 tablespoon water
4 large ears of corn, kernels cut off, about 2²/₃ cups
2 large eggs
¹/₃ cup milk (regular or 2 percent)
¹/₄ teaspoon each: salt, freshly grated nutmeg
Freshly ground pepper to taste
2 thick slices applewood-smoked bacon (See Midwestern Sources, page 376), cooked crisp, crumbled

1. Put a rack in the center of the oven; preheat the oven to 325 degrees. Generously grease a 4- to 5-cup-capacity shallow baking dish. Set aside.

2. Heat the butter in a 10-inch nonstick skillet over high heat. When it is hot, add the onion. Cook for 1 minute until hot, stirring often. Add the water; cook the onion until slightly tender, about 3 minutes more. Remove from the heat and stir in the corn.

3. Whisk the eggs in a 2-quart bowl until frothy. Add the milk and seasonings. Stir in the corn mixture and transfer to the prepared dish. The flan can be prepared ahead to this point and refrigerated overnight (refrigerate the bacon separately, wrapped in plastic). Garnish with the crumbled bacon just before baking.

4. Bake until the custard is set in the center, about 40 minutes (slightly longer if the flan was refrigerated). To test for doneness, gently shake the dish—the center should not jiggle if set. Serve hot.

5. The flan can also be made ahead and refrigerated overnight. Reheat, covered, in a preheated 300-degree oven for 30 minutes. Alternately, reheat in a microwave oven at medium power (50 percent), covered with waxed paper, until hot, about 4 minutes.

Goose Island Honey-Roasted Root Vegetables

This is a simple vegetable dish that enhances roasted meats and poultry. These vegetables are so named for the rich Chicago-area farmlands where vegetables once grew in profusion. Root cellars kept these root vegetables crisp and fresh during the cold winter months. I've seen several root cellars in the Midwest; it's amazing that these primitive damp and cold, dirt-floored areas kept vegetables longer than our refrigerators seem to do today.

YIELD: 4 SERVINGS

4 each: medium carrots, medium parsnips, peeled, cut
 into 1¹/₄-inch diagonal chunks, about 2 cups each
2 medium turnips, peeled, quartered, about 2 cups
6 large cloves garlic, peeled
1 tablespoon unsalted butter
3 tablespoons honey
2 tablespoons fresh lemon juice
¹/₄ teaspoon each: salt, cinnamon
Freshly ground pepper to taste

1. Put a rack in the center of the oven; preheat the oven to 350 degrees. Grease a shallow baking dish, large enough to hold the vegetables in a single layer without crowding them too much. Set aside.

2. Bring 6 cups salted water to a boil in a 4-quart pot. Add the carrots, parsnips, and turnips. Cook 4 minutes. Add the garlic and cook 2 minutes more. The vegetables will just be blanched, they will not be tender. Drain in a colander.

3. Melt the butter with the remaining ingredients in the same pot. When hot, add the vegetables and toss gently to coat them. Transfer them to the prepared dish. The vegetables can be made 2 days ahead to this point and refrigerated, covered airtight.

4. Roast the vegetables, uncovered, for 40 minutes; use a spatula to turn them twice during roasting. Increase the heat to 425 degrees. Continue to roast until they are lightly browned, about 20 minutes more, turning once. Lightly sprinkle with salt. Serve hot.

Sautéed Woodland Mushrooms with Sliced Green Onions

These mushrooms have a great taste and a lively look. Serve them as a garnish with simply roasted or grilled beef, lamb, poultry, or game. They are also delicious on an open-face grilled cheese sandwich.

YIELD: 4 SERVINGS

1¹/₂ tablespoons each: olive oil, unsalted butter
2 large cloves garlic, sliced paper-thin,
    about 1 tablespoon
1 pound wild mushrooms (shiitake and/or cremini),
    trimmed, sliced, about 6 cups
¹/₄ cup Beef Stock (page 366) or broth
2 tablespoons ruby red port wine
¹/₄ teaspoon salt
Freshly ground pepper to taste
4 medium scallions, thinly sliced, about 1 cup

1. Heat the oil and butter in a 12-inch nonstick skillet over medium-high heat. When hot, add the garlic and mushrooms. Cook, uncovered, until the mushrooms are just beginning to turn limp, about 3 minutes, stirring often.

2. Add the beef stock or broth, the port wine, salt, and pepper. Simmer until the mushrooms are just softened but still have texture, about 2 minutes. Remove from the heat. They can be cooked several hours ahead to this point and kept at room temperature.

3. To serve, gently reheat just until hot. Toss with the scallions and continue to heat through, about 20 seconds. Adjust the seasoning. Serve hot.

Morels

Morel mushrooms—exotic, pricey, sophisticated, sought-after, and prevalent in the Midwest—are veritable treasures, never to be taken for granted. At about $20 a pound during their brief spring season, morels are dark brown and shaped like a rounded hollow tree with a spongy texture and pitted cap. Varying in size from a small wild strawberry to a large lamb chop, morels grow prolifically in Wisconsin, Michigan, Iowa, and some parts of northwestern Illinois. A successful mycophile can count on a cache of several pounds, and will eat the prized morels in every way imaginable, from the simplest sauté in butter with shallots to batter-fried.

How to Cook Hard Squash into
Soft Submission . . .

Squash needs to be cooked until completely soft and squooshy in order to be smoothly pureed. This can be accomplished by baking, microwaving, or steaming the squash. For all methods, pierce the surface of the squash in several places with a fork. Cooking times vary with the size of the vegetable; the following times are based on large squashes weighing about 2¼ pounds. For smaller sizes, just decrease the cooking time accordingly.

❖ To bake, place it on a baking sheet and bake in 375-degree oven, turning it over once halfway through the cooking, until very soft, about 1 hour, 20 minutes.

❖ To microwave, place it on a paper plate and cook on high power (100 percent), turning once, until very soft, about 19 minutes.

❖ To steam, cut it in half. Put the halves in a large steamer basket, cut side down, over rapidly boiling water. Cover and cook until very soft, about 23 minutes. Drain on paper toweling.

❖ To puree cooked squash, cut it in half when cool enough to handle and then remove seeds and stringy membrane. Spoon the flesh into a processor or, in batches, into a blender. Puree until completely smooth, about 2 minutes, stopping once to scrape down the sides of the container.

Spiced Squash Pancakes

Leftover squash has many uses, one of the best is in pancakes. Be sure to put some extra squash in the oven while you're at it. Any winter squash will do (except spaghetti squash); it must be baked until soft so it purees into a smooth batter. These pancakes are deliciously lowfat and light-tasting; they're excellent plain or with currants, dried cranberries, or pecans added for texture, if you desire. Serve them as a vegetable side dish with any simply roasted or grilled meat, poultry, or game dinner. They're also an option for breakfast, brunch, lunch, or supper, topped with maple syrup or maple cream, apple butter, applesauce, or sautéed sliced apples. The recipe can be easily doubled or tripled.

YIELD: ABOUT 2 TO 4 SERVINGS AS A SIDE DISH; EIGHT 4-INCH PANCAKES

1 cup pureed cooked winter squash
4 large egg whites
$1/3$ cup milk (1 percent or regular)
2 tablespoons dark brown sugar
$1/2$ teaspoon ground cinnamon
$1/4$ teaspoon freshly grated nutmeg (see page 289)
$2/3$ cup cake flour
Scant $1/2$ teaspoon baking soda
Generous pinch of salt
Unsalted butter, for sautéing

1. Put all the ingredients except the butter in a food processor fitted with the metal blade or in a blender. Mix until smooth.

2. Heat a nonstick griddle with just enough butter to coat the surface. When it is hot, spoon the batter into 4-inch rounds. Cook them in batches over medium heat until well browned on both sides, turning only once, about 6 minutes altogether. Keep the pancakes warm in a preheated 200-degree oven while the remaining pancakes are being cooked. Serve hot.

Harvest Ratatouille

I find the fall harvest in the Midwest colorful and exciting, with all the vegetables for ratatouille loaded up at the farmer's markets. Between my passion for the harvest and my love of ratatouille, I've made many versions of this dish over the years. The secret to this version is the slow-cooking onions, which I learned from Richard Olney and Lulu Peyraud in their wonderful cookbook Lulu's Provençal Table *(HarperCollins, 1994); the onions caramelize and sweeten the whole mixture. The only other vegetable I cook separately is the eggplant, to develop its flavor and to add it toward the end of cooking so that it doesn't end up mushy. This proportion of vegetables can be varied according to your taste; for me, it just turns out to be an optimum balance. The vegetables are cut rather chunky so that they are discernible in the final mix. If the tomatoes lack sweetness and flavor, add a little tomato paste to bolster them. This recipe makes a large batch; you can decrease it easily by a third. Adding a tablespoon of the oil at the end of cooking gives a seemingly rich finish without using much oil. Try to make this a day or two ahead of serving it; like any stew-type mixture, its flavor improves as it stands.*

YIELD: 8 TO 10 SERVINGS

¹/₄ cup olive oil

2 medium Spanish onions, halved, thinly sliced, about
   4¹/₂ cups

7 small (not baby) zucchini, cut into ¹/₂-inch-wide by
   1¹/₂-inch-long matchsticks, about 7 cups

3 large cloves garlic, thinly sliced, about 1¹/₂ tablespoons

1 teaspoon salt

1 each: large red, yellow, and green bell pepper, cut
   into 1-inch squares, about 4 cups

3 firm, ripe large tomatoes, seeded, cut into
   1-inch chunks, about 2¹/₄ cups

3 bay leaves

1¹/₂ teaspoons dried thyme

¹/₂ teaspoon freshly ground black pepper

2 medium eggplants, unpeeled, cut into 1-inch-square
   dice, about 8 cups

1 to 2 tablespoons tomato paste (optional)

1. Heat 1 tablespoon of the oil in a wide (about 10 inches across) heavy pot. When the oil is very hot, add the onions. Cook over medium heat, covered, for 10 minutes (until there's some moisture from the onions). Stir the onions occasionally. After 10 minutes, cook, uncovered, over medium-high heat, stirring often until the onions turn a light brown (but do not burn), about 8 to 10 minutes more.

2. Add the zucchini, garlic, and ¹/₂ teaspoon of the salt. Cook 5 minutes, stirring often. Add the red, yellow, and green peppers, the tomatoes, bay leaves, thyme, and pepper. Simmer, covered, until the vegetables are just about tender, about 20 to 30 minutes, stirring often to prevent burning. Check often to avoid overcooking (unless you want a very cooked-down, soft mixture).

3. Meanwhile, heat 1 more tablespoon of the oil in a 12-inch nonstick skillet. When hot, add half of the eggplant, sprinkled with $1/4$ teaspoon of the remaining salt. Brown it quickly over medium-high heat, about 2 to 3 minutes, shaking the pan to brown the eggplant evenly. Remove from the pan and set aside. Repeat with 1 more tablespoon oil, the remaining salt, and the remaining eggplant.

4. When the vegetables are almost as tender as desired, add the eggplant to the pot. Stir well. Cook, covered, until the eggplant is just tender, about 10 minutes: The vegetables will continue to cook after they're removed from the stove. Stir in the remaining oil. Cool. Adjust the seasoning. Refrigerate 1 to 2 days before serving.

5. To serve, stir the ratatouille and adjust the seasoning. Remove and discard the bay leaves. Serve hot, at room temperature, or chilled. Gently reheat if serving hot.

Baked Sweet and Sour Red Cabbage

This delicious hearty version of sweet and sour cabbage bakes in the oven, requiring very little attention from the cook. Adding some of the vinegar after the cabbage is cooked restores its wonderful deep red color. Serve it with Brisket of Beef with Caramelized Onion Sauce (page 121) or grilled sausage.

YIELD: 6 SERVINGS

1 tablespoon vegetable oil

3 thick slices bacon, cut into small dice, about 1/2 cup

1 medium onion, chopped, about 1 1/4 cups

1 medium red cabbage, thinly sliced, about 10 cups

1 large apple, unpeeled, cored, thinly sliced, about 2 cups

3/4 cup dry red wine

7 tablespoons red wine vinegar

3 1/2 tablespoons sugar

1/2 teaspoon salt

Freshly ground pepper to taste

1. Put a rack in the lower third of the oven; preheat the oven to 350 degrees.

2. In a large nonaluminum ovenproof pot, heat the oil over medium-high heat. When hot, add the bacon and onion. Cook until the onion is lightly browned, about 4 minutes, stirring often. Add the cabbage, apple, wine, 3 tablespoons of the vinegar, the sugar, 1/2 teaspoon salt, and the pepper. Mix well.

3. Bake, covered, about 1 1/2 hours, stirring every half-hour. Stir in the remaining vinegar. Adjust the seasoning, sugar, and vinegar as needed. The cabbage can be made a day ahead and refrigerated.

4. To serve, reheat, covered, in a preheated 350-degree oven until hot, about 30 minutes, stirring occasionally. Adjust the seasoning.

Corn Fritters

What I especially like about these lowfat fritters is their texture; the batter is light and the kernels of corn are very evident. When sweet young corn is not available, coarsely chop (do not puree) larger kernels in the food processor and add a pinch of sugar to the batter. Serve the fritters as a vegetable side dish with any simply prepared entree or as an hors d'oeuvre with a dollop of salsa on top. This recipe can also be made with leftover cooked corn, cut off the cob.

**YIELD: ABOUT 4 TO 6 SERVINGS;
FOURTEEN TO SIXTEEN 2 1/2-INCH FRITTERS**

4 young medium ears of corn, kernels cut off, about 2 cups
2 tablespoons flour
3 tablespoons minced green onion or 2 tablespoons snipped fresh chives
4 large egg whites
3/4 teaspoon ground cumin
1/2 teaspoon salt
Freshly ground pepper to taste
2 tablespoons peanut oil, for frying

1. Put all the ingredients except the oil in a mixing bowl. Mix until well combined.

2. Heat 2 teaspoons of the oil in a nonstick griddle or a 12-inch nonstick skillet over medium-high heat. When the oil is hot, swirl the pan to coat the entire surface with oil. Use a generous tablespoon of batter for each fritter. Cook until both sides are well browned, about 3 minutes total. Add 1 teaspoon oil, heat the pan until hot, and fry the remaining fritters the same way. Repeat until all are fried. Keep the cooked fritters warm in a preheated 200-degree oven while the remaining fritters are frying. Serve hot.

Corn, Right off the Cob . . .

It often comes as a shock that fresh young corn-at-its-prime can be eaten (and savored) without first cooking it. If munching it right off the cob seems too barbaric, the kernels can be cut and used in a variety of ways, just as they are. Here's how:

❖ As a summer corn salad with onion, tomatoes, and peppers in a fresh herb dressing, or as an ingredient in potato, pasta, or mixed green salads.

❖ As a garnish for cold or hot soups.

❖ Mixed into sandwich spreads, grilled cheese sandwiches, and tortillas.

❖ Stirred into muffins, breads, or pancakes as well as pilafs and polentas.

❖ To make a corn salsa with corn, green onions, lime juice, and herbs.

Grilling Vegetables

The barbecue grill and the taste and character of fresh farmstand vegetables were made for each other. To grill favorite vegetables such as tomatoes, onions, zucchini, peppers, and eggplant, cut them into slices or slabs and brush them lightly with garlic oil or herbed oil or just season them, without any oil at all. Set them on a clean, greased grill that is medium hot . . . not too hot. The cooking time will vary depending on the heat and the vegetable. Keep a watchful eye to prevent them from burning.

Grilled Portobellos with Garlic Oil

Portobellos are abundant (and at a fraction of their supermarket price) at the farmers' markets. This is an appealing mushroom presentation, a great platter garnish for meats, game, and poultry, or a perfect buffet option. The hot mushrooms are served on red leaf lettuce leaves, garnished with paper-thin slices of fresh garlic (which can be pushed aside), and a sprinkle of diced fresh tomato. A magnificent sight, especially to mushroom (and garlic) lovers. Generously brush both sides of the mushrooms with the warm oil at least 10 minutes in advance of cooking to flavor them. Be sure to save enough oil for brushing both before they are grilled (or broiled) and after.

YIELD: 4 SERVINGS

4 portobello mushroom caps, each about 4 to 5 inches in diameter, gently cleaned with a soft brush
¹/₄ cup Garlic Oil (page 363), warm
Salt and freshly ground pepper to taste
8 to 12 leaves red leaf lettuce
2 small cloves garlic, sliced paper-thin (the ultra-thin slicing disc of the processor does a great job), about 1 teaspoon
¹/₄ cup diced outer shell of plum tomatoes

1. Prepare a medium-hot fire for grilling or put the broiler rack 10 inches from the heat source and preheat the broiler.

2. Arrange the mushroom caps on a jelly roll pan (cookie sheet with sides). Generously brush warm oil on both sides of the mushrooms. Let the mushrooms stand at least 10 minutes.

3. To cook, lightly brush both sides of the mushroom caps again with the warm oil. Sprinkle generously with salt and pepper. To grill, place them rounded side down until they are very hot and sizzling, about 4 minutes. Turn with tongs and continue to grill until they are totally tender but not mushy, about 2 to 3 minutes more. To broil, place the caps rounded side down on the jelly roll pan. Broil until lightly browned and sizzling, about 3 minutes; do not overcook. Turn with tongs and continue to broil until they are browned and tender but not mushy (do not overcook), about 3 minutes more.

4. To serve, arrange the lettuce leaves attractively on a platter. Arrange mushrooms on the lettuce leaves. Garnish with sliced garlic and diced tomato. Gently brush the mushrooms, garlic, and tomato with the remaining oil. Serve immediately.

Stuffed Onions with Garlicky Spinach

Ring any platter with these onions; they're very decorative as well as delicious,
pairing well with beef, lamb, pork, poultry, or fish.

YIELD: 4 SERVINGS

2 quarts salted water
4 small-to-medium onions, peeled but with tops intact
   (so they do not fall apart)
1 pound young spinach, stemmed, about 6 cups leaves
1 1/2 tablespoons olive oil
2 large cloves garlic, minced, about 1 tablespoon
3 anchovy fillets, washed, blotted dry, finely chopped
Salt and freshly ground pepper to taste
1 to 1 1/2 cups Chicken Stock (page 364)
   or lower-salt broth

1. Bring salted water to a boil in a 4-quart pot. Cut off the upper quarter of the onion (this top piece will be the "lid" on the stuffed onion). Use a melon baller to scoop out the flesh from the bottom part, leaving about a 1/3-inch shell (reserve the scooped onion for another use).

2. Simmer the onion lids and bottoms, in the boiling salted water, covered, until just tender but still very much intact, about 4 minutes. Use a slotted spoon to remove the onion bottoms and lids. Reserve the water. Invert the onions on paper towels to drain. The onions can be cooked several hours ahead and kept at room temperature.

3. Bring the onion water back to a boil. Add the spinach leaves (use a wooden spoon to push the leaves into the water). After 1 minute, drain the spinach in a colander. Do not press out the liquid but let it drain naturally.

4. Heat the oil in a 12-inch nonstick skillet over medium heat. When hot, add the garlic and stir-fry until it is fragrant and golden, about 10 seconds; do not burn. Add the spinach and anchovies. Increase the heat to high. Use tongs or a fork to keep tossing the spinach so that the garlic and anchovies are well distributed. Cook until the mixture is hot, about 1 minute. Adjust the seasoning with salt and pepper.

5. Divide the spinach stuffing among the onions; top with the lids. Use a fork to arrange the spinach so that it's visible around the edge of the lid. The onions can be stuffed several hours ahead and kept at room temperature.

6. To cook, arrange the onions in a single layer in a shallow lidded pan just large enough to hold them tightly. Add enough broth to come halfway up the sides of the onions. Bring the liquid to a boil. Simmer, covered, until the onions are hot, about 5 to 7 minutes. Use a slotted spoon to remove the onions (reserve the broth for another use). Serve hot.

The Blackhawk's Creamed Spinach

The Blackhawk in Chicago was Don Roth's landmark restaurant and a much-sought-after destination for Chicagoans and tourists alike. It was the home of the spinning salad assembled and tossed at tableside, huge rib roasts in large covered carts . . . and creamed spinach. Here's The Blackhawk's delicious recipe; I've decreased the cream and increased the milk without any compromise in taste.

YIELD: ABOUT 3 TO 4 SERVINGS

2 tablespoons finely chopped salt pork
1 small onion, finely chopped, about ¹/₂ cup
Two 10-ounce packages frozen chopped spinach,
*   thawed, gently squeezed of moisture but*
*   not squeezed dry*
2 tablespoons each: unsalted butter, flour
¹/₄ cup heavy cream
1 cup milk (regular or 1 percent)
¹/₂ teaspoon salt
Freshly ground pepper to taste

1. Cook the salt pork, covered, in a 10-inch skillet over medium heat until the fat is rendered, about 6 minutes. Add the onion and cook until it is golden brown, about 8 minutes, stirring often. Stir in the spinach. Remove from the heat and set aside.

2. Heat the butter in a 1-quart saucepan over medium heat until it is melted. Stir in the flour. Cook 2 minutes, stirring often. Slowly stir in the cream and milk. Bring to a simmer gradually and cook until thickened, about 2 minutes, stirring constantly. Add the seasonings and reserved spinach. Stir well. Heat through. Adjust the seasoning.

3. The spinach can be made a day ahead and refrigerated, covered airtight; the nice green color may diminish a bit but not the taste. To serve, gently reheat in a saucepan or, alternately, in a microwave oven on high power (100 percent) until hot, about 1 to 1¹/₂ minutes. Adjust the seasoning.

Mashed Potatoes with Celery Root and Parsnip

A simple blending of roots—celery root, potatoes, and parsnip—makes this mashed potato dish as smooth as silk without much fat. The russet potatoes have just the right starchy texture to thicken the mixture. Celery root browns quickly once its surface is exposed to the air, so have the salted water boiling, ready for the peeled celery root (and potatoes). This is a great accompaniment for the Venison Stew with Red Onions, Dried Cranberries, and Wild Mushrooms (page 140) or the Orange-Roasted Chicken on Tossed Greens (page 152).

YIELD: 6 SERVINGS

2 medium celery roots, peeled, cut into 2-inch chunks,
    about 4 cups
2 large russet or Idaho potatoes, peeled, cut into 2-inch
    chunks, about 3¹/₂ cups
1 large parsnip, peeled, cut into 2-inch chunks,
    about 1²/₃ cups
1¹/₂ quarts boiling salted water
4 large cloves garlic, peeled
1¹/₂ tablespoons unsalted butter
³/₄ teaspoon each: salt, freshly grated nutmeg
    (see page 289)
Freshly ground pepper to taste

1. Put a rack in the center of the oven: preheat the oven to 300 degrees. Grease a 5-cup soufflé or baking dish. Set aside.

2. Plunge the celery roots, potatoes, and parsnip into the boiling water. Simmer, covered, 15 minutes. Add the garlic cloves. Cook until the vegetables are soft, about 10 minutes more. Drain the vegetables.

3. Put the hot drained vegetables, the butter, salt, nutmeg, and pepper into a food processor fitted with the metal blade. Puree until the mixture is

very smooth, about 1 to 2 minutes, stopping to scrape down the sides of the bowl. Adjust the seasoning. Transfer the mixture to the prepared baking dish. Cover the dish with foil. The mashed potatoes can be made several hours ahead to this point and kept at room temperature.

4. To serve, bake, covered, until hot, about 30 minutes. Alternately, reheat in a microwave oven on high power (100 percent) until hot, about 2 to 3 minutes. Serve hot.

Celery Root

Celery root, also known as celeriac, is a wonderful, deep-flavored root vegetable widely used in European cooking. This special celery has been cultivated specifically for its root (although the leaves can be used as an herb); it's totally different from the bunches of celery we know so well. It delivers an intense celery taste with an edge of parsley.

At farmers' markets in the Midwest, you can find creamy celery roots with long green stems and leaves still intact; these vegetables command your attention. The celery root with the leaves detached, however, may be the most homely member of the vegetable family, what with its shaggy brown skin mottled with lots of irregular nooks and crevices.

Like many root vegetables, celery root stores well throughout the winter and is available until spring. But it is best in the fall, when it's freshly harvested.

Remove the peel with a very sharp knife so that there is little waste. Toss the tough peels straight into the trash rather than the disposal or they're apt to cause a visit from the plumber. Peeled root, soaked briefly in lemon or vinegar water, won't discolor. A food processor slices and shreds celery root with quick and easy perfection. Otherwise, a firm serrated knife should be used for slicing it.

Double-Baked Potatoes with Horseradish

Here, two big Midwest crops—horseradish and potatoes—work together to produce great taste in this twice-baked preparation. Serve with simply grilled meats, poultry, or fish. It's a great do-ahead, and the recipe can be easily increased to serve a crowd.

YIELD: 4 SERVINGS

2 large russet or Idaho potatoes
1 teaspoon vegetable oil
2 tablespoons unsalted butter
1 small onion, minced, about $^1/_2$ cup
1 medium clove garlic, minced, about $^3/_4$ teaspoon
$^1/_3$ cup heavy cream
1 tablespoon drained white horseradish
Generous $^1/_4$ teaspoon salt
Freshly ground pepper to taste
$^3/_4$ cup grated imported Parmesan cheese

1. Put a rack in the center of the oven; preheat the oven to 400 degrees. Lightly coat the potatoes with oil. Bake the potatoes until they are tender (to test, pierce with a knife), about 50 minutes. Alternately, cook them in a microwave oven on high power (100 percent) for 6 minutes, then bake in a 400-degree oven until they are tender and the skins are crisp, about 10 to 15 minutes. When they are cool enough to handle, split the potatoes lengthwise and scoop out the flesh, leaving about a $^1/_4$-inch shell.

2. Melt the butter in small nonstick skillet over medium-high heat. Add the onion and garlic. Cook until the onion is softened, about 4 minutes, stirring often. Transfer the mixture to a 2-cup mixing bowl. Add the scooped-out potato, the cream, horseradish, salt, pepper, and half the cheese. Use a potato masher to make the mixture as smooth as possible. Adjust the seasoning. Divide the potato mixture among the 4 half skins. Sprinkle evenly with the remaining cheese. The potatoes can be made a day ahead to this point. Arrange them on a cookie sheet, cover airtight, and refrigerate.

3. To serve, bake, uncovered, in a preheated 375-degree oven until the cheese has browned, about 20 minutes, slightly longer if potatoes have been refrigerated. Serve hot.

Potatoes

We may consider the potato a staple, but not to the extent expressed in *Buckeye Cookery and Practical Housekeeping*, circa 1880. "Potatoes in Seven Ways" instructs the cook to mash them on Sunday, bake them in their jackets on Monday, bake them with roast beef on Tuesday, slice and serve them Kentucky-style on Wednesday, steam them whole on Thursday, fry them as pancakes on Friday, and boil them unskinned on Saturday. Potatoes for every day of the week.

Oven Country "Fries"

These potatoes are double-cooked. First, they are seared on the stove. Fortunately, this can be done several hours in advance. About a half-hour before dinner, pop them into the preheated oven. At the last minute of baking, the potatoes are tossed with the garlic and cheese (mince the garlic, red pepper flakes, and cheese in the food processor for a uniformly fine texture) and baked until the cheese melts and the garlic is fragrant. Easy enough. Use Parmigiano-Reggiano; it makes a big difference.

YIELD: 4 TO 6 SERVINGS

5 large russet or Idaho potatoes, peeled, quartered
  lengthwise, placed in cold water to cover
2¹/₂ tablespoons olive oil (not extra-virgin)
¹/₃ cup grated imported Parmesan cheese
3 large cloves garlic, finely minced,
  about 1¹/₂ tablespoons
¹/₄ teaspoon red pepper flakes
Salt to taste

1. Put a rack in the center of the oven; preheat the oven to 425 degrees. Set aside a heavy shallow roasting pan large enough to hold the potatoes in a single layer without crowding them.

2. Drain the potatoes; blot them very dry with paper towels.

3. Heat the oil in the roasting pan over medium-high heat. When it is hot, add the potatoes in a single layer. Brown them on all sides, turning them with a metal spatula as they brown, about 9 minutes total. Remove from the heat. The potatoes can be made several hours in advance to this point and kept in the pan at room temperature.

4. Put cheese, garlic, and red pepper flakes into a food processor fitted with a metal blade or in blender. Process until finely textured. Set aside.

5. To finish, place the potatoes in the hot oven. Bake until they are tender, about 25 minutes. Use tongs to turn them once midway through cooking. Just before removing them from the oven, sprinkle with the cheese mixture. Bake 1 minute longer, or until the cheese melts.

6. To serve, transfer the potatoes to a heated serving dish. Sprinkle with salt. Serve hot.

Warm Russet Potato Pancakes

These potato pancakes are really good; their simplicity is their success. It's a recipe from Mark Baker, the executive chef of Chicago's Four Seasons Hotel restaurant, Seasons. They can be served with the simplest roasted meats and poultry or with stews. They also make a great brunch or supper dish, topped with poached eggs and a sprinkling of chives or apple slices sautéed in a combination of butter and maple syrup. Russet and Idaho potatoes are interchangeable and the processor does a quick shredding job. These are successful do-aheads, although they are great right off the griddle.

YIELD: ABOUT 4 SERVINGS, TWELVE 3-INCH-DIAMETER PANCAKES

3 large russet or Idaho potatoes, peeled, coarsely
   shredded, about 7 cups
¼ cup each: flour, milk
1 large egg
2 large green onions, thinly sliced, about ½ cup
¾ teaspoon salt
¼ teaspoon freshly grated nutmeg (see page 289)
Freshly ground pepper to taste
3 tablespoons each: unsalted butter, vegetable oil,
   for frying

1. When you are ready to cook the pancakes, combine all the ingredients except the butter and oil in a large bowl. The potatoes will darken considerably if the mixture is allowed to stand. Even so, the mixture will lose its white color but that's not apparent in the cooked pancake.

2. Heat 1 tablespoon each of the butter and oil on a nonstick griddle or in a 12-inch nonstick skillet over medium heat. When it is very hot, use a ¼-cup measure of the potato mixture for each pancake. Drop onto hot griddle, leaving 1-inch space between each. Use a fork to shape each pancake into a 3-inch round. Lightly compress the pancake with a metal spatula. As the liquid accumulates in the bowl, stir the mixture to moisten it and drain off the excess but do not squeeze it dry.

3. Cook until the underside is brown, about 4 to 5 minutes. Turn and cook until the other side is brown and the potato is tender, about 4 to 5 minutes more. Keep the pancakes warm in a preheated 250-degree oven while you cook the remaining pancakes, adding equal quantities of butter and oil to the griddle as needed. Serve hot.

4. These pancakes can be made several hours ahead. Once they are cool, stack them, separated by pieces of waxed paper, and refrigerate. To serve, arrange the pancakes in a single layer on baking sheets. Put the racks in the center area of a preheated 300-degree oven. Bake 10 minutes. Use a spatula to turn the pancakes. Bake 10 minutes longer. Serve hot.

Chive Cream

This mixture is great spooned onto the Warm Russet Potato Pancakes, baked potatoes, or as a spread on thick slices of grilled bread.

YIELD: 1 1/2 CUPS

1¹/₂ cups crème fraîche or sour cream
¹/₂ cup finely snipped fresh chives
2 tablespoons olive oil
1 to 2 teaspoons fresh lemon juice
Salt and freshly ground white pepper to taste

Combine the ingredients (using only 1 teaspoon lemon juice) in a 1-quart bowl. Adjust the lemon and seasoning. The chive cream can be prepared a day ahead and refrigerated, covered airtight.

Aunt Mary's Stuffed Artichokes

*This makes a wonderful meal, served with an Herb Garden Salad with Tomato and
Olive Vinaigrette (page 85). Medium (not huge) whole artichokes are stuffed with a
garlic–bread crumb mixture that becomes moist during cooking and adheres to the leaves.
The artichokes become perfectly tender and the flavor is great! Serve them hot, with a cruet
of fruity olive oil and a pepper grinder on the table. Use your fingers to remove the leaves,
then eat the breading and the "meat" on each leaf. You'll need a knife and fork for the
remaining stuffing and the heart. Bread crumbs made from day-old bread are far superior
to any that are commercially packaged. Whenever you have leftover high-quality bread, let
it sit on the counter overnight, trim away the crusts, cut the bread into small chunks and
crumb them in the food processor fitted with a metal blade. Wrap the crumbs in airtight
double plastic bags and freeze them until needed.*

YIELD: 4 SERVINGS

4 medium artichokes

STUFFING:
2 cups day-old bread crumbs
$^1/_3$ cup grated imported Parmesan cheese
   (Parmigiano-Reggiano)
1 large clove garlic, minced, about $^1/_2$ tablespoon
$^1/_3$ cup minced fresh parsley leaves
$3^1/_2$ tablespoons olive oil
$^1/_4$ teaspoon salt
Freshly ground black pepper to taste

Olive oil, coarsely cracked pepper, for serving

1. Set aside a deep casserole just large enough to
hold the artichokes snugly. Keep a kettle of water
boiling.

2. Remove the dark green outer leaves from the
artichokes. Trim the stems flat so that the
artichokes are stable. Cut $^3/_4$ inch off the top of the
artichokes with a stainless-steel serrated knife. Turn
the artichokes over and press on the stem end
firmly to spread and loosen the inner leaves. Under
cold running water, spread the outer leaves and pull
out the light inner leaves. Use a sharp grapefruit
spoon to remove the hairy choke. Rinse thoroughly.
Invert the artichokes on paper towels to drain.

3. For the stuffing, combine the bread crumbs with
$^1/_2$ cup of the cheese, the garlic, parsley, 2
tablespoons of the oil, the salt, and the pepper in a
small dish. Alternately, these ingredients can be
mixed in the food processor fitted with the metal
blade.

4. To assemble, divide the stuffing evenly among
the artichokes, first filling the centers, then tucking

small amounts down between the leaves. Stand the artichokes in the casserole.

5. To cook, carefully pour the boiling water to a depth of 1 inch around the artichokes. Lightly salt the water. Drizzle the remaining olive oil over the artichokes; sprinkle the remaining cheese over each. Simmer, with the cover slightly askew to let out a little steam, until tender (a paring knife should go through the center easily), about 30 minutes. Check the water level occasionally; add more as needed.

6. To serve, use tongs to transfer the artichokes to a heated serving platter. Pass the olive oil separately along with a pepper grinder. Serve hot.

Eggplant Rolatini

One of my favorite neighborhood restaurants in the northern suburbs of Chicago is Gusto Italiano in Glenview. Their Eggplant Rolatini is a great specialty. It takes a little time to assemble, but it can be completely prepared up to 2 days in advance and baked just before dinner. Papery-thin slices of eggplant are sautéed and rolled around a creamy ricotta and spinach filling; tomato sauce and mozzarella cheese finish it off. Serve with a tossed green salad.

YIELD: 4 TO 6 SERVINGS

1 large eggplant (at least 1 pound), peeled
4 large eggs
¼ cup water
½ cup grated Romano cheese
¾ teaspoon salt
¾ cup flour
¼ cup olive oil
1 cup loosely packed spinach leaves
One 15-ounce carton ricotta cheese, drained

TOPPING:
2 cups store-bought spaghetti sauce
1½ cups shredded mozzarella cheese

1. Put a rack in the center of the oven; preheat the oven to 325 degrees. Set aside a 9-inch-square baking dish.

2. Cut one long side of the eggplant flat. Rest it on this flat side and cut the eggplant into at least 12 long, very thin slices. Ideally, each slice should be about ⅛ inch thick.

3. Put 3 of the eggs, the water, ¼ cup of the Romano cheese, and ¼ teaspoon of the salt in a shallow dish or pie plate. Whisk until mixed. Put the flour in another shallow dish or pie plate. Heat

1½ tablespoons of the oil in a large nonstick skillet over medium-high heat until it is hot.

4. Use tongs to dip the eggplant slices first in flour, then in the egg mixture. Shake off any excess. Fry the eggplant in batches, turning once, until they are very lightly browned on both sides, about 6 minutes total. Drain on paper towels. Add more oil and reheat the skillet as needed for remaining slices.

5. Mince the spinach leaves in a food processor fitted with a metal blade or by hand. Put the spinach leaves, the remaining Romano cheese, egg, salt, and the ricotta cheese in a bowl. Use a fork to combine.

6. To assemble, fill each eggplant slice as follows: spoon a generous 2 tablespoons of the filling at the bottom of the slice. Roll it up as tightly as possible without letting the filling come out the sides.

7. Spread 1 cup of spaghetti sauce in the baking dish; arrange the eggplant rolls, seam side down, over the sauce. Top with the remaining sauce. Sprinkle the mozzarella cheese evenly over the rolls. The eggplant rolatini can be prepared to this point up to 2 days in advance, covered tightly, and refrigerated. Bring them to room temperature before baking.

8. To serve, bake, uncovered, until sizzling hot, about 45 to 50 minutes. Serve hot. Leftovers can be reheated, covered, in a preheated 325-degree oven or, alternately, in a microwave oven on high power (50 percent) until hot, timing dependent on amount being reheated.

Spaghetti Squash Lasagna

Crisp, crunchy golden strands of spaghetti squash stand in for the usual lasagna noodles in this baked vegetable dish. It can be completely cooked in advance and reheated, which makes it a great choice for family gatherings and potluck dinners.

YIELD: 4 TO 5 SERVINGS

SPAGHETTI SQUASH:

1 medium spaghetti squash, surface pricked with a fork, cooked until tender in the microwave oven on high power (100 percent) for about 12 minutes or baked in a 375-degree oven for 40 to 60 minutes, cooled until it can be handled
3 tablespoons flour
1 medium clove garlic, minced, about 3/4 teaspoon
1/2 teaspoon salt

RICOTTA MIXTURE:

One 15-ounce carton lowfat ricotta cheese, drained
1 cup packed spinach leaves
1/3 cup grated imported Parmesan cheese
 (Parmigiano-Reggiano)

1 cup store-bought spaghetti sauce
6 ounces sliced mozzarella cheese

1. Put a rack in the center of the oven; preheat the oven to 350 degrees. Set aside a shallow 6-cup-capacity baking dish and a cookie sheet.

2. Split the squash lengthwise. Remove the seeds and the stringy portion. Use a fork to "comb" the squash flesh, pulling it off in long strands. Put the flesh in a large mixing bowl and toss it with the flour, garlic, and salt until well combined.

3. For the ricotta mixture, put the ricotta, spinach, and Parmesan cheese in a food processor fitted with the metal blade or in a blender. Process until smooth.

4. To assemble, spread 1/2 cup of the spaghetti sauce on the bottom of the baking dish. Top with the spaghetti squash, arranging it evenly and compactly. Spread the ricotta mixture evenly over the squash. Spread the remaining sauce over the ricotta. Cover with the sliced mozzarella. Place the dish on the cookie sheet (to catch any juices).

5. Bake, uncovered, until the cheese is lightly browned on the edges and the juices bubbling, about 40 to 50 minutes. Cut into squares. Serve hot.

6. The lasagna can be cooked a day ahead, cooled completely, then refrigerated, covered airtight. To serve, reheat, uncovered, in a preheated 300-degree oven until hot, about 30 minutes.

Pizza Bread Pudding

*Serve this homey bread pudding with a salad of mixed greens for a perfect supper.
You can add other typical pizza ingredients to the pudding—green pepper, pepperoni,
cooked sausage, and mushrooms—although it is very tasty with just these basic
ingredients. When tomatoes are at their summer best, substitute 2 cups diced fresh
tomatoes and their juices for the canned diced tomatoes. This pudding can be baked
in advance and successfully reheated.*

YIELD: 4 TO 6 SERVINGS

2 cups crustless 1-inch day-old bread cubes
1 large egg
1 large egg white
One 14^1/$_2$-ounce can diced tomatoes in their juice
^{3}/$_4$ cup tomato juice
^{1}/$_2$ cup minced red onion
2 tablespoons finely julienned fresh basil
1 teaspoon dried oregano
1 tablespoon each: brown sugar, balsamic vinegar
^{1}/$_8$ teaspoon each: salt, red pepper flakes
^{3}/$_4$ cup shredded mozzarella cheese

1. Put a rack in the center of the oven; preheat the oven to 325 degrees. Lightly grease a 6-cup-capacity shallow baking dish. Set it aside with a jelly roll pan (a cookie sheet with sides).

2. Spread the bread cubes on the jelly roll pan. Bake until they are lightly toasted, about 15 minutes.

3. Meanwhile, put the egg and egg white in a 2-quart bowl. Froth with a fork. Add the diced tomatoes and their juice, the tomato juice, onion, basil, oregano, sugar, vinegar, salt, and red pepper flakes. Mix well. Add the baked bread cubes and toss well. Let the mixture stand until all the liquid is absorbed, about 15 minutes, tossing occasionally.

4. Transfer the mixture to the prepared baking dish and spread it evenly. Sprinkle with the cheese.

5. Bake, uncovered, until the cheese is lightly colored, about 45 minutes. Serve hot.

6. The pizza bread pudding can be made a day ahead and refrigerated. To serve, reheat, covered, in a preheated 350-degree oven until heated through, about 25 minutes.

Lightly Spiced Pilaf

Sautéed Wild Rice with Fennel, Currants, and Orange

Curried Garden Rice Casserole

Bulgur Wheat and Rice Pilaf with Vegetables

Toasted Barley and Mushroom Risotto

Vegetable Polenta with Mushroom-Tomato Sauce

Couscous with Vegetables and Wheat Berries

White Beans with Two Tomatoes

Quick Braised Cabbage with Bacon and Navy Beans

Chili Bean Bake

Casserole of Spinach, Black Beans, and Spicy Yellow Rice

Orzo with Goat Cheese, Tomato, and Fresh Basil

Penne with Escarole and Bacon

Farfalle (Bow Ties) with Broccoli, Red Pepper, and Garlic

Gremolata Fettuccine

Lemon Noodles with Poppy Seeds

Sweet Noodle and Apple Pudding

Chapter 9

Grains, Beans, and Pastas

❖

Even a casual glance at the new food pyramid (either one, actually: the USDA version or the Mediterranean diet version) and it is plain to see that grains, beans, and pastas are the foods of the nineties. Here in the Midwest, that could mean 1890s just as easily as the last of the twentieth century. The tradition runs deep.

North Dakota and Kansas are famous for the country's durum wheat crop, which provides the flour that ends up in all manner of pasta. Michigan is the leading producer of dried beans. Wild rice and Minnesota are all but synonymous.

What we have here isn't just the base of the pyramid (a sure indication that of these foods you can eat as much as you like, guilt free) but the base of inspired, delicious meals. With this in mind I have developed recipes that pull in two directions. On the one hand, you will find side dishes, some of which include vegetables. You will also find main-course dishes that celebrate the integrity of these base-line products and the ways in which they can hold up underlying ingredients for a flavorful display.

A Lightly Spiced Pilaf will have any dinner guest reaching for more. Toasted Barley and Mushroom Risotto; Couscous with Vegetables and Wheat Berries; Farfalle (Bow Ties) with Broccoli, Red Pepper, and Garlic: these dishes can stand alone just as easily as they complement a roast chicken or a slice of brisket. You just can't get much more Midwest than wild rice with currants. This is a dish that tastes like the lands that surround us.

There is something liberating about grains, beans, and pastas—a subtle permission to move beyond baked beans and macaroni and cheese and rice casseroles. Here at the base of the food pyramid are the beginnings of great dishes to come.

Lightly Spiced Pilaf

This is a simple combination of angel-hair pasta and rice that works well with meat or poultry recipes with highly flavored sauces. I like to serve it with Skewered Turkey, Red Peppers, and Onions (page 166).

YIELD: 6 SERVINGS

2 tablespoons safflower oil
4 ounces angel-hair pasta, broken into pieces
1¹/₂ cups uncooked rice
3 cups Chicken Stock (page 364) or lower-salt broth
¹/₄ teaspoon each: cinnamon, allspice
Freshly ground pepper to taste

1. Heat the oil in a 2-quart saucepan over medium-high heat. Add the pasta and rice. Cook until they are lightly browned, about 4 minutes, stirring constantly.

2. Add the stock or broth, the cinnamon, allspice, and pepper. Bring the liquid to a boil and simmer, covered, until the liquid is absorbed and the rice is tender, about 15 minutes. Remove from the heat and let stand 10 minutes. Adjust the seasoning and serve hot.

3. The pilaf can be made a day ahead and refrigerated. To serve, gently reheat in a double boiler or in a microwave oven at high power (100 percent) in 1-minute increments. Adjust the seasoning.

Sautéed Wild Rice with Fennel, Currants, and Orange

The flavor and crunch of this wild rice dish enhances game, beef, lamb, and poultry.

YIELD: 6 SERVINGS

2 tablespoons unsalted butter
Grated zest (colored rind) of 1 large orange, removed
    with a zester or fine grater (see page 14),
    about 1 tablespoon
1 small clove garlic, minced, about ³/₄ teaspoon
2 small onions, chopped, about 1¹/₂ cups
¹/₂ large fennel bulb, diced small, about 1¹/₃ cups
4 cups chilled, cooked Wild Rice (page 360)
³/₄ teaspoon salt
Freshly ground pepper to taste
¹/₃ cup each: orange juice, currants

1. Heat the butter in a 12-inch nonstick skillet over medium-high heat. When hot, add the orange zest, garlic, onions, and fennel. Cook, uncovered, stirring often, until the onions are softened, about 5 minutes.

2. Add the wild rice and salt and pepper. Cook until very hot and fragrant, about 2 minutes. Add the orange juice and currants and heat through. Serve hot.

3. The rice can be served immediately or prepared to this point a day ahead and refrigerated. Reheat it, covered, in a preheated 350-degree oven until hot, about 30 minutes, adding a little water as needed. Adjust the seasoning.

Wild Rice

The Chippewa Indians called wild rice *manomin* (the good berry). Early French settlers named it *folle avoine* (crazy oat). Scientists dubbed it *Zizania aquatica* (water weed). I side with the Chippewas.

Wild rice is actually more tame than wild and more of a grass than it is a rice—nonetheless it was important enough to the Indians that they fought wars over it. Until 30 years ago, the Minnesota Chippewas were still the country's major harvesters of wild rice, guiding their canoes through the paddies while beating the ripe stalks with wooden sticks to make the grains fall into the canoe. Today, most wild rice crops are planted and harvested by machine.

After harvesting, the rice was first dried in the sun and then placed in a wide, shallow hole lined with animal hides. Male members of the tribe, wearing special moccasins, would walk on the rice until the hulls came off. The wind blew the chaff away and then the rice was poured into a blanket. Boiled with bacon or salt pork, the crop provided a satisfying meal rich in protein and iron.

In the 1990s machinery has replaced canoes and special moccasins, but some people think the end result is even chewier and more delicious than in days of old.

Curried Garden Rice Casserole

Here, mixed vegetables cook along with the rice for a fairly spicy accompaniment to grilled fish, shellfish, and poultry. If you are planning to make the casserole in advance and reheat it, stir the peas in just before serving.

YIELD: 6 SERVINGS

1 tablespoon each: safflower oil, curry powder
2 large cloves garlic, minced, about 1 tablespoon
1 medium onion, minced, about 1 1/4 cups
1 cup long-grain rice
1 cup each: chopped cabbage, carrots, zucchini
1/2 cup dried currants
2 cups Chicken Stock (page 364) or lower-salt broth, boiling hot
1 cup thawed frozen tiny peas
Salt and red pepper flakes to taste

1. Put a rack in the center of the oven; preheat the oven to 350 degrees. Set aside a 10-cup-capacity stove-to-oven casserole.

2. Heat the oil over medium-high heat. When hot, add the curry powder, garlic, and onion. Cook until the onion is heated through and fragrant, stirring often, about 3 minutes. Add the rice, cabbage, carrots, zucchini, and currants. Stir well. Cook until heated through, about 2 minutes. Add the stock or broth. Cover and transfer to the oven.

3. Bake, covered, until the rice is tender, about 20 to 22 minutes. Stir in the peas. Season with salt and red pepper flakes. The casserole can be served immediately or refrigerated overnight (without the peas); let it cool at room temperature, uncovered, before refrigerating.

4. Reheat, covered, in a preheated 350-degree oven until hot, about 30 minutes. Then stir in the peas and adjust the seasoning.

Rice Reserves

Cooking rice can be a do-ahead preparation. With the exception of arborio used in risottos, most types of rice freeze and reheat extraordinarily well.

To do so, cook the rice according to the instructions on the package, only ever-so-slightly less. Drain and rinse it under cold water until it is cool. This stops the cooking. Spread the rice out on paper towels to blot any excess moisture. Then divide it into convenient portions in airtight plastic bags. Refrigerate the rice for up to 3 days or freeze it for as long as 3 months.

To thaw frozen rice quickly, use the microwave oven. Just remove the wire twist tie, place the plastic bag on a paper plate, and zap it at high power (100 percent) in 30-second increments. Every minute, work through the bag to separate the grains of rice as they thaw.

If you don't have a microwave oven, rice can be thawed at room temperature or by putting it in a fine strainer and immersing it in boiling water, then draining it.

Once the rice is thawed, it can be used in any recipe that calls for cooked rice.

Bulgur Wheat and Rice Pilaf with Vegetables

*The white rice perks up the texture and appearance of the bulgur wheat,
a brownish grain that has a tender texture. Bulgur wheat consists of
wheat kernels that have been steamed, dried, and crushed.*

YIELD: 6 SERVINGS

1 tablespoon vegetable oil
1 medium onion, chopped, about 1¼ cups
1 small carrot, chopped, about ⅓ cup
2 medium ribs celery, chopped, about 1 cup
¾ cup uncooked bulgur wheat
½ cup uncooked rice
2⅔ to 3 cups Chicken Stock (page 364)
    or lower-salt broth
Salt and freshly ground pepper to taste

1. Heat the oil in a 2-quart saucepan over medium-high heat. When hot, add the vegetables. Cook, stirring often, until they are very hot and fragrant, about 4 minutes.

2. Add the bulgur wheat, rice, and 2⅔ cups of the stock or broth. Bring the liquid to a boil. Simmer, covered, until the liquid is absorbed and the grains are tender, about 15 minutes. Add the remaining broth, if mixture is too dry. Season with salt and pepper. Serve hot.

3. The pilaf can be made a day ahead and refrigerated. Let it come to room temperature before reheating, covered, in a preheated 350-degree oven until hot, about 20 minutes, adding stock, broth, or water if the pilaf is too dry. Alternately, gently reheat in a microwave oven on medium power (50 percent) for about 3 minutes. Adjust the seasoning.

Toasted Barley and Mushroom Risotto

The creamy texture and rich taste of this dish closely resemble risotto, though it's made with barley instead of arborio rice. This version is bursting with mushrooms, which are so wonderful with barley. Adding a bit of butter at the end gives a buttery impression without actually adding much. Toast the barley to deepen its natural flavor, although, if you're in a hurry, this is not a critical step. Serve the risotto with Maple Carrots and Leeks (page 195) and a salad of mixed greens.

YIELD: 3 TO 4 MAIN-COURSE SERVINGS

3 cups Chicken Stock (page 364) or lower-salt broth
1 tablespoon olive oil
1 cup quick-cooking pearl barley
1 large clove garlic, minced, about $1/2$ tablespoon
2 large shallots, minced, about $1/3$ cup
$2^{1}/_{2}$ cups coarsely chopped trimmed mushrooms
  (try a mix of domestic and wild)
1 tablespoon each: minced fresh rosemary,
  snipped fresh chives
2 teaspoons unsalted butter
2 tablespoons grated imported Parmesan cheese
  (Parmigiano-Reggiano), plus additional for serving
$1/4$ teaspoon salt
Freshly ground pepper to taste

1. Heat the stock or broth in a saucepan or in a microwave oven; keep it hot until the risotto is finished cooking.

2. Heat the oil in a 2-quart saucepan until hot. Shake the pan to coat the bottom of the pan with oil. Add the barley. Cook over medium heat until lightly toasted, about 5 minutes, stirring often. Add the garlic, shallots, and $1^{1}/_{2}$ cups of the fresh mushrooms. Cook until the mushrooms are heated through, about 2 minutes, stirring often.

3. Add $1/2$ cup of the hot stock or broth and simmer gently over medium heat, stirring often with a wooden spoon. As the broth is absorbed by the barley, add more broth by the $1/2$ cup. Stir often. The barley is done when it is tender but firm to the bite, about 20 minutes. About 5 minutes before the barley is finished, add the remaining fresh mushrooms. It's okay if you do not use all of the broth. On the other hand, if you run out (add water as needed). Toward the end of the cooking process, add the broth cautiously to avoid having excess liquid when the barley is done. The risotto should be creamy but not runny. Stir in the rosemary, chives, butter, the 2 tablespoons of cheese, and the salt and pepper. Serve hot. Pass the additional cheese separately.

4. The risotto can be made ahead and refrigerated (reserve the herbs and add them when you are ready to serve). To serve, gently reheat on top of the stove over low heat until hot, stirring constantly and adding hot broth or water as needed. Alternately, reheat in microwave oven on medium power (50 percent), for about 2 to $2^{1}/_{2}$ minutes, stopping to stir and check the liquid. Stir in the rosemary and chives.

Vegetable Polenta with Mushroom-Tomato Sauce

Here, a mix of vegetables gives tantalizing flavor and texture to this delicious version of polenta. It's unbelievably easy to make, considering its impact. Stefano Panozza, the chef/partner of Café Luciano in Evanston, Illinois, prefers using instant polenta in this recipe; it's a finely textured cornmeal that cooks to a very creamy consistency in 5 minutes. This recipe can be made 2 days ahead.

YIELD: 6 SERVINGS

2 tablespoons olive oil
1 cup each: chopped red bell pepper, green bell pepper,
    Spanish onion, mushrooms
2 tablespoons dry white wine or dry vermouth
9 cups water
³/₄ cup heavy cream
3 tablespoons crumbled blue cheese
1 tablespoon each: salt, freshly ground pepper
4 cups instant polenta (1¹/₂ pounds)
³/₄ cup grated imported Parmesan cheese
    (Parmigiano-Reggiano)
3 tablespoons butter
¹/₄ cup minced fresh parsley
Mushroom-Tomato Sauce (recipe follows)

1. Lightly oil a 10¹/₂ × 15¹/₂-inch jelly roll pan (cookie sheet with sides). Set aside.

2. Heat the 2 tablespoons oil in a 12-inch nonstick skillet over medium-high heat. When hot, add the vegetables. Cook, uncovered, until they are softened, about 5 minutes, stirring often. Add the wine and cook 1 minute longer. Remove from the heat and set aside.

3. Bring the water, cream, blue cheese, salt, and pepper to a boil in a 3-quart pot. Add the reserved vegetables and slowly stir in the polenta. Cook over medium heat until it is thickened, about 5 minutes, stirring constantly with a wooden spoon. Remove from the heat.

4. Immediately add the grated Parmesan, butter, and parsley. Stir until the butter is melted. Adjust the seasoning (you may need more salt, depending on the saltiness of the blue cheese).

5. Spread the hot mixture on the prepared pan; it should be about 1 inch thick. Cut the polenta into squares, then cut the squares diagonally into triangles. Arrange the triangles overlapping on a large, warm serving platter. Spoon the hot mushroom-tomato sauce over the triangles. Serve hot.

6. The polenta can be made 2 days ahead and refrigerated, covered airtight, once completely cooled. Reheat the polenta, uncovered, in a preheated 350-degree oven until it is hot, about 20 minutes. It develops a nice crust in this reheating.

Mushroom-Tomato Sauce

YIELD: ABOUT 2 1/4 CUPS

2 tablespoons olive oil
12 medium mushrooms, sliced
3 tablespoons dry white wine or dry vermouth
2 cups thick store-bought spaghetti sauce
2 tablespoons minced fresh parsley
2 teaspoons unsalted butter
Salt and freshly ground pepper to taste

1. Heat the oil in a 12-inch nonstick skillet over medium heat. When hot, add the mushrooms. Cook, uncovered, until soft, about 5 minutes, stirring often to avoid any browning. Add the wine and cook 1 minute more. Add the spaghetti sauce. Cook, uncovered, until the sauce is thickened to the consistency of a loose marmalade, about 5 to 8 minutes, stirring often.

2. Stir in the parsley and butter. Season with salt and pepper. The sauce can be made several days ahead and refrigerated, covered airtight. Gently reheat until hot before using.

Couscous with Vegetables and Wheat Berries

As good as couscous—a granular semolina—can be by itself, it's even better with wheat berries—whole, unprocessed wheat berry kernels. The contrast between the soft couscous and the chewy wheat berries is very appealing. Because these wheat berries are hard, they must be soaked overnight (see Note) before adding them to the couscous. Soak more than you need and freeze them, adding them to other grains, chili, casseroles, and salads.

Any vegetables, fresh or leftover, can be used in this recipe—about 2 cups are required. The couscous can accompany any simple main course or it can be the main meal served with a green garden salad.

YIELD: 3 TO 4 SIDE SERVINGS

1½ cups Chicken Stock (page 364) or lower-salt broth
½ cup wheat berries, presoaked (see Note)
1 tablespoon olive oil
1 medium onion, diced, about 1¼ cups
½ large red bell pepper, diced, about ⅔ cup
4 medium mushrooms, diced, about ⅔ cup
1 medium zucchini, diced, about 2 cups
¾ cup quick-cooking couscous
3 tablespoons julienned fresh basil
Salt and red pepper flakes to taste

1. Bring the stock and wheat berries to a boil in a 2-quart saucepan. Simmer until the berries are chewable, about 10 minutes.

2. Meanwhile, heat the oil in an 8-inch nonstick skillet over medium-high heat. When it is hot, add the vegetables. Cook until they are very hot but still textured, about 5 minutes.

3. Add the vegetables and couscous to the stock and berries. Stir well, cover, and remove from the heat. Let the couscous rest 5 minutes. Add the basil, salt, and red pepper flakes. Fluff with a fork until well combined. Serve hot.

NOTE: To presoak wheat berries, put them in a bowl and add water to cover by 3 inches. Soak for 12 hours or overnight at room temperature. Drain them well; pat them dry with paper towels. Presoaked and drained berries can be refrigerated for up to 3 days, or frozen for as long as 3 months, sealed airtight.

Wheat Berries

Wheat berries, the unprocessed wheat kernels that are the primary source of many wheat flours, may indeed be good for you. But more than that, they are chewy and have a great, slightly sweet taste all their own. They add delicious dimensions to many different dishes.

The wheat berry includes the bran, germ, and endosperm of wheat. Wheat bran supplies fiber; wheat germ packs a concentrated source of vitamins, minerals, and protein; the endosperm, which accounts for the majority of the kernel, is full of starch, protein, niacin, and iron. For something that actually tastes good, you can't ask for much more than that.

Wheat berries, like all other hard, dry whole grains, must be softened before using them in recipes (except in soups and stews where the grains can soften as the liquid simmers).

To soften wheat berries, soak them overnight in water to cover, or, if you're in a hurry, simmer them in water for about an hour until tender. After soaking or cooking them, a cup of wheat berries will swell to about 2½ cups. Once softened and drained well in a strainer, they can be refrigerated for as long as 3 days or frozen for up to 6 months.

The berries freeze separately when they aren't wet. The best method for drying them out is to spread them on a baking sheet lined with paper towels and refrigerate them, uncovered, for about 2 days. Once they're packed away in airtight plastic food bags in the freezer, they will be within easy reach for salads, chili, casseroles, breads, cookies, stir-fries, and stews.

White Beans with Two Tomatoes

Here, canned beans are used as a shortcut, but dried beans, soaked and cooked, always have a preferable texture and taste. Cook the canned beans quickly, over high heat, so they don't become mushy. A mix of sun-dried and fresh plum tomatoes brings up their flavor. The sun-dried tomatoes that require soaking have the better flavor for this dish.

YIELD: 4 SERVINGS

1 tablespoon olive oil

2 medium cloves garlic, minced, about 1¹/₂ teaspoons

2 large shallots, minced, about 5 tablespoons

12 sun-dried tomato halves softened in ²/₃ cup hot water for 15 minutes, drained, cut into ¹/₄-inch dice, soaking liquid reserved

2 teaspoons Worcestershire sauce

Dash of hot sauce

Two 15-ounce cans Great Northern beans, rinsed in cold water, drained, or 1 cup dried beans, soaked, cooked, drained

4 ripe medium plum tomatoes, outer shells only, cut into ¹/₄-inch dice, about 1¹/₃ cups

¹/₄ teaspoon salt

Freshly ground black pepper to taste

1. Heat ¹/₂ tablespoon of the oil in a 10-inch nonstick skillet over medium heat. When hot, add the garlic and shallot. Cook until they are fragrant, about 2 minutes, stirring often. Add the diced sun-dried tomatoes and their liquid along with the Worcestershire and hot sauce. Gently simmer for 2 minutes. Remove from the heat; add the beans and the remaining oil. Stir well.

2. The beans can be prepared to this point several hours ahead and kept at room temperature. Quickly heat the beans over high heat until hot.

3. To serve, add the diced fresh tomatoes, salt, and pepper to the hot beans. Heat through. Adjust the seasoning and serve hot.

Quick Braised Cabbage with Bacon and Navy Beans

Savoy cabbage is a delicious, delicate variety. This dish makes a quick and wonderful Sunday night supper served with crusty bread, or it can be served as an accompaniment to roast duck or lamb for a great fall dinner party. High-quality smoked ham or sausage can be substituted for the bacon. As in the previous recipe, canned beans are used as a shortcut; soaked and cooked dried beans are preferable.

YIELD: 3 TO 4 MAIN-COURSE SERVINGS

3 thick slices bacon, preferably applewood-smoked
  (see Midwestern Sources, page 376)
2 medium cloves garlic, minced, about 2 teaspoons
2 small leeks, tough green leaves trimmed, split, rinsed,
  thinly sliced, about 1 cup
1 large Savoy cabbage, core removed, thinly sliced,
  about 6 cups
1 cup Chicken Stock (page 364) or lower-salt broth
$^1/_4$ cup dry white wine or dry vermouth
One 15-ounce can Great Northern beans, rinsed in
  cold water, drained or $^1/_2$ cup dried beans, soaked,
  cooked, drained
1 tablespoon each: finely julienned fresh sage, snipped
  fresh chives
Freshly ground pepper to taste

1. Cook the bacon in a 12-inch nonstick skillet over medium-high heat until it is crisp, about 3 minutes. Use a slotted spoon to set the bacon aside on paper towels. Drain off all but 2 tablespoons of the fat in the pan.

2. Add the garlic and leeks to the skillet. Cook until they are fragrant, about 2 minutes. Add the cabbage, chicken stock, white wine, and beans. Gently toss until combined. Simmer until the

cabbage is just beginning to wilt, about 3 minutes. Crumble the bacon and add it to the skillet along with the herbs and pepper. Toss until well combined. Adjust the seasoning. Serve hot.

Chili Bean Bake

These baked beans pack a solid chili flavor, perfect with grilled hot dogs, brats, and hamburgers—meats that are not basted with barbecue sauce. Start with dried beans for this recipe, which may take a long time to become tender—anywhere from 3 to 6 hours, depending on the beans. Luckily, they require only occasional stirring and adjusting of water as they cook. These are best baked ahead and refrigerated so that the flavors have time to develop fully.

YIELD: 8 SERVINGS

8 ounces each: dried black beans, dried Great Northern
   white beans
2 large cloves garlic, minced, about 1 tablespoon
1 large onion, minced, about 2 cups
1 cup each: tomato sauce, ketchup
1 tablespoon safflower oil
1/4 cup packed dark brown sugar
2 1/2 tablespoons chili powder
2 tablespoons each: molasses, maple syrup
1 teaspoon each: cumin, dried oregano
1 to 4 cups water
1/2 to 3/4 teaspoon salt
2 green onions, thinly sliced, for garnish
Sour cream, for serving

1. Sort through the beans, discarding any small pebbles. Cover the beans with cold water. Soak 12 hours or overnight. Rinse and drain well.

2. Put a rack in the center of the oven; preheat the oven to 350 degrees. Set aside a 10-cup-capacity casserole.

3. Combine the garlic, onion, tomato sauce, ketchup, oil, sugar, chili powder, molasses, maple syrup, cumin, oregano, and 1 cup of the water in the casserole. Stir in the drained beans. Adjust the liquid to just cover the beans.

4. Bake, covered, for 3 to 6 hours, stirring well every hour, until the beans are tender, adding the remaining water as needed. Stir in the salt. Adjust the seasoning. Serve hot, garnished with the green onions. Pass the sour cream separately.

5. The beans can be made up to 4 days ahead and refrigerated. To serve, stir in enough water so the beans are just covered with liquid. Bake, covered, in a preheated 350-degree oven until they are hot, about 45 minutes.

Midwestern Beans

Baked beans came to the Midwest from Boston, and they were standard food on the Michigan farm where Della T. Lutes grew up in the early 1900s. To make baked beans for her father's birthday, she remembers soaking the beans overnight, boiling them twice the next morning "until the outer skin burst," and then draining them before adding mustard, vinegar, and brown sugar. The mixture was baked in a heavy tin pan with small bits of pork until "the beans were brought to a mealy consistency suitable for slicing when cold."

Casserole of Spinach, Black Beans, and Spicy Yellow Rice

This is an addictive casserole mix that is spooned into tortillas and rolled up with dollops of salsa, guacamole, light sour cream, and more Chihuahua cheese. Eaten out of hand, it's a mess to handle but well worth it. Each component—the rice, beans, and spinach—stands out fresh and clear. If you keep the frozen spinach very moist, it works well in place of the 16 cups of fresh spinach leaves that you would have to cook to end up with the same quantity of cooked spinach. Turmeric is a yellow-orange spice that turns the rice a bright neon yellow. This casserole can be set up a day in advance and baked at the last minute.

YIELD: 4 SERVINGS

YELLOW RICE:
1 tablespoon vegetable oil
1 large clove garlic, minced, about ¹/₂ tablespoon
1 medium onion, minced, about 1¹/₄ cups
³/₄ cup uncooked long-grain rice
³/₄ teaspoon turmeric
1¹/₂ cups Chicken Stock (page 364) or lower-salt broth, boiling hot
¹/₄ teaspoon salt

BLACK BEANS:
One 15-ounce can black beans, rinsed and drained
1 tablespoon chili powder

SPINACH:
1 tablespoon vegetable oil
1 large clove garlic, minced, about ¹/₂ tablespoon
Two 10-ounce packages frozen leaf spinach, thawed (do not squeeze dry)
¹/₄ teaspoon salt
Freshly ground pepper to taste
2 to 4 tablespoons water, as needed

1 cup shredded Chihuahua cheese (Monterey Jack can also be used)
Cilantro leaves, for garnish
4 large tortillas, light sour cream, salsa, and Guacamole (recipe follows), for serving

1. Set aside a 2-quart casserole.

2. For the yellow rice, heat the oil in a 2-quart saucepan over medium-high heat. Add the garlic, onion, rice, and turmeric. Cook, stirring often, until the onion is softened. Add the chicken stock or broth, the salt and pepper. Mix well. Simmer, covered, until the liquid is absorbed, about 15 minutes. Let the rice rest off the heat for 5 minutes. Fluff with a fork. Adjust the seasoning.

3. Meanwhile, combine the black beans with the chili powder. Set them aside.

4. For the spinach, heat the oil in a 10-inch nonstick skillet over high heat. When it is hot, add the garlic, spinach, salt, pepper, and 2 tablespoons of the water. Cook, stirring often, until the garlic is fragrant, about 2 minutes. Add more water if the spinach is not moist, with loose leaves (it should not be compacted together).

5. To assemble, spoon half the spinach into the bottom of the casserole, spreading it out evenly. Layer the rice on top, then the beans, the remaining spinach and the cheese. The casserole can be made a day in advance and refrigerated, covered airtight.

6. Put a rack in the center of the oven; preheat the oven to 375 degrees. Bake the casserole, covered, until it is sizzling, about 45 minutes. Garnish the casserole with cilantro leaves.

7. To serve, heat the tortillas: sprinkle the tortillas with hot water, wrap them in foil, and bake them in a preheated 375-degree oven until hot, about 10 minutes. Alternately, layer the tortillas between paper towels and microwave them on high power (100 percent) until hot, about 45 seconds. Place the casserole on the table, accompanied by the tortillas, sour cream, salsa, and guacamole, all in separate serving dishes. Each person should spoon the hot casserole mixture onto a tortilla, garnish it as desired, and roll it up.

Guacamole

YIELD: 3/4 CUP

1 very ripe avocado, preferably Haas
1/4 teaspoon minced garlic
1 teaspoon fresh lime juice
1 tablespoon tomato salsa
2 teaspoons chopped cilantro leaves
Pinch of each: salt, cayenne pepper

Use a fork to mash the avocado in a small bowl until chunky. Stir in the remaining ingredients. Adjust the seasoning. The guacamole tastes best when freshly made. It can be refrigerated up to 3 hours, covered closely with plastic wrap. Serve chilled or at room temperature.

Orzo with Goat Cheese, Tomato, and Fresh Basil

In this pasta dish, half the goat cheese is melted into the sauce while the remaining half is crumbled over the orzo just as the dish is finished and served. This is simple cooking at its best.

YIELD: 2 TO 3 MAIN-COURSE SERVINGS

1 tablespoon olive oil
2 medium cloves garlic, minced, 1¹/₂ teaspoons
4 ounces soft mild goat cheese
¹/₂ to ³/₄ cup Chicken Stock (page 364)
   or lower-salt broth
8 ounces orzo, cooked according to package directions
1 large ripe but firm tomato, juiced and seeded,
   cut into ¹/₃-inch dice, about 1¹/₃ cups
³/₄ teaspoon salt
Red pepper flakes to taste
3 tablespoons julienned fresh basil leaves

1. Heat the oil in a 12-inch nonstick skillet over medium-high heat. When hot, add the garlic, half the goat cheese, and ¹/₂ cup of the stock. Simmer until the cheese is melted, about 2 minutes, stirring often. Add the orzo and heat thoroughly, about 1 to 2 minutes, adding the remaining stock if the mixture is too dry. Toss in the tomatoes, salt, and red pepper flakes. Cook 1 minute more. Remove from the heat.

2. To serve, add the remaining goat cheese, crumbled into small bits, and the basil leaves. Adjust the seasoning. Serve hot.

Penne with Escarole and Bacon

The smokiness of the small amount of bacon adds just the right edge to this summery mixture. Escarole, a variety of endive, has broad, slightly curved, pale green leaves with a sweet mild flavor once it's cooked. This is a subtle-tasting dish that goes down easy in hot weather. It looks cool, too.

YIELD: 2 TO 3 MAIN-COURSE SERVINGS

1 thick slice bacon, preferably applewood-smoked (see Midwestern Sources, page 376), cut into small dice, about 2¹/₂ tablespoons

1 tablespoon olive oil

2 medium cloves garlic, minced, 1¹/₂ teaspoons

¹/₂ large red onion, cut into ¹/₃-inch dice, about 1¹/₂ cups

4 cups torn escarole (about one 7-ounce head)

8 ounces penne pasta (tubes), cooked

³/₄ cup Chicken Stock (page 364) or lower-salt broth

¹/₄ cup freshly grated imported Parmesan cheese (Parmigiano-Reggiano), plus additional for serving

¹/₈ teaspoon red pepper flakes

¹/₄ teaspoon salt

1. Cook the bacon in a 12-inch nonstick skillet over medium-high heat until it is well browned. Use a slotted spoon to transfer the bacon to a paper towel. Pour off the fat from the pan.

2. Add the oil to the skillet. When hot, add the garlic and red onion. Cook until they are just heated through and fragrant, about 2 minutes, stirring often. Stir in the escarole and cook until it is just wilted, about 1 minute.

3. Stir in the penne and broth. Bring the liquid to a boil. Add the bacon, ¹/₄ cup of the cheese, the red pepper flakes, and the salt. Toss well and remove from the heat. Adjust the seasoning. Serve hot. Pass the additional grated Parmesan separately.

Pasta Pizzazz . . .

The simplest flourish can brighten the basic pasta formula—fettuccine tossed with olive oil, garlic, and Parmesan cheese:

❖ Fresh herbs such as minced parsley, basil, oregano, and snipped chives, used together or individually.

❖ Diced fresh tomato cut only from the shell.

❖ Roasted red or green bell peppers (the combination is also great) or pimiento cut into strips or diced.

❖ Thinly sliced green onions.

❖ Lemon juice and cracked pepper.

❖ Crunchy surprises such as a topping of sautéed garlic bread crumbs tossed with fresh herbs; or barely cooked diced fennel, asparagus, broccoli, or thin carrot slices, black and green olives, thinly sliced raw mushrooms, your choice(s) all tossed into hot seasoned pasta.

Farfalle (Bow Ties) with Broccoli, Red Pepper, and Garlic

Colorful and light, this hot pasta dish can easily be served as a salad with a splash of red wine vinegar added.

YIELD: 2 TO 3 MAIN-COURSE SERVINGS

1 tablespoon olive oil
3 medium cloves garlic, minced, about 2¼ teaspoons
2 large stems broccoli, florets separated from the stems, florets broken apart so they are tiny, stems peeled and thinly sliced, about 4 cups total
¼ teaspoon salt
1 large red bell pepper, seeded, diced, about 1¼ cups
1¼ to 1¾ cups Vegetable Stock (page 367) or broth
8 ounces farfalle pasta, cooked according to package directions
⅓ cup freshly grated imported Parmesan cheese (Parmigiano-Reggiano), plus additional for serving
Red pepper flakes to taste

1. Heat the oil in a 12-inch nonstick skillet over medium-high heat. When hot, add the garlic, broccoli stems, and salt. Cook, uncovered, until very hot, about 2 minutes, stirring often.

2. Add the florets, sliced stems, red pepper, and 1¼ cups of the vegetable stock. Bring the liquid to a boil and simmer 1 minute. Add the pasta. Simmer, uncovered, until the pasta is hot and the broccoli is just beginning to be tender, about 3 minutes, adding more broth as needed if the pan becomes too dry. Add the ⅓ cup cheese and the red pepper flakes. Toss well. Heat through, about 1 minute more. Adjust the seasoning. Serve hot. Pass the additional cheese separately.

Pasta Convenience

Purists claim that pasta must be served freshly cooked from the pot, but I have had great success cooking pasta in large batches and freezing it. It works especially well with penne (tubes), farfalle (bow ties), and orzo because these pastas are less delicate than other shapes. I also find that pasta reheats very well, a convenience that eliminates last-minute effort.

For best results, cook the pasta until al dente—still firm to the bite. Rinse under cold water to stop the cooking. Drain well and toss gently with oil (about 1 teaspoon of oil to each 8 ounces of cooked pasta keeps the pasta from sticking together). Refrigerate for up to 3 days or freeze for up to 1 month in airtight plastic bags. You can use this cooked, chilled pasta for any pasta recipe—from salads (pasta salads made with chilled pasta hold up much better flavor-wise than those made with hot, freshly cooked pasta) to hot pastas in various sauces.

Gently thaw the pasta, if frozen, in the microwave oven at high power (100 percent) in 30-second increments or by submerging the airtight bags in a bowl of hot water. Or put the pasta in a colander and run it under hot water to separate and make it supple again. Then, reheat it in the sauce of your choice.

Gremolata Fettuccine

*Gremolata, the Italian garnish of minced parsley, garlic, and lemon zest,
is typically sprinkled over osso bucco for a fresh, flavorful uplift to braised veal shanks.
Here, the gremolata is made with orange zest as well and tossed right into the fettuccine
for a great flavor impact. Serve this fettuccine with Braised Veal Shanks with Vegetables
(page 132); it makes great informal dining. The fettuccine is also delicious served with
grilled meats, poultry, or seafood.*

YIELD: 6 SERVINGS

1⅓ cups loosely packed parsley leaves

1 tablespoon each grated orange and lemon zest
(colored rind) removed with a zester or fine grater
(see page 14)

3 medium garlic cloves

3 tablespoons unsalted butter

8 ounces hot fettuccine, cooked al dente, reserving
about ¼ cup of the pasta cooking liquid

Salt and freshly ground pepper to taste

1. Put the parsley leaves (be sure that they are dry, without any moisture) and the zests in a food processor fitted with the metal blade. Turn the processor on. Drop the garlic cloves through feed tube and process until the mixture is minced as fine as possible.

2. Put the butter into a shallow pasta bowl. Transfer the contents of the processor bowl to the pasta bowl. Add the hot pasta and ¼ cup of the cooking liquid. Toss until well mixed. Add salt and pepper as needed. Serve hot.

3. The fettuccine can be made a few hours ahead, kept at room temperature, and reheated in a microwave oven at high power (100 percent) for about 2½ to 3½ minutes, adding a little water if mixture is too dry. Adjust the seasoning.

Lemon Noodles with Poppy Seeds

Simple as these Hungarian-inspired noodles are, they offer a delicious alternative to richer noodle dishes. Serve them with ham, smoked turkey, brisket, grilled chicken, or broiled fish.

YIELD: 4 TO 6 SERVINGS

1/4 cup each: sugar, fresh lemon juice
2 tablespoons unsalted butter
1 teaspoon grated lemon zest (colored rind), removed
   with a zester or fine grater (see page 14)
Pinch of salt
8 ounces egg noodles, cooked according to package
   directions
1 teaspoon poppy seeds

1. Combine the sugar, lemon juice, butter, zest, and salt in a small nonaluminum pan or microwavable dish. Heat the mixture on the stove over medium heat or in the microwave oven on high power (100 percent) for about 30 to 50 seconds until hot. Stir until combined.

2. Keep the hot drained noodles in their pot. Toss with the lemon mixture and poppy seeds until the noodles are well coated. Serve hot.

3. These noodles can be made ahead, kept at room temperature, and reheated quickly in a nonstick skillet or in the microwave oven at high power (100 percent) for about 2½ to 3½ minutes, tossing the noodles during cooking. Do not overcook. Adjust the seasoning and lemon balance.

Sweet Noodle and Apple Pudding

This slightly sweet, old-fashioned noodle pudding with apples and raisins (actually an adaptation of a recipe from the turn-of-the-century included in a personal collection of Nebraska recipes) makes an ideal homey accompaniment to the Brisket of Beef with Caramelized Onion Sauce (page 121) or any roasted beef or poultry.

YIELD: 6 SERVINGS

2 tablespoons unsalted butter

4 large eggs, separated

²/₃ cup sugar

¹/₈ teaspoon salt

¹/₂ cup milk

12 ounces egg noodles, cooked according to package
   directions, rinsed and well drained

¹/₂ cup raisins

3 large Granny Smith apples, peeled, cored, thinly
   sliced (best done in food processor with the thin
   slicing disc), about 5 cups

¹/₂ cup sliced almonds with skins

2 tablespoons sugar mixed with ¹/₄ teaspoon cinnamon,
   for topping

1. Put a rack in the center of the oven; preheat the oven to 350 degrees. Grease a 6-cup-capacity shallow baking dish or a 9-inch square baking pan, preferably ceramic or Pyrex. Set aside.

2. Use an electric mixer to beat the butter, egg yolks, sugar, and salt until light and fluffy, about 3 minutes. Add the milk. Mix until combined. Stir in the cooked noodles and raisins.

3. Whip the egg whites until they hold their shape but are still moist. Fold the whites into the noodle mixture.

4. To assemble, arrange half of the apple slices over the bottom of the prepared dish. Spread half of the noodle mixture over the apples. Repeat the layering; spread the top layer of noodles evenly.

5. Bake for 40 minutes. Sprinkle the casserole with sliced almonds, then with the cinnamon sugar. Continue to bake until the almonds are golden brown and the pudding is set, about 20 minutes more. Serve hot.

6. This pudding can be made a day ahead and refrigerated. Reheat, covered with foil, in a preheated 300-degree oven until heated through, about 40 minutes.

YEAST BREADS:
Basic White Bread
Light Cracked Whole-Wheat Bread
Garlic Rolls with Fresh Rosemary
Whole-Wheat Pepper-Cheese Baguettes with Chopped Onion
Potato Dill Rolls
Cinnamon-Raisin Pull-Apart Bread
Bread Dough for the Grill
Pizza Batter-Bread
Chicago Deep-Dish Pizza with Sausage, Mushrooms, and Green Pepper
Basic Pizza Crust Dough

QUICK BREADS:
Peppered Buttermilk Biscuits
Parmesan Oatmeal Muffins
Warm Buttermilk Corn Bread Pie
Deep Apple-Cinnamon Bread
Winter Dried Fruit Bread
Lemon Popovers with Lemon Maple Butter

SANDWICHES:
Vegetable Pitas
Turkey Salad Sandwich with Sprouts
Double-Grilled Vegetable Sandwich
Toasted Gruyère, Red Cabbage, and Apple Sandwich
Garlic Bread with Parmesan Cheese and Fresh Basil

Chapter 10

Yeast Breads, Quick Breads, and Sandwiches

❖

There is nothing that compares to fresh, home-baked goods—no other aroma, no other flavor. Nothing. Yet many good cooks shy away. And for no good reason. To me, the actual process of making good bread, putting the warm loaf on the table, telegraphs a statement that says a great deal about the cook and the attention to quality a fine meal deserves. This is just as true at home as it is in a restaurant.

If I sound passionate about baking bread, that's good. Because I am very passionate about this subject and I want you to succeed. So I am going to follow the lead of the old Midwestern cookbooks and lean heavily on the basics—both the basics of how to achieve great bread each time you try, and the basic breads: white, whole-wheat, potato, and cinnamon breads, rolls, biscuits, corn bread, and quick breads. But I also want you to see that there is a very broad landscape of possibilities out there.

So you will find recipes for the likes of Garlic Rolls with Fresh Rosemary (imagine serving those with Orange-Roasted Chicken on Tossed Greens), Whole-Wheat Pepper-Cheese Baguettes with Chopped Onion, Parmesan Oatmeal Muffins, Deep Apple-Cinnamon Bread. You will find pizza doughs and bread dough made specially for the grill.

And since the ultimate use for terrific bread is to make a delicious sandwich, I am also including some of my favorite sandwich recipes in this chapter: the Vegetable Pitas, the Turkey Salad Sandwich with Sprouts, and the Double-Grilled Vegetable Sandwich.

Once you discover this world of bread dough and baking and experience how comfortable and rewarding it can be, I don't think you will ever turn back.

Basic White Bread

This is a soft, multipurpose bread, perfect for sandwiches and toast. The dry milk makes a soft crumb without adding much cholesterol; the oil helps keep the bread fresh for a few days, but it's best to freeze any extra to maintain its original freshness. After the dough rises once, it can be shaped in the pan, covered with plastic wrap, and refrigerated overnight. The second rising time will be at least doubled when using chilled dough.

YIELD: 1 LOAF

BREAD:
1 package active dry yeast
1 teaspoon sugar
1 cup plus 2 tablespoons warm water
   (105 to 115 degrees)
3 cups bread or unbleached flour (bread flour gives
   a softer texture—a perfect balance is 1 cup bread
   flour, 2 cups unbleached flour)·
$^1/_4$ cup instant nonfat dry milk
2 tablespoons vegetable oil
1 teaspoon salt

GLAZE:
1 large egg white, frothed with a fork

1. Fifteen minutes before baking, put a rack in the center of the oven; preheat the oven to 375 degrees. Lightly grease and sprinkle with cornmeal an 8-cup-capacity (9-inch) bread pan, preferably black steel. Set it aside.

2. Stir the yeast and the sugar into the water; set aside until the yeast is foamy, about 5 minutes.

3. To mix and knead the dough in a food processor fitted with the metal blade or in a mixer with the dough hook, put the remaining bread ingredients into the bowl. Turn the machine on and slowly add the yeast mixture. Mix until the dough cleans the sides of the bowl. If the dough is too wet, add more flour by the tablespoon, working it in before adding more. If the dough is dry and crumbly, add more water by the tablespoon, again working it in before adding more. Once the desired consistency is achieved (moist but not sticking to the sides), mix the dough until well kneaded, uniformly supple, and elastic, about 40 seconds in the food processor, about 6 minutes in a mixer. Or by hand, put the remaining bread ingredients into a large bowl and make a well in the center. Pour the yeast mixture into the well and work it into the ingredients in the bowl. Knead on a floured board until the dough is elastic and smooth, about 10 minutes.

4. Transfer the dough to a large enough plastic bag for the dough to double, squeeze out the air, and seal the top. Place the bag in a bowl and let the dough rise in a warm spot until doubled in bulk, about 1 to 1$^1/_2$ hours.

5. Punch the dough down and fit it into the pan. Cover it loosely with plastic and let it rise in a warm spot until doubled, about 1 hour. When it has doubled, brush the top with egg white.

6. Bake until golden and sounds hollow when rapped on the bottom, about 35 minutes. Immediately remove from the pan to cool on a wire rack.

Freezer Freshness

Home-baked yeast breads, rolls, muffins, and scones taste best when freshly baked because they have no preservatives and, typically, little fat. Freeze any bread that will not be used the day it's baked. Breads freeze beautifully when you go about it in a specific way. Here's how:

❖ Cool breads completely on a wire rack. Place them in the freezer, unwrapped, until they are frozen solid. Remove them from the freezer and place each loaf (or roll) in a plastic food bag, squeeze out all the air and twist the top of the bag into a tight coil. Fold the coiled part over itself and seal it in place with a twist tie. Repeat the plastic bagging a second time. This double-bagging eliminates potential off-odors. Bread can be frozen for as long as 2 months.

❖ When ready to use frozen bread, thaw it at room temperature, keeping the bread in its wrapping. Remove it from the bag and reheat in a 350-degree oven until just warmed through, not hot, about 8 to 10 minutes. Wrap it in foil for a soft crust; reheat it unwrapped—right on the oven rack—for a firmer crust.

Light Cracked Whole-Wheat Bread

This is a light cracked-wheat bread, versatile because it's not dense. It makes great sandwich bread as well as great toast. If you want to increase the bulgur wheat to make the loaf denser, it will be necessary to use 2 packets of yeast.

YIELD: 1 LOAF

BREAD:
1 package active dry yeast
1 tablespoon sugar
1 cup plus 2 tablespoons warm water
   (105 to 115 degrees)
2 cups bread flour
3/4 cup whole-wheat flour
2 tablespoons bulgur wheat
Generous 3/4 teaspoon salt
1 tablespoon vegetable oil

GLAZE:
1 large egg
1/2 teaspoon salt
2 teaspoons bulgur wheat, for sprinkling

1. Fifteen minutes before baking, put a rack in the lower third of the oven; preheat the oven to 400 degrees. Lightly grease a 7-cup-capacity (8-inch) bread pan, preferably black steel. Set it aside.

2. Stir the yeast and the sugar into the water; set aside until the yeast is foamy, about 5 minutes.

3. To mix and knead the dough in the food processor fitted with the metal blade or in a mixer with the dough hook, put the remaining bread ingredients into the bowl. Turn the machine on and slowly add the yeast mixture. Mix until the dough cleans the sides of the bowl. If the dough is too wet, add more flour by the tablespoon, working it in before adding more. If the dough is dry and crumbly,

add more water by the tablespoon, again working it in before adding more. Once the desired consistency is achieved (moist but not sticking to the sides), mix the dough until well kneaded, uniformly supple, and elastic, about 50 seconds in the food processor, about 7 minutes in a mixer. Or by hand, put the remaining bread ingredients into a large bowl and make a well in the center. Pour the yeast mixture into the well and work it into the ingredients in the bowl. Knead on a floured board until the dough is elastic and smooth, about 12 minutes.

4. Transfer the dough to a large enough plastic bag for the dough to double, squeeze out the air, and seal the top. Place the bag in a bowl and let it rise in a warm spot until doubled in bulk, about 1 to 1½ hours.

5. Punch the dough down and shape it to fit the prepared pan. Cover it loosely with plastic wrap. Let it rise in a warm spot until doubled, about 1 hour.

6. For the glaze, use a fork to mix the egg and salt in a small bowl until frothy. When the dough has doubled, brush the top with the glaze. Sprinkle with the bulgur wheat.

7. Bake 30 minutes. Gently remove the loaf from the pan. Place the loaf directly on the oven rack and bake until the bottom is browned and sounds hollow when rapped, about 5 minutes more. Cool on a wire rack.

Garlic Rolls with Fresh Rosemary

The dough for these little flat rolls rises only once, just like flatbread or focaccia.

YIELD: EIGHT 4-INCH ROLLS

1 recipe Light Cracked Whole-Wheat Bread dough
*   made with olive oil instead of vegetable oil*
*   (page 255), allowed to rise only once*
3 tablespoons olive oil
2 large cloves garlic, minced, about 1 tablespoon
1 tablespoon chopped fresh rosemary
Bulgur wheat, red pepper flakes, kosher salt,
*   for sprinkling*

1. Fifteen minutes before baking, set 2 racks in the center area of the oven; preheat the oven to 450 degrees. Grease 2 baking sheets, preferably black steel. Set them aside.

2. Punch the dough down in the plastic bag and refrigerate it for 1/2 hour for easier handling.

3. On a lightly floured board, divide the dough into 8 equal parts. With your hands, gently stretch each piece into a 4-inch round (rolling is not necessary).

4. Place the rounds on the prepared baking sheets, spacing them 2 inches apart. Use a sharp knife to cut through each round to make 2 parallel slashes about 1 inch in from opposite edges of dough.

5. Combine the oil, garlic, and rosemary. Spoon the mixture onto each round, dividing the ingredients evenly. Use the back of a spoon to gently spread the oil mixture to the edges of each round. Sprinkle with bulgur wheat, red pepper flakes, and kosher salt.

6. Bake until the rounds are just golden on top and well browned on the bottom, about 12 minutes. Do not overbake. Let them cool on a rack. Serve warm.

7. The rolls can be reheated, wrapped in foil, in a preheated 350-degree oven for about 12 minutes.

Roasted Garlic . . .

Garlic roasted until buttery soft becomes sweet. The taste is both delicate and refined. Squeeze each roasted clove to extract the soft flesh from the skin and spread it on warm bread sprinkled with salt and fresh coarsely cracked pepper, or add it to sauces, soups, sandwich spreads, and salad dressings for wonderful flavor. Most recipes for roasting garlic use olive oil, but here's a simple preparation that uses no oil at all:

❖ Wrap each firm, plump garlic head in foil, twisting the foil closed at the top. Place the heads on a baking sheet. Roast in a 400-degree oven for 1 hour. These roasted garlic heads can be kept for 3 days in the refrigerator, stored in a plastic bag. The heads tend to weep a bit but don't worry about it.

Whole-Wheat Pepper-Cheese Baguettes with Chopped Onion

This baguette splits slightly as it bakes, revealing the cheese filling. Served warm, the bread complements salads, soups, and informal meals.

YIELD: TWO 9-INCH BAGUETTES

1 recipe Light Cracked Whole-Wheat Bread dough
  made with olive oil instead of vegetable oil
  (page 255), allowed to rise only once
1 tablespoon each: olive oil, water
1 large sweet onion, chopped, about 2 cups
1/2 cup each: shredded mozzarella, shredded aged Asiago
  cheese
1 teaspoon each: dried oregano, cracked pepper
1/4 teaspoon salt
1 recipe glaze for Lightly Cracked Whole-Wheat Bread
  (page 255)

1. Fifteen minutes before baking, set a rack in the lower third of the oven; preheat the oven to 400 degrees. Grease a baking sheet, preferably black steel. Set it aside.

2. Punch the dough down in the plastic bag and refrigerate it in the bag for 1/2 hour for easier handling.

3. Meanwhile, heat the oil and water in a 10-inch nonstick skillet over high heat. Add the onion and cook until just seared, about 4 minutes, stirring often. Transfer the onion to a small mixing bowl. Let it cool slightly, then add the cheeses, oregano, pepper, and salt. Toss until well combined.

4. Divide the chilled dough in half. On a lightly floured board, roll each half to about a 5 × 9-inch rectangle. Divide the filling, mounding it along the center down the length of the bread. Close the loaf by pinching the sides together along the top; pinch the ends together as well. Place the loaves, pinched side up, on the prepared pan. Lightly brush the glaze over the loaves.

5. Bake 20 minutes. Brush the glaze once more over the loaves, especially over any newly opened edges. Bake until the loaves are well browned, about 10 more minutes. Let them rest on a wire rack for 30 minutes before serving. Serve warm.

6. The baguettes can be reheated, wrapped in foil, in a preheated 350-degree oven for about 15 minutes.

Potato Dill Rolls

These rolls have a soft texture, perfect for absorbing gravy and sauces.
The dough can also be baked as a baguette or a standard loaf.

YIELD: TWELVE 3 TO 4-INCH-DIAMETER ROLLS

ROLLS:
2 small potatoes, about 5 ounces total
1 package active dry yeast
1 tablespoon sugar
1 cup warm water including the potato cooking liquid
   (105 to 115 degrees)
2 cups bread flour
1 cup all-purpose flour
1 tablespoon safflower oil
2 teaspoons dried dillweed
³/₄ teaspoon salt

GLAZE:
1 egg
¹/₂ teaspoon salt

1. Fifteen minutes before baking, put a rack in the lower third of the oven; preheat the oven to 375 degrees. Grease a large baking sheet, preferably black steel. Set it aside.

2. For the rolls, cook the potatoes in water to cover until they are soft, about 15 minutes. Drain, reserving both the potatoes and their cooking liquid. Let the liquid cool slightly.

3. Stir the yeast and sugar into the cooking liquid combined with enough warm water to measure 1 cup; set it aside until the yeast is foamy, about 5 minutes.

4. Put the potatoes (it is not necessary to peel them, but cut them in half) and the flours into a food processor fitted with the metal blade. Mix until the potato is crumbled. With the processor running, add the yeast mixture, oil, dillweed, and salt. Mix until the dough just cleans the sides of the work bowl. If the dough is too sticky, add more flour by the tablespoon, working it in before adding more. If the dough is dry and crumbly, add more water by the tablespoon, again working it in before adding more. Once the desired consistency is achieved (moist but not sticking to the sides), mix the dough until well kneaded, uniformly supple, and elastic, about 40 seconds.

5. Transfer the dough to a large plastic food bag. Squeeze out the air and seal the top. Place the bag in a bowl and let the dough rise in a warm place until it has doubled in bulk, about 1¹/₄ hours.

6. Punch the dough down. Place the dough on a floured board. Cut it into 12 equal pieces. Shape each piece into a ball by pinching one end. Place the balls, pinched side down, on the prepared baking sheet, spacing them 2 inches apart. Lightly drape oiled plastic wrap over the rolls and let them rest in a warm place until they are puffy but not quite doubled, about 30 minutes.

7. For the glaze, use a fork to mix the egg and salt in a small bowl. When the rolls have puffed, lightly brush the surface with glaze.

8. Bake until the rolls are well browned, about 20 minutes. Transfer them to a rack to cool. Serve warm.

9. The rolls can be reheated, wrapped in foil, in a preheated 350-degree oven for about 12 minutes.

Cinnamon-Raisin Pull-Apart Bread

*This loaf is rich, generously studded with plump raisins, and swirled with cinnamon
sugar. It's delicious served warm and pulled apart or sliced, toasted, and spread with
Honey Pecan Butter (page 36).*

YIELD: 1 LOAF

BREAD:
1 package active dry yeast
3 tablespoons sugar
1/4 cup warm water (105 to 115 degrees)
2 1/2 cups bread flour
3 tablespoons unsalted butter, softened
3/4 teaspoon salt
2/3 cup evaporated milk
3/4 cup raisins

TOPPING:
5 tablespoons sugar
1 1/2 teaspoons cinnamon
4 tablespoons unsalted butter

1. Fifteen minutes before baking, put a rack in the center of the oven; preheat the oven to 350 degrees. Grease a 7-cup-capacity (8-inch) loaf pan. Set it aside.

2. Stir the yeast and 1 teaspoon of the sugar into the warm water; let it stand until it is foamy, about 5 minutes.

3. To mix and knead the dough in the food processor fitted with a metal blade or in a mixer with the dough hook, put the remaining sugar, flour, butter, and salt into the bowl. Turn the machine on and slowly add the yeast mixture and the evaporated milk. Mix until the dough cleans the sides of the bowl. If the dough is too wet, add more flour by the tablespoon, working it in before

adding more. If the dough is dry and crumbly, add more water by the tablespoon, again working it in before adding more. Once the desired consistency is achieved (moist but not sticking to the sides), mix the dough until well kneaded, uniformly supple, and elastic, about 40 seconds in the food processor, about 6 minutes in a mixer. Add the raisins and mix until they are just worked into the dough, 4 to 5 seconds. Or by hand, put the remaining sugar, flour, butter, and salt into a large bowl and make a well in the center. Pour the yeast mixture into the well and work the ingredients together, then add the evaporated milk and work it in. Knead the dough on a floured board until it is elastic and smooth, about 10 minutes. Knead in the raisins.

4. Transfer the dough to a large plastic food bag, squeeze out the air, and seal the top. Place the bag in a bowl. Let the dough rise in a warm spot until doubled in bulk, about 2 hours.

5. For the topping, mix 1 tablespoon of the sugar and 1/4 teaspoon of the cinnamon in a small dish. Lightly sprinkle the inside of the prepared pan with the cinnamon-sugar. Set aside the remaining cinnamon-sugar. Melt the butter, add the remaining 4 tablespoons of sugar and 1 1/4 teaspoons of cinnamon; cook just until the sugar dissolves, about 2 minutes.

6. On a lightly floured board, punch the dough down. Divide it into 24 pieces. Spoon 2

tablespoons of the butter mixture into the bottom of the pan, then fill the pan with a single layer of the bread dough, placing the pieces in an irregular pattern. Spoon approximately 2 more tablespoons of the butter mixture over the dough and add another layer of the bread dough. Cover the pan loosely with plastic wrap and let the dough rise in a warm spot until it is doubled in bulk, about 1 hour.

7. Bake until the loaf is well browned and sounds hollow when rapped on the bottom, about 40 minutes. Let it cool in the pan for 5 minutes. Use a sharp knife to loosen the bread from the sides of the pan and transfer it to a wire rack. While the bread is still warm, brush the remaining butter mixture over the top and sprinkle with the reserved cinnamon sugar.

When the Clock Runs Out . . .

It's just not true that bread-making is time-constrained, inflexible, or uninterruptible. Here are some timesaving tips for when you are in the midst of making bread and find that your time does not work out as you anticipated:

❖ When the dough has risen once, you can totally forget about it until the following day. Just punch it down, and refrigerate it airtight right in the plastic bag it was rising in. The next day, shape the dough and let it rise again. Chilled dough will take 1 to 2 hours longer to double in volume. Dough for a pizza can be rolled, topped, and baked right away, without any delay.

❖ To be sure the dough will rise in the time indicated in the recipe, pick a warm spot, away from any drafts. A 75- to 80-degree environment is ideal; your oven is the perfect space. A gas oven is sufficiently warmed from the pilot without turning it on, while an electric oven must be turned on to any setting for 2 minutes, then turned off before placing the dough in it.

❖ If you can't wait for the bread dough in the pan to completely double as directed, you can put the almost-doubled loaf into a cold oven, turn it to the specified temperature and bake as usual, adding a few extra minutes since the oven was not preheated. I have found that, without fail, as the oven comes up to temperature, the bread comes up, too, baking to perfection.

Bread Dough for the Grill

This is a basic dough for the grill. It produces a bread that's crusty on the outside with a pleasantly chewy interior. The dough can be refrigerated for as long as 5 days; I've found that it actually improves in taste and texture as each day passes. This dough also bakes very well into baguettes or round loaves, developing a great sour flavor as well as a crustier finish when it has been refrigerated for a few days. You can also use store-bought ready-made dough on the grill although it doesn't have quite the same texture; about 8 ounces or 1 cup of dough is the right amount for each grilled bread round.

YIELD: THREE 8-INCH GRILLED BREAD ROUNDS, 12 WEDGES

BREAD:

1 package active dry yeast
2 teaspoons honey
1 cup plus 2 tablespoons warm water
    (105 to 115 degrees)
2 cups bread flour
1 cup all-purpose flour
1¼ teaspoons salt
2 tablespoons olive oil

Thick Herbed Oil, heated, for grilling (recipe follows)
Salt to taste

1. Prepare a medium-hot (not too hot) barbecue fire with a few chunks of water-soaked mesquite wood.

2. Stir the yeast and honey into the water; set aside until the yeast is foamy, about 5 minutes.

3. To mix and knead the dough in the food processor fitted with a metal blade or in a mixer with the dough hook, put the remaining bread ingredients into the bowl. Turn the machine on and slowly add the yeast mixture. Mix until the dough cleans the sides of the bowl. If the dough is too wet, add more flour by the tablespoon, working it in before adding more. If the dough is dry and crumbly, add more water by the tablespoon, again working it in before adding more. Once the desired consistency is achieved (moist but not sticking to the sides), mix the dough until well kneaded, uniformly supple, and elastic, about 40 seconds in the food processor, about 6 minutes in a mixer. Or by hand, put the remaining bread ingredients into a large bowl and make a well in the center. Pour the yeast mixture into the well and work the ingredients together. Knead the dough on a floured board until the dough is elastic and smooth, about 10 minutes.

4. Transfer the dough to a large plastic food bag, squeeze out the air, and seal the top. Place the bag in a bowl. Let the dough rise in a warm spot until doubled in bulk, about 1 hour. Punch the dough down. The dough can be used immediately, refrigerated for up to 5 days, or frozen for up to 3 months, wrapped airtight. Thaw frozen dough, still wrapped, in the refrigerator.

5. When you are ready to grill the bread, on a heavily floured board, divide the dough into 3 equal

portions, roughly 8 ounces (or about 1 cup) each. Roll each into a 7½-inch round. Stack the rounds between oiled sheets of waxed paper. The dough can be rolled several hours in advance and refrigerated, covered loosely with plastic.

6. To grill, prepare a medium barbecue fire with a few chunks of water-soaked mesquite wood. Brush one side of the dough round with the herbed oil; flip the oiled side down onto the grill and brush the top side with oil. Repeat with the remaining rounds. Cover the grill for 3 to 4 minutes until rounds are browned on underside. Use a spatula to turn the rounds; brush the grilled surfaces with oil. Close grill for 3 to 4 minutes more. Sprinkle lightly with salt. Use kitchen shears to cut the rounds into 4 wedges each. Serve warm.

Thick Herbed Oil

This oil is more than is actually needed for brushing 3 grilled breads, but it's so good just tossed with diced summer tomatoes and julienned fresh basil for an improvised tomato topping on the breads or mixed greens that it is wise to have some on hand. Use it on vegetables, fish, and chicken as well. It will be necessary to stir up the oil before using it. Gently warming the oil in the microwave oven or in a saucepan helps to thin it out and make it go farther.

YIELD: 2/3 CUP

1 large clove garlic, peeled, about ½ tablespoon
2 large green onions, trimmed, cut into 1-inch lengths, about ½ cup
½ cup each: olive oil, loosely packed fresh herbs (a mix of basil, sage, thyme, rosemary)
½ teaspoon salt
Red pepper flakes to taste

In a food processor fitted with the metal blade or in a blender, mix all the ingredients until they are as smooth as possible. The oil can be made up to 2 days ahead and refrigerated, covered airtight. Warm it slightly in the microwave oven or in a saucepan and stir the oil just before using.

Pizza Batter-Bread

The flavor of this batter-bread is reminiscent of pizza. It's quick and easy to make since it only rises once. It's best served warm from the oven; it can be reheated several hours after baking, but the flavor of the seasonings will diminish.

YIELD: ONE 9 × 13-INCH BREAD, TWELVE 3 × 3 1/3-INCH SQUARES

BREAD:
1 package active dry yeast
2 tablespoons sugar
1 1/4 cups warm water (105 to 115 degrees)
3 cups bread flour
1 teaspoon each: dried oregano leaves, dried basil leaves
1/4 teaspoon red pepper flakes
1 1/4 teaspoons salt
2 tablespoons olive oil

GLAZE:
1 large egg
1/2 teaspoon salt
1/4 teaspoon freshly ground pepper

1/4 cup finely grated imported Parmesan cheese,
    for sprinkling

1. Fifteen minutes before baking, put a rack in the center of the oven; preheat the oven to 350 degrees. Grease a 9 × 13-inch pan. Set it aside.

2. Stir the yeast and sugar into the water; set it aside until the yeast is foamy, about 5 minutes.

3. To mix and knead the dough in a food processor fitted with the metal blade or in a mixer with the dough hook, put the remaining bread ingredients into the bowl. Turn the machine on and slowly add the yeast mixture. Mix until the dough cleans the sides of the bowl. If the dough is too wet, add more

flour by the tablespoon, working it in before adding more. If the dough is dry and crumbly, add more water by the tablespoon, again working it in before adding more. Once the desired consistency is achieved (moist but not sticking to the sides), mix the dough until well kneaded, uniformly supple, and elastic, about 40 seconds in the food processor, about 6 minutes in a mixer. Or by hand, put the remaining bread ingredients into a large bowl and make a well in the center. Pour the yeast mixture into the well. Work the yeast mixture into the ingredients in the bowl. Knead the dough on a floured board until it is elastic and smooth, about 10 minutes.

4. Transfer the dough to the prepared pan. Pat it out evenly and set it aside to rest in a warm place, lightly draped with plastic wrap, until it's somewhat puffy (not necessarily doubled), about 40 minutes.

5. For the glaze, put the egg, salt, and pepper in small bowl. Whisk until frothy. Brush the puffed surface of the bread with the glaze. Sprinkle cheese evenly over the top.

6. Bake until lightly browned on the edges, about 30 minutes. Cut into 12 squares and serve warm.

Chicago Deep-Dish Pizza with Sausage, Mushrooms, and Green Pepper

If deep-dish pizza wasn't actually born in Chicago, it certainly was catapulted to celebrity status right here. This is one of the most popular renditions of Chicago-style pizza, loaded with rich, gooey cheese, spicy sausage, and pungent green peppers, all topped with a tomato-mushroom sauce. If you'd rather have onions than green pepper, olives instead of mushrooms, go for it. Pizza recipes are meant to be improvised.

YIELD: ONE 14-INCH DEEP-DISH PIZZA, 6 WEDGES

1 pound mild or hot Italian sausage, casing removed, meat crumbled

1 large green bell pepper, seeded, cut into 1- to 3-inch-wide strips, about 1 1/4 cups

10 ounces Herkimer or white Cheddar cheese, shredded, about 2 1/2 cups

1 tablespoon flour

1/2 teaspoon each: fennel seed, dried oregano, red pepper flakes

1/4 teaspoon salt

4 large mushrooms, trimmed, thinly sliced, about 1 cup

2 cups store-bought pizza sauce

One Basic Pizza Crust Dough (recipe follows)

2 tablespoons olive oil, plus additional for oiling the pan

1. Put a rack in the center of the oven; line the oven rack with unglazed quarry tiles or a pizza stone (optional). Preheat the oven to 425 degrees. Oil the bottom and sides of a 14-inch deep-dish pizza pan, preferably black steel. Sprinkle the inside surface with cornmeal. Set aside.

2. Cook the sausage in an 8-inch nonstick skillet over medium-high heat, stirring occasionally, until browned, about 7 minutes. Use a slotted spoon to transfer the sausage to paper towels, then to a large mixing bowl.

3. Add the green pepper, cheese, flour, and seasonings to the sausage. Toss until combined.

4. Put the mushrooms and pizza sauce in a small bowl. Mix well. Set aside.

5. On a floured board, roll the pizza dough into a 20-inch circle. Fold the dough into quarters and transfer it to the prepared pan. Unfold the dough and adjust it to fit the pan. Press it into the bottom and sides of the pan, then gently ease the dough up the sides until it extends above the rim. Trim away the excess leaving 1/2 inch of the dough. Brush the bottom and sides of the dough with the oil.

6. Add the cheese filling in an even layer. Spread the mushroom-and-pizza sauce evenly over the top. Fold the 1/2-inch dough down and pinch it to form a rim.

7. Bake until the topping is sizzling and the rim of the crust is well browned, about 22 minutes. Let it rest 10 minutes and serve warm, cut into wedges.

Basic Pizza Crust Dough

This is a good basic pizza crust recipe; it also makes great baguettes.

YIELD: DOUGH FOR ONE 14-INCH DEEP-DISH PIZZA

1 package active dry yeast
1 cup warm water (105 to 115 degrees)
2³/4 cups unbleached all-purpose flour
1/4 cup whole-wheat flour
1¹/4 teaspoons salt
3 tablespoons extra-virgin olive oil

1. Stir the yeast into the water and let it stand until the yeast is foamy, about 5 minutes.

2. To mix and knead the dough in a food processor fitted with the metal blade or in a mixer with the dough hook, put the remaining ingredients into the bowl. Turn the machine on and slowly add the yeast mixture. Mix until the dough cleans the sides of the bowl. If the dough is too wet, add more flour by the tablespoon, working it in before adding more. If the dough is dry and crumbly, add more water by the tablespoon, again working it in before adding more. Once the desired consistency is achieved (moist but not sticking to the sides), mix the dough until well kneaded, uniformly supple, and elastic, about 40 seconds in the food processor, about 6 minutes in a mixer. Or by hand, put the remaining ingredients into a large bowl and make a well in the center. Pour the yeast mixture into the well. Work the yeast mixture into the ingredients in the bowl. Knead the dough on a floured board until the dough is elastic and smooth, about 10 minutes.

3. Transfer the dough to a large plastic bag, squeeze out the air and seal the top. Place the bag in a bowl and let the dough rise in a warm spot until doubled in bulk, about 1¹/2 hours. The dough can be used right away for the Chicago Deep Dish Pizza with Sausage, Mushrooms, and Green Pepper (page 265), or it can be refrigerated for up to 2 days or frozen for as long as 2 months, wrapped airtight. Thaw frozen dough, still wrapped, in the refrigerator.

Peppered Buttermilk Biscuits

Biscuits are the easiest type of bread to make at home. Here, they are peppery, moist, and soft-textured. Cut into rectangles, they have a great homespun appeal that goes perfectly with soups, stews, and salads. This recipe is easily doubled or tripled.

YIELD: 6 BISCUITS

BISCUITS:
2 cups flour
1 tablespoon baking powder
1/2 teaspoon salt
1 teaspoon coarsely ground pepper
5 tablespoons unsalted butter, cut into small pieces
3/4 cup buttermilk

GLAZE:
1 large egg
1/2 teaspoon salt

1. Put a rack in the center of the oven; preheat the oven to 400 degrees. Grease a cookie sheet and set it aside.

2. For the biscuits, combine the flour, baking powder, salt, and pepper in a food processor fitted with the metal blade or in a small bowl. Work the butter into the dry ingredients in the food processor or with a pastry blender until the mixture resembles coarse meal. Add the buttermilk. Mix just until the ingredients clump together.

3. Transfer the dough to a floured board and knead it, folding and pressing it back on itself, until it holds together and is smooth, about 30 seconds. Pat the dough into a 6 × 8-inch rectangle, about 1/2 inch thick. Cut it evenly into 6 pieces. Transfer the biscuits to the prepared cookie sheet, spacing them 1 inch apart.

4. For the glaze, use a fork to mix the egg and salt until frothy. Brush the glaze over the biscuits. (The glaze will keep a week in the refrigerator.)

5. Bake the biscuits until they are golden, about 18 minutes. Transfer to a wire rack to cool. The biscuits can be served immediately or kept at room temperature for several hours. Gently reheat in a preheated 300-degree oven for 10 minutes or in a microwave oven on medium power (50 percent) until just heated through, about 40 seconds. Serve warm.

Parmesan Oatmeal Muffins

These big, round-topped muffins are savory in a most delicious way. Aromatic herbs, zesty cheese, and oatmeal give them just the right character for serving with a steaming bowl of soup or a hearty stew.

YIELD: 8 MUFFINS

1/3 cup safflower oil

1 large egg

2 large egg whites

3 dashes of red pepper sauce

1 tablespoon minced parsley leaves

1 medium clove garlic, minced, about 3/4 teaspoon

3/4 cup grated imported Parmesan cheese

1 cup flour

2/3 cup rolled oats

2 teaspoons baking powder

1 1/2 tablespoons sugar

1/2 teaspoon baking soda

1/4 teaspoon salt

1/8 teaspoon each: dried thyme, dried oregano

3/4 cup plain lowfat yogurt

1. Place a rack in the center of the oven; preheat the oven to 375 degrees. Line 8 standard muffin cups with paper liners and set them aside.

2. Put the oil, egg, egg whites, pepper sauce, parsley, and garlic in a large mixing bowl; whisk until just combined. Add the dry ingredients and mix well. Fold in the yogurt. Do not overmix. Divide the batter among the muffin cups.

3. Bake until they are lightly browned and a toothpick inserted in the center comes out clean, about 25 minutes. Let the muffins cool in the pan for 5 minutes. Serve warm.

Warm Buttermilk Corn Bread Pie

Recipes similar to this one are usually loaded with fat and cheese. Here, the cheese is used where it counts—right on the top. Serve this moist corn bread warm, cut into wedges, with Oven "Fried" Chicken (page 154) or Meat Loaf with Greens (page 123). Spoon Vegetable Chili (page 73) over the wedges for a great one-dish supper, and serve it with coleslaw on the side.

YIELD: 6 SERVINGS

1 tablespoon unsalted butter

1 small onion, minced, about $^1/_2$ cup

2 large eggs

2 large egg whites

One 17-ounce can salt-free whole-kernel corn, drained

1 cup plus 2 tablespoons buttermilk

3 tablespoons sugar

1$^3/_4$ teaspoons ground cumin

$^3/_4$ teaspoon salt

$^1/_4$ teaspoon red pepper flakes

1 cup flour

$^2/_3$ cup yellow cornmeal, plus additional for the pan

2 teaspoons baking powder

$^1/_2$ teaspoon baking soda

2 small plum tomatoes, outer shells only, cut into
 $^1/_4$-inch dice, about $^2/_3$ cup

3 ounces Colby cheese, grated, about $^3/_4$ cup

1. Put a rack in the center of the oven; preheat the oven to 425 degrees. Generously grease a deep 9-inch pie plate or a 5$^1/_2$-cup capacity shallow baking dish. Lightly sprinkle the bottom and sides with cornmeal and set it aside.

2. Heat the butter in a small nonstick skillet over medium-high heat. When hot, add the onion and cook until it is softened, about 2 minutes, stirring often.

3. Meanwhile, put the eggs, egg whites, drained corn, buttermilk, sugar, cumin, salt, and red pepper flakes into a large mixing bowl. Add the onion mixture. Use a wooden spoon to mix well. Add the flour, the $^2/_3$ cup cornmeal, the baking powder and soda. Stir until well combined. Fold in the tomatoes. Transfer the batter to the prepared baking dish.

4. Bake until the corn bread is browned and a toothpick inserted into the center comes out clean, about 18 to 20 minutes.

5. Scatter the cheese evenly toward the edges with only a meager sprinkling in the center. Continue to bake until the cheese is melted, about 2 minutes more. Let the corn bread rest 15 to 20 minutes before serving. Serve warm, cut into 6 wedges. The corn bread can be made several hours ahead and kept at room temperature.

6. To serve, gently reheat in a microwave oven on medium power (50 percent) for about 1 minute, or in a preheated 350-degree oven until just warmed through, about 10 minutes. Do not overheat.

Deep Apple-Cinnamon Bread

Old-fashioned, moist, and full of apple flavor, this quick bread is moderately sweet. Serve it with salads and soups; it also makes great toast for breakfast or tea. As with many quick breads, this loaf is best served the day after it's baked, when the flavors have had a chance to develop.

YIELD: ONE 8-INCH LOAF

$^1/_2$ cup dried apple slices
$^3/_4$ cup walnuts
1 stick unsalted butter, softened
1 cup sugar
2 large eggs
1$^1/_3$ cups applesauce
2 cups cake flour
1 teaspoon baking soda
$^1/_2$ teaspoon salt
2 teaspoons cinnamon

1. Put a rack in the center of the oven; preheat the oven to 350 degrees. Generously grease a 7-cup-capacity (8-inch) loaf pan, preferably aluminum or Pyrex; dust it lightly with flour. Set it aside.

2. Mince the apple slices and the walnuts together in a food processor fitted with the metal blade; pulse on/off to control the texture. Set aside.

3. Use an electric mixer to cream the butter and sugar. Add the eggs and mix until fluffy and smooth. Add the applesauce and mix well. Add the apples and nuts to the batter. Mix well.

4. Sift the flour, baking soda, salt, and cinnamon together and add them to the batter. Mix until well combined. Transfer the batter to the prepared pan.

5. Bake until the loaf is dark brown and a toothpick inserted in the center comes out clean,

about 55 to 60 minutes. Let the loaf rest in its pan on a wire rack for 10 minutes. Gently remove the loaf from the pan and cool completely. The bread can be served immediately but it is best when wrapped in foil and allowed to rest at room temperature overnight. It can be frozen, wrapped airtight, for up to 2 months (thaw in the wrapping).

Winter Dried Fruit Bread

Packages of mixed dried fruits contain a delicious combination of pears, apples, apricots, and prunes. Steeped in tea and flavored with the citrus zest and cinnamon, the fruits are baked into a luscious, moist, and rich tea bread. It can be served plain or further embellished with sweet butter or cream cheese.

YIELD: ONE 7-INCH LOAF

One 8-ounce package mixed dried fruits
1 cup plus 2 tablespoons sugar
1/2 cup strong-brewed tea
Grated zests (colored rind) of 1 lemon and 1 orange,
    removed with a zester or grater (see page 14)
1/2 teaspoon cinnamon
6 tablespoons unsalted butter, melted
2 large eggs
1/3 cup buttermilk
2 cups unbleached all-purpose flour
1 teaspoon baking powder
1/2 teaspoon each, baking soda, salt
1 cup toasted walnuts (page 358)

1. Put a rack in the center of the oven; preheat the oven to 350 degrees. Butter a 6-cup-capacity (7-inch) loaf pan; dust the inside with flour. Set it aside.

2. Remove the stones from the prunes. Place all the fruit in a small nonaluminum pan with 2 tablespoons of the sugar, the tea, zests, and cinnamon. Cook, uncovered, over medium heat until the fruit has softened and the mixture has thickened, about 10 minutes.

3. Transfer the fruit to a food processor fitted with the metal blade; process 3 seconds to roughly chop the fruit.

4. Use an electric mixer to combine the remaining sugar, the butter, and the eggs until fluffy, about 2 minutes. Add the buttermilk and mix thoroughly. Spoon the flour, baking powder, baking soda, and salt over the batter, then the fruit and walnuts. Mix on low speed until just combined. Transfer the batter to the prepared loaf pan.

5. Bake for 45 minutes. Reduce the oven temperature to 300 degrees and continue to bake until browned and a toothpick inserted in the center comes out clean, about 15 minutes longer. If the top browns too quickly, loosely tent the pan with aluminum foil during the last 15 minutes. Let the bread cool in the pan for 5 minutes, then turn it onto a wire rack to cool completely. When it is cool, wrap it airtight in foil. The bread is best left to mellow for 1 to 2 days at room temperature before serving. It can also be frozen for up to 3 months, wrapped airtight. Thaw in the wrapping at room temperature.

Lemon Popovers with Lemon Maple Butter

Popovers are always an appealing form of bread; consider serving these crusty popovers for breakfast, lunch, or supper. The clove brings out some of the lemon flavor but the Lemon Maple Butter really does it.

YIELD: 6 POPOVERS

POPOVERS:
1 cup flour, sifted
1¹/₂ cups milk
4 large eggs
¹/₈ teaspoon ground cloves
¹/₂ teaspoon salt
Zest (colored rind) of 2 large lemons, removed with a zester or a fine grater, about 2 tablespoons

Lemon Maple Butter (page 40), for serving

1. Put a rack in the center of the oven; preheat the oven to 400 degrees. Grease a 6-cup popover pan with shortening or a thin coat of cooking spray. Heat the pan in the oven for 15 minutes.

2. Meanwhile, use an electric mixer, a food processor fitted with the metal blade, or a blender to combine all the popover ingredients until smooth. Transfer the mixture to a 1-quart measuring cup.

3. Carefully pour the batter into the hot popover pans, filling them about seven-eighths full.

4. Bake for 10 minutes. Decrease the heat to 350 degrees, and continue to bake until the popovers are very dark and crisp, about 40 to 45 minutes longer. Serve them hot, with the lemon maple butter.

Vegetable Pitas

This tasty vegetarian pita is the creation of Marvin Vigadi, the former chef/owner of Beverly's Café in Winnetka, Illinois. Served heaping-full and warm, this sandwich is very sustaining. As a shortcut, use a 16-ounce bag of mixed frozen vegetables to substitute for the fresh broccoli, cauliflower, and carrots.

YIELD: 3 PITA SANDWICHES

1 to 1¼ cups water
¼ teaspoon salt
1⅓ cups each: cauliflower florets, broccoli florets, sliced carrots (4 cups total)
1 cup diced mushrooms
1 tablespoon unsalted butter
¼ cup each: diced red onion, seeded and diced tomato, store-bought Caesar dressing
Freshly grated pepper to taste
Three 6-inch-diameter fresh pita rounds
½ cup grated Muenster or Monterey Jack cheese

1. Bring 1 cup of water and the salt to a boil in a 12-inch skillet over medium-high heat. Add the cauliflower, broccoli, and carrots. Cook, uncovered, stirring often, until the vegetables are almost tender, about 10 minutes. Add the mushrooms and continue to cook until the vegetables are just tender. Add the remaining water as necessary if the pan becomes too dry. When the vegetables are done, drain off the water and stir in the butter. Remove the pan from the heat.

2. Add the onion, tomato, and Caesar dressing to the vegetables. Mix until combined and season with salt and pepper. The mixture can be made a few hours ahead and kept at room temperature. Gently reheat it before using, adding a little water if the mixture is too dry (but it should not be runny).

3. Put a rack in the center of the oven; preheat the oven to 300 degrees. Set aside a baking sheet.

4. To finish the sandwiches, wrap the pitas in foil and bake them until they are warm, about 10 minutes. Remove the foil. Carefully cut the pitas in half. Gently open the pita halves and spoon a generous tablespoon of cheese inside each half. Place the halves on the reserved baking sheet.

5. Bake the pitas until the cheese is melted, about 5 minutes. Spoon the warm vegetable mixture inside the warm pita halves, heaping it generously. Serve warm.

Turkey Salad Sandwich with Sprouts

Here, turkey is combined with celery, Calamata olives, red onion, and tomato. The alfalfa sprouts are arranged over the turkey salad once it's spread on the bread. The result is crunchy and delicious.

YIELD: 4 SANDWICHES

2 cups roughly chopped turkey meat

2 large ribs celery, finely diced, about 1 cup

8 Calamata olives, pitted, flesh cut into small pieces

2¹/₂ tablespoons each: finely diced outer tomato shell, red onion

¹/₃ cup plus 1 tablespoon light mayonnaise

2 teaspoons balsamic vinegar

Salt and freshly ground pepper to taste

Softened unsalted butter or mayonnaise, | for spreading on the bread

8 slices high-quality bread

1 cup alfalfa sprouts

Leaf lettuce

1. Put the turkey, celery, olives, tomato, onion, mayonnaise, and balsamic vinegar in a small bowl. Mix well. Season with salt and pepper.

2. Spread one side of the bread with butter or mayonnaise. Divide the turkey salad among 4 bread slices, spreading it to the edge. Place the sprouts on the turkey, then the lettuce. Close the sandwiches, cut them in half, and serve immediately.

Double-Grilled Vegetable Sandwich

Here vegetables are grilled, then layered between slices of bread, and the sandwich is grilled again. That's what makes this sandwich special. The basil-garlic mayonnaise just melts into the warm vegetables. The grilling vinegar reduces the amount of oil typically used on these grilled vegetables . . . but not the flavor.

YIELD: 2 LARGE SANDWICHES

GRILLING VINEGAR:

1/4 cup minced fresh basil leaves

2 large cloves garlic, minced, about 1 tablespoon

1/3 cup balsamic vinegar

1 tablespoon olive oil

VEGETABLES:

1/2 medium eggplant, peeled, cut into 3/4-inch-thick round slices

1 medium zucchini, trimmed, cut into 1/2-inch-thick lengthwise slices

1 large sweet onion, cut into 1/2-inch-thick slices

1 large red bell pepper, sides cut off into lengthwise slabs, seeds discarded

Salt and freshly ground pepper to taste

BASIL-GARLIC MAYONNAISE:

1/4 cup light mayonnaise

1/4 cup minced fresh basil leaves

1 large clove garlic, minced, about 1/2 tablespoon

4 large slices high-quality crusty bread

1. For the grilling vinegar, combine all the ingredients in a small bowl. Set aside.

2. For the vegetables, prepare a medium-hot barbecue fire with a few chunks of water-soaked mesquite wood. Use tongs to place the vegetables in a single layer on the preheated grill. Immediately brush the grilling vinegar on the vegetables and turn them over. Brush the top side of the vegetables with the vinegar. Keep turning the vegetables to cook them evenly, brushing them generously with the vinegar. When the vegetables are just tender but still intact, about 6 minutes, remove them from the grill. Brush them with the remaining grilling vinegar and sprinkle them with salt and pepper. The vegetables can be made a day ahead and refrigerated. Let them come to room temperature before finishing the sandwiches.

3. For the basil-garlic mayonnaise, combine all the ingredients in a small dish.

4. To assemble the sandwich, spread the mayonnaise on one side of the 4 bread slices. Layer the vegetables on 2 slices, dividing them equally. Close the sandwiches, pressing down lightly.

5. To serve, lightly brown the sandwiches on an oiled griddle or, alternately, wrap them in foil and heat them on the grill until they are very warm. Cut the sandwiches in half. Serve warm.

Toasted Gruyère, Red Cabbage, and Apple Sandwich

Ina's, a popular homestyle café in Chicago, serves this sandwich; with a mix of rye bread, Dijon mustard, and unique filling, it's a winner. The apples and cabbage can be cooked in advance and gently reheated before assembling the sandwiches.

YIELD: 4 SANDWICHES

RED CABBAGE:

2 tablespoons unsalted butter
1 medium red onion, thinly sliced, about 1¼ cups
½ small head red cabbage, quartered, cored, thinly sliced, about 3½ cups
2 tablespoons red wine vinegar
2 tablespoons sugar
½ teaspoon caraway seeds
Generous ¼ teaspoon salt
Freshly ground pepper to taste

CARAMELIZED APPLES:

1 large Granny Smith apple, peeled, halved, cored, sliced, about 1½ cups
½ tablespoon sugar
1 tablespoon unsalted butter

Dijon mustard to taste
8 slices each: hearty rye bread, Gruyère cheese

1. For the red cabbage, heat the butter in a 10-inch nonstick skillet over medium-high heat. When the butter is sizzling, add the onion and cook, stirring often, until it is softened but not brown, about 4 minutes. Add the cabbage and vinegar and cook gently, covered, until the cabbage is tender but still textured, about 12 minutes. Add the sugar, caraway seeds, salt, and pepper. Cook gently 5 minutes longer, stirring often to prevent burning. The cabbage can be made a day ahead and refrigerated. Gently reheat in a skillet and adjust the seasoning before assembling the sandwich.

2. For the caramelized apples, toss the apple slices with the sugar in a large bowl. Heat the butter in an 8-inch nonstick skillet over medium-high heat. When the butter starts to brown, add the sliced apples. Cook until golden and tender but still intact, about 6 to 8 minutes, stirring often. The apples can be made a day ahead and refrigerated. Gently reheat in a skillet before assembling the sandwich.

3. To assemble, generously spread Dijon mustard on 4 bread slices. Cover the mustard with warm apple slices. Cover the apples with a cheese slice. Divide the warm cabbage among the remaining 4 slices of bread. Place a cheese slice on the cabbage. Leave the sandwiches open-face for cooking; they will be closed after they are cooked.

4. To cook, heat a griddle over medium heat. Lightly grease the hot griddle. Place a 2-part open-face sandwich on the griddle. Cook, tented with foil, until the cheese is melted, about 4 minutes. Close the sandwich, pressing it lightly together. Turn it over and place it on a baking sheet. Keep it warm in a preheated 250-degree oven while cooking the remaining sandwiches. Serve warm.

Garlic Bread with
Parmesan Cheese and Fresh Basil

Here, garlic-infused oil is brushed on baguettes that have been cut in half lengthwise, then lightly seasoned with salt and pepper and sprinkled with grated Parmesan cheese. When the loaf is fresh from the oven, julienned fresh basil leaves are strewn over the surface.

YIELD: 1 LARGE BAGUETTE LOAF, SPLIT IN HALF, ABOUT 8 PIECES, ABOUT 6 TO 8 SERVINGS

2¹/₂ tablespoons olive oil
5 large cloves garlic, minced, about 2¹/₂ tablespoons
1 baguette loaf, split lengthwise
Salt and pepper to taste
¹/₂ cup each: finely grated (not minced or ground)
 imported Parmesan cheese (Parmigiano-Reggiano),
 julienned fresh basil leaves

1. Put a rack in the lower third of the oven; preheat the oven to 375 degrees. Set aside a cookie sheet.

2. Combine the oil and garlic in a small skillet. Heat the mixture until the garlic is fragrant but not browned, about 4 minutes, watching closely. Strain the oil through a fine sieve, pressing firmly to extract all the flavor and oil.

3. While it is still warm, brush the oil over the surface of the baguette halves. Season them lightly with salt and pepper. Sprinkle them evenly with cheese. The bread can be made to this point and refrigerated overnight or frozen for up to 1 month, wrapped airtight. Thaw in the wrapping at room temperature, if frozen.

4. Place the baguette halves, cheese side up, on the cookie sheet. Bake in the preheated oven until they are well browned, about 15 minutes. Remove them from the oven and distribute the julienned basil leaves evenly over each half. Cut each half into 4 equal portions. Serve hot.

CAKES:

Red River Valley Rich Chocolate Cake

Lemon Angel Cake

Warm Spiced Pumpkin Cake with
  Caramel Sauce

Chocolate Cappuccino Pound Cake

Lazy Daisy Vanity Cake

Caramel-Glazed Apple Chunk Cake

Truly "Old-Fashioned" Strawberry
  Shortcake

Annella Campbell's Company Cake

Fresh Gingerbread Cakes with Diced
  Pears

Petoskey Carrot Cake

Sunshine Cake

Fresh Blueberry-Lemon Bundt Cake

Glazed Maple Pecan Tea Cake

Frozen Deep Chocolate Ice Cream Roll
  with Hot Fudge Sauce

COOKIES:

Deep Chocolate Cinnamon Cookies

Allspice Orange Poppy Seed Cookies

Peanut Butter Cookies

Chewy Oatmeal Toffee Crunch Cookies

Caramel Apple Squares with Pecans

Orange Cornmeal Crisps

Lemony Clove Icebox Cookies

Rocky Road Brownies

Two-Cereal Crisps

Blueberry Bar Cookies

Spice Cookies with Candied Ginger

Chocolate Chip Brownie Blobs

PIES, CRISPS, AND COBBLERS:

All-American Apple Pie

Buttery Lemon Meringue Pie

Warm Maple Cranberry Apple Pie

Warm Rhubarb Streusel Pie

Chocolate Caramel Tart

Very Berry Deep-Dish Pie

Nancy's Upside-Down Apple Pie

Family's Favorite Pumpkin Chiffon Pie

Strawberry-Rhubarb Crisp

Caramel Pecan Apple Crisp

Warm Fall Fruit Streusel Cake

Fresh Peach-Plum Cobbler

OTHER VARIED DESSERTS:

Simply Peaches

Warm Rosy Berry Compote

Baked Caramel Pears with Vanilla Ice
  Cream

Red Plum and Raspberry "Fool"

Persimmon Pudding

Maple Syrup Eggnog Custards

Baked Chocolate Mousse Puffs

Chocolate Mint Ice Cream

100 Percent Fresh Strawberry Sherbet

Chapter 11

Desserts

❖

The "First Law of Midwestern Dining" is as true today as it was a hundred years ago: save room for dessert. Since many of the nineteenth-century Midwest cookbooks are all devoted to desserts, how could I not make desserts a significant part of this cookbook? Besides, I truly love the idea of dessert and I love serving it. It's like putting happiness on the table.

I have come to think of cake as the epicenter of the Midwestern dessert experience. Homey cakes, not fancy, fussy cakes. Cakes with that soft, moist texture and buttery flavor that all but shout home-made. Sunshine Cake is a good example, and recipes for it appear in many of the early cookbooks. As its name suggests, it is as yellow as the sunshine, with a light texture very much like an angel cake. And as old an inspiration as it may be, it stands right up to its more modern cousins such as Chocolate Cappuccino Pound Cake or Warm Spiced Pumpkin Cake with Caramel Sauce.

The homespun nature of Midwestern desserts continues right through pies, crisps, cobblers, puddings, custards, and cookies. Simply Peaches is simply delicious. Persimmon Pudding is a standout. The pies and crisps follow the seasons, starting in late spring with Strawberry-Rhubarb Crisp, then into Fresh Peach-Plum Cobbler, or the Very Berry Deep-Dish Pie, and finally arriving at All-American Apple Pie and Pumpkin Chiffon Pie in fall. What's in season in winter? Chocolate Caramel Tart.

You'll find I have a preference for thin, crisp cookies when you try the likes of Peanut Butter Cookies or Orange Cornmeal Crisps. But the Blueberry Bar Cookies and Caramel Apple Squares with Pecans are so loaded with fruit they are like little tarts cut into squares.

The nicest thing about taking to heart the homey nature of Midwestern desserts is the ease with which delicious results can be achieved.

Red River Valley Rich Chocolate Cake

*Raw grated potato is the secret ingredient in this marvelously moist
and fine-crumbed chocolate cake.*

YIELD: ONE 9 × 13-INCH CAKE

1³/₄ cups cake flour
³/₄ cup unsweetened cocoa powder
1¹/₂ teaspoons baking soda
¹/₂ teaspoon salt
1 small potato, unpeeled, grated, about 1 cup
1³/₄ cups sugar
1 stick unsalted butter, softened
2 large eggs
2 cups sour cream
1 teaspoon pure vanilla extract
Ivory Frosting (recipe follows)

1. Put a rack in the center of the oven; preheat the oven to 350 degrees. Grease a 13 × 9-inch cake pan; lightly dust it with flour, tapping out the excess. Set it aside.

2. Sift the flour, cocoa, baking soda, and salt onto a sheet of waxed paper. Set it aside.

3. Use a mixer to cream the potato, sugar, butter, and eggs until they are light and fluffy. Add the sour cream and vanilla; combine well. Add the dry ingredients in 3 batches, mixing each addition very well. Transfer the batter to the prepared pan.

4. Bake until a toothpick inserted in the center comes out clean, 35 to 40 minutes. Cool the cake completely on a wire rack before frosting.

Ivory Frosting

**YIELD: ENOUGH FROSTING FOR ONE
9 × 13-INCH CAKE**

3 cups confectioners' sugar, sifted
4 tablespoons unsalted butter, softened
3 tablespoons sour cream
1 tablespoon pure vanilla extract

Use a mixer or food processor fitted with the metal blade to combine all the ingredients until smooth, scraping down the sides as necessary.

Lemon Angel Cake

According to food historian Meryle Evans, the Dover rotary beater, patented in 1869, should be credited with the boom in popularity of angel cakes. It reduced the amount of time it took a cook to beat egg whites from hours to minutes, which is fortunate for me, since angel cake is my favorite. I've made them in a varying range of flavors . . . from maple pecan, coffee, and orange to chocolate. They're cakes for modern times . . . lowfat and luscious! Here, a lemony version makes a perfect foil for summer's fresh berries. Although the cake is delicious unfrosted, the lemon yogurt glaze gives it a festive finish.

YIELD: ONE 10-INCH TUBE CAKE

$1^1/_2$ cups superfine sugar
$^3/_4$ cup plus $1^1/_2$ tablespoons cake flour
2 cups egg whites (about 16 large),
   at room temperature
$1^1/_2$ teaspoons cream of tartar
$^1/_4$ teaspoon salt
3 tablespoons fresh lemon juice
Grated zest (colored rind) of 2 large lemons,
   removed with a zester or fine grater (see page 14),
   about 2 tablespoons
Lemon Yogurt Glaze (recipe follows) (optional)
   or 1 tablespoon confectioners' sugar, for sprinkling

1. Put a rack in the center of the oven; preheat the oven to 375 degrees. Set aside an ungreased 10-inch tube pan.

2. Divide the sugar in half. Sift one half 3 times. Sift the other half with the flour 3 times.

3. Use a mixer on low speed to beat the egg whites in a 4-quart grease-free bowl until they are frothy. Add the cream of tartar and salt. Increase the mixer speed to medium and slowly add the lemon juice. Beat until the whites are thick and hold their shape but are still soft and moist, about 3 minutes.

4. Add the plain sifted sugar, 1 tablespoon at a time, beating well after each addition. Increase the speed to high and beat until the whites have increased in volume about fivefold, hold their shape, and are very thick, shiny, and smooth, about $1^1/_2$ minutes more.

5. Gently but thoroughly, in 3 batches, fold in the sugar and flour mixture and the lemon zest. Transfer the batter to the tube pan and smooth the surface with a spatula. Use a sharp knife to cut through the batter in 10 places to break up any large air pockets.

6. Bake until the surface is very brown and a toothpick inserted in the center comes out clean, about 35 minutes. If the top of the cake is getting too brown, gently tent a piece of foil over it during the last 5 minutes of baking. Invert the pan on the counter or, if it has risen beyond the cake pan prongs, invert it onto a funnel or an empty wine bottle. Let it cool completely.

7. Use a sharp, flexible knife to loosen the cake from the sides, tube, and bottom of the pan. Invert it onto a rack. The cake will keep at room

temperature up to 2 days, well covered, or it can be frozen, wrapped airtight, for up to 3 months. Thaw the cake in the wrapping at room temperature.

8. To serve, frost with lemon yogurt glaze, or press 1 tablespoon of confectioners' sugar through a fine sieve over the top of the cake.

Lemon Yogurt Glaze

YIELD: 1/2 CUP

1¹/2 cups confectioners' sugar, sifted
2 tablespoons plain nonfat yogurt
1 teaspoon fresh lemon juice
¹/4 teaspoon finely grated lemon zest, removed with a zester or fine grater (see page 14)

Combine all the ingredients in a small bowl until smooth.

Baking Basics . . .

❖ **Position the oven rack and preheat the oven. Use a mercury oven thermometer to make certain the heat is accurate. If not, adjust the oven setting until the thermometer registers the required temperature.**

❖ **Be sure you have the size baking pan specified for the recipe.**

❖ **Prepare the pan as directed.**

❖ **Use unsalted butter.**

❖ **Measure flour by first stirring it to make it less compact; scoop it into specific quantity dry (not liquid) measuring cups and level it off with the straight edge of a knife.**

❖ **Use a mixer to cream sugar and butter until fluffy.**

❖ **Beat in the eggs thoroughly.**

Warm Spiced Pumpkin Cake with Caramel Sauce

*During a Midwestern autumn, pumpkins are everywhere you look. While the taste
of fresh pumpkin is wonderful, it's not as dense as canned pumpkin. Canned pumpkin
is a good product, compromising neither the flavor nor the quality of this recipe.
Topped with a butter-rich caramel sauce that's not too sweet, this luscious cake
represents nostalgic homecomings—ideal for Thanksgiving or other family
get-togethers. Be sure to serve it warm.*

YIELD: ONE 10-INCH BUNDT CAKE

2 cups cake flour
1 tablespoon baking powder
¹/₂ teaspoon each: baking soda, salt
2¹/₄ teaspoons cinnamon
1¹/₄ teaspoons allspice
3 large egg yolks
1¹/₃ cups granulated sugar
1¹/₂ sticks unsalted butter, at room temperature
3 tablespoons each: bourbon, buttermilk
1¹/₄ cups canned solid-pack pumpkin
3 large egg whites, at room temperature
2 teaspoons confectioners' sugar
Caramel Sauce (recipe follows)

1. Put a rack in the center of the oven; preheat the oven to 350 degrees. Generously grease a 12-cup-capacity (10-inch) Bundt pan, and lightly dust it with flour, tapping out any excess. Set it aside.

2. Sift the flour, baking powder, baking soda, salt, 2 teaspoons of the cinnamon, and 1 teaspoon of the allspice onto a sheet of waxed paper. Set aside.

3. Use a mixer to cream the egg yolks, granulated sugar, and butter until light and fluffy, about 2

minutes. Add the bourbon, buttermilk, and pumpkin and mix until smooth, scraping down the sides of the bowl. Add the sifted dry ingredients and mix until well combined.

4. Use clean beaters to whip the egg whites in a clean, grease-free bowl until they hold soft peaks yet are still moist. Stir one quarter of the egg whites into the batter. Fold in the remaining whites. Transfer the batter to the prepared pan. Tap the pan on the counter several times to settle the batter. Use a knife to cut through the batter in several places to break up any remaining air bubbles.

5. Bake until the cake is lightly browned and a toothpick inserted in the center comes out clean, about 55 minutes. Let the cake cool in the pan for 5 minutes, then gently invert it onto a wire rack.

6. The cake can be made 1 day ahead and kept at room temperature, covered airtight, or it can be wrapped airtight and frozen for up to 3 months. Thaw the cake in the wrapping at room temperature. The cake should be served warm. To reheat it, return the cake to the pan. Cover it with foil and reheat in a preheated 350-degree oven until it is warmed through, about 15 minutes. Or, alternately, warm the cake, uncovered, in a microwave oven on a microwavable serving plate at medium power (50 percent) until just warm (not steamed), about 3 to 4 minutes.

7. To serve, combine the confectioners' sugar and the remaining cinnamon and allspice. Press the mixture through a fine sieve over the cake. Cut the warm cake into slices and serve with warm caramel sauce.

Caramel Sauce

YIELD: 1 1/4 CUPS

^{1}/2 cup sugar
4 tablespoons unsalted butter
3 tablespoons dark corn syrup
1 cup heavy cream
Pinch of salt

1. Combine the sugar, butter, syrup, ^{1}/2 cup of the cream, and the salt in a heavy 1^1/2-quart saucepan. Bring to a boil over medium-high heat. Boil, uncovered, until the sauce is thickened (there will be large, deep bubbles) and turning a deep tan color, about 11 minutes, stirring almost constantly.

2. Stir in the remaining ^{1}/2 cup of cream. Bring back to a boil, stirring until the caramel melts and the mixture is smooth, about 30 seconds more. The sauce can be made several days ahead and refrigerated. Gently reheat in a double boiler or a microwave oven at high power (100 percent), for 30-second increments. Serve warm.

Good to the Last Drop . . .

Recipes using solid-pack pumpkin always seem to leave a little bit behind in the can. But there's no need to waste it:

❖ Add pumpkin to mashed potatoes, celery root, or carrots.
❖ Swirl pumpkin into pureed vegetable soups.
❖ Substitute pumpkin in recipes specifying pureed squash.
❖ Make pumpkin pancakes, waffles, quick breads, or muffins.
❖ Freeze the pumpkin (as long as 3 months) until you can use it.

Chocolate Cappuccino Pound Cake

The ultimate in dense chocolate cakes, this is like a pound cake in texture but is more moist and very rich. Served at the Starbucks Coffee Shops in the Chicago area, this recipe goes perfectly with a steaming cup of java on a cold afternoon in the Windy City. The pound cake was created by Suzanne Weisler, a former stockbroker, who started Hot Cakes, a Chicago-based baking operation.

YIELD: ONE 10-INCH BUNDT CAKE

1²/₃ cups flour
¹/₂ teaspoon each: baking powder, salt
1¹/₂ cups (3 sticks) unsalted butter, softened
2³/₄ cups sugar
5 large eggs
1 teaspoon pure vanilla extract
1 cup unsweetened cocoa, preferably Dutch processed, sifted
1 tablespoon finely ground deep-roasted coffee
1 cup buttermilk
¹/₄ cup water
Cocoa, for sprinkling

1. Put a rack in the center of the oven; preheat the oven to 350 degrees. Grease a 12-cup-capacity (10-inch) Bundt pan, and lightly dust it with flour, tapping out any excess. Set it aside.

2. Sift the flour, baking powder, and salt onto a sheet of waxed paper.

3. Use a mixer to beat the butter until light and fluffy. Add the sugar slowly, beating at slow speed. Increase the speed to high and beat for 5 minutes. Add the eggs, one at a time, and the vanilla; beat until fluffy, stopping as needed to scrape down the sides of the bowl. Add the cup of cocoa and the coffee. Blend well.

4. Add the sifted dry ingredients, alternating with the buttermilk and water, until the batter is smooth, scraping the bowl as needed. Pour the batter into the prepared pan and smooth it with a spatula.

5. Bake until the cake pulls away from sides of the pan and a toothpick inserted in the center comes out clean, about 70 to 80 minutes. If the edges of the cake brown too much, tent them with foil. It's okay if the surface cracks. Transfer the cake to a wire rack to cool for 30 minutes. (The cake deflates as it cools and sometimes the top crust layer separates from the cake. That's okay, too. Just carefully peel it off.) Invert the cake onto the rack to cool completely.

6. The cake will keep at room temperature up to 2 days, well covered, or it can be frozen, wrapped airtight, up to 3 months. Thaw the cake in the wrapping at room temperature.

7. To serve, sift cocoa through a fine sieve over the top of the cake.

Lazy Daisy Vanity Cake

This cake combines the best of two classic recipes—plain vanity cake and the broiled coconut topping from the Lazy Daisy cake. In Victorian Cakes (Caxton Printers, Ltd., 1941, reprinted by Aris Books, Berkeley, Calif., 1986), Caroline King writes about an ambrosial vanity cake served in her home in Chicago in the late 1800s. The texture and taste of her basic recipe reminded me of the Lazy Daisy cake made by Chicago's Heinemann's Bakeries. So I adapted her cake and added a broiled topping similar to Heinemann's to give the cake a sweet crunch and to keep it moist.

YIELD: ONE 8-INCH ROUND CAKE

CAKE:
1 1/2 cups flour
1/2 cup cornstarch
1 1/2 teaspoons baking powder
Pinch of salt
1 stick unsalted butter, softened
1 1/2 cups sugar
2 teaspoons pure vanilla extract
1/2 cup milk
6 large egg whites, at room temperature

LAZY DAISY TOPPING:
3 tablespoons unsalted butter
1 tablespoon milk
3/4 cup firmly packed dark brown sugar
1/2 cup sweetened coconut flakes

1. Put a rack in the center of the oven; preheat the oven to 350 degrees. Grease an 8-inch springform pan and lightly dust it with flour, tapping out any excess. Set it aside.

2. For the cake, sift the flour, cornstarch, baking powder, and salt onto a sheet of waxed paper. Set aside.

3. Use a mixer to cream the butter, sugar, and vanilla, about 2 minutes. Slowly pour in the milk and mix until smooth. Fold in the dry ingredients.

4. Use clean beaters to whip the egg whites in a clean, grease-free bowl until they hold their shape but are still moist and soft. Use a rubber spatula to fold the egg whites into the cake batter. Transfer the batter to the prepared pan.

5. Bake until a toothpick inserted in the center comes out clean, about 50 minutes. Let the cake rest in the pan set on a rack for at least 30 minutes, or until somewhat cooled.

6. For the topping, preheat the broiler with the rack about 8 inches from the heat source.

7. Put all the topping ingredients into a small saucepan. Bring to a boil, stirring constantly. Pour the hot topping evenly over the cake. Broil the cake until the topping is bubbly and somewhat darkened, about 1 to 2 minutes. Watch it constantly to avoid burning. Let the cake cool completely. The cake can be made 1 day ahead, covered airtight, in a cake tender, and kept at room temperature.

Caramel-Glazed Apple Chunk Cake

Moist, full-flavored, and generously studded with diced apples, this is one of the best apple cakes I have ever tasted. The recipe was developed by Elizabeth Sanchez, a pastry chef in Chicago. Serve it warm for a late breakfast, a morning coffee get-together, or for dessert following an informal family meal. It's important to use tart apples for the best flavor.

YIELD: ONE 10-INCH BUNDT CAKE

CAKE:

2¹/₂ cups plus 1 tablespoon flour
1¹/₄ teaspoons cinnamon
¹/₄ teaspoon freshly grated nutmeg (see page 289)
1 teaspoon each: baking soda, salt
1 cup vegetable oil
2 cups sugar
3 large eggs
1¹/₂ teaspoons pure vanilla extract
3 tablespoons orange juice
1¹/₂ large Granny Smith apples, peeled, cored, cut into ¹/₂-inch chunks, about 3¹/₄ cups
1 cup chopped pecans

GLAZE:

1 stick unsalted butter
1 cup packed light brown sugar
¹/₄ cup heavy cream

1. For the cake, put a rack in the center of the oven; preheat the oven to 350 degrees. Generously grease a 12-cup-capacity (10-inch) Bundt cake pan; lightly dust it with flour, tapping out the excess. Set it aside.

2. Sift the 2¹/₂ cups of flour, the cinnamon, nutmeg, baking soda, and salt onto a sheet of waxed paper. Set aside.

3. Use a mixer to beat the vegetable oil, sugar, eggs, and vanilla for 3 minutes (the mixture will be thick and smooth). Add the sifted ingredients and the orange juice and mix until combined. Toss the apples and pecans with the remaining tablespoon of flour and stir them into the batter with a wooden spoon; it will be very thick. Transfer the batter to the prepared pan and smooth the surface.

4. Bake until a toothpick inserted in the center comes out clean, about 1 hour.

5. While the cake is baking, bring all the ingredients for the glaze to a simmer in a small saucepan for 3 minutes, uncovered.

6. When the cake is done, let it rest on a cooling rack for 5 minutes. Invert the cake onto a rack placed on a sheet of foil. Brush the warm cake with the glaze, reapplying the glaze as it drips onto the foil. Let the cake rest 1 hour before serving it.

7. The cake is best served warm. To reheat it, place the cake on a baking sheet lined with foil. Bake it in a preheated 350-degree oven until it is just warm, about 8 to 10 minutes. Cut the warm cake into slices. Serve immediately.

Nutmeg

Freshly grated nutmeg is far superior in flavor and aroma to the commercial product, just as freshly ground pepper is preferred for its seasoning effect. Rub the whole nutmeg across the fine (and sharp) surface of a nutmeg grater. As a seed, it keeps for years without deteriorating. But once ground, its flavor and aroma diminish.

Truly "Old-Fashioned" Strawberry Shortcake

This shortcake recipe is loaded with nostalgia and is absolutely delicious. It's adapted from Home Grown, a small, charming book by Della Lutes, written in 1937. The book contains many heartwarming accounts of her mother's cooking in southern Michigan in the late 1800s. Her memories of this shortcake are compelling . . . "try as I may I cannot persuade my palate that a shortcake made today, using exactly the same component parts, tastes quite as did those [shortcakes] so inextricably mingled in memory with the rare, sweet Junes of my childhood." Few changes were made from the original recipe, only milk and sour cream substituted for "clabbered" milk, a naturally soured milk that is thick and curdly. Try to make the shortcake close to serving time as it's best assembled and served warm. It can, however, be reheated, if necessary.

YIELD: ONE 7-INCH SQUARE CAKE

2 cups flour
1 teaspoon baking soda
3/4 teaspoon salt
1 tablespoon sugar
2 tablespoons vegetable shortening
2 tablespoons chilled unsalted butter,
  plus 1 1/2 tablespoons, softened
2/3 cup sour cream
1/3 cup milk
1 1/2 pints very ripe strawberries mashed with a fork,
  sweetened to taste, about 3 cups
4 to 6 strawberries with hulls, for garnish
Heavy cream, chilled, for serving (optional)

1. Put a rack in the center of the oven; preheat the oven to 450 degrees. Grease a 7-inch square baking pan. Line the bottom of the pan with a square of parchment paper. Butter the paper. Set the pan aside.

2. Sift the flour, baking soda, salt, and sugar into a mixing bowl. Add the shortening and chilled butter. Work the butter and shortening into the flour mixture with your hands or with a pastry blender until it is in small bits.

3. Make a well in the center. Put the sour cream and milk in a small dish. Stir the mixture lightly; do not make it smooth. Pour the mixture into the well. Use a wooden spoon to stir the ingredients together until well combined.

4. Transfer the dough to a well-floured board. Compress it into a ball, and knead it, folding it back on itself, just until smooth, no longer than 1 minute. Flatten the ball lightly with your hand. Sprinkle the surface with flour and gently roll the dough into a 7-inch square, about 3/4 inch thick. Transfer the dough to the prepared pan, patting it lightly into place.

5. Bake until the top is golden brown, about 20 minutes. Let it cool on a wire rack 15 minutes before serving. Alternately, the shortcake can be baked several hours ahead and kept at room temperature. Reheat it, covered with foil, in a preheated 300-degree oven until warmed through but not hot, about 10 to 12 minutes.

6. To serve, transfer the warm cake to a serving platter. Use a serrated knife to split the cake horizontally, making the top piece somewhat thicker than the bottom. Set the top piece aside. Spread half the softened butter on the cut surface of the bottom piece. Spoon half the mashed strawberries over the entire cake to the edges. Close the shortcake with the top piece, cut side up. Spread the remaining butter on the surface, then the remaining mashed strawberries. Garnish with the whole strawberries. Serve warm, cut into squares. Pass the cream in a pitcher, if desired.

Annella Campbell's Company Cake

An old family recipe of Annella Campbell's, this festive cake was the grand finale at a potluck dinner in Fargo, North Dakota, on a warm fall evening in 1990. It's called "company" cake because the layers are baked with a delicious meringue topping, then filled with a vanilla custard cream. Serve the cake plain, with fresh strawberries or raspberries, raspberry sauce, or a dollop of whipped cream.

YIELD: ONE 8-INCH LAYER CAKE

1 cup flour
1 teaspoon baking powder
$1/8$ teaspoon salt
$1/2$ cup each: vegetable shortening, sugar
4 large egg yolks
2 teaspoons pure vanilla extract
$1/3$ cup milk

TOPPING:
5 large egg whites, at room temperature
$2/3$ cup sugar
$1/2$ cup chopped walnuts

Vanilla Custard Filling (recipe follows)

1. Put a rack in the center of the oven; preheat the oven to 325 degrees. Generously grease two 8-inch layer cake pans; lightly dust them with flour, tapping out any excess. Set the pans aside.

2. Sift the flour, baking powder, and salt together onto a sheet of waxed paper. Set aside.

3. Use a mixer to cream the shortening and sugar until fluffy, about 2 minutes. Add the egg yolks, one at a time, beating well after each addition. Add the vanilla and combine well. Add the flour mixture alternately with the milk, mixing until smooth.

Divide the batter between the prepared pans; use a spatula to spread it evenly.

4. For the topping, use clean beaters to beat the egg whites in a grease-free bowl until they are thick and hold their shape but are still soft and moist. Add the sugar, 1 tablespoon at a time, beating well after each addition. Divide the topping between the pans; use a spatula to spread it over the batter. Sprinkle with the nuts.

5. Bake until the top is lightly colored and a toothpick inserted in the center comes out clean (it's okay if the meringue cracks), about 30 minutes. Let the cakes rest 10 minutes in their pans on wire racks. Use a small knife to release the cakes from the sides of the pans. Use a metal spatula to gently remove the cakes and place them on the racks, meringue side up, to cool completely.

6. Spread one layer, meringue side up, with the filling. Top with the other layer, also meringue side up. This cake is best served the day it is made, but it can be made one day ahead and kept in a cool dry place (not in the refrigerator because the meringue will weep), well covered.

Vanilla Custard Filling

YIELD: ENOUGH FILLING
FOR ONE 8-INCH LAYER CAKE

2 tablespoons each: sugar, cornstarch
Pinch of salt
1 large egg yolk
1 cup milk
1 teaspoon pure vanilla extract

Combine the sugar, cornstarch, and salt in a heavy 1-quart saucepan. Add the egg yolk and milk and stir over medium heat until the mixture coats a spoon, about 4 minutes. Remove from the heat, stir in the vanilla, and let the custard cool completely. If the mixture is lumpy, whisk it vigorously until smooth before using.

Fresh Gingerbread Cakes with Diced Pears

These gingerbread cakes bridge the gap between a sweet muffin and a dessert; they satisfy without being too sweet. They are especially nice served warm, in individual soufflé dishes, with a small dollop of rich vanilla ice cream melting in the center.

YIELD: 10 MEDIUM CAKES

One ³/₄-inch piece fresh ginger, peeled and minced, about 1¹/₄ teaspoons
¹/₂ cup firmly packed dark brown sugar
2 large egg whites
1 stick unsalted butter, softened
3 tablespoons each: molasses, light corn syrup
1¹/₂ cups cake flour
1¹/₄ teaspoons baking soda
¹/₂ teaspoon cinnamon
¹/₄ teaspoon salt
¹/₈ teaspoon freshly ground pepper
1 large firm pear, cored, peeled if desired, cut into ¹/₃-inch dice, about 2 cups
1 tablespoon confectioners' sugar, for sprinkling
Vanilla ice cream, for serving (optional)

1. Put a rack in the center of the oven; preheat the oven to 350 degrees. Line 10 medium muffin cups with paper liners or grease ten 8-ounce-capacity individual soufflé dishes. Set them aside.

2. Use an electric mixer to combine the ginger, sugar, egg whites, butter, molasses, and corn syrup until smooth and flowing. Put the flour, baking soda, cinnamon, salt, and pepper on top of the batter. Spoon the pears on top of the dry ingredients. Use a rubber spatula to fold in these ingredients until they are completely combined. Spoon the batter into the prepared muffin cups or soufflé dishes. (Place the soufflé dishes on a baking sheet.)

3. Bake until a toothpick inserted in the center comes out clean, about 17 minutes. Let the cakes cool in their pans for 5 minutes. Press the confectioners' sugar through a fine sieve to dust the tops of the cakes. Serve warm, with ice cream, if desired.

4. The cakes can be made a day ahead and kept at room temperature, well covered, or it can be frozen, wrapped airtight, for up to 3 months. Frozen cakes do not need to be thawed before reheating. Reheat them in a preheated 300-degree oven until warm, about 12 minutes (longer if frozen) or in a microwave oven on medium power (50 percent) until they are just warm.

Petoskey Carrot Cake

*Here, great-tasting dried fruits—wild blueberries, cranberries, and tart cherries—
are baked into a moist carrot cake batter. American Spoon Foods (see Midwestern
Sources, page 377), based in Petoskey, Michigan, is the source for these highly flavorful
dried fruits. If it's difficult to find this variety, you can use a cup of dried cranberries.
Like most fruitcakes, this carrot cake develops more flavor a few days after it is baked;
keep it at room temperature, wrapped airtight, for at least a day before serving.
It also freezes very well.*

YIELD: ONE 10-INCH BUNDT CAKE

*⅓ cup each: dried tart cherries (coarsely chopped),
  cranberries, wild blueberries*

or

1 cup dried cranberries
3 tablespoons Scotch whiskey
1¾ cups plus 2 tablespoons cake flour
1½ teaspoons each: baking powder, baking soda
¾ teaspoon salt
*¼ teaspoon each: freshly grated nutmeg
  (see page 289), allspice*
2 teaspoons cinnamon
1½ cups sugar
2 sticks unsalted butter, softened
3 large eggs
2 teaspoons pure vanilla extract
*2 large carrots, scrubbed, trimmed, grated,
  about 2¼ cups*
¾ cups pecan, toasted (page 358), chopped
1 tablespoon confectioners' sugar, for sprinkling

1. Put a rack in the center of the oven; preheat the oven to 325 degrees. Generously grease a 12-cup-capacity (10-inch) Bundt pan; lightly dust it with flour, tapping out the excess. Set it aside.

2. Combine the dried fruit and Scotch whiskey in a small bowl. Set aside. Sift the dry ingredients with all the spices. Set aside.

3. Use an electric mixer to cream the sugar and the butter. Add the eggs, one at a time, and the vanilla. Beat until very smooth, about 2 minutes. Add the carrots. Mix well. Add the flour mixture with the nuts and dried fruit mixture. Use a wooden spoon to combine all the ingredients. Transfer the batter to the prepared pan and smooth the top with a spatula.

4. Bake until a toothpick inserted in the center comes out clean, about 45 minutes. Allow the cake to cool upright in the pan on a wire rack for 10 minutes. Then invert the cake onto the wire rack to cool completely. The cake keeps up to 3 days at room temperature, wrapped in foil, or can be frozen for up to 2 months, wrapped airtight. Thaw the cake in the wrapping at room temperature.

5. To serve, press confectioners' sugar through a fine sieve over the top of the cake.

Sunshine Cake

Here's a special-occasion cake for guests of all ages. Appearing in many of the early Midwestern cookbooks, it's a universally appealing yellow cake that is very light in texture, much like an angel cake. Many frostings would complement this cake, but I've chosen lemon for its wonderful tart contrast.

YIELD: ONE 10-INCH TUBE CAKE

1 cup cake flour
1¼ cups sugar
4 large egg yolks
8 large egg whites, at room temperature
½ teaspoon each: cream of tartar, salt
½ teaspoon lemon extract
Grated zest (colored rind) of 1 lemon, removed with a zester or fine grater (see page 14), about 1 tablespoon
Lemon Frosting (recipe follows)

1. Put a rack in the center of the oven; preheat the oven to 350 degrees. Set aside an ungreased 10-inch tube pan.

2. Sift the flour 3 times. Sift the sugar 3 times. Set them aside.

3. Use an electric mixer to beat the egg yolks until thick and light-colored, about 4 minutes.

4. Use clean beaters to beat the egg whites in a clean, grease-free bowl until foamy. Add the cream of tartar and salt; beat until the egg whites are thick and hold their shape but are still soft and moist. Use a rubber spatula to gently fold the sugar, in 3 batches, into the whites. Fold in the lemon extract, zest, and beaten egg yolks until blended. Gently fold in the flour. Transfer the batter to the tube pan and use a rubber spatula to spread it evenly.

5. Bake until the top is lightly browned and a toothpick inserted in the center comes out clean, about 45 minutes. Invert the pan onto a funnel or the neck of a wine bottle to cool.

6. When cool, use a small knife to release the cake from the sides and bottom of the pan. Spread the top and sides with lemon frosting. Once frosted, the cake will keep overnight at room temperature, well covered.

7. The cake, covered airtight, will keep 1 day at room temperature, or it can be frozen for as long as 2 months, wrapped airtight. Thaw the cake in its wrapping at room temperature.

Lemon Frosting

YIELD: ENOUGH FROSTING FOR
ONE 10-INCH TUBE CAKE

3³/4 cups confectioners' sugar, sifted

4 tablespoons unsalted butter, melted

Pinch of salt

*Grated zest (colored rind) of 1 large lemon, removed
with a zester or fine grater (see page 14), about
1 tablespoon*

¹/4 cup fresh lemon juice

*¹/2 to 1 teaspoon milk or water, as necessary for
consistency*

Put all the ingredients except the milk or
water in a mixing bowl. Combine until
smooth. Add the milk or water for the
spreading consistency.

Fresh Blueberry-Lemon Bundt Cake

This is one of those old-fashioned Bundt cakes where one slice is never enough.

YIELD: ONE 10-INCH BUNDT CAKE

3¼ cups plus 3 tablespoons cake flour
1 teaspoon each: baking soda, salt
2 sticks unsalted butter, softened
2 cups sugar
Grated zest (colored rind) of 2 large lemons, removed
    with a zester or fine grater (see page 14), about 2
    tablespoons
3 large eggs
1 teaspoon lemon extract
¼ cup buttermilk
2½ cups blueberries
Tart Lemon Glaze (recipe follows)

1. Put a rack in the center of the oven; preheat the oven to 350 degrees. Generously grease a 12-cup-capacity (10-inch) Bundt cake pan; lightly dust it with flour, tapping out the excess. Set it aside.

2. Sift 3¼ cups of the flour, baking soda, and salt onto a sheet of waxed paper; set aside.

3. Use an electric mixer to cream the butter, sugar, and lemon zest in a large bowl until light and fluffy. Add the eggs and lemon extract. Beat 3 minutes (the mixture will become thick and smooth). Add the sifted ingredients and the buttermilk. Mix well until combined. Toss the blueberries with the remaining flour to coat them. Use a wooden spoon to stir them into the batter; the batter will be very thick. Transfer the batter to the prepared pan. Bang the pan on the counter to settle the batter. Use a spatula to smooth the surface.

4. Bake until a toothpick inserted in the center

comes out clean, about 55 to 60 minutes. Let the cake rest in its pan on a wire rack for 10 minutes. Then gently invert it onto the rack. Place the rack on a sheet of aluminum foil and brush the warm cake with glaze, reapplying the glaze as it drips onto the foil.

5. Let the cake cool completely. It can be made a day ahead and stored at room temperature, covered airtight. This cake does not freeze well.

Tart Lemon Glaze

YIELD: 1/2 CUP

Grated zest (colored rind) of 1 lemon, removed with
    a zester or fine grater (see page 14), about 1
    tablespoon
1 cup confectioners' sugar
3 tablespoons fresh lemon juice
4 tablespoons unsalted butter, melted
Pinch of salt

Put the lemon zest and sugar in a blender or food processor fitted with the metal blade and process until the zest is finely minced. Add the remaining ingredients and mix until smooth. Set the glaze aside at room temperature until ready to use.

Glazed Maple Pecan Tea Cake

Flecked with pecans and glazed with a thin maple icing, this cake is perfect for more than just tea. Consider it for buffet desserts and morning coffee. Plan to make the cake 2 days in advance as it will slice much more neatly once it's had a chance to rest at room temperature, wrapped airtight.

YIELD: ONE 9-INCH LOAF CAKE

CAKE:

1½ sticks unsalted butter, at room temperature

1 cup plus 2 tablespoons sugar

2 teaspoons pure vanilla extract

1½ teaspoons maple flavoring

2 large eggs

One 3-ounce package cream cheese, at room
   temperature

1¾ cups cake flour

1¼ teaspoons baking powder

¼ teaspoon salt

½ cup minced pecans

⅔ cup buttermilk

GLAZE:

½ cup confectioners' sugar, sifted

2 teaspoons each: pure vanilla extract, maple flavoring,
   buttermilk

1. Put a rack in the center of the oven; preheat the oven to 325 degrees. Generously grease a 9-inch (8-cup-capacity) loaf pan; lightly dust it with flour, tapping out the excess. Cut a piece of parchment or waxed paper to fit the bottom of pan. Grease the paper. Set the pan aside.

2. For the cake, use an electric mixer to cream the butter, sugar, vanilla, and maple flavoring until fluffy. Add the eggs, one at a time, beating each

until the batter is smooth. Add the cream cheese. Mix until smooth.

3. Sift the flour, baking powder, and salt together. Combine the dry ingredients with the pecans. Add the flour mixture to the batter, alternating with the buttermilk. Mix until it is smooth. Transfer the batter to the prepared pan and smooth the surface with a spatula.

4. Bake until the top is well browned and a toothpick inserted in the center comes out clean, about 1 hour, 35 minutes. The cake will crack on the top. Let it rest in the pan for 10 minutes after baking.

5. Meanwhile, for the glaze, combine the sugar, flavorings, and buttermilk in a small bowl. Stir until smooth.

6. Use a sharp knife to separate the cake from the sides of the pan. Invert the cake onto a wire rack. Spread the glaze over the top of the warm cake, then let the cake cool completely. The cake should be stored at room temperature for 2 days before it is served. To store, wrap the cake in foil and then place it in an airtight plastic bag.

7. The cake can also be frozen, wrapped airtight, for up to 3 months. Thaw the cake in the wrapping at room temperature.

Frozen Deep Chocolate Ice Cream Roll with Hot Fudge Sauce

This is one dessert almost everyone has tasted at some point. I must confess I have always loved it, sauced with hot fudge. Before serving, it's important to let it rest briefly at room temperature so that it can be easily sliced. You could use any number of ice cream or frozen yogurt flavors for the filling: coffee, chocolate chip, Heath Bar crunch, maple walnut, or raspberry sherbet. Take your choice!

YIELD: 8 TO 12 SERVINGS

$^3/_4$ cup cake flour
1 teaspoon baking powder
$^1/_2$ teaspoon baking soda
Pinch of salt
3 large eggs, separated
$^1/_2$ cup sugar
1 tablespoon cocoa powder, preferably Dutch processed
4 ounces semisweet chocolate, melted
$^1/_3$ cup water
2 teaspoons pure vanilla extract
2 pints ice cream, yogurt, or sherbet of choice, softened but not melted, for filling
1 tablespoon confectioners' sugar, for sprinkling
Hot fudge sauce (recipe follows), for serving

1. Put a rack in the center of the oven; preheat the oven to 350 degrees. Line a $10^1/_2 \times 15^1/_2$-inch jelly roll pan (cookie sheet with sides) with aluminum foil, leaving a 2-inch overhang. Wrap the overhang around the ends of the pan. Grease the foil and lightly dust it with flour, tapping out the excess. Set the pan aside.

2. Sift the flour, baking powder, baking soda, and salt together on a sheet of waxed paper. Set aside.

3. Use an electric mixer to beat the egg yolks and sugar until they are light and fluffy, about 3 minutes. Add the cocoa and melted chocolate to the yolks. Beat until combined. Add the water and vanilla. Mix until smooth, scraping down the sides of the bowl. Add the flour mixture and mix until combined.

4. Use clean beaters and a clean grease-free bowl to whip the egg whites into soft, moist peaks that hold their shape but are not stiff. Use a rubber spatula to gently fold the egg whites into the chocolate mixture. Pour the batter into the center of the prepared pan. Use a rubber spatula to spread it evenly in the pan.

5. Bake until a toothpick inserted in the center comes out clean, about 8 to 9 minutes. Place the pan on a wire rack and use a small knife to release any part of the cake sticking to the sides of the foil. Cover the cake with a cookie sheet and invert it. Remove the jelly roll pan and peel off the foil carefully to avoid tearing the cake. Place the clean side of the foil on the cake with a large wire rack over it; invert the cake so it is right side up, resting on the foil. Cool the cake completely.

6. To fill, spread the cake with softened ice cream, frozen yogurt, or sherbet, leaving a ¼-inch border. Starting at short end, use the foil to gently roll the cake as compactly as possible. Wrap it securely and freeze. When frozen, double-wrap it. The roll can be frozen for as long as 1 month.

7. To serve, unwrap the cake and place it, seam side down, on a serving platter. Let it rest at room temperature for 10 minutes or until slightly softened. Sprinkle the cake with confectioners' sugar pressed through a fine sieve. Use a serrated knife to cut the cake into diagonal slices. Serve the sauce separately.

Hot Fudge Sauce

YIELD: 1 3/4 CUPS

4 ounces unsweetened chocolate, broken into pieces
4 tablespoons unsalted butter
1¼ cups sugar
½ cup whole milk
1 teaspoon baking powder
1 tablespoon pure vanilla extract

1. Cook the chocolate, butter, sugar, and milk in the top of a double boiler over gently simmering water until smooth.

2. Off the heat, stir in the baking powder, then the vanilla. Serve hot. The sauce can be made in advance and refrigerated up to 1 week, or frozen, covered airtight. Reheat gently before using.

Deep Chocolate Cinnamon Cookies

*The triple dose of chocolate with a touch of cinnamon permeates the kitchen while
these cookies bake. Chewy and crisp at the same time, they are—not surprisingly—
very, very rich and very delicious.*

YIELD: THIRTY-TWO 2 1/2-INCH COOKIES

¹/₄ cup flour
¹/₄ teaspoon baking powder
Pinch of salt
6 tablespoons unsalted butter, softened
Scant ¹/₂ cup sugar
2 large eggs
8 ounces semisweet chocolate, melted
¹/₄ cup cocoa powder, preferably Dutch processed
1¹/₂ teaspoons cinnamon
1 cup milk chocolate chips
1 cup chopped walnuts, toasted (page 358)
1 tablespoon confectioners' sugar, for sprinkling

1. Put a rack in the center of the oven; preheat the oven to 350 degrees. Line 2 cookie sheets with parchment paper. Set them aside.

2. Sift the flour, baking powder, and salt onto a sheet of waxed paper. Set aside.

3. Use an electric mixer to beat the butter, sugar, and eggs until smooth. Add the melted chocolate, cocoa, and cinnamon. Mix well. Add the flour mixture and combine. Stir in the chocolate chips and walnuts.

4. By the tablespoon, place the dough on the prepared cookie sheets, spacing the cookies 1 inch apart. Dip your finger in water and gently flatten the tops.

5. Bake until just set, not gooey or hard, about 11 minutes. Let the cookies rest 5 minutes on the sheets. Then, use a metal spatula to transfer them to a wire rack to cool completely. Sprinkle the tops with confectioners' sugar, pressed through a fine sieve. These cookies are best when freshly baked but will keep up to 2 days at room temperature in an airtight container.

Allspice Orange Poppy Seed Cookies

*The combination of allspice and orange zest lends a distinctive tang
to these crunchy poppy seed cookies.*

YIELD: ABOUT THIRTY-SIX 2 1/2-INCH COOKIES

2 cups cake flour
1/4 teaspoon salt
1 cup sugar
2 sticks unsalted butter, at room temperature
*Grated zest (colored rind) of 1 1/2 large oranges,
    removed with a zester or fine grater (see page 14),
    about 1 1/2 tablespoons*
2 large egg yolks
2 teaspoons allspice
2 tablespoons poppy seeds, plus additional for garnish

GLAZE:
1 large egg
1/8 teaspoon salt

1. Put a rack in the center of the oven; preheat the
oven to 350 degrees. Grease 2 cookie sheets and set
them aside.

2. Combine the flour and salt on a sheet of waxed
paper. Set aside.

3. Use an electric mixer to cream the sugar, butter,
and orange zest until light and fluffy. Add the egg
yolks and combine well. On low speed, add the
flour mixture and 2 tablespoons of the poppy seeds;
mix well.

4. Use 1 tablespoon of dough per cookie, spacing
them 2 inches apart on the cookie sheets. With
your fingers, gently flatten the dough into 2-inch
rounds.

5. For the glaze, use a fork to froth the egg and salt
in a small bowl. Lightly brush the glaze over the
cookies with a feather brush. (The remaining glaze
can be refrigerated for up to 5 days and used for
other baking.) Sprinkle the cookies with additional
poppy seeds.

6. Bake until the cookies just begin to brown
around the edges, about 9 to 10 minutes. Let them
rest 3 minutes on the cookie sheet, then use a
metal spatula to transfer them to a wire rack to cool
completely.

7. Store them at room temperature in an airtight
tin for up to 1 week, or freeze, wrapped airtight, for
up to 1 month.

Freezing Cakes and Cookies . . .

Most cakes and cookies freeze very well:

❖ Let baked goods cool completely on a rack.

❖ For cakes: place them on a baking sheet lined with waxed paper. Place in the freezer until frozen solid. Wrap the frozen cake in a plastic bag, seal tightly, then wrap and seal it in another bag to make sure it is airtight. Return to the freezer for up to 3 months. Thaw at room temperature while still wrapped in the plastic bag. Double-bagging may seem excessive, but this process effectively removes the possibility of freezer burn and off-flavors.

❖ For cookies: place single layers between sheets of waxed paper in an airtight tin. Freeze up to 3 months. Thaw at room temperature in the closed tin.

Peanut Butter Cookies

These cookies are best made with chunky—not smooth—peanut butter.

YIELD: ABOUT THIRTY-TWO 3-INCH COOKIES

1 stick unsalted butter, softened
³/₄ cup each: granulated sugar, firmly packed
   light brown sugar
2 large egg whites
1¹/₂ teaspoons pure vanilla extract
1¹/₄ cups chunky peanut butter
1 cup unbleached all-purpose flour
¹/₂ teaspoon baking soda
¹/₄ teaspoon salt

1. Put a rack in the center of the oven; preheat the oven to 375 degrees. Set aside 2 cookie sheets.

2. Use an electric mixer to cream the butter and both sugars on high speed until light and fluffy. Add the egg whites and vanilla; mix well. Add the peanut butter and mix until smooth. Add the flour, baking soda, and salt; mix just until the flour disappears. Do not overmix.

3. Roll the dough into 1¹/₂-inch balls; put them on the cookie sheets spaced 2¹/₂ inches apart. Flatten with the tines of a fork.

4. Bake until set (not browned), about 12 minutes. Let them rest 3 minutes on the cookie sheet, then use a metal spatula to transfer them to a wire rack to cool completely. They can be stored in an airtight container for several days or frozen, wrapped airtight, for up to 2 months.

Chewy Oatmeal Toffee Crunch Cookies

Loaded with oats and chopped pecans, these cookies become even more enticing made with the Heath Bar chunks.

YIELD: ABOUT SIXTEEN 4-INCH COOKIES

³/₄ cup packed dark brown sugar

¹/₂ cup granulated sugar

1¹/₂ sticks unsalted butter, at room temperature

1 large egg

1 teaspoon pure vanilla extract

1 cup all-purpose flour

¹/₂ teaspoon baking soda

¹/₈ teaspoon salt

1³/₄ cups rolled oats

³/₄ cup coarsely chopped pecans

4 small (1.2 ounces each) Heath Bars, chopped into ¹/₂-inch pieces

1. Put a rack in the center of the oven; preheat the oven to 350 degrees. Lightly grease 2 cookie sheets. Set them aside.

2. Use an electric mixer to beat the sugars, butter, egg, and vanilla until smooth. Add the flour, baking soda, salt, and oats; mix well. Use a wooden spoon to stir in the pecans and chopped Heath Bars.

3. Put ¹/₄-cup portions of dough 2 inches apart on the prepared cookie sheets. Press down lightly with your fingers.

4. Bake until lightly colored, about 15 minutes. Cool on the cookie sheets for 3 minutes. Then, use a metal spatula to transfer the cookies to a wire rack to cool completely. They can be stored in an airtight container at room temperature for 4 days, or wrapped airtight and frozen for up to 1 month.

Caramel Apple Squares with Pecans

These squares are loaded with apples and just enough caramel to make them irresistible.

YIELD: TWENTY-FOUR 1 1/2 × 2 1/4-INCH RECTANGLES

CRUST AND TOPPING:
1 large egg, separated
1¹/₂ cups firmly packed light brown sugar
2 sticks unsalted butter, softened
¹/₈ teaspoon salt
2 cups flour

APPLE AND CARAMEL FILLING:
2 tablespoons flour
1 tablespoon sugar
1 teaspoon cinnamon
Twenty ³/₄-inch caramels (I used Kraft caramels),
    about 6 ounces
1 tablespoon water
4 large Granny Smith apples, peeled, cored,
    thinly sliced, about 5 cups

¹/₂ cup coarsely chopped pecans

1. Put a rack in the center of the oven; preheat the oven to 350 degrees. Set aside a 13 × 9 × 2-inch baking pan.

2. For the crust and topping, put the egg white in a small dish and froth it with a fork. Set aside. Use an electric mixer to cream the egg yolk, sugar, butter, and salt. Add the flour. Mix until just combined.

3. Refrigerate about 1¹/₂ cups of the mixture (for the topping) until ready to use. Spoon the remaining mixture into the baking pan, distributing

it as evenly as possible. Place a piece of plastic over the dough—or put your hand in a small plastic food bag—and press the dough into a thin, even layer.

4. Bake until it is lightly browned, about 15 minutes. Cool about 15 minutes.

5. For the filling, combine the flour, sugar, and cinnamon in a small dish. Melt the caramels in the water in the microwave oven at high power (100 percent, for 1¹/₂ minutes) or in a double boiler over boiling water for 20 minutes until completely melted, stirring occasionally.

6. To assemble, toss the apple slices with the flour mixture. Overlap the apple slices tightly over the slightly cooled crust. Use all the apple slices—they cook down. Drizzle the melted caramel evenly over the apples. Crumble the refrigerated topping evenly over the caramel. Brush the surface with the reserved egg white. Scatter the pecans over the top.

7. Bake until the top is nicely browned, about 45 minutes. Cool completely on a rack. Cut into 1¹/₂ × 2¹/₄-inch rectangles. To do this easily, cut the cake into quarters, then cut each quarter into 6 rectangles. These are best served the day that they are baked, but they can be made a day in advance. To store overnight, place them in a single layer on a cookie sheet, cover with foil and refrigerate. To serve, uncover and bring to room temperature.

Orange Cornmeal Crisps

*Plain, buttery, and crispy with the addition of the cornmeal, these cookies
pair well with fresh fruit, ice cream, or sorbets.*

YIELD: TWENTY-FOUR 2 3/4-INCH COOKIES

1 stick unsalted butter, softened
¹/₂ cup firmly packed light brown sugar
1 large egg, separated
Grated zest (colored rind) of 1 large orange,
    removed with a zester or fine grater (see page 14),
    about 1 tablespoon
1 cup cake flour
¹/₄ cup yellow cornmeal
¹/₈ teaspoon salt

1. Put a rack in the center of the oven; preheat the oven to 350 degrees. Lightly grease 2 cookie sheets. Set them aside.

2. Use an electric mixer to beat the butter, sugar, and egg yolk until fluffy. Add the zest, cake flour, cornmeal, and salt. Mix until smooth. For easier handling, chill the dough, wrapped in plastic, until firm (briefly in the freezer, about 45 minutes in the refrigerator).

3. Shape the dough into 1-inch balls. Place them on the prepared cookie sheets spaced 1¹/₂ inches apart. Use your fingers to flatten the balls into discs about 2 inches in diameter and ¹/₄ inch thick. Froth the egg white with a fork and lightly brush the surface of the cookies.

4. Bake until the edges are browned, about 10 minutes. Let the cookies rest 1 minute before transferring them to a wire rack to cool. These can be made ahead and kept at room temperature in an airtight container for 3 days, or frozen, wrapped airtight, for up to 3 months.

Lemony Clove Icebox Cookies

The complementary essences of lemon and clove give these cookies an especially lively flavor. Mince the lemon zest with the sugar in a food processor or blender to release the lemon oil and develop the lemon flavor to its fullest.

YIELD: TWENTY-FOUR 2-INCH COOKIES

1¼ cups flour
1 teaspoon baking powder
½ teaspoon ground cloves
¼ teaspoon salt
Grated zest (colored rind) of 2 large lemons,
    removed with a zester or fine grater (see page 14),
    about 2 tablespoons
¾ cup sugar
1 stick unsalted butter, softened
1 large egg
24 whole cloves, for garnish (optional)

GLAZE:
1 large egg
Pinch of salt

1. Put a rack in the center of the oven; preheat the oven to 350 degrees. Lightly grease 2 cookie sheets. Set them aside.

2. Sift the flour with the baking powder, cloves, and salt onto a sheet of waxed paper. Set aside.

3. Use a food processor fitted with the metal blade or a blender to mince the lemon zest with the sugar until the zest becomes small specks.

4. Use an electric mixer to cream the butter and lemon sugar until fluffy. Add the egg and mix until smooth. Add the flour mixture; mix well.

5. Wrap the dough airtight and chill until firm (briefly in freezer, about 45 minutes in refrigerator).

6. Shape balls with 1 tablespoon of dough; place them on the prepared cookie sheets, spaced 1½ inches apart. Press lightly with your fingers to flatten them. Press a clove lightly in the center of each cookie, if desired.

7. For the glaze, use a fork to froth the egg with the salt in small bowl. Lightly brush the glaze over the cookies. (The remaining glaze can be refrigerated for up to 3 days and used for other baking.)

8. Bake until lightly browned, about 10 to 12 minutes. Let the cookies rest 3 minutes on the cookie sheet. Then, use a metal spatula to transfer them to a wire rack to cool. When completely cool, store in an airtight container at room temperature for up to 1 week, or freeze, wrapped airtight, for up to 1 month.

Rocky Road Brownies

These brownies are candy-like, dense and chewy; they are best served chilled. Space regular-size marshmallows on the bottom of the prepared pan and cover them with the batter to prevent them from browning too much.

YIELD: TWELVE 2 1/2-INCH SQUARES

1³/4 cups sugar

1¹/2 sticks unsalted butter, softened

3 large eggs

2 teaspoons pure vanilla extract

4 squares unsweetened chocolate, melted and cooled

¹/2 cup cocoa powder, preferably Dutch processed

³/4 cup flour

¹/4 teaspoon salt

1 cup each: milk chocolate chips, chopped walnuts

12 regular-size marshmallows

1. Put a rack in the center of the oven; preheat the oven to 350 degrees. Generously grease a 9 × 13-inch pan; lightly dust it with flour, tapping out the excess. Set it aside.

2. Use an electric mixer to cream the sugar and butter until fluffy. Add the eggs and mix until thick and lemon-colored, about 2 minutes. Add the vanilla and chocolate. Mix until combined. Add the cocoa, flour, and salt. Slowly mix into the batter until combined. Stir in the chips and walnuts.

3. Lay the marshmallows on their sides in the prepared pan, starting in the center and leaving a 1¹/2-inch border around the edge, spacing them evenly. Spoon the batter (it's very thick) over the marshmallows to cover them as much as possible (it's okay if they are not completely covered). Add the remaining batter evenly in the center of the pan; do not add batter to the spaces between the marshmallows and the sides of the pan (the batter will spread as it bakes to reach the sides).

4. Bake until a toothpick inserted into the center comes out moist but not gooey, about 25 minutes. Do not overbake. Let the brownies cool completely in the pan placed on a wire rack. Cut into 12 squares. Refrigerate in the pan until they are chilled. Use a wide metal spatula to carefully transfer the brownies to a serving platter. Wrap airtight. These can be made a day in advance and refrigerated, or frozen, wrapped airtight, for up to 3 months. Serve chilled.

Two-Cereal Crisps

These cookies have great texture, which derives from the combination of cornflakes, oatmeal, and coconut.

YIELD: SIXTEEN 2 1/2-INCH COOKIES

2 tablespoons unsalted butter, softened
$^1/_2$ cup sugar
2 large eggs
$^3/_4$ cup quick-cooking oatmeal
$^2/_3$ cup coconut flakes
2 cups cornflakes
1 teaspoon baking powder
$^1/_2$ teaspoon salt

1. Put a rack in the center of the oven; preheat the oven to 350 degrees. Lightly grease 2 cookie sheets. Set them aside.

2. Use an electric mixer to cream the butter, sugar, and eggs until they are light and smooth. Add the remaining ingredients and mix only until combined.

3. Drop the batter by the tablespoon onto the prepared cookie sheets, spacing the cookies 1 inch apart.

4. Bake until the edges are browned, about 12 minutes. Let the cookies rest for 2 minutes. Then, use a metal spatula to transfer them to a wire rack to cool completely. These cookies will keep up to 5 days at room temperature in an airtight container, or they can be frozen, wrapped airtight, for up to 2 months.

Blueberry Bar Cookies

These delicate bar cookies mean summer to me. When early tart blueberries start showing up in the farmers' markets, this recipe is the first on my cooking agenda. Both the crust and the fruit have a fresh lemon flavor. Served with a dollop of vanilla ice cream, a good thing becomes even better.

YIELD: EIGHTEEN 2 × 3-INCH BARS

CRUST:

$1/2$ cup sugar

1 stick unsalted butter, chilled, cut into small pieces

Grated zest (colored rind) of 1 large lemon, removed with a zester or fine grater (see page 14), about 1 tablespoon

1 large egg yolk

$1^1/3$ cups flour

$1/4$ teaspoon salt

CRUMB TOPPING:

Grated zest (colored rind) of 1 large lemon, removed with a zester or fine grater, about 1 tablespoon

1 cup sugar

1 stick unsalted butter, chilled, cut into small pieces

1 cup flour

FILLING:

1 large egg white

$1^1/2$ teaspoons fresh lemon juice

$1^1/2$ tablespoons sugar

4 cups blueberries

Vanilla ice cream, for serving (optional)

1. Put a rack in the center of the oven; preheat the oven to 400 degrees. Set aside an ungreased 13 × 9-inch baking pan.

2. For the crust, put the sugar, butter, zest, egg yolk, $1^1/4$ cups of the flour, and the salt into a food processor fitted with the metal blade. Mix until the ingredients are uniformly granular.

3. Or, to make by hand, cut the butter into $1^1/4$ cups of the flour and the salt with a pastry blender or 2 knives until it is uniformly granular. Add the zest, sugar, and egg yolk; use a fork to mix until combined.

4. Transfer the crust to the baking pan, pressing it evenly into the bottom and $1/2$ inch up the sides. Use a piece of plastic wrap under your fingers to help spread the dough. Sprinkle with the remaining flour.

5. For the crumb topping, put all the ingredients in the same processor bowl and mix until the butter is the size of small peas.

6. Or, to make by hand, mince the zest and set aside. Cut the butter into the flour with a pastry blender or 2 knives until it is the size of small peas. Lightly mix in the sugar and zest.

7. For the filling, use an electric mixer to beat the egg white and lemon juice until foamy. Add the sugar and beat until the egg white holds soft peaks. Fold the blueberries into the egg white.

8. Carefully spread the filling over the crust. Sprinkle the crumb topping evenly over the blueberries.

9. Bake until the top begins to turn a medium brown, about 55 minutes. Cut into 2 × 3-inch bars. Serve warm or at room temperature, with ice cream, if desired. These bars are best served the day they are baked.

Spice Cookies with Candied Ginger

Minced candied ginger provides a sharp burst of flavor in these cookies.

YIELD: THIRTY-FIVE 2 1/2-INCH COOKIES

1³/₄ cups plus 2 tablespoons flour
1 teaspoon baking soda
¹/₄ teaspoon salt
1¹/₄ teaspoons each: cinnamon, ground cloves,
    ground ginger
1¹/₂ sticks unsalted butter, softened
¹/₂ cup plus 2 tablespoons sugar
2 tablespoons finely minced candied ginger
1 large egg white
2 tablespoons dark Karo syrup
Additional sugar, for rolling
70 paper-thin slices of candied ginger, for garnish

1. Put a rack in the center of the oven; preheat the oven to 350 degrees. Lightly grease 2 cookie sheets. Set them aside.

2. Sift the flour, baking soda, salt, and spices onto a sheet of waxed paper. Set aside.

3. Use an electric mixer to cream the butter, sugar, and minced ginger until light and fluffy. Add the egg white and syrup; mix well. Add the flour mixture; mix well again. Put the sugar for rolling into a shallow dish.

4. Roll level tablespoons of dough into balls with your fingers. Roll the balls in the sugar; place them on the prepared baking sheets spaced 2 inches apart. Dip the bottom of a glass in sugar and press each ball into a 2¹/₂-inch round. Overlap 2 thin slices of candied ginger in the center of each round, pressing them in lightly.

5. Bake until lightly browned on the edges, about 12 to 13 minutes. Let the cookies rest 5 minutes on the baking sheet. Then, use a metal spatula to transfer them to a wire rack to cool. When they are completely cool, store in an airtight container at room temperature for up to 1 week or freeze, wrapped airtight, for up to 1 month.

Chocolate Chip Brownie Blobs

Here, the deep richness of brownies is translated into a truly irresistible thick cookie that delivers the same satisfaction without the problem of getting them out of the pan.

YIELD: TWELVE 3 3/4-INCH COOKIES

1⅓ cups sugar
1 stick unsalted butter, at room temperature
2 large eggs
1½ tablespoons instant coffee granules
1 tablespoon pure vanilla extract
5 ounces unsweetened chocolate, broken into pieces,
   melted, cooled
1 cup all-purpose flour
¼ teaspoon salt
2 cups semisweet chocolate morsels

1. Put a rack in the center of the oven; preheat the oven to 350 degrees. Lightly grease 2 cookie sheets. Set them aside.

2. Use an electric mixer to beat the sugar, butter, eggs, coffee, and vanilla until smooth. Add the melted chocolate and mix until combined. Add the flour and salt and mix well. Use a wooden spoon to stir in the chocolate morsels.

3. Use ⅓ cup dough for each cookie and space them 2 inches apart on the prepared cookie sheets.

4. Bake until they are set, about 15 minutes. Let them rest for 5 minutes. Then, use a metal spatula to transfer them to a wire rack to cool completely. The cookies can be stored in an airtight container for 3 days at room temperature or frozen, wrapped airtight, for up to 3 weeks.

All-American Apple Pie

Warm apple pie is one of those treasured desserts that everyone loves. I, personally, have never been able to resist one. I recommend using a food processor for preparing an apple pie. First, make the pastry, then use the same work bowl (without washing it) to slice the apples. Not only is the job done faster, there are fewer bowls to clean up afterward. As a shortcut, use Pillsbury pie crusts, enough for two 9-inch crusts, available in the refrigerated sections of supermarkets, instead of making your own pastry dough.

YIELD: ONE 9-INCH PIE

1 recipe Double-Crust Pastry Dough (page 370)

APPLE FILLING:
3/4 cup sugar
3 tablespoons unbleached all-purpose flour
2 teaspoons pure vanilla extract
1 teaspoon cinnamon
1/4 teaspoon freshly grated nutmeg (see page 289)
1/8 teaspoon salt
6 medium Granny Smith apples, peeled, cored,
    cut into 1/4-inch-thick slices, about 7 cups
2 tablespoons unsalted butter

TOPPING:
1 teaspoon sugar
1/8 teaspoon cinnamon

Vanilla ice cream, for serving

1. Put a rack in the center of oven; preheat the oven to 450 degrees. Set aside a deep 9-inch Pyrex pie plate and a cookie sheet.

2. For the pastry, transfer the dough to a plastic bag; compress it into a ball, then flatten the dough into an 8-inch disc. Divide the dough into 2 parts, using one third for 1 piece and two thirds for the other. Flatten each piece into a disc. Refrigerate in plastic bags (or briefly place them in the freezer) until firm enough to roll out. On a floured board, roll the larger piece (keep the smaller piece refrigerated) into a 12-inch-diameter circle. Wrap it around the rolling pin and unroll over the pie plate, centering it. Gently press the dough into the bottom and sides of the plate.

3. For the filling, put the sugar, flour, vanilla, and spices in a large plastic bag or mixing bowl. Combine well. Add the apples and shake or toss until the apples are coated with the sugar mixture. Carefully arrange the apples on the bottom crust, making sure they fill the pan to the edges. Cut the butter into small pieces and dot them over the top.

4. Roll the smaller piece of dough into a 10-inch diameter circle. Wrap it around the rolling pin and unroll it over the top of the pie, carefully centering it. Trim the edges, leaving a 1/2-inch overhang. With floured fingers, tuck the overhang under to seal it tightly; then form a decorative edge with the tines of a fork. Use a sharp paring knife to make several slashes in the top crust to allow steam to escape during baking. Combine the sugar and cinnamon and sprinkle it over the top.

5. Place the pie plate on the cookie sheet (to catch any juices), and bake for 15 minutes. Reduce the oven temperature to 425 degrees and continue to bake until the crust is golden, about 40 to 45 minutes longer. Transfer the pie to a wire rack to cool for at least 1½ hours before serving. This pie is best served the day that it is made.

6. To serve, the pie should be warm. Reheat it in a preheated 350-degree oven until warm, about 12 minutes. Cut it into wedges and top each serving with a scoop of vanilla ice cream.

Buttery Lemon Meringue Pie

Lemon meringue pie takes its rightful place alongside apple pie as an all-American favorite. A creamy, sweet froth of meringue contrasts with the puckery lemon filling, a taste combination that can't be improved on. Instead of a filling thickened with cornstarch, I've substituted a light buttery custard that has a perfectly smooth consistency.

YIELD: ONE 9-INCH PIE

1 recipe single-crust Sweet Butter Pastry Dough
   (page 369), prebaked in a 9-inch pie plate

FILLING:
Grated zest (colored rind) of 1 large lemon, removed
   with a zester or fine grater (see page 14),
   about 1 tablespoon
1 1/3 cups sugar
4 large eggs
1/4 cup sour cream
1 stick unsalted butter, melted
1/2 cup fresh lemon juice

MERINGUE TOPPING:
5 large egg whites
1/4 teaspoon cream of tartar
1 cup sugar

1. Put a rack in the center of the oven; preheat the oven to 375 degrees. Set aside the prebaked butter pastry crust in the 9-inch pie plate along with a cookie sheet. Let the crust cool completely.

2. For the filling, use a food processor fitted with the metal blade or an electric mixer. For the food processor, mince the zest with the sugar until it is as fine as possible. Leave it in the work bowl. Add the eggs, sour cream, and butter. Mix for 1 minute,

stopping once to scrape down the sides of the bowl. Add the lemon juice and mix 5 seconds.

3. To make the filling with an electric mixer, mince the zest with the sugar in a blender. Put the sugar mixture in the mixer bowl. Add the eggs and butter. Mix on high speed until thick. Add the sour cream and mix until it is smooth. Reduce to low speed and add the lemon juice.

4. Pour the filling into the prebaked pastry shell. Place the pie plate on the cookie sheet (for easier handling).

5. Bake until the filling is still slightly soft in the center, about 25 minutes. It will firm up more as it cools. Cool to room temperature. The pie can be made a day in advance to this point and refrigerated. Bring it to room temperature before adding the meringue.

6. For the meringue, preheat the oven to 425 degrees. Use an electric mixer to beat the egg whites on medium speed until foamy. Add the cream of tartar and beat on high speed until they hold soft peaks. Gradually add the sugar by the tablespoon, beating well after each addition. Continue to beat until the egg whites are thick and shiny.

7. Spread the meringue over the pie, mounding it in the center and extending it over the edge of the crust. Use the back of a spoon to make peaks and swirls.

8. Bake just until the meringue is lightly browned, 6 to 8 minutes. The pie is best served shortly after the meringue is baked, but it can be held up to 5 hours in a cool, dry place (do not refrigerate).

Warm Maple Cranberry Apple Pie

Here, cranberries give apple pie a deliciously different dimension. The cranberries are first simmered with maple syrup and sugar, then combined with the sliced raw apples. Served with a scoop of ice cream, this is a winner. Here, too, Pillsbury pie crusts, available in the refrigerated sections of supermarkets, are an acceptable shortcut.

YIELD: ONE 9-INCH PIE

1 recipe Double-Crust Pastry Dough (enough for a
   2-crust 9-inch pie), Cinnamon Variation
   (page 370)

FILLING:
4 cups fresh cranberries
1 cup sugar
1/3 cup maple syrup
1/2 teaspoon each: cinnamon, maple flavoring
1/8 teaspoon salt
5 medium Golden Delicious apples, peeled, cored,
   cut into 1/3-inch slices, about 4 cups
3 tablespoons flour
2 tablespoons unsalted butter, cut into small bits

GLAZE:
1 large egg yolk
1 tablespoon heavy cream

Strawberry or vanilla ice cream, for serving

1. Put a rack in the center of the oven; preheat the oven to 450 degrees. Set aside a deep 9-inch Pyrex pie plate and a cookie sheet.

2. For the pastry, transfer the dough to a plastic bag; compress it into a ball, then flatten the dough into an 8-inch disc. Divide the dough into 2 parts, using one third for 1 piece and two thirds for the other. Flatten each piece into a disc. Refrigerate in plastic bags (or briefly place them in the freezer) until firm enough to roll out. On a floured board, roll the larger piece (keep the smaller piece refrigerated) into a 12-inch-diameter circle. Wrap it around the rolling pin and unroll over the pie plate, centering it. Gently press the dough into the bottom and sides of the plate.

3. For the filling, put the cranberries, sugar, and maple syrup into an 8-inch nonaluminum skillet. Cook over medium heat, uncovered, stirring often, until the cranberries have popped and thickened, about 20 minutes. Remove from the heat. Stir in the cinnamon, maple flavoring, and salt.

4. Toss the apples with the flour in a plastic bag or in a mixing bowl. Add the apples with any loose flour to the cranberries. Mix well. Let the mixture cool to room temperature.

5. Transfer the cranberry-apple filling to the lined pie plate, mounding it slightly. Dot with the butter.

6. Roll the smaller piece of dough into a 10-inch-diameter circle. Wrap it around the rolling pin and unroll it over the top of the pie, carefully centering it. Trim the edges, leaving a 1/2-inch overhang. With floured fingers, tuck the overhang under to seal it tightly; then form a decorative edge with the tines of a fork. Use a sharp paring knife to make several slashes in the top crust to allow steam to escape during baking.

7. For the glaze, put the egg yolk and cream in a small dish. Mix with a fork. Lightly brush the glaze over the crust.

8. Place the pie on the cookie sheet (to catch any juices), and bake for 10 minutes. Reduce the oven temperature to 425 degrees and continue to bake until the bottom crust is golden brown, about 40 to 45 minutes longer. Transfer the pie to a wire rack for at least 2 hours before serving. The pie can be baked a day ahead, cooled completely, and refrigerated.

9. To serve, the pie should be warm. Reheat, uncovered, in a preheated 300-degree oven until warm, about 15 minutes. Cut into wedges and top each serving with a scoop of strawberry or vanilla ice cream.

Warm Rhubarb Streusel Pie

Long before I fully appreciated rhubarb (I'm now totally converted), I couldn't stop eating this pie. It's not even necessary to serve it with ice cream; it's that good.

YIELD: ONE 9-INCH DEEP-DISH PIE

1 recipe single-crust Sweet Butter Pastry Dough,
   prebaked in a 9-inch pie plate (page 369)
   (a Pillsbury pie crust works well here)

RHUBARB FILLING:
2 pounds rhubarb, unpeeled, cut into 1/3-inch slices,
   about 8 cups
1 3/4 cups sugar
Grated zest (colored rind) of 1 large orange,
   removed with a zester or fine grater (see page 14),
   about 1 tablespoon
2 tablespoons orange juice
3 tablespoons quick-cooking tapioca
2 teaspoons pure vanilla extract
1/4 teaspoon allspice
Pinch of salt

STREUSEL TOPPING:
1 stick unsalted butter, chilled, cut into tablespoon-size
   pieces
2/3 cup packed dark brown sugar
1 cup plus 2 tablespoons flour
Grated zest (colored rind) of 1/2 large orange,
   removed with a zester or fine grater (page 14),
   about 1/2 tablespoon
1 teaspoon cinnamon
Pinch of salt

1. Put a rack in the center of the oven; preheat the oven to 350 degrees. Set aside the prebaked crust in the pie plate along with a cookie sheet. Let the crust cool completely.

2. For the rhubarb filling, put the rhubarb and all the remaining ingredients in a bowl. Mix until well combined. Let the filling rest 15 minutes, then transfer it to the prebaked crust, spreading it evenly.

3. Bake for 1 hour.

4. Meanwhile, make the streusel. Put all the topping ingredients in a food processor fitted with the metal blade, or in a mixing bowl. Mix until the topping is crumbled, using the pulse on/off or a pastry blender. Spread the topping over the pie after it has baked for 1 hour. Gently pat it into place.

5. Return the pie to the oven and bake until the top is browned and the juices bubbling, about 25 to 30 minutes longer. Transfer it to a wire rack for at least 1 1/2 hours. The pie can be made a day ahead and refrigerated when completely cooled.

6. To serve, reheat it in a preheated 350-degree oven until warm, about 10 to 12 minutes.

Rhubarb

Those who love rhubarb rue the day it leaves the market, but there's no reason not to enjoy it on a 12-month basis, especially since it freezes so well. Buy the freshest rhubarb you can find, wash and dry it, and cut it into 1/2-inch chunks. Put it into airtight bags and freeze.

Chocolate Caramel Tart

Since the combination of caramel and chocolate always undoes me, this is one of my favorite desserts to make for festive dinners. A cookie-like crust holds a dark chocolate fudge filling, topped with a smooth layer of tawny caramel and garnished with a ring of toasted pecans. Back when Jill Sigrist and Larry Quaglia co-owned Jilly's Café in Evanston, Illinois, Jill baked this mouthwatering tart daily.

YIELD: ONE 9-INCH TART

1 recipe single-crust Sweet Butter Pastry Dough (page 369), prebaked in a 9-inch pie plate

FILLING:
5$\frac{1}{2}$ ounces semisweet chocolate
7 tablespoons unsalted butter
2 large eggs
$\frac{1}{4}$ cup sugar
2 tablespoons flour

CARAMEL:
$\frac{1}{4}$ cup heavy cream
2 tablespoons unsalted butter
1 tablespoon light corn syrup
$\frac{1}{2}$ cup sugar
$\frac{1}{2}$ teaspoon pure vanilla extract

$\frac{1}{2}$ cup chopped pecans, toasted (page 358), for garnish

1. Put a rack in the center of the oven; preheat the oven to 325 degrees. Set aside the prebaked crust and a cookie sheet. Let the crust cool completely.

2. For the filling, gently melt the chocolate and butter in a saucepan or in a microwave oven on medium power (50 percent), stirring often. Use an electric mixer to beat the eggs, sugar, and flour until smooth and thick. Add the chocolate mixture and combine until smooth.

3. Pour the filling into the cooled crust; use a rubber spatula to smooth the surface.

4. Bake until the filling is set around the edges, 18 to 20 minutes. Cool on a wire rack. Make the caramel while the tart is cooling.

5. For the caramel, bring the cream and butter to a boil in a small saucepan; keep it hot.

6. Cook the corn syrup in a 1$\frac{1}{2}$-quart pan until it is hot. Add the sugar and mix until combined. Cook over medium-high heat without stirring. When the syrup starts to color, begin to stir it constantly until the sugar has dissolved and the mixture is a deep tan, about 8 minutes. Carefully pour in the cream and butter—it will spatter. Stir well, then cook over high heat, still stirring constantly, until smooth, about 2 minutes. Immediately transfer the caramel to a bowl and stir in the vanilla. If the mixture becomes too thick to pour as it cools, gently reheat it on the stove, adding several drops of cream, as needed.

7. Pour the caramel over the tart, tilting it to spread the caramel evenly. Garnish the outer edge with pecans. The tart can be made a day in advance and refrigerated.

8. To serve, bring it to room temperature and cut into wedges.

Very Berry Deep-Dish Pie

This pie is an extravagance, but it's worth it! Make it at the height of berry season. Nine cups of berries are bursting between the crusts. Select a mix of berries or just one type, whatever the season dictates, but be sure to use 9 cups. Serve the pie warm with a scoop of strawberry or raspberry ice cream. Pillsbury pie crusts, available in the refrigerated sections of supermarkets, are a viable shortcut for the double-crust pastry dough.

YIELD: ONE 9-INCH DEEP-DISH PIE

1 recipe Double-Crust Pastry Dough
   (enough for a 2-crust 9-inch pie) (page 370)

FILLING:
9 cups mixed berries (5 cups blueberries, 2 cups each:
   raspberries, strawberries, hulled, quartered, or
   halved if small)
1 tablespoon each: fresh lemon juice, flour
²/₃ to 1 cup sugar, depending on the sweetness
   of the berries
¹/₄ cup quick-cooking tapioca
Pinch of salt
2 tablespoons unsalted butter, cut into small bits

Ice cream, for serving

1. Set aside a deep 9-inch Pyrex pie plate and a cookie sheet.

2. For the pastry, transfer the dough to a plastic bag; compress it into a ball, then flatten the dough into an 8-inch disc. Divide the dough into 2 parts, using one third for 1 piece and two thirds for the other. Flatten each piece into a disc. Refrigerate in plastic bags (or briefly place them in the freezer) until firm enough to roll out. On a floured board, roll the larger piece (keep the smaller piece

refrigerated) into a 12-inch-diameter circle. Wrap it around the rolling pin and unroll over the pie plate, centering it. Gently press the dough into the bottom and sides of the plate.

3. For the filling, put the berries in a large bowl. Toss with the lemon juice. Combine the flour, sugar, tapioca, and salt in a small dish. Add this to the berries and toss well until combined. Let the mixture stand for 20 minutes, then transfer the filling to the pie plate, gently mounding the berries in the center. Dot the surface with the butter.

4. Roll the smaller piece of dough into a 10-inch-diameter circle. Wrap it around the rolling pin and unroll it over the top of the pie, carefully centering it. Trim the edges, leaving a ¹/₂-inch overhang. With floured fingers, tuck the overhang under to seal it tightly; then form a decorative edge with the tines of a fork. Use a sharp paring knife to make several slashes in the top crust to allow steam to escape during baking. Place the pie on the cookie sheet (to catch any juices).

5. Put the pie in the oven and immediately decrease the oven temperature to 400 degrees. Bake until the crust is a deep brown and the fruit is

bubbling, about 1 hour. If the edges are becoming too dark, protect them with strips of aluminum foil. Let the pie cool on a wire rack until the juices are thickened, about 2 hours, before serving. The pie is best served the day it is made.

6. To serve, the pie should be slightly warm. Gently reheat at 300 degrees until warmed through, about 15 minutes. Cut into wedges and top each serving with ice cream.

Nancy's Upside-Down Apple Pie

You already know that apple pie is one of my passions and this one is surely a winner. Picture this: pecans arranged close together in an attractive design in a heavily buttered pie plate with an apple-filled double-crust pie placed on top of them. The baked pie is inverted onto a serving platter to reveal a totally pecan-covered crust, all gleaming. It's easy to do and you can't beat the presentation . . . or the taste! Thanks to my friend Nancy Fraiman, this unusual recipe now belongs to a world of apple-pie lovers.

YIELD: ONE 9-INCH DEEP-DISH PIE

4 tablespoons unsalted butter, softened but not melted,
　for the pie plate

PECAN CRUST:
1³/₄ cups large pecan halves
¹/₂ cup packed brown sugar
1 recipe Double-Crust Pastry Dough (page 370) or
　Pillsbury pie crusts (enough for a 2-crust 9-inch pie)

FILLING:
5 large Granny Smith apples, peeled, cored,
　thinly sliced, about 7¹/₂ cups
1 tablespoon each: fresh lemon juice, flour
¹/₂ cup sugar
1 teaspoon each: cinnamon, freshly grated nutmeg
　(see page 289)
Pinch of salt
2 tablespoons unsalted butter, cut into small bits
Vanilla ice cream or crème fraîche, for serving
　(optional)

1. Put a rack in the center of the oven; preheat the oven to 400 degrees. Generously coat the inside of a 9-inch deep-dish pie plate with the softened butter. Set it aside, along with a cookie sheet.

2. For the pecan crust, arrange the pecans, rounded side down, in the prepared pie plate, starting at the center and working up to 1 row on the sides, pressing them into the butter. Sprinkle the brown sugar evenly over the pecans. Gently compact the pecans into place with your hands.

3. For the pastry, transfer the dough to a plastic bag; compress it into a ball, then flatten the dough into an 8-inch disc. Divide the dough into 2 parts, using one third for 1 piece and two thirds for the other. Flatten each piece into a disc. Refrigerate in plastic bags (or briefly place them in the freezer) until firm enough to roll out. On a floured board, roll the larger piece (keep the smaller piece refrigerated) into a 12-inch-diameter circle. Wrap it around the rolling pin and unroll over the pecan mixture, centering it. Gently press the dough into the bottom and sides of the plate.

4. For the filling, put the apples into a large bowl and toss them with the lemon juice. Combine the flour, sugar, cinnamon, nutmeg, and salt in a small dish. Add the flour mixture to the apples and toss until combined. Place the apple slices on the pastry crust, mounding them slightly in the center. Dot the surface with butter.

5. Roll the smaller piece of dough into a 10-inch-diameter circle. Wrap it around the rolling pin and unroll it over the top of the pie, carefully centering it. Trim the edges, leaving a $\frac{1}{2}$-inch overhang. With floured fingers, tuck the overhang under to seal it tightly; then form a decorative edge with the tines of a fork. Raise the rim of the crust slightly from the edge of the pan. Use a sharp paring knife to slash the top crust to allow steam to escape.

6. Place the pie on the cookie sheet (for easy handling) and bake until well browned, about 1 hour. Pierce through the crust with the point of a small knife to be sure the apples are tender. If they seem firm, bake the pie longer, using foil to protect the edges of crust from burning. Let the pie rest on a wire rack at room temperature for 5 minutes. Then, gently invert it onto a sturdy oven-to-table serving plate. As the pie settles, the outer crust may crack. That's okay, just push it together with your hands. This pie is best served the day that it's baked.

7. To serve, the pie should be warm. Place the platter on the reserved cookie sheet and reheat in preheated 300-degree oven until just warmed through, about 10 minutes. Cut the pie into wedges and top each serving with a dollop of vanilla ice cream or crème frâiche.

Family's Favorite
Pumpkin Chiffon Pie

This pumpkin chiffon pie appealed to me many years ago because it seemed lighter than the traditional pumpkin custard pie that was an obligatory part of my family's Thanksgiving get-togethers. I have liked it enough to include it in my Thanksgiving dessert selection ever since, improving on it as the years have gone by. By now it's become a family favorite, as much a part of the holiday as the family itself.

YIELD: ONE 9-INCH DEEP-DISH PIE

CRUST:

1 1/3 cups gingersnap cookie crumbs

5 tablespoons unsalted butter, melted

3 tablespoons light brown sugar

1/2 teaspoon cinnamon

FILLING:

2 tablespoons dark rum

1 tablespoon each: water, fresh lemon juice

2 teaspoons unflavored gelatin

3 large egg yolks

3/4 cup sugar

1/2 cup milk

1 1/2 cups canned pumpkin

1/2 teaspoon each: cinnamon, freshly grated nutmeg
  (see page 289)

Pinch of salt

4 large egg whites (see Note)

1/4 teaspoon cream of tartar

1 cup heavy cream, whipped with 1 tablespoon
  confectioners' sugar, for garnish

1. Put a rack in the center of the oven; preheat the oven to 350 degrees. Set aside a 9-inch deep-dish pie plate and a cookie sheet.

2. For the crust, combine the crumbs, butter, sugar, and cinnamon in a food processor fitted with a metal blade or in a mixing bowl. Press the mixture into the bottom and up the sides of the pie plate.

3. Bake until the crust is set but not browned, about 6 minutes. Set it aside on a wire rack to cool.

4. For the filling, combine the rum, water, and lemon juice in a small dish. Sprinkle the gelatin over the mixture. Let it stand until the gelatin is softened, about 5 minutes.

5. Whisk the egg yolks and sugar together in the top of a double boiler placed on the counter. Add the milk, pumpkin, cinnamon, nutmeg, and salt; mix well. Cook the mixture in the double boiler over boiling water until it is hot and has thickened slightly, about 10 minutes. Remove from the heat and stir in the gelatin mixture. Refrigerate until the mixture is chilled but has not begun to set, about 2 hours.

6. Meanwhile, in an electric mixer, beat the egg whites until foamy. Add the cream of tartar and continue to beat until they hold soft peaks. Stir the chilled pumpkin mixture and gently fold in the egg whites.

7. Transfer the filling to the cooled crust and refrigerate until it is set, about 4 hours or overnight.

8. To serve, spoon the sweetened whipped cream into a pastry bag fitted with a star tip and decorate the top of the pie. Refrigerate the decorated pie for up to 4 hours before serving chilled.

NOTE: This recipe uses raw egg whites. Some cases of salmonella have been traced to raw eggs, although this is rare. It is even rarer to find salmonella in raw egg whites as opposed to yolks.

Strawberry-Rhubarb Crisp

This is a delicious crunchy fruit crisp. The strawberries balance the intensity of the rhubarb, but both flavors are very evident.

YIELD: 6 TO 8 SERVINGS

FRUIT:

1 1/2 pounds rhubarb, cut into 1/3-inch slices,
about 6 cups

2 pints strawberries, washed, patted dry, hulled,
cut in half if large

Grated zest (colored rind) of 1 orange,
removed with a zester or fine grater (see page 14),
about 1 tablespoon

2 tablespoons orange juice

3 1/2 tablespoons quick-cooking tapioca

2 teaspoons pure vanilla extract

1/4 teaspoon allspice

TOPPING:

2/3 cup packed dark brown sugar

1 cup flour

Grated zest (colored rind) of 1/2 orange,
removed with a zester or fine grater

1 teaspoon cinnamon

Pinch of salt

1 stick unsalted butter, softened, cut into
tablespoon-size pieces

Vanilla ice cream or crème fraîche, for serving

1. Put a rack in the center of the oven; preheat the oven to 350 degrees. Set aside a 10-cup-capacity shallow baking dish and a cookie sheet.

2. For the fruit, put all the ingredients in a large mixing bowl. Toss well until combined, then let the fruit rest 15 minutes while preparing the topping.

3. For the topping, put the sugar, flour, zest, cinnamon, and salt into a food processor fitted with the metal blade or into a mixing bowl. Mix well. Cut the butter into the flour mixture until crumbly, using the pulse on/off or a pastry blender.

4. Transfer the fruit mixture to the baking dish. The surface will be uneven. Spoon the topping evenly over the fruit and gently pat it in place.

5. Place the baking dish on the cookie sheet (to catch any juices) and bake until the top is well browned and the juices are bubbling, about 50 to 60 minutes. Let the crisp rest 30 minutes before serving. It can be made a day ahead and refrigerated once it is completely cool.

6. To serve, the crisp should be warm. Reheat it in a preheated 350-degree oven until warm, about 10 to 12 minutes. Serve with a dollop of crème fraîche or a scoop of vanilla ice cream.

Caramel Pecan Apple Crisp

*If you love homey apple desserts, this ranks right up there with the best.
Tucked under a cookie-like crust is a bevy of cinnamon-flavored apples.*

YIELD: ONE 9-INCH CRISP, 6 SERVINGS

FILLING:

6 medium Granny Smith apples, peeled, cored,
   sliced ¼ inch thick, about 7 cups
¼ cup sugar
3 tablespoons flour
1½ teaspoons cinnamon
2 teaspoons fresh lemon juice

TOPPING:

1 large egg, separated
¾ cup packed light brown sugar
1 stick unsalted butter, frozen, cut into 8 pieces
¾ cup flour
Pinch of salt
2 tablespoons coarsely chopped pecans

Vanilla or butter pecan ice cream, for serving

1. Put a rack in the center of the oven; preheat the oven to 375 degrees. Set aside a 9-inch round shallow Pyrex pie plate or baking dish and a cookie sheet.

2. For the filling, put the apples in a large bowl. Toss them with the sugar, flour, cinnamon, and lemon juice until well coated. Mound the apples high in the pie plate or baking dish and set them aside.

3. For the topping, you will use only half the egg yolk (or 2 teaspoons) for the recipe, discarding the other half. Put the egg white into a small dish and froth it with a fork. Set aside. Put the ½ egg yolk, along with all the remaining ingredients, *except* the pecans, in a food processor fitted with the metal blade. Mix until the topping is finely crumbed and just beginning to clump together. Do not overprocess. Distribute the topping evenly over the apples: Pat it to cover the apples, pressing down so that it adheres. Brush the topping with the egg white. Scatter the pecans over the top and gently press them into the crust. Brush the pecans with more of the egg white.

4. Place the pie plate on the cookie sheet (to catch any juices) and bake until the top is dark brown, about 45 to 50 minutes. Transfer to a wire rack to cool at least 1½ hours before serving.

5. To serve, the crisp should be warm. Reheat it, uncovered, in a preheated 350-degree oven until warm, about 10 minutes. Serve with a scoop of vanilla or butter pecan ice cream.

Warm Fall Fruit Streusel Cake

It's hard to describe the total charm of this warm dessert, but I'll try since it's one of my all-time favorites. A tender cake layer with a crumb topping bakes over a tumble of plums, pears, and raspberries. The idea for this homey dessert is a variation of a peach cake I made long ago as a bride and re-created from memory years later. The raspberries, available in the fall, add a wonderful nuance, but they're not essential to the success of the dessert. This is an efficient food processor preparation since the batter can be mixed in the same work bowl as the streusel, without washing it between steps.

YIELD: 6 TO 8 SERVINGS

STREUSEL:
1/2 cup flour
1/3 cup packed light brown sugar
4 tablespoons unsalted butter, chilled
1/4 teaspoon cinnamon
Pinch of salt

CAKE:
1/3 cup sour cream
1/4 teaspoon baking soda
1 large egg
1/3 cup sugar
4 tablespoons unsalted butter, softened
1 1/2 teaspoons pure vanilla extract
3/4 cup flour
1/2 teaspoon baking powder
1/4 teaspoon salt

FRUIT:
3 firm, ripe medium pears, peeled only if desired,
    cored, cut into 1-inch cubes, about 2 cups
6 firm, ripe large plums, cut into 1/3-inch slices,
    about 5 cups
1/2 cup sugar
1 tablespoon quick-cooking tapioca
2 tablespoons fresh lemon juice

1/4 teaspoon cinnamon
2 to 6 tablespoons water
2/3 cup raspberries (optional)

Vanilla or butter pecan ice cream, for serving (optional)

1. Put a rack in the center of the oven; preheat the oven to 375 degrees. Butter a 5-cup-capacity shallow baking dish or an 8-inch shallow square baking pan, preferably Pyrex. Set aside along with a cookie sheet.

2. For the streusel, put all the ingredients in a food processor fitted with the metal blade or in a large mixing bowl. Pulse on/off or use a pastry blender to combine until the butter is the size of small peas. Set aside in the refrigerator.

3. For the cake, stir the sour cream and baking soda together in a small dish. Beat the egg, sugar, and butter in a food processor fitted with the metal blade or beat in an electric mixer until light and fluffy. Add the vanilla and the sour cream mixture; mix well. Add the flour, baking powder, and salt; pulse on/off just until mixed (do not overprocess) or combine with the electric mixer. Set aside.

4. For the fruit, put the pears, plums, sugar, tapioca, lemon juice, and cinnamon, in a large skillet with 2 tablespoons of the water. Gently toss until combined. Cook over medium-high heat, uncovered, until the pears are somewhat tender but not soft; this will take from 4 to 10 minutes depending on the pears. Stir often to avoid burning. Add the remaining water if mixture becomes too dry.

5. To assemble, transfer the hot fruit and juices to the prepared pan (the fruit mixture must be hot when the cake is assembled in order for the batter to bake through all the way). Use a spatula to spread it evenly. Tuck the raspberries, if using them, into the fruit. Spoon the cake batter evenly over the hot fruit and spread it in a thin, even layer with

a spatula. It's okay if the fruit is not completely covered. Sprinkle the streusel over the batter.

6. Place the pan on the cookie sheet (to catch any juices) and bake until the surface is a deep brown and a toothpick inserted in the center of the cake layer comes out clean, about 30 minutes. Transfer to a wire rack to cool at least 45 minutes before serving. Serve while it is still warm. The dessert can also be baked a day ahead and refrigerated when it is completely cool.

7. To serve, the cake should be warm. To reheat, bake it in a preheated 300-degree oven until heated through but not hot, about 15 minutes. Serve topped with vanilla or butter pecan ice cream if you wish.

Fresh Peach-Plum Cobbler

*Cobblers are among those old-fashioned desserts whose appeal is timeless.
This one combines two of my favorite seasonal fruits under a tender sugar-crusted
cinnamon biscuit. Cooking the fruit on top of the stove before baking the cobbler is
essential; I've tried the recipe without doing this and the juices did not thicken satisfactorily.
I like to serve this warm, with a small scoop of ice cream melting over the top.*

YIELD: 6 TO 8 SERVINGS

TOPPING:
1 cup plus 2 tablespoons flour
1/4 cup sugar
1 1/2 teaspoons baking powder
1/2 teaspoon cinnamon
1/4 teaspoon salt
4 tablespoons unsalted butter, chilled, cut in 8 pieces
1/2 cup heavy cream

FRUIT:
8 large peaches, pitted, cut into 1/2-inch-thick slices,
    about 7 cups, tossed with 1 tablespoon lemon juice
5 dark-skinned plums, cut into 1/2-inch-thick slices,
    about 3 cups
2 tablespoons quick-cooking tapioca
1/2 cup plus 2 tablespoons sugar
    (less if fruit is very sweet)
1/4 teaspoon cinnamon

Vanilla ice cream, for serving (optional)

1. Put a rack in the center of the oven; preheat the oven to 425 degrees. Set aside a 9- to 10-cup-capacity baking or soufflé dish and a cookie sheet.

2. For the topping, combine the flour, sugar, baking powder, cinnamon, and salt in a food processor fitted with the metal blade or in a mixing bowl.

Use the pulse on/off or a pastry blender to cut in the butter until it resembles a coarse meal. Add the cream and mix just until the dough clumps together. The dough will be sticky. Transfer the dough to a large plastic food bag. Working through the bag, press the dough into a firm ball. Remove it from the bag and place it on a well-floured board. Knead the dough, folding and pressing it back on itself, until it holds together and is smooth, about 30 seconds. Refrigerate while you prepare the fruit.

3. For the fruit, put the peaches tossed with lemon juice in a 10-inch nonaluminum skillet. Add the plums, tapioca, sugar, and cinnamon. Gently toss until well mixed. Cook, just until the mixture begins to simmer, about 4 minutes, stirring occasionally. Transfer to the baking dish.

4. To finish the topping, roll out the dough on a heavily floured board to roughly the shape of the baking dish. Use a soft brush to remove any excess flour. Place the dough on top of the fruit (no matter if the fruit is hot or cooled). Gently tuck the edges down into the fruit. Patch the dough where necessary, although it does not need to cover the entire surface of the fruit.

5. Place the dish on the cookie sheet (to catch any juices) and bake until the crust is lightly browned

and the fruit is bubbling, about 40 to 45 minutes. Transfer to a wire rack to cool at least 2 hours before serving. The cobbler is best served the day that it is made, while it is still warm, but it can also be made a day ahead and refrigerated, uncovered, once it's completely cooled.

6. To serve, the cobbler should be warm. Reheat, uncovered, in a preheated 350-degree oven until it is warm (not hot), about 12 minutes. Serve with ice cream, if desired.

Peeling Peaches . . .

Many people don't mind those fuzzy peach skins and leave them on when cooking peaches. Others peel peaches for anything other than out-of-hand eating. Many peaches, especially those you buy at large supermarkets, are hybridized so the skins are less fuzzy and more tender than the old-fashioned varieties you're apt to find at farm stands and orchards. To peel or not, the choice is yours.

To peel 1 or 2 peaches, you can carefully use a sharp swivel-bladed vegetable peeler, unless the peach is very ripe. With a light hand, use a sawing motion to remove the skin with the peeler.

If you have a lot of peaches to peel, you might find it easier to blanch them quickly in boiling water. Bring enough water to a boil to cover the peaches. Carefully drop them in for 15 to 30 seconds, depending on how ripe the peaches are (less time for ripe peaches). Immediately transfer them to a bowl of ice water to keep them from cooking further. The skin should slip right off.

Simply Peaches

Given the great flavor of sun-ripened peaches in season, the best way to enhance them is to do so simply. This recipe is inspired by a dish of fresh strawberries served in much the same way at a wonderful Provençale restaurant, La Merenda, in Nice, France. These simple ingredients bring out the flavor of peaches as well as strawberries. It's not necessary to peel the peaches but you can do so if you wish.

YIELD: 6 SERVINGS

6 firm but ripe medium peaches, unpeeled,
   sliced ⅓ inch thick, about 6 cups
½ tablespoon pure vanilla extract
2 to 3 tablespoons sugar, to taste
¼ cup fresh lemon juice
2 tablespoons grated orange zest (colored rind),
   removed with a zester or grater (see page 14)

1. Put the peaches in a 2-quart bowl with the remaining ingredients. Toss until they are coated evenly. Refrigerate for at least 30 minutes or for up to 3 hours.

2. Serve chilled, in a glass bowl.

Warm Rosy Berry Compote

This thick, berry-filled compote resembles the best of pie fillings. The compote can also be thinned with additional orange juice and served as a sauce over puddings, cakes, and frozen desserts.

YIELD: 6 SERVINGS

2 pints strawberries, hulled
1/3 to 1/2 cup sugar, depending on sweetness of berries
2 teaspoons cornstarch
Grated zest (colored rind) of 1 large orange, removed with a zester or fine grater (see page 14), about 1 tablespoon
1/2 cup orange juice
1 pint blueberries
2 tablespoons orange-flavored liqueur
1 pint raspberries
Raspberry, peach, or vanilla ice cream or frozen yogurt, for serving (optional)

1. Puree 1 pint of the strawberries until smooth with the sugar, cornstarch, orange zest, and juice in a blender or a food processor fitted with the metal blade.

2. Transfer the puree to a 1-quart nonaluminum saucepan. Stir in 1 cup of the blueberries. Cook over medium heat until the mixture is simmering and thickened, about 5 minutes, stirring to avoid burning. The sauce can be made 2 days ahead and refrigerated.

3. To serve, gently reheat the sauce. When hot, add the remaining strawberries (quartered if large, otherwise halved) and blueberries. Heat through, about 30 seconds. Remove from the heat, stir in the liqueur, and gently fold in the raspberries. Serve warm, in stemmed goblets, topped with a dollop of ice cream or frozen yogurt, if you wish.

Berries

Berries, unadorned, are one of summer's simple pleasures. Eating them out of hand or served simply in a lovely dish can be the ultimate delight. However, there comes a time when embellishments and flourishes are in order, transforming berries into a more festive dessert. Here are some quick and easy berry tossings and toppings that will do the trick. Remember always to use berries that are firm and in the peak of flavor.

Toss berries with:

❖ Grated orange zest and sugar.
❖ A splash of orange juice, liqueur (framboise or orange-flavored), rum, or balsamic vinegar, each usually with a bit of sugar added to taste.
❖ A sauce of strained, pureed raspberries or strawberries.

Top berries with:
❖ Softened vanilla or strawberry ice cream or frozen yogurt. Keep the consistency like sour cream. Don't let it melt into a liquid.
❖ Sour cream sprinkled with light brown sugar.
❖ Lowfat vanilla yogurt.

Baked Caramel Pears with Vanilla Ice Cream

Baking reinforces the delicate flavor of pears much more than poaching them. Here, they're double-baked, once to tenderize, then to reheat in a thick caramel sauce. High-quality caramels make the difference in this dessert. The rum is barely perceptible, it just deepens the caramel flavor, but if you want to omit it, substitute an equal amount of water.

YIELD: 4 SERVINGS

PEARS:
2 tablespoons each: *light brown sugar, dark rum*
1/2 teaspoon fresh lemon juice
1 tablespoon unsalted butter
3 ripe but firm large Bartlett pears, peeled, split lengthwise, cored with a melon baller

CARAMEL SAUCE:
Pan juices from the pears
Thirteen 3/4-inch-square good-quality caramels (about 4 ounces total)
1 teaspoon dark rum

Vanilla ice cream, for serving

1. Put a rack in the center of the oven; preheat the oven to 400 degrees. Set aside a 9-inch Pyrex pie plate.

2. For the pears, combine the sugar, rum, lemon juice, and butter in a small saucepan. Heat until the butter is just melted. Stir until mixed.

3. Arrange the pears, cut side down, in the pie plate with the tops pointing toward the center. Brush the warm butter mixture over the pears.

4. Bake, uncovered, until the pears are just tender, about 20 to 35 minutes, depending on the ripeness of the pears, brushing them with the pan juices twice during baking. The pears can be baked a day ahead and refrigerated, covered airtight. Let them come to room temperature before reheating.

5. For the sauce, transfer the pan juices from the pears to the top of a double boiler. Add the caramels and the rum. Cook in a double boiler over boiling water for about 15 minutes until the caramels are melted. Stir until smooth.

6. To serve, cut the pear halves lengthwise into 2 quarters; leave them in the plate and pour the warm sauce evenly over the pears. Gently reheat, uncovered, in a preheated 300-degree oven, basting once with the caramel sauce, until the pears are heated through but not hot, about 12 minutes. Arrange 3 warm pear quarters in each of 4 warm shallow soup dishes. Top each serving with a scoop of ice cream. Spoon some of the caramel sauce over the ice cream.

Red Plum and Raspberry "Fool"

Here is a "fool" for sure since this version features a tart puree of plums and raspberries swirled into a puff of meringue instead of the traditional rich whipped cream. Because it's an Italian meringue, it's very creamy, dense, and glossy. It's easy to make an Italian meringue when you use a candy thermometer; otherwise, you have to test the syrup by immersing a drop into cold water. The syrup should form a soft ball in the water. Many other fruits can be substituted for the plums and raspberries; just be sure the cooked fruit puree measures ⅔ cup and is very tart.

YIELD: 4 SERVINGS

FRUIT PUREE:

4 tart but ripe large red plums, split and pitted
½ pint raspberries
2 tablespoons sugar
1 tablespoon water mixed with ½ teaspoon gelatin
¼ cup raspberry fruit spread

ITALIAN MERINGUE:

3 tablespoons water
½ cup sugar
2 large egg whites
1 teaspoon pure vanilla extract
24 fresh raspberries, for garnish

1. For the fruit puree, put the plums (cut into small pieces), raspberries, and sugar in a food processor fitted with the metal blade or in a blender. Puree until smooth. The mixture should be very tart. Press it through a fine sieve (to remove the seeds) into a small nonaluminum saucepan.

2. Simmer the puree, uncovered, over medium heat until it is slightly thickened, about 10 minutes. Remove from the heat and stir in the gelatin mixture and raspberry fruit spread. (You should have about ⅔ cup fruit puree.) Refrigerate until chilled.

3. For the Italian meringue, boil the water and sugar in a very small saucepan over high heat until it reaches the soft-ball stage or registers 240 degrees on a candy thermometer (it may be necessary to carefully tip the saucepan so there is enough depth to measure the syrup with the thermometer), about 4 minutes. As the temperature approaches 200 degrees, use a mixer to start beating the egg whites until they hold their shape but are still shiny and moist. With the mixer running, slowly (and carefully) pour the hot syrup in a thin, steady stream into the egg whites; this will take about 1 minute. Continue to beat the meringue until it is very thick and cool (feel the exterior of the mixer bowl), about 3 more minutes. Stir in the vanilla.

4. To finish, gently fold the fruit puree into the meringue, leaving it slightly marbled. Spoon half the mixture into 4 long-stemmed goblets, dividing it equally. Dot each serving with 3 raspberries. Spoon in the remaining mixture. Garnish each with 3 more raspberries. Chill at least 3 hours or overnight. Serve chilled.

Persimmon Pudding

Quite a surprise to find Indiana persimmons in a dessert at Topolobampo, Rick and Deann Bayless's more formal Mexican restaurant in Chicago, adjoining their popular, casual Frontera Grill. Rick created this recipe for old-fashioned creamy persimmon pudding after coming across Dillman Farm's frozen persimmon pulp (see Midwestern sources, page 378) in an Indiana food shop. It's mouthwatering and easy to make with the frozen pulp. Without this product, Midwest persimmons (if you can find them) are a struggle to deal with since they are small, mostly pit with very little flesh; you would need a load of them to yield 1 cup of puree. Occasionally at Topolobampo, I have had the pudding served with persimmon ice cream.

YIELD: 4 SERVINGS

¹/₃ cup plus 1 tablespoon flour
¹/₂ cup sugar
¹/₂ teaspoon cinnamon
¹/₈ teaspoon salt
¹/₄ teaspoon each: baking soda, baking powder
1 cup frozen persimmon pulp, thawed (see Headnote)
1 large egg
2 large egg yolks
¹/₂ cup heavy cream
¹/₃ cup milk
¹/₂ cup chopped pecans
Slightly sweetened cinnamon-flavored whipped cream
    or vanilla ice cream, for serving

1. Put a rack in the center of the oven; preheat the oven to 275 degrees. Grease four 6-ounce-capacity individual soufflé dishes. Set them aside with a shallow baking pan large enough to hold them. Bring a kettle of water to a boil.

2. Put the flour, sugar, cinnamon, salt, baking soda, and baking powder in a large bowl. Stir well.

3. Put the persimmon pulp, egg, egg yolks, cream, and milk in a 1-quart bowl. Whisk until smooth and flowing. Add the dry ingredients and stir until smooth.

4. Divide the mixture among the prepared dishes. Top with the pecans, dividing them equally. Place the dishes in the baking pan. Balance the pan on the edge of the oven rack and carefully pour the boiling water into the pan to reach halfway up the sides of dishes. Gently slide the pan into the center of the oven.

5. Bake until the pudding has risen and cracked slightly on the surface, about 40 minutes. A toothpick inserted in the center will come out moist but not wet. The pudding should not be firm. Use a spatula to transfer the dishes from the water bath to a wire rack for at least an hour before serving. The pudding can be made a day ahead and refrigerated, covered airtight, once it is completely cooled.

6. To serve, the pudding should be just barely warm. Reheat it in a preheated 275-degree oven until slightly warmed through, about 8 minutes (less if the pudding has been held at room temperature). Serve with cinnamon-flavored whipped cream or vanilla ice cream.

Maple Syrup Eggnog Custards

The subtlety of the maple syrup makes a nice sauce for these eggnog custards.
This is a do-ahead dessert since the custards must be well chilled before serving.

YIELD: 6 SERVINGS

¹/₂ cup pure maple syrup, plus additional, for serving
   (optional)
4 large eggs
¹/₃ cup sugar
¹/₄ cup nonfat dry milk
2¹/₂ cups whole milk
1 teaspoon each: pure vanilla extract, dark rum
¹/₄ teaspoon salt
1 teaspoon freshly grated nutmeg (see page 289),
   plus additional, for garnish

1. Put a rack in center of the oven; preheat the oven to 350 degrees. Generously butter six ¹/₂-cup-capacity individual soufflé dishes or custard cups. Place the cups in a baking pan just large enough to hold them. Set aside. Bring a kettle of water to a boil.

2. Boil the maple syrup in a small saucepan until somewhat thickened, about 3 minutes. Chill 10 minutes. Divide it equally among the prepared dishes.

3. Put the eggs in a 1-quart mixing bowl and whisk until frothy. Whisk in the sugar and nonfat dry milk until well combined. Add the remaining milk, vanilla, rum, salt, and the 1 teaspoon nutmeg, and whisk until combined. Strain the custard through a fine sieve. Divide the strained custard equally among the dishes, filling them to the rims. Set the pan on the oven rack. Pour enough hot water into the pan to reach halfway up the sides of the dishes.

4. Bake until a knife inserted in the center of a custard comes out clean, about 30 to 35 minutes. Use a metal spatula to carefully transfer the custards to a wire rack to cool. When cool, cover and refrigerate them until well chilled, at least 5 hours or overnight.

5. To serve, run a knife around the edge of each dish. Carefully invert the custards onto individual serving plates, coating each with the syrup from the bottom of the dish. Lightly sprinkle the tops with freshly grated nutmeg and pass additional maple syrup separately, if you wish.

Baked Chocolate Mousse Puffs

This is a chocolate lover's dream. One of the easiest, most practical dessert preparations there is, it really delivers in terms of taste and presentation, arriving at the table puffed and still hot from the oven. The mousse is made in advance and slipped into the oven in the middle of the meal. Baked, it is more like a partially baked, hot, flourless chocolate cake. It can also be served unbaked as a chilled mousse. I prefer to serve the puffs hot, topped with whipped cream, or with ice cream that melts into the center.

YIELD: 8 SERVINGS

8 ounces unsweetened chocolate
4 tablespoons unsalted butter
$1/2$ cup strong coffee
4 large eggs, separated, at room temperature
2 cups sugar
1 tablespoon plus 1 teaspoon pure vanilla extract
Whipped cream, or vanilla or coffee ice cream,
   for serving

1. Put a rack in the center of the oven; preheat the oven to 400 degrees. Grease eight 8-ounce-capacity soufflé dishes. Lightly coat the inside of the dishes with sugar, tapping out the excess. Set them aside with a cookie sheet.

2. Gently melt the chocolate and butter in the coffee in a microwave oven on medium power (50 percent) for about 3 to 4 minutes, stirring once midway, or in the top of a double boiler over boiling water, about 4 minutes. Transfer the mixture to a bowl and stir well. The mixture will be thick.

3. Put the egg yolks and $1\,1/3$ cups of the sugar in a 2-quart bowl. Whisk until light in color and fluffy. Whisk in the vanilla. Add a small amount of the chocolate mixture (it doesn't need to be completely cool) to the egg yolks and stir well. Add the remaining chocolate and stir well again.

4. Use an electric mixer to beat the egg whites. As they thicken, add the remaining sugar, a small amount at a time. Continue beating the whites until they hold their shape but are still moist and shiny. Stir one third of the whites into the chocolate mixture. Fold in the remaining whites with a flexible rubber spatula. Divide the mixture among the prepared dishes (it can come up to the top of the dish). The puffs can be baked immediately or refrigerated for up to 8 hours. Let the refrigerated mousse come to room temperature before baking it.

5. About 20 minutes before serving, place the soufflé dishes on the baking sheet, spacing them about 1 inch apart, and bake until the mousses are puffed, slightly cracked on the surface, but not too firm, about 12 minutes.

6. To serve, place the hot chocolate mousse puffs on serving plates; gently insert a spoon into each center and tuck a small dollop of whipped cream or a tiny scoop of ice cream inside each one. Serve immediately.

Chocolate Mint Ice Cream

With so many excellent ice creams available, it seems unnecessary to make ice cream at home. This uniquely wonderful ice cream proves an exception. Peggy Ryan, chef and co-owner of Va Pensiero restaurant in Evanston, Illinois, created this recipe for the Best of the Midwest Market barbecue many summers ago. She tucked the ice cream into brioche rolls. They were ice cream sandwiches to swoon over.

YIELD: 1 1/2 QUARTS

2 cups each: heavy cream, half-and-half
Grated zest (colored rind) of 3 oranges,
*   removed with a zester or fine grater (see page 14)*
¹/₂ cup chopped fresh peppermint
8 ounces bittersweet chocolate
8 large egg yolks
1 cup sugar
1 teaspoon pure vanilla extract

1. Bring the cream, half-and-half, orange zest, and mint to a boil in a heavy 2-quart nonaluminum saucepan. Remove from the heat and let stand at room temperature for 2¹/₂ hours.

2. Gently melt the chocolate in the top of a double boiler over boiling water, stirring often. Remove from the heat.

3. Strain the cream mixture through a fine sieve, return it to the saucepan, and bring it to a boil. Put the egg yolks and sugar in a mixing bowl and whisk until light-colored and smooth. Slowly stir 1 cup of the hot cream mixture into the beaten egg yolks. Then whisk the egg yolk mixture into the hot cream remaining in the saucepan.

4. Cook over medium heat until very hot but not boiling (about 180 degrees on an instant-read thermometer). Be sure not to let the cream boil.

Remove from the heat and whisk in the chocolate and vanilla. Strain through a fine sieve. Chill the mixture. Then freeze in an ice cream machine according to the manufacturer's instructions. Freeze in an airtight container no longer than 2 days for the best taste.

100 Percent Fresh Strawberry Sherbet

I usually get carried away and buy far more seasonal fruit than I can use. I freeze the surplus to use in a food processor sherbet. Then I can enjoy these summer fruits throughout the year. The food processor is the only piece of kitchen equipment that can transform a quantity of frozen fresh fruit into a fruit "blizzard" as my friend Marion Cunningham, the well-known cook and author, calls it, and then into a smooth, full-flavored sherbet. Three cups of almost any fruit can be substituted for the strawberries (see Note), making this a great recipe to count on as seasonal fruit comes to market.

YIELD: ABOUT 3 CUPS

1 pint strawberries, hulled, cut in half
2 tablespoons sugar or to taste
1 teaspoon fresh lemon juice
⅓ cup thawed strawberries, lowfat yogurt,
   or cranberry juice (to smooth out the sherbet)

1. Arrange the strawberries on a cookie sheet lined with waxed paper and freeze until solid, about 40 minutes. Once frozen, they can be used right away or stored for several months in an airtight plastic bag.

2. Let the frozen strawberries rest at room temperature about 10 minutes; they should still be frozen, but not rock-hard. Put them in a food processor fitted with the metal blade. Add the sugar and pulse on/off several times to chop the berries; then process continuously until the berries are minced into tiny frozen chips, stopping often to scrape down the sides of the work bowl with a rubber spatula.

3. With the processor on, slowly add the lemon juice and strawberries, yogurt, or cranberry juice; continue to process until the mixture is smooth, about 5 to 8 minutes, stopping as necessary to scrape down the sides of the work bowl. This can be served immediately as a soft sherbet or frozen up to 3 months, covered airtight.

4. To serve the frozen sherbet, reprocess (thaw it slightly to spoon it into the work bowl) until smooth. It's best served immediately but it can be frozen up to 3 hours before serving so it will still have a wonderfully smooth texture.

NOTE: Fruits can be used singly or in combination. Any fruit used for this sherbet must be cut into 1-inch pieces, then frozen like the strawberries. Peaches, nectarines, and apricots do not need to be peeled; the peel becomes minuscule specks in the sherbet. Pineapple, bananas, kiwi, and apples must be peeled. Put up to 3 cups of the frozen fruit into the food processor and proceed as for the strawberry sherbet. Mix fruits for variety. Some favorite combinations are strawberry and banana, peach and a small handful of raspberries, pineapple and banana.

Cranberry Mustard

State Fair Corn Relish

Sweet Dill Cucumber Crisps

Apple Chutney with Dried Cranberries

Orange Pickled Beets and Shallots

Chicago "Hot"

Fresh Cranberry Relish

Chapter 12
Condiments

❖

It used to be necessary in the Midwest to put up pickles and fruits to have any hope of delicious meals in the middle of winter. But times have changed, and we now have a year-round supply of fresh fruits and vegetables. So, today it is pleasure not necessity that leads us to pickling and preserving the bounty of our farmers' markets.

Just consider the pleasure to be found in Cranberry Mustard or State Fair Corn Relish. Making your own condiments does not have to be complicated or technically challenging. In fact, the most delightful results come from the simplest recipes. Sweet Dill Cucumber Crisps, Apple Chutney with Dried Cranberries, Orange Pickled Beets and Shallots—these are taste elements that enliven any meal.

I have eliminated the involved ritual of canning in favor of the refrigerator, even though refrigerator-held preserves have a shorter shelf life. I like to respond to the harvest as it pours into the market, then make small quantities of condiments. Fresh ingredients are essential to success, so make your pickles and preserves as soon as you get home with your produce, then let them sit for at least a few days to develop their unique, exciting flavors. Any of these recipes can be doubled or tripled, depending on your needs.

Cranberries:

Cranberries were first harvested from the wetlands of Wisconsin by the Menominee and Chippewa Indians hundreds of years ago. Today they are the state's most important fruit crop, making Wisconsin the nation's second-leading producer of the ruby-red berries after Massachusetts.

❖ When buying cranberries, select plump, lustrous, firm berries that are red to reddish black in color.

❖ Cranberries will keep in the refrigerator for as long as 8 weeks. Store in their bags, securing with a twist-tie if opened. Do not wash them until ready to use.

❖ Cranberries freeze extraordinarily well, right in their original bags, for as long as a year (until the next crop is ready).

❖ Cranberries cook easily and quickly in the microwave oven without having to stir them constantly since they won't stick or burn. Four cups of cranberries cook in about 12 to 14 minutes at full power (100 percent), stirring only once after 6 minutes.

❖ Cranberries can be chopped or sliced in the food processor while still frozen. It is not necessary to thaw them; in fact, thawed cranberries are too soft to chop neatly or to slice.

❖ Add cranberries to quick breads, muffins, scones, pancakes, cakes, applesauce, ice cream, sorbet, sweet desserts and savory sauces, puddings as well as stews, grains, casseroles, and game dishes.

Cranberry Mustard

In 1993, at the Best of the Midwest Market at Ravinia (Highland Park, Illinois), I tasted a cranberry mustard product from Wisconsin Wilderness that sent me right to the stove. It was such a good idea. Here's my own version of this condiment; a bright-colored, tangy mustard, thick enough to serve as a sauce and just right for spreading on a sandwich. Serve it in a small dish with hot or cold meats and poultry and/or as a sandwich spread with cheeses as well as vegetables, poultry, and cold cuts. It's also a wonderful gift from the kitchen, easy to make and versatile on the table.

YIELD: ABOUT 2 3/4 CUPS

One 12-ounce bag of cranberries, about 4 cups
2 medium Granny Smith apples, peeled, cored, diced,
    about 4 cups
$^2/_3$ cup water
1 cup sugar
$^1/_8$ teaspoon allspice
1 tablespoon each: cider vinegar, Dijon mustard
2 tablespoons prepared mustard
$^1/_4$ teaspoon salt

1. Put the cranberries, apples, water, sugar, and allspice into a 3-quart nonaluminum pot. Bring to a boil and simmer, uncovered, until the apples are tender, about 20 minutes.

2. Transfer the mixture to a blender or a food processor fitted with a metal blade. Mix until smooth. Add the remaining ingredients and mix until well combined. Let cool to room temperature. Adjust the salt and mustard to your taste. The mustard can be kept refrigerated for up to 2 weeks, covered airtight. Serve chilled.

State Fair Corn Relish

*This is a wonderful summer harvest recipe, a welcome condiment for hot dogs,
brats, and hamburgers as well as cold cuts. It's best to let the relish mellow for
at least a day before serving it.*

YIELD: 7 CUPS

LIQUID:
2 cups cider vinegar
1 tablespoon fresh lemon juice
³/4 cup packed light brown sugar
3 tablespoons sugar
¹/2 teaspoon dry mustard
2 teaspoons each: mustard seed, celery seed
Scant 1 tablespoon salt
¹/4 teaspoon red pepper flakes

VEGETABLES:
4¹/2 cups fresh corn kernels, about 7 large ears
2 cups sliced cabbage
1 medium onion, chopped, about 1¹/4 cups
2 medium ribs celery, diced, about 1 cup
1 large red bell pepper, seeded, diced, about 1¹/4 cups

1. For the liquid, combine all the ingredients in a
3-quart nonaluminum pot. Bring to a boil.

2. For the vegetables, add all ingredients to the
boiling liquid and simmer, covered, for 20 minutes,
stirring occasionally. Continue to simmer,
uncovered, to reduce the liquid, for about 10
minutes more. Cool to room temperature. Once
cooled, the relish can be refrigerated in airtight
containers or jars for up to 3 weeks.

Sweet Dill Cucumber Crisps

These homemade crisps are bright green and very fresh-tasting,
quite different from those you can buy.

YIELD: 4 CUPS

1 pound pickling cucumbers, unpeeled, scrubbed, thinly
    sliced, about 3 cups
1 large green bell pepper, seeded, quartered, thinly
    sliced, about 1 cup
1 medium red onion, quartered, thinly sliced, about
    1 cup
1¹/₂ tablespoons salt
¹/₂ cup each: sugar, white vinegar
1¹/₂ teaspoons dried dill
1 teaspoon mustard seed

1. Put the cucumbers, green pepper, red onion, and salt in a 2-quart bowl. Add cold water to cover. Soak for 2 hours. Drain in a colander and return the vegetables to the bowl. Set aside.

2. Meanwhile, combine the sugar, vinegar, dill, and mustard seed in a 1-quart nonaluminum pan. Bring to a boil and simmer until the sugar is dissolved, about 5 minutes. Remove from the heat and cool to room temperature.

3. Pour the cooled mixture over the cucumbers. Toss until combined. Refrigerate, covered airtight, for at least 2 days before using to allow the flavors to meld. The pickles can be kept up to 1 month, refrigerated covered airtight.

Apple Chutney with Dried Cranberries

Chutneys dress up any meal. And don't forget to spread them on meat, cheese, and vegetable sandwiches. Homemade chutney has a much fresher taste than those that are commercially available. The contrasting flavors, colors, and textures of the cranberries and apples are especially appealing in this recipe.

YIELD: 3 CUPS

1 large clove garlic, minced, about ¹/₂ tablespoon
1 medium onion, minced, about 1¹/₄ cups
5 medium apples, peeled, cored, diced,
  cut into ¹/₃-inch dice, about 5 cups
¹/₂ cup firmly packed light brown sugar
6 tablespoons white wine vinegar
¹/₄ teaspoon each: dry mustard, ground ginger, ground
  allspice, ground cloves, red pepper flakes
Pinch of salt
³/₄ cup dried cranberries
1 tablespoon cornstarch mixed with 2 tablespoons
  cold water

1. Put the garlic, onion, apples, sugar, vinegar, and spices in a 1¹/₂-quart nonaluminum saucepan. Bring the liquid to a boil over high heat and simmer, uncovered, stirring occasionally, until the apples are tender, about 10 to 12 minutes.

2. Add the cranberries and cornstarch mixture to the pan. Stir until well combined. Cook until the cranberries are plumped and the mixture thickened, about 3 minutes. Refrigerate 2 days before serving. The chutney can be refrigerated for up to 1 month, or frozen for as long as 2 months, covered airtight. Serve chilled or at room temperature.

Orange Pickled Beets and Shallots

Beets elicit a strong response—positive or negative! Here, they're combined with thinly sliced shallots in a spicy orange juice mixture. These beets are great in a composed salad paired with portions of Curried Celery Root and Apple Salad (page 103) or as an addition to green salads. They also make a flavorful condiment that goes with a wide variety of simple meals.

YIELD: 2 CUPS

1 teaspoon grated orange zest (colored rind),
   removed with a grater or zester (see page 14)
$1/3$ cup orange juice
$1/2$ tablespoon vegetable oil
$1^1/2$ teaspoons Dijon mustard
$1^1/4$ teaspoons sugar
$1/8$ teaspoon allspice
$1/4$ teaspoon salt
Freshly ground pepper to taste
2 large beets, cooked (see Note), julienned,
   about $1^3/4$ cups
3 large shallots, thinly sliced, about $1/2$ cup

1. Put all the ingredients except the beets and shallots in a $1^1/2$-quart bowl. Whisk until well combined. Add the beets and shallots and toss until the vegetables are mixed and well coated. Refrigerate at least overnight, and for up to 3 weeks before serving.

2. To serve, mix well. Adjust the seasoning.

NOTE: To cook beets, wash, trim, and wrap each one in foil. Place the beets on a cookie sheet and bake in a preheated 450-degree oven for 1 to $1^1/2$ hours, depending on their size. To determine if tender, insert a small sharp knife right through the foil.

Chicago "Hot"

This chunky tomato relish is adapted from a recipe in America Cooks: Favorite Recipes from the 48 States, a charming and homespun book written by Cora, Rose, and Bob Brown in 1940. The book has 48 chapters, one for each of the states that then comprised the Union. From Illinois come such temptations as haystack hash and Chicago "Hot." In truth, this savory relish is not all that hot, horseradish being the only ingredient that contributes to its spicy nature.

YIELD: 1 PINT

$1/3$ cup plus 1 tablespoon cider vinegar

2 tablespoons light brown sugar

1 teaspoon salt

2 teaspoons pickling spice, tied in a cheesecloth bag

2 medium tomatoes, cored, seeded, cut into $1/2$-inch dice, about $1 1/2$ cups

4 medium ribs celery, cut into $1/4$-inch dice, about 2 cups

1 large red bell pepper, seeded, cut into $1/4$-inch dice, about $1 1/2$ cups

1 small sweet onion, cut into $1/4$-inch dice, about $3/4$ cup

3 tablespoons well-drained white horseradish

1. Put the vinegar, sugar, salt, and pickling spice in a nonaluminum saucepan. Simmer until the sugar dissolves, about 5 minutes.

2. Put the tomatoes, celery, pepper, and onion in a large bowl. Toss until combined. Pour the hot liquid, including the spice bag, over the vegetables. Add the horseradish and toss gently until combined. Cover and refrigerate at least 12 hours or for up to 1 week before serving. Stir well, drain the liquid, and remove the spice bag. Adjust the vinegar, salt, or sugar to your taste. The relish, covered airtight, can be refrigerated for up to 1 month.

Fresh Cranberry Relish

For its very ease, this simple, uncooked relish is remarkable. It's delicious and refreshing when served with turkey, chicken, game, cold cuts, or any other meats. Combined with a little mayonnaise, it makes a tangy sandwich spread. The apples and pear help to sweeten the mixture. It's almost no recipe at all. It can be varied as your taste dictates; the cranberries are the key component. Just be sure to make it at least 2 days in advance to allow time for the flavor and color to deepen.

YIELD: 3 1/2 CUPS

One 12-ounce bag of fresh cranberries, about 4 cups
$^1/_2$ medium orange, seeded, rind and flesh cut into
   1-inch chunks
1 medium pear, unpeeled, cored,
   cut into 1-inch chunks
2 small sweet apples, unpeeled, cored,
   cut into 1-inch chunks
$^3/_4$ cup sugar or to taste

Combine the ingredients and put them, in batches, in a food processor fitted with the metal blade, and process each batch until finely minced but not absolutely smooth; this should have some texture. The relish should be refrigerated at least 2 days before serving. Covered airtight, it can be refrigerated for up to 3 weeks or frozen for up to 3 months. Stir well before serving and adjust the sugar. Serve chilled or at room temperature.

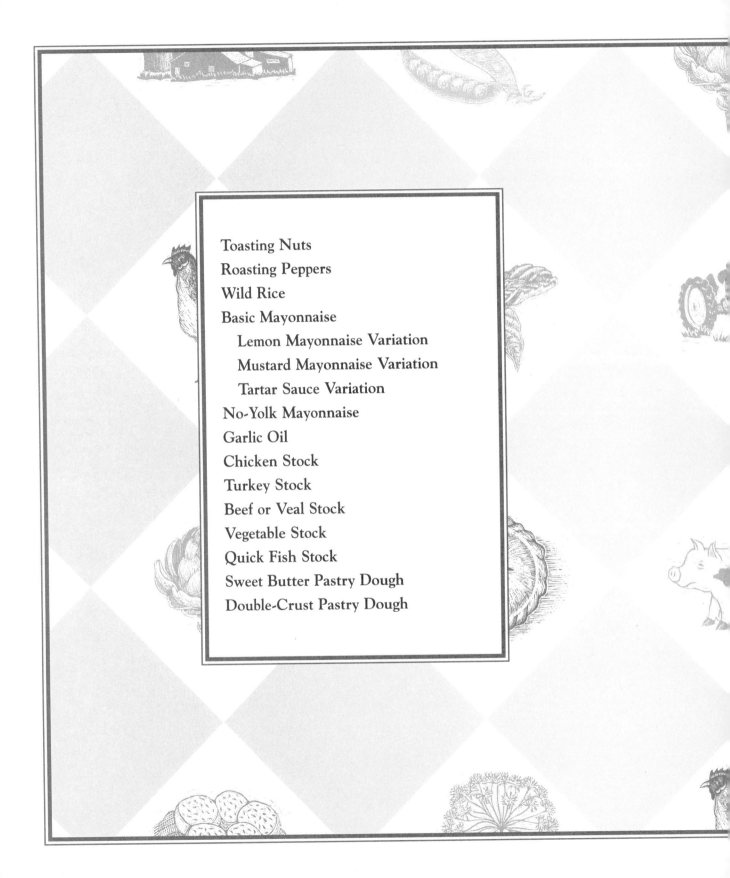

Toasting Nuts

Roasting Peppers

Wild Rice

Basic Mayonnaise

    Lemon Mayonnaise Variation

    Mustard Mayonnaise Variation

    Tartar Sauce Variation

No-Yolk Mayonnaise

Garlic Oil

Chicken Stock

Turkey Stock

Beef or Veal Stock

Vegetable Stock

Quick Fish Stock

Sweet Butter Pastry Dough

Double-Crust Pastry Dough

Chapter 13

Basics

❖

Toasting Nuts

Toasting nuts brings out their flavor; it does make a difference. To use your time wisely, toast more than you need and store them in the freezer up to 6 months, wrapped airtight and clearly labeled. They will be available to you for recipes that require them, without having to toast them each time.

To toast nuts, spread them in a single layer on a baking sheet. Bake in a preheated 350-degree oven until lightly browned and fragrant—about 8 to 10 minutes for pine nuts, about 10 minutes for walnuts and pecans—watching carefully so they do not burn.

Roasting Peppers

Roasting peppers brings out their sweetness; they add color, flavor, and a unique texture to many preparations, such as salads, pastas, sandwiches, and spreads, to name just a few. It came as a surprise to me that they also freeze beautifully. This method of cutting off the pepper sides and then broiling them reduces the time and attention typically required for roasting peppers.

To prepare peppers for roasting, stand them on a board; cut off the sides in 4 slabs, following the natural flat contours as much as possible. Cut off the bottom piece. Discard the seeds and core and trim away the membrane. To roast peppers in the broiler, put a rack 6 inches from the heat source and preheat the broiler. Line a cookie sheet with aluminum foil. Arrange the pepper pieces (including stem end) on the prepared cookie sheet, skin side up. Broil until the skin is blackened, about 8 minutes. Remove from the oven and use the foil lining to wrap up the peppers and steam them. Let them rest on the counter for about 10 minutes. Slip off the skins. To roast peppers on the barbecue, prepare a hot barbecue fire. Place the pepper pieces, skin side down, on the rack. Grill until the skin is blackened, about 5 minutes. Wrap the peppers in foil to steam them. After 10 minutes, slip off the skins.

Wild Rice

Wild rice adds an earthy taste and interesting texture to pilafs, soups, casseroles, stuffings, and salads. It freezes extremely well, so make 2 or 3 times this recipe while you're at it. Freeze the wild rice in convenient-size portions in airtight plastic bags.

YIELD: 3 1/2 CUPS

2 cups water
1 cup wild rice

Bring the water to a boil in a 2-quart saucepan. Add the wild rice and bring back to a boil. Simmer, covered, until the water has evaporated and the rice is done to taste (it can be al dente or fluffy), 30 to 50 minutes depending on the freshness of the rice and the desired texture. The rice, covered airtight, can be refrigerated for 3 days or frozen for up to 1 month.

Basic Mayonnaise

Different oils will change the flavor of the mayonnaise as will the addition of herbs, spices, nuts, and grated citrus zest.

YIELD: 1 3/4 CUPS

1 large egg
1 teaspoon each: red wine vinegar, fresh lemon juice,
    Dijon mustard
1/2 teaspoon salt
Freshly ground pepper to taste
3/4 cup each: olive oil, safflower oil

1. Process the egg, vinegar, lemon juice, mustard, salt, pepper, and 3 tablespoons olive oil for 30 seconds in a food processor fitted with the metal blade or in a blender. With the machine running, slowly add the remaining oils in a thin steady stream. The mayonnaise will thicken as the oil is added. Adjust the seasoning. The mayonnaise can be refrigerated for up to 10 days, covered airtight.

Lemon Mayonnaise Variation: To 1/2 cup basic mayonnaise, add 1 tablespoon fresh lemon juice and 1 1/2 teaspoons grated lemon zest (see page 14).

Mustard Mayonnaise Variation: To 1/2 cup basic mayonnaise, add 1 tablespoon Dijon mustard or any other mustard of your choice.

Tartar Sauce Variation: To 1/2 cup basic mayonnaise, add 1 tablespoon each minced parsley and sweet pickle relish; 1 teaspoon each Dijon mustard and minced shallot; 1/2 teaspoon fresh lemon juice; and 1/2 riced, hard-cooked egg or 1 whole riced, hard-cooked egg white.

No-Yolk Mayonnaise

*This is a thick, flavorful mayonnaise that can be used in all recipes calling for mayonnaise.
Depending on the oil you use, it can be virtually free of cholesterol.*

YIELD: 1 1/2 CUPS

2 large egg whites
1 tablespoon Dijon mustard
2 teaspoons red wine vinegar
Salt and freshly ground pepper to taste
1¹/₂ cups oil (I use ³/₄ cup each safflower and olive oil)

Mix the egg whites, mustard, vinegar, salt, pepper,
and 3 tablespoons of the oil for 30 seconds in a
food processor fitted with the metal blade or in a
blender. With the machine running, add the
remaining oil in a thin, steady stream. The mixture
will thicken as the oil is added. The mayonnaise
can be refrigerated for up to 10 days, covered
airtight.

Garlic Oil

Garlic lovers take note . . . and I am right in there with you. I use this oil on salads, pasta, breads, fish, and vegetables. But take heed! It's important to make the oil in small quantities, use it up quickly, and keep it refrigerated to avoid any possibility of botulism.

YIELD: 1/2 CUP

4 to 6 large cloves garlic, minced, about 2 to 3
　　tablespoons
$^1/_2$ cup olive oil

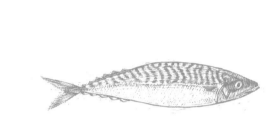

1. Heat the garlic and oil in a small pan over medium-low heat just until the garlic becomes aromatic, about 4 minutes.

2. Strain it into a jar, cover tightly, and refrigerate for up to 3 days.

Chicken Stock

YIELD: 5 CUPS

5 pounds chicken bones and backs
2 medium onions, peeled, cut into chunks
1 large leek, cut into chunks
1 large carrot, cut into chunks
2 medium ribs celery, cut into chunks
8 parsley sprigs
1 bay leaf
2 whole cloves
1 teaspoon dried thyme

1. Combine all the ingredients in a 6-quart pot and add water to cover. Bring to a boil, and simmer gently, uncovered, for 1½ hours, skimming the top to discard the foam as necessary.

2. Discard the bones and vegetables. Pour the stock through a strainer lined with a double thickness of cheesecloth. Refrigerate until the fat solidifies, then remove and discard it. Pour the stock into convenient-sized containers and refrigerate for up to 2 days, or freeze, covered airtight, for up to 3 months.

Turkey Stock

If you have pan juices leftover from roasting a turkey, add them to the stockpot with the other ingredients. These juices will deepen the flavor of the stock.

YIELD: 4 CUPS

1 turkey carcass, broken up
1 medium carrot, cut into chunks
1 large onion, cut into chunks
2 medium ribs celery, cut into chunks
6 cups lower-salt chicken broth
4 cups water
$^1\!/_2$ teaspoon dried thyme leaves
2 bay leaves
3 peppercorns

Put all the ingredients in a 4-quart stockpot. Bring the liquid to a boil and simmer, covered, for $1^1\!/_2$ hours. Strain the stock and discard the solids. Cool the stock, then refrigerate until the fat solidifies. Remove and discard it. Pour the stock into convenient-sized containers and refrigerate for up to 3 days, or freeze, covered airtight, for up to 3 months.

Beef or Veal Stock

Making beef or veal stock is time-consuming but easy and well worth the effort.

YIELD: 2 1/2 QUARTS

10 pounds beef or veal bones, cut in 3- to 4-inch pieces
   (have your butcher do this)
4 medium onions, peeled, quartered
3 small carrots, peeled, cut into 1-inch pieces
3 medium ribs celery, cut into 1-inch pieces
10 parsley sprigs

1. Put a rack in the center of the oven; preheat the oven to 425 degrees.

2. Place the bones in a single layer in 2 large roasting pans and bake for 1 hour, turning them once after 30 minutes.

3. Add the onions and carrots to the roasting pans. Bake 30 minutes longer.

4. With a slotted spoon, transfer the bones and vegetables to an 8- to 10-quart stockpot. Discard the fat from the roasting pans, then add water and scrape up the browned bits sticking to the bottom of the pans. Pour this water into the stockpot. Add additional water to cover the bones.

5. Bring to a boil over high heat and simmer gently, uncovered, for 1 hour, skimming the top to discard the foam as necessary. Add the celery and parsley and continue to simmer gently for 10 hours. As the water evaporates, add more to maintain the original level.

6. Discard the bones and vegetables and pour the stock through a strainer lined with a double thickness of cheesecloth. Return the strained stock to the pot and boil uncovered until it is reduced to 10 cups, about 1 to 2 hours.

7. Refrigerate the stock until the fat has solidified, then remove and discard it. Pour the defatted stock into convenient-sized containers and refrigerate for up to 2 days, or freeze, covered airtight, for up to 3 months.

Vegetable Stock

Add any other vegetables you might happen to have on hand; the point is to pack the water with vegetables to obtain depth of flavor. When tomatoes are in season, add 2 tomatoes, quartered, instead of the tomato paste.

YIELD: 2 QUARTS

4 quarts water
4 each: medium leeks, carrots, celery stalks, sliced
2 tablespoons tomato paste
1 large bunch of parsley
6 large cloves garlic, peeled, split
6 whole peppercorns
4 bay leaves
1 tablespoon cider vinegar

Combine all the ingredients in an 8-quart pot. Bring to a boil and simmer, uncovered, for 1$\frac{1}{2}$ hours. Strain, pressing as much liquid from the vegetables as possible. Discard the vegetables and pour the stock into convenient-sized containers; refrigerate for up to 3 days, or freeze, covered airtight, for up to 3 months.

Quick Fish Stock

Here's a quick fish stock, well flavored and timesaving. Add salt to taste after the stock has been added to a recipe, since clam juice is usually salty. Make a double quantity while you're at it; freeze the excess in plastic ice cube trays for other soups, sauces, and lowfat fish dishes. Once frozen, the stock cubes can be popped out and stored in a plastic bag, tied airtight.

YIELD: ABOUT 5 CUPS

1 large leek, thinly sliced, about 1 cup
2 small onions, thinly sliced, about 1¹/₂ cups
3 cups bottled clam juice
2 cups water
¹/₄ cup dry white wine or dry vermouth
1 bay leaf
¹/₂ teaspoon dried thyme

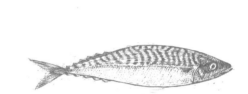

Put all the ingredients into a 3-quart nonaluminum pot. Bring to a boil and simmer, uncovered, for 20 minutes. Pour through a strainer lined with a double thickness of cheesecloth. Pour the stock into convenient-sized containers (or ice cube trays) for freezing; refrigerate for up to 3 days or freeze, covered airtight, for up to 3 months.

Sweet Butter Pastry Dough

This is an excellent crust for fruit tarts as it seldom becomes soggy
For ease of preparation, make it in the food processor.

YIELD: ONE 11-INCH CRUST

¹/₂ cup plus 2 tablespoons unsalted butter, chilled,
*   cut in small pieces*
3 tablespoons sugar
2 large egg yolks
3 tablespoons ice water
1 teaspoon pure vanilla extract
¹/₂ teaspoon salt
1²/₃ cups unbleached all-purpose flour

1. Put a rack in the center of the oven; preheat the oven to 425 degrees. Set aside a 9-inch round, 1-inch-deep tart pan with a removable bottom, or a 9-inch pie plate and a cookie sheet.

2. Put the butter and sugar in a food processor fitted with a metal blade or in a mixing bowl. Cut the butter into the sugar using pulse on/off or, if you're doing this by hand, with a pastry blender until the butter is finely chopped. Add the egg yolks, water, vanilla, and salt; mix well. Add the flour and mix just until the dough clumps together.

3. Transfer the dough to a large plastic bag; compress it into a ball, then flatten it into a disc. Place the disc in the freezer for about 10 to 15 minutes until it is firm enough to roll. The dough can also be refrigerated for up to 2 days or frozen, wrapped airtight, for up to 1 month. If too firm to roll, let it stand at room temperature until pliable enough to roll out without splitting.

4. On a floured board, roll the dough into a circle ¹/₈ inch thick. Carefully fold the dough into

quarters. Place it on the tart pan or pie plate centering the point of the triangle. Unfold the dough and gently press it into the bottom and sides of the pan; trim the excess dough ¹/₂ inch above the rim. Pinch the edges to form a decorative edge. Refrigerate or freeze briefly, about 15 minutes, until the pastry is firm. Prick the bottom with a fork in several places.

5. To prebake, line the pastry with aluminum foil and fill it with dried beans or rice. Place the pan on the cookie sheet (for easier handling), and bake for 15 minutes. Remove the foil and beans and continue baking until the pastry is lightly browned, about 10 minutes longer. Cool for at least 20 minutes before filling.

Double-Crust Pastry Dough

Pastry for a double-crust pie is most easily made in the food processor.

YIELD: ONE DOUBLE-CRUST FOR 9-INCH DEEP-DISH PIE

2^1/$_4$ cups unbleached all-purpose flour
^{1}/$_2$ cup each: chilled vegetable shortening,
   chilled unsalted butter, cut in small pieces
^{3}/$_4$ teaspoon salt
^{1}/$_2$ cup ice water

1. Put the flour, shortening, butter, and salt in a food processor fitted with the metal blade or in a mixing bowl. Cut the shortening and butter into the flour using pulse on/off or, if you're doing this by hand, with a pastry blender until the mixture resembles coarse meal. Drizzle the water over the mixture. Use pulse on/off or a fork to mix just until the dough begins to clump. Do not overprocess by letting the dough form a ball. Little flecks of butter should be visible in the dough.

2. Transfer the dough to a plastic bag; compress it into a ball, then flatten the dough into an 8-inch disc. Divide the dough into 2 parts, using one third for 1 piece and two thirds for the other. Flatten each piece into a disc. Refrigerate in plastic bags (or briefly place them in the freezer, about 15 minutes) until firm enough to roll out. The dough can also be refrigerated for up to 2 days or frozen, covered airtight. If too firm to roll, let the dough stand at room temperature until pliable enough to roll without splitting.

3. On a floured board, roll the larger piece (keep the smaller piece refrigerated) into a 12-inch-diameter circle. Wrap it around the rolling pin and unroll it over the pie plate, centering it. Gently press the dough into the bottom and sides of the plate.

4. Fill the pie as directed in the individual recipe.

5. Roll the smaller piece of dough into a 10-inch-diameter circle. Wrap it around the rolling pin and unroll it over the top of the pie, carefully centering it. Trim the edges, leaving a ^{1}/$_2$-inch overhang. With floured fingers, tuck the overhang under to seal it tightly; then form a decorative edge with the tines of a fork. Use a sharp paring knife to make several slashes in the top crust to allow steam to escape during baking. Sprinkle or glaze the crust as specified in the recipe. Bake as directed.

Cinnamon Variation: Add ^{3}/$_4$ teaspoon cinnamon and 1 tablespoon sugar to the Double-Crust Pastry Dough recipe.

Midwestern Sources

Produce and Herbs

Angelic Organics
1547 Rockton Road
Caledonia, Illinois 61011
815-389-2746
Heirloom and specialty tomatoes, cucumbers,
watermelons, muskmelons, cantaloupes, potatoes,
and bouquets of dried flowers

Applesource
Route 1
Chapin, Illinois 62628
217-245-7589
Gala and many other apple varieties

Barry's Berries
68640 42nd Avenue
Covert, Michigan 49043
616-621-4272
Blueberries, raspberries, blackberries, apricots, peaches,
plums, and nectarines

Broadlands Organic Farm, Inc.
1445 West Cullom Avenue
Chicago, Illinois 60613
312-871-2560
Heirloom and garden variety tomatoes, summer and
winter squash, zucchini, and eggplant

Chadwick Farms
Route 2, Box 26
Chadwick, Illinois 61014
815-684-5625
Blueberries, raspberries, blackberries, apricots, plums,
peaches, and nectarines

Chicago's Indoor Garden, Inc.
2708 West Belmont Avenue
Chicago, Illinois 60618
312-463-2848
Nine sprout varieties, seed salads (sprouted garbanzos
and Alaskan peas with spices), snow pea shoots,
sunflower greens, and wheatgrass juice

Clausen Road Produce
1223 Clausen Road
Burlington, Wisconsin 53105
Bi-color super-sweet corn, melons, beans, peppers,
tomatoes, carrots, beets, squashes, and pickles

Doud Orchards
R.R. 1
Dencer, Indiana 46926
317-985-3937
Heirloom and specialty apples, pears, plums; apple
butter, applesauce; jams and fruit butters; cider and
comb honey

Ela Orchard
P.O. Box 73
Rochester, Wisconsin 53167
414-534-2565
Apples and apple cider

Forest Resource Center
Route 2, Box 156A
Lanesboro, Minnesota 55949
507-467-2437
Freeze-dried shiitake mushrooms and shiitake
wild rice soup mix

Geneva Lakes Produce
1223 Clausen Road
Burlington, Wisconsin 53105
414-763-2449
Bi-color sweet corn, beans, melons, peppers, pickles,
beets, cucumbers, and gladiolas

Gourmet Gardens
1211 North Wilkins Place
Plainfield, Illinois 60544
815-436-5365
Potted and cut herbs, assorted lettuces and salad greens,
tomatoes, peppers, celeriac, shallots, leeks, and tomatoes

Gourmet Herbs, Inc.
P.O. Box 703
New Lenox, Illinois 60451
815-485-3330
Herbs, flowers, and greens

Green Feet Organic Enterprises
8364 South State Road 39
Clayton, Indiana 46118
317-539-6935
Organic tomatoes, potatoes, squashes, corn, hot peppers,
dried mushrooms, and mesclun mix

Harmony Valley Farm
Route 2, Box 116
Viroque, Wisconsin 54665
608-483-2143
Salad mix, French petite beans, celeriac, garlic braids
and bulbs

Heartland Growers Association
Route 2, Box 239
Carthage, Illinois 62321
217-746-2112
Fresh and dried shiitake mushrooms

Hickory Hill Farm
South 6555 Highway 23
Loganville, Wisconsin 53943
608-727-2941
Herbs and vegetables

Hoosier Organic Marketing Enterprises
R.R. 2, Box 182
Clayton, Indiana 46118
317-539-6935
Organic specialties and unusual varieties of tomatoes,
potatoes, fresh herbs, edible flowers, seasonal green salad
mixes, and an unusual garlic pepper

Kingsfield Gardens
Route 1
Blue Mounds, Wisconsin 53517
608-924-9341
Many organic vegetables, including baby bok choy,
Middle Eastern cucumbers, haricots verts, eggplants,
button onions, cipollini onions, leeks, gray shallots,
garlic and onion braids, Japanese pink and yellow
tomatoes

Missouri Dandy Pantry
212 Hammons Drive
Stockton, Missouri 65785
417-276-5121
Black walnuts, black walnut cream, black walnut syrup,
black walnut candies

Pepin Heights Orchard
Route 4, Box 18
Lake City, Minnesota 55041
612-463-7272
Sparkling apple cider

The Potato Company
54281 State Road 13
Middlebury, Indiana 46540
219-825-7811
Exotic potatoes and herbs, beans, tomatoes, melons,
salad greens, and cut flowers

Prairie Crossing Farm
32400 North Harris Road
Grayslake, Illinois 60030
708-548-4030
Specialty tomatoes, sweet peppers, beets, summer
squashes, cucumbers, Swiss chard, and basil

Renaissance Farm
P.O. Box 268
Spring Green, Wisconsin 53588
608-588-2230
Pestos: sweet basil, lemon basil, cilantro; basil, lemon basil, dill, and cilantro; pine nuts

River Valley Ranch
P.O. Box 898
New Munster, Wisconsin 53152
800-SHROOMS (800-747-6667)
Portobello, shiitake, cremini, button, and oyster mushrooms

Schaeffer Family Farm
H.C.R. 64, Box 221
West Plaines, Missouri 65775
417-257-0670
Garlic braids with herbs and flowers, herb wreaths, and dried flower bouquets

Solar Gardens
2720 North Pitcher Street
Kalamazoo, Michigan 49004
616-382-3117
Edible flowers; nasturtium-herb butter; dried cherries, blueberries, and strawberries; dried morel, chanterelle, and porcini mushrooms

Specialty Game, Inc.
4444 Lawndale Avenue
Lyons, Illinois 60534
708-447-9400
Specialty mushrooms: portabello, shiitake, cremini, oyster, baby blue oyster, golden chanterelle, lobster, hedgehog, and porcini

Star Valley Flowers
Route 1, Box 1168
Soldiers Grove, Wisconsin 54655
608-624-3325
Sunflowers, mixed bouquets, bittersweet, hydrangea, gladiola, amaranth, and decorative gourds

Sundial Gardens
11238 Sequoya Lane
Indian Head Park, Illinois 60525
708-246-1668
Herbs and oils

Thyme from Rosemary
N6535 State Road 120
Elkhorn, Wisconsin 53121
414-642-4042
Herb plants, wreaths, and ropes; herb flower honey; herb jellies; and seasonal vegetables

Trailside Farms
321 South Clark Lane, P.O. Box 456
Elizabeth, Illinois 61048
815-858-2245
Organic herb gifts: culinary herb crate, bushel of basil, mint tea drinking jars, and assorted herb packets

Unique Herbs
90 Acorn Lane
Highland Park, Illinois 60035
708-831-3758
Potted herbs: basil, caraway, chamomile, chervil, coriander, lemon verbena, horseradish, mint, rosemary, sage, sorrel, and sweet woodruff

Wauconda Orchards
1201 Gossell Road
Wauconda, Illinois 60084
708-526-8553
Apples

Willow Run Farms
49350 North I-94 Service Drive
Belleville, Michigan 48111
313-699-6202
Hydroponic lettuce and greens, cut and potted herbs, and shiitake mushrooms

Cheeses and Breads

Auricchio Cheese, Inc.
5810 Highway NN
Denmark, Wisconsin 54208
414-863-2123
Specialty Italian cheeses, such as Asiago, fontina, and provolone

Bass Lake Cheese Factory
598 Valley View Trail
Somerset, Wisconsin 54025
715-247-5586
Old-fashioned Colby, raw-milk Cheddar, plus goat's milk, Colby-style, and Jack-style cheeses

Besnier America
218 Park Street
Belmont, Wisconsin 53510
608-762-5173
Brie: plain, cracked pepper, and herbed

Blue Mont Dairy
302 Tuedt Drive
Mt. Horeb, Wisconsin 53572
608-437-3178
Swiss Emmental, cultured organic butter

Capriole
10329 Newcut Road
Greenville, Indiana 47124
812-923-9408
Goat cheeses: fresh chèvre logs, Banon (chèvre in brandied chestnut leaves), Festiva (marbled with pesto and sun-dried tomatoes), and Fromage à Trois Tortas (low in calories and fat)

Corner Bakery
516 North Clark Street
Chicago, Illinois 60610
312-644-8100
Breads: garlic and thyme, raisin pecan, and rosemary olive oil; harvest, country, and sesame baguettes; pretzel rolls; assorted muffins and croutons

Country Connection, Inc.
421 Ridge Road
Wilmette, Illinois 60091
708-256-1968
Specialty farmhouse cheeses from southwestern Wisconsin

Dancing Winds Farm
686 County 12 Boulevard
Kanyon, Minnesota 55946-9159
507-789-6066
Goat cheeses such as chèvre; Brie, and aged cheeses

Dietrich's Dairy
Route 1, Box 83
Fowler, Illinois 62338
217-434-8460
Fresh goat blue cheeses and hard cheeses

Eichten's Hidden Acres Cheese Farm
16705 310th Street
Center City, Minnesota 55012
612-257-4752
Gouda, baby Swiss, Havarti, Tilsit, and raw-milk Cheddar

Fantome Farm
6378 Rosey Lane
Ridgeway, Wisconsin 53582
Goat cheese: fresh chèvre, Moreso (with ash), Provençal (in olive oil), and Boulot (aged raw milk)

Heavenly Hallah
P.O. Box 47
Lincolnshire, Illinois 60069
708-680-2200
Challah braids and crowns: regular, raisin, no yolk; Challah rings: apricot, apple cinnamon, cranberry, and chocolate chip

La Paysanne, Inc.
Route 3, Box 10
Hinckley, Minnesota 55037
612-384-6612

Sheep's milk products: Ewe Scream (reduced-fat sheep's milk ice cream), Ewegurt (frozen sheep's milk yogurt), and cheeses

Loomis Cheese Co.
220 Felch Street
Ann Arbor, Michigan 48103
313-741-8512
Great Lakes Cheshire cheese and garden garlic-chive cheese

Maytag Dairy Farms
P.O. Box 806
Newton, Iowa 50208
515-792-1133
White Cheddar cheese, blue cheese, blue and Edam goat cheeses

Mossholder Farms Cheese Factory
4007 North Richmond Street
Appleton, Wisconsin 54915
414-734-7575
Mossholder-style brick cheese (semisoft), various ages

Nature's Bakery
1019 Williamson Street
Madison, Wisconsin 53703
608-257-3649
Pitas, whole-grain breads, fruit and vegetable muffins, and granola

Nauvoo Mill and Bakery
1530 Mulholland Street
Nauvoo, Illinois
217-453-6734
Blue cheese, whole-wheat flour

Sunrise Bakery
1813 3rd Avenue East
Hibbing, Minnesota
218-263-3544
Potica and specialty cakes and breads

Tolibia Cheese Company
45 East Scott Street
Fond du Lac, Wisconsin 54935
414-921-3500
Gorgonzola and specialty Italian cheeses

Warren Cheese Plant, Inc.
415 Jefferson Street
Warren, Illinois 61087
815-745-2627
Apple Jack cheese and string cheese

Wisconsin Meadows, Inc.
472 Random Drive
Amery, Wisconsin 54001
715-268-7053
Sheep's milk cheeses

Meat, Poultry, and Fish

Brotherson's Meats
824 West 36th Street
Minneapolis, Minnesota 55408
612-823-7227
Smoked chicken, turkey, and ham; venison sausage

Carolyn Collins Caviar Company
925 West Jackson Boulevard, 3rd Floor
Chicago, Illinois 60607
312-226-0342
Pepper, citron, and Great Lakes Golden Caviar

Cherokee Bison Farms
H4225 Elm Road
Colby, Wisconsin 54421
715-223-3644
Bison: steaks, roasts, stew meat, burgers, brats, summer sausage, jerky, and bacon

Culver Duck Farms
P.O. Box 910
Middlebury, Indiana 46540
219-825-9537
Boneless duck breasts, teriyaki or honey-orange marinated duck breasts, and chicken breasts

Eichten's Hidden Acres
16705 310th Street
Center City, Minnesota 55012
Bison, all cuts, and specialty bison products such as jerky

Gateway Natural Meats
37443 385th Street
Bellevue, Iowa 52031-9514
319-872-4327
Beef: steaks, roasts, liver, and ground. Pork: chops, roasts, fresh and smoked hams, bacon, cutlets, sausage, brats, and spareribs

Lewright Meats
108 North Iowa Street
Eagle Grove, Iowa 50533
515-448-4286
Smoked pork loin, chops, sausages, cured ham, bacon

MacFarlane Pheasant Farm, Inc.
2821 South U.S. Highway 51
Janesville, Wisconsin 53546
608-757-7881
Smoked pheasant products

Maple Leaf Farms
P.O. Box 308
Milford, Indiana 46542
800-348-2048
Duck products: roasted with orange sauce, Szechuan style, stuffed legs Florentine, cajun or honey-orange marinated breasts, duck sausage

M Bar D Buffalo Company
Route 1, Box 77
Kampsville, Illinois 62053
618-653-4254
Buffalo

Morey Fish Company
742 Decatur Avenue North
Golden Valley, Minnesota 55427
612-541-0129
Smoked salmon

Morris Farms
7292 40th Street North
Oakdale, Minnesota 55128
612-777-4037
Free-range chickens and turkeys

Nest Eggs
P.O. Box 14599
Chicago, Illinois 60614
312-525-4952
Naturally-raised chicken eggs

Nueske's Hillcrest Farm Meats
Route 2
Wittenberg, Wisconsin 54499
715-253-2226
Applewood-smoked bacon, ham, and specialty meats

Plath's Meats, Inc.
P.O. Box 7
Rogers City, Michigan 49779
517-734-2232
Applewood-smoked pork loin, chops, sugar-cured hams and bacon, turkey breast, chicken, whitefish

Rainbow Ridge Farm
20175 Rhoda Avenue
Welch, Minnesota 55089
612-437-7837
Range-fed geese

Rushing Waters Trout Farm
P.O. Box 308
Milford, Indiana 46542-0308
800-348-2048
Fresh and smoked rainbow trout

Rush River Deer Farm, Inc.
Box 33
New Prague, Minnesota 56071
612-758-2106
Venison chops, medallions, summer sausage and Polish sausages; smoked pheasant; stuffed quail, and Minnesota sweet corn chowder

Sausages by Amy
1143 West Lake Street
Chicago, Illinois 60607
312-829-2250
Variety of sausages: chicken sausage with apples and
apple sugar, Jamaican jerk chicken, Santa Fe–style
chicken, andouille, and veal and pork bratwursts

Star Prairie Trout Farm
400 Hill Avenue
Star Prairie, Wisconsin 54026
715-248-3633
Fresh salmon and trout

Sweet Meadow Farms
R.R. 1, Box 123
Zumbrota, Minnesota 55992
507-732-7400
Lamb: loin and sirloin chops, tenderloins, racks,
summer sausage, and lentil and rice sausage

Underhill Farms
R.R. 2
Moundridge, Kansas 67107
316-345-8415
Venison steaks, burgers, summer sausage, and sticks

Welsh Family Organic Farm
1509 Dry Ridge Drive
Lansing, Iowa 52151
Organic chicken breasts, turkey breasts, ground pork
and beef

Whistling Wings
113 Washington Street
Hanover, Illinois 61041
815-591-2206
Mallard ducks

Sweets:

Anna, Ida & Me, Ltd.
1117 West Grand Avenue
Chicago, Illinois 60622
312-243-ANNA (312-243-2662)
Mondel bread and rugelach

Ganache Bakery
1511 Sherman Avenue
Evanston, Illinois 60201
708-864-4424
Chocolate heart cookies

Nikki's Cookies, Inc.
2018 South 1st Street
Milwaukee, Wisconsin 53207
414-481-4899
Assorted cookies: key lime, amaretto, shortbread,
chocolate-chip, and lemon

Norman's Nordic Kringla
121 Main, Box 488
Roland, Iowa 50236
515-388-4738
Almond, lemon, lemon poppy seed, and nutmeg kringles

Star Struck Baking Co.
4032 Tower Circle
Skokie, Illinois 60076
708-328-7407
Amaretto and Raspberry Caz bars (cross between
a brownie and fudge)

Sweet Sally's Inc.
1660 North LaSalle Street #3309
Chicago, Illinois 60614
312-654-1669
Flavored toffees: espresso, sugar, lemon, and cinnamon,
covered in milk or semisweet chocolate

Top Hat Company, Inc.
P.O. Box 66
Wilmette, Illinois 60091
708-256-6565
Dessert sauces including hot fudge, raspberry fudge,
caramel

Miscellaneous

American Spoon Foods, Inc.
P.O. Box 566
Petoskey, Michigan 49770
800-222-5886

Fruit preserves; butters; spoonfruit (preserves without sugar); salad dazzlers (dressings without sugar or oil); dried cherries, cranberries, blueberries, and persimmons

Best Products Co.
3806 Fon du Lac Drive
Richfield, Wisconsin 53076
414-644-6239
Whipped honey: amaretto, apple, black raspberry, cinnamon, lemon, mint, and natural

Bonamego Farms
62200 Territorial Road
Lawrence, Michigan 49064
616-674-8885
Jams, jellies, dried fruits, and honey

Bowman's Landing Epicurean Co.
605 E. Chicago Avenue
Hinsdale, Illinois 60521
708-850-7405
Infused vinegars

Burhop Family Recipe Ocean's Prime
1438 West Cortland
Chicago, Illinois 60622
312-278-5815
Fish marinades

Clear Creek Orchard
2648 340th Street S.W.
Tiffin, Iowa 52340
319-654-2670
Jams: black raspberry, dark sweet cherry, rhubarb, plum, peach; chunky fruit toppings: blueberry, marion blackberry, red cherry; apple butter

Country Grown Foods
12202 Woodbrine Street
Redford, Michigan 48239
313-535-9222
Specialty grain products

Dillman Farm
4955 West State Road 45
Bloomington, Indiana 47403
812-825-5525
Frozen persimmon pulp

East Shore Specialty Foods
P.O. Box 138
Nashotah, Wisconsin 53058
414-367-8988
Flavored mustards; seasoned pretzels; popcorn seasoning, and jalapeño jelly

Frontier Soups
970 North Shore Drive
Lake Bluff, Illinois 60044
708-615-0551
Hand-packed heartland soup mixes

Granny Gator's Specialty Foods, Inc.
4021 Radcliffe
Northbrook, Illinois 60062
708-291-9654
Cajun barbecue sauce

Grey Owl Foods
P.O. Box 88
Grand Rapids, Minnesota 55744
218-327-2281
Hand-finished wild rice

Heartland Mill, Inc.
Route 1, Box 2
Marienthal, Kansas 67863
316-379-4472
Organic stone-ground flours, blue and yellow corn meal, oats, tortilla chips, and noodles

Homestead Mills
P.O. Box 1115
Cook, Minnesota 55723
218-666-5233
Buckwheat pancake mix, natural-grain cereals

Manitok Wild Rice
Box 97
Callaway, Minnesota 56521
218-375-3425
Wild rice, rice blends, wild rice pancake and muffin mix,
wild berry jellies, syrup, and honey

Maple Acres Sugar Bush
HCR01
Caroline, Wisconsin 54928
715-754-2724
Maple syrup, maple sugar leaves, maple cream,
and golden maple root beer

Minnesota Specialty
69 Airport Boulevard
McGregor, Minnesota 55760
800-328-6731
Wild rice and berry syrups

Nature's Garden
7867 30th Road
Rapid River, Michigan 49878
906-474-6729
Pure maple syrup, cream, and candy; pure honey,
creamed honey, and honey-flavored sticks

Oak Creek Farms
218 North C Street
Edgar, Nebraska 68935
402-224-3038
Blue and white corn chips, tutti frutti pasta,
whole-wheat/carrot pasta, cinnamon crisp corn chips

Ole Salty's of Rockford, Inc.
3131 Summerdale Avenue
Rockford, Illinois 61101
815-963-3355
Potato Chips

Prairie Thyme Ltd.
2 South 13th Street
Kansas City, Kansas 66102
913-371-1315
Gourmet flavored vinegars and raspberry jalapeño
ambrosia sauce (a condiment sauce for cheeses or glazes)

Roadhouse, Inc.
1753 Cora
Des Plaines, Illinois 60018
708-296-5333
Roadhouse Original Recipe, Not For Amateurs
Bar-B-Que sauces, and Casa De Camino Bar-B-Que salsa

Scenic Waters Wild Rice Company
H. C. R. 3, Box 126
Blackduck, Minnesota 56630
Natural hand-harvested wild rice

Special Edition Foods
650 South Lee Avenue
Vicksberg, Michigan 49097
616-649-4372
Suzie Q Sweet/Sour and Greek salad dressings

Thompson Berry Farms
525 Lake Avenue South
Duluth, Minnesota 55802
218-722-2529
Raspberries and raspberry products

Wallace Honey Farm
W811, Highway 18
Sullivan, Wisconsin 53178
414-593-8915
Nine varieties of honey; pollen; comb; beeswax candles,
and bulk beeswax

Wisconsin Wilderness
101 West Capitol Drive
Milwaukee, Wisconsin 53212
800-359-3039
Cranberry mustard and chutney, garden salsa, cranberry
cinnamon bread mix, apple cranberry crisp mix

Yoder Popcorn Company, Inc.
P.O. Box 147
Shipshewana, Indiana 46565
219-768-4051
White and yellow popcorns, flavored popcorns, popcorn
oils, and salts

Bibliography and Reading List

Along the Northern Border: Cookery in Idaho, Minnesota and North Dakota; contains *Library Ann's Cook Book,* Minneapolis, 1928, and *YMCA Cook Book,* Grand Forks, N.D., 1924 (reprint published by Arno Press, New York, 1973).

American Heritage Cookbook. New York: American Heritage Press, 1969.

Aresty, Esther. *The Delectable Past.* New York: Simon and Schuster, 1964.

Beard, James. *James Beard's American Cookery.* Boston: Little, Brown and Company, 1972.

Brown, Dale. *American Cooking.* New York: Time-Life Books, 1968.

Buckeye Cookery and Practical Housekeeping. Estelle Woods Wilcox, ed. Minneapolis: Buckeye Publishing Co., 1880 (reprint published by Minnesota Historical Society Press, St. Paul, 1988).

Chicago Record Cook Book, Chicago: Chicago Record, 1896.

Coyle, L. Patrick. *The World Encyclopedia of Food.* New York: Facts on File, Inc., 1982.

Cummings, Richard Osborn. *The American and His Food.* Chicago: University of Chicago Press, 1940.

The Flavor of Dubuque, by the Women's Auxiliary of the Dubuque Symphony Orchestra. Dubuque, Iowa, 1971.

Fussell, Betty. *I Hear American Cooking.* New York: Viking Penguin, 1986.

Hachten, Harva. *The Flavor of Wisconsin.* The State Historical Society of Wisconsin, Madison, Wis., 1986.

Harris, Marvin. *Good to Eat: Riddles of Food and Culture.* New York: Simon and Schuster, 1985.

Holden, Emery May, and Katherine Davis Holden. *The Aunts' Cook Book.* Cleveland: Horace Carr, 1937.

Hooker, Richard J. *A History of Food and Drink in America.* Indianapolis: Bobbs-Merrill Co., 1981.

Idone, Christopher. *Glorious American Food.* New York: Random House, 1985.

Jones, Evan. *American Food.* New York: E. P. Dutton and Co., 1975.

Kander, Mrs. Simon. *The New Settlement Cook Book.* New York: Simon and Schuster, 1954.

Kander, Mrs. Simon, and Mrs. Henry Schoenfeld. *The Settlement Cook Book.* Milwaukee, Wis. 1903 (reprint published by New American Library, New York, 1985).

Kerr, Mary Brandt. *America: Regional Recipes from the Land of Plenty.* London: Quarto Publishing, nd.

King, Caroline B. *Victorian Cakes.* Caxton Printers, Ltd., 1941 (reprint published by Aris Books, Berkeley, Calif., 1986).

Kreidberg, Marjorie. *Food on the Frontier: Minnesota Cooking from 1850 to 1900.* St. Paul, Minn.: Minnesota Historical Society Press, 1975.

Levenstein, Harvey. *Revolution at the Table: The Transformation of the American Diet.* New York: Oxford University Press, 1988.

Lutes, Della. *The Country Kitchen.* Boston: Little, Brown and Co., 1941.

McGee, Harold. *On Food and Cooking*. New York: Scribner's, 1984.

Makanowitzky, Barbara. *Tales of the Table*. Englewood Cliffs, N.J., Prentice Hall, 1972.

Mariani, John F. *Dictionary of American Food and Drink*. New Haven, Conn.: Ticknor and Fields, 1983.

Mickelson, Bonnie Stewart. *Hollyhocks and Radishes*. Bellevue, Wash.: Pickle Point Publishing, 1989.

Midwestern Home Cookery; contains *The Presbyterian Cook Book*, Dayton, Ohio, 1875, and *The Capital City Cook Book*, Madison, Wis., 1906 (reprints published by New York: Arno Press, 1973).

Paddleford, Clementine. *How America Eats*. New York: Charles Scribner's Sons, 1960.

Palmer House Old and New. Chicago: The Chicago Hotel Company, 1925.

Periam, Jonathan. *Home and Farm Manual*. New York: Greenwich House, 1884.

Root, Waverly, and Richard de Rochemont. *Eating in America: A History*. New York: William Morrow, 1976.

Rosengarten, Frederic. *The Book of Edible Nuts*. New York: Walker and Company, 1984.

Sesqui-Samplings: 150 Years of Cooking in Indianapolis, by the Indianapolis Sesquicentennial Commission, Indianapolis, 1971.

Shapiro, Laura. *Perfection Salad*. New York: Henry Holt and Co., 1986.

Simon, André L., and Robin Howe. *Dictionary of Gastronomy*. New York: McGraw Hill Book Co., 1970.

Stobart, Tom. *Cook's Encyclopedia*. New York: Harper and Row, 1981.

Tarr, Yvonne Young. *The Farm-House Cookbook*. New York: Quadrangle/The New York Times Book Company, 1973.

The United States Regional Cook Book. Ruth Berolzheimer, ed. Chicago: Culinary Arts Institute, 1947.

Waldo, Myra. *The International Encyclopedia of Cooking*. New York: Macmillan, 1967.

Weaver, William Woys. *America Eats: Forms of Edible Folk Art*. New York: Harper and Row, 1989.

Wilder, Laura Ingalls. *The Long Winter*. New York: Harper and Row, 1940.

Williams, Susan. *Savory Suppers and Fashionable Feasts: Dining in Victorian America*. New York: Pantheon Books, 1985.

Wilson, José. *American Cooking: The Eastern Heartland*. New York: Time-Life Books, 1971.

The World Atlas of Food: A Gourmet's Guide to the Great Regional Dishes of the World. New York: Simon and Schuster, 1974.

Index